Rhetorics for Community Action

Public Writing and Writing Publics

Phyllis Mentzell Ryder

LEXINGTON BOOKS
A division of
ROWMAN & LITTLEFIELD PUBLISHERS, INC.
Lanham • Boulder • New York • Toronto • Plymouth, UK

Published by Lexington Books
A division of Rowman & Littlefield Publishers, Inc.
A wholly owned subsidiary of The Rowman & Littlefield Publishing Group, Inc.
4501 Forbes Boulevard, Suite 200, Lanham, Maryland 20706
www.lexingtonbooks.com

Estover Road
Plymouth PL6 7PY
United Kingdom

British Library Cataloguing in Publication Information Available

Library of Congress Cataloging-in-Publication Data

Ryder, Phyllis Mentzell, 1963-
  Rhetorics for community action : public writing and writing publics / Phyllis Mentzell Ryder.
    p. cm.
  Includes bibliographical references and index.
  ISBN 978-0-7391-3766-6 (cloth : alk. paper) — ISBN 978-0-7391-3768-0 (electronic)
  1. Rhetoric—Social aspects. 2. Rhetoric—Political aspects. 3. Communication in politics. I. Title.
  P301.5.S63R93 2011
  808'.066361—dc22

                                                                          2010043810

Printed in the United States of America

∞ ™ The paper used in this publication meets the minimum requirements of American National Standard for Information Sciences—Permanence of Paper for Printed Library Materials, ANSI/NISO Z39.48-1992.

Contents

List of Figures

Acknowledgments

I am indebted to many people who have helped bring this book together. I thank the leaders and staff at the many inspiring community organizations in DC who have embraced me and my students and taught me so much about what it means to do public work: Mary Brown and Aikta Suri at Life Pieces to Masterpieces; Dennis Chestnut at Groundwork, Anacostia River, DC; Laura Osuri and Abby Strunk at *Street Sense*; Ashley Lawson and Jennifer Roccanti at Miriam's Kitchen; Heather Prince Doss and Nathan Mishler at Thrive, DC; Matt Thornton at Higher Achievement Program; Irma Rivera and Shahidah Abdul-Latiff at CentroNía; Sam D'Agostino at LIFT; MJ Parks at Little Friends for Peace; and many, many more.

I am indebted to my colleagues in the University Writing Program at George Washington University, whose generosity and curiosity helped inspire and motivate me. I especially thank two instructional librarians, Jennifer Nutefall and Bill Gillis, who helped me think through what it means to research communities and community organizations, and three dedicated readers in my writing group, Cayo Gamber, Sandie Friedman, and Christy Zink. The encouragement and intellectual prodding of Rachel Riedner and Randi Kristensen helped get me started and saw me through.

A heart full of gratitude to Angela Hewett, a fervent and demanding organizer, whose friendship I hold dear.

And, perhaps most of all, I owe a great deal to many students through the years, whose dedication, reflections, and scholarship have taught me so much.

Chapter 1

Introduction

I believe in the power of the people. I am inspired by people who come together and make things happen. I love to hear stories like the one about DC's Meridian Hill Park: after a young boy was shot, a neighborhood association rose up and reclaimed that park. They got together and patrolled. They recruited neighbors and interviewed their elders about what the park was like in the past. They pulled weeds. They started taking up space, using the park, and reclaiming it. They pressured the police to come by more often. They pressured the DC government to fix the fountains and replace the benches. They invited people in. And now, every weekend, the park is flooded with drummers and dancers, with couples strolling through to enjoy the festive atmosphere and children twirling around and stomping their feet. The people who made it happen kept going; they are now an organization called Washington Parks and People, reclaiming parks all over DC.

I love to walk into Life Pieces to Masterpieces. Suspended along the hallway wall is a painting of an American flag. Strips of textured, red acrylic canvas are sewn in rows, alternating with cross-hatched, lighter strips. In the top-left blue box, cut-out shapes like small paper dolls replace the traditional stars. This canvas was jointly created by all the young African-American boys and artists at Life Pieces to Masterpieces. It is captioned, "America, what about your children IV," and has this explanation: "By replacing the stars on the flag with children, we ask America to put children first." Down the hallway and around the corner in a large, well-lit gallery, more paintings shout out from the walls. The canvases are big, imposing, and dramatic.

The sewn acrylic collage paintings are manifestations of the nonprofit's premise: Love + Security + Expression = Life. In a city once known as the murder capital of the United States and where in the first years of this decade,

1

a juvenile was murdered on average once a month, this affirmation is no mere slogan; it signifies a profound act of hope and power. Cofounder Mary Brown told me that a teenager, part of a drug crew who worked a nearby city block, walked a young boy to her door. "You take care of Shorty here," he told her. "It's too late for me," he implied, "but Shorty can have a different life, and it can begin here, with Mary Brown and the artists and people who create a safe and uplifting place for young boys to find their way."

I love these stories. They are treasures I collect. They affirm for me the power of people: their vibrancy, their creativity, their optimism, and their ability to come together as a strong force for good.

I suppose I'm attracted to stories about public action because I was surrounded by it in my childhood. I had a taste of the giddy power of community building when my family settled in the small town of Winchester, tucked into the rolling hills of southwestern New Hampshire. Winchester is one of the poorest towns in the state. The regional newspaper generally reported crimes and high unemployment rates and other stories that painted our town as a sad and unworthy place. When I was in high school, a man who lived up the dirt road from our house proposed that we start a town newspaper. He made it happen: he brought together a group of Winchester citizens of all ages and all parts of town, including my mother and me. We went to work. Each month, we published *The Winchester Star,* and we shouted to the world that Winchester was a proud and productive place. We interviewed people who had just moved to town. We interviewed our town elders. We researched the proposals that would be put before the community in our traditional New England Town Hall Meetings. Sometimes, I made up crossword puzzles. Being part of that team was hard and demanding, but it was also rejuvenating and fun.

The man who got us started on that newspaper was Dr. Dennis Littky. He soon focused his attention on Thayer, our local high school. What happened there was eventually documented (with some embellishment) by Susan Kammeraad-Campbell in *Doc: The Story of Dennis Littky and His Fight for a Better School.*[1] Though I had graduated from Thayer the year before, I heard regular updates from my mother, a community activist in her own right, who was on the school board and just about every other committee in town. At Thayer, Littky threw out the hard-and-fast rules, and he designed learning communities based on student interests and aspirations. When he met a young artist who planned to drop out of school, Littky hired him to paint a mural in the cafeteria. The young man did, then came back to school in the fall. Littky used the techniques of grassroots organizing to build a school. He met with students, he listened, and he identified student leaders—not just the ones who were on the student government, but the rebellious ones who had a power among those who stayed on the edges of school. He gave them meaningful responsibilities and won them over to help build a school they could believe in. Thayer was one of the first schools to be part of education reformer Ted Sizer's Coalition for Essential Schools, at the front-end of whole-school reform movements.[2]

But the transformation was not without controversy, and soon the town was in dramatic turmoil, with some people galvanized to oust Littky and others rallying to keep him in. Seats on the school board—including my mother's—were hard-fought. The school budget, which was regularly approved at town hall meetings, was scrutinized fiercely. The whole experience was terrifying and energizing, a lesson in politics and power, in how deeply people believe, in how widely people could disagree, and about how quickly small things could be distorted.

The stories from my immediate family have also guided the way I think about public action and my concern that it begins at the grassroots. My father worked in international public health. One of the more powerful stories he told about his work in Africa was a wrenching epiphany that public health workers had to look at the consequences of their "help" from the perspective of the community they professed to be helping. He and my mother moved first to Gondar, Ethiopia, where he taught Ethiopian nurses, sanitation work-ers, and health officers to go into the country, show villagers everyday behav-iors that would keep them healthy, and support them as they incorporated these new habits into their village routines. Then he, my mom, and my two older sisters traveled to Bamako, Mali, where one more sister was born and Ouagadougou, Upper Volta (where I was born. Upper Volta is now Burkina Faso). In these West African countries, my father worked with the Ministries of Health, coordinating an international team brought in to vaccinate the countries against measles.

Decades later, back in Winchester, when my father was dying, he pinched the skin on his arm and watched it. "See how the skin sticks together like this?" my father asked, always the teacher. "This means I'm dehydrated," and he told the story of working with a measles vaccination team. When he and his crew came to the village, all the children were lined up, waiting to offer their arms for the shots. He reached for a young boy and pinched his arm. The skin stuck together, and the little peak on his arm remained long after my father let go. My father vaccinated the boy, lowered his arm, and vac-cinated the next. When he came home from that trip, he wrote a letter to his supervisors back in the United States. "For whom are we trying to eradicate measles?" he asked. The boy would survive measles and die of starvation. From the perspective of the villagers, my father came to realize, measles vaccinations were only one small part of a much more holistic public health need. He switched his specialty to population control, and he told us this story often to remind us that "doing good" needs to begin by listening to the people on the ground and by working *with* them. I understood that doing good *for* people, instead of *with* people, was stepping into a dangerous zone where one couldn't be too sure of one's motives or consequences.

I spent nine years of my childhood in Indonesia, where my father served as a family planning advisor to the Indonesian government, which eventually had not only a Ministry of Public Health but also a Ministry of Family Planning. A recent Ford Foundation report about the massive effort to transform public attitudes about family planning describes the evolution of the project:

> With assistance from like-minded donors from overseas, including the Ford Foundation, a few doctors, social activists and bureaucrats began in 1952 to organize efforts to provide women with the means to control their fertility—the family planning movement was born, first through the actions of inspired individuals, then as a small nongovernmental service provider, but later to develop into a huge, multi-sectoral government program dedicated to reducing the levels of fertility across the nation.[3]

As part of the process, my father helped train teams who in turn trained local men and women to teach their communities about the benefits and methods of family planning. These efforts were bolstered with a big communications campaign. Big billboards shouted the slogan "dua anak cukup" (two children is enough). The results were impressive: within a decade, the large country, spread across hundreds of islands in the archipelago, had new attitudes and new awareness about family planning. The average family size declined steeply from 5.6 children in the late sixties to close to 3 in the late eighties, and down to 2.6 in the late nineties.[4] As a child happily romping with my sisters first in Jakarta, Java, and later in Sanur Beach, Bali, I didn't fully understand the complex interactions between civil society, international and local nonprofits, or the changes in the Indonesian government, but I did come away with a sense of what is possible. How could I doubt the power to persuade millions of people to make dramatic and personal changes in their own lives?

I didn't fully understand that I had learned these lessons about the power and potential of people to effect change until a few years ago when I was reading the autobiography of that great community educator, Miles Horton. Horton was the founder of the Highlander Folk School in Appalachia. Highlander was a gathering place for community organizers, from the labor leaders of the thirties to the civil rights activists of the fifties and sixties. Rosa Parks went there, as did Dr. King and Septima Clark. Horton's philosophy of community organizing put learning first. As his cowriter, Herbert Kohl, writes in the preface of Horton's autobiography, Horton felt that "if in the course of

[a] struggle, you had learned nothing about the fundamental values you were struggling for or did not understand your own role in the process, you might end up becoming just another oppressor of people weaker than you are."[5] His autobiography is heady stuff—the danger and thrills of taking moral stances, of working behind the scenes with great leaders, and of understanding how to bring communities together in a spirit of hope and with a sense of power.

When I turned the book over, I saw on the back cover a blurb from Dennis Littky. Littky wrote, "It is exciting reading—the kind of book I underlined and returned to monthly for inspiration and for keeping me on track." I hadn't thought of Dennis for years, and I hadn't seen him for decades. Yet, suddenly, it seemed that I could see a thread connecting me with my one-time neighbor, my parents, and many generations of activists. This book is my attempt to add a small piece of insight to the broad community of activists, especially those of us who are also educators.

INVENTING THE PUBLIC

When I talk about "publics" in this book, I refer to the social entities that come together with particular visions of people's role within democracy. People come together as a public when they repeatedly encounter texts that have invoked that role, when they start to feel that a particular way of describing what is happening is most accurate, and when they accept and perpetuate that vision. I talk about publics in the plural, rather than the more common "public" or "public sphere" or "the people," to highlight the many conflicting ideas about what the public looks like and how it does and should operate. "Public writing" has the power to bring people together with a shared sense of how the world works, how democracy works, and how their power as the people can effect change. Public writing happens in all sorts of places, sometimes literally written (such as brochures, letters, articles, agendas, or Tweets) and sometimes manifest in other forms (such as speeches, slogans chanted at a rally, or protesters silently barricading a street). My question in this book is how does public writing turn people into publics? What is it in public writing that people respond to? How can we create writing that brings people together in this way? How can we teach others to do so?

I see my task here as taking the same approach that composition scholar David Bartholomae laid out when he considered how teachers help newcomers write within a particular kind of community: an academic one. In "Inventing the University," Bartholmae admonishes composition teachers to respond generously as students—especially first-generation college students—invent the university audience whom they are trying to address.[6] Overusing jargon, constructing oddly-shaped sentences, and inserting inflated diction are all ways that students try their best to appropriate the markers they attribute to academic discourse. The job of academic writing teachers, Bartholomae tells us, is to help students understand the values of the university—its assumptions about knowledge-making, its ethos of scholarly transparency in method and attribution, the pleasure that academics feel in the intellectual pursuit—and how all of these values translate into specific rhetorical choices as they write. Academic writing teachers should see students' successes and missteps as evidence of how well they understand the unique and strange new rhetorical situation that is university writing. Every time academics write, he notes, they invent the university.

Public writers make a parallel move: they have to invent the publics they wish to address, and they need practice doing it. Understanding a public is a complex task with many components to keep track of: an exigency that brings people together, a sense of agency and capacity, a sense of how the world is, and what it can become. All these components constantly compete against other public conceptions—opposing ideas about who *really* has power and who *really* can create change. Teachers of public writing must adopt an equally generous response to those who venture into this arena. Inventing a public is a difficult, vital work. I offer this book as a guide to help teachers and students gain a richer understanding of the values and rhetorical moves of public writing.

THE DANGERS OF NARROWLY DEFINED PUBLICS

One of the most important lessons I have learned as I have ventured into studying, teaching, and creating public writing is to define "public" broadly. I've noticed that many activists, teachers, and scholars are quick to categorize some groups as democratic and some as not, some groups as doing "real" public work and some as not. I sympathize with this move. As one drawn to ideals of community organizing, I find myself shying away from hierarchical organizations that bring in service professionals to attend to public "good"; as one drawn to an ideal of a multicultural democracy, I find myself shying away from reified ideals of rational, critical civil debate and toward a more cacophonous space of hybrid languages and genres and expanded notions of reasonableness. But if we are to understand public writing in all its complexity, we need to recognize how this very move of laying out what counts as public is at the heart of public writing. The struggle to be seen as *the* public is such a fundamental part of the work of public formation that we need to be very self-conscious about how we deploy this move. Analyzing and engaging in public struggles means operating in a space where multiple publics fight to be recognized. To work in that space, we need an expansive understanding, one that lays out not just one vision but also how each vision butts up against competing or complementary definitions. If we don't see the full range, we may dismiss or overlook the rhetorical moves that have solidified other groups around other kinds of values. Without such an understanding, we are limited in our abilities to engage with those publics in a spirit of inquiry and in our abilities to resist and challenge those publics whose visions we find incompatible with our own.

I learned this lesson over several years as I regularly taught and revised my college-level courses about public writing. My first course designs did not interrogate any of the competing definitions of democracy and public work but assumed that every nonprofit operated within a grassroots, community-organizing framework. I praised those activists who approached their community members as fellow activists, who worked together to identify and analyze their needs, and who demanded that those in power account for their needs. I sent students to work at places like soup kitchens and after-school tutoring programs, places that (at least at first glance) seem designed to help citizens assimilate into the current social structures. As a result, I inadvertently taught my students to scorn the very organizations I had asked them to work with. My response was not to abandon nonprofits whose methods seemed to conflict with the democratic theory I valued, but instead to look more closely at the public visions of those organizations and to think more critically about how I was defining "real" democratic actions.

I'll share the story of the evolution of my course as a way to illustrate why we need to be expansive in our definition of what is public.

Rhetorics of Social Protest

I found my way into my current course design, in which my students partner with multiple community organizations, after several years of teaching the rhetorics of social protest. I loved teaching the social protest class because it was exciting to introduce students to the power of social action and to see them begin to appreciate how people can tackle head-on issues that are deeply embedded in the fabric of society. In one version of the course, I immersed students in the history of the Civil Rights Movement, drawing especially on Charles Payne's *I've Got the Light of Freedom*, an insightful and thorough book about the persistent, dangerous work of the Student Nonviolent Coordinating Committee within Mississippi.[7] Payne recounts SNCC's philosophy, the ways that organizers adapted to the local conditions in which they worked, their methods of gaining trust of black men and women, and how they relied on local leaders to persuade a community that it had the power to fight institutional and state-sanctioned racism. Teaching about SNCC was especially moving, since the young Bob Moses, Charles Sherrod, and Charlie Cobb (among others) who spoke truth to power were not much older than the students I was teaching. And some of them, like Stokely Carmichael, had joined the organization as students at Howard University, just down the street from George Washington, where I teach.

I also liked to begin with SNCC because its history is less well known to my students (and to many people), who associate the Civil Rights Movement with Dr. King and the March on Washington. Through a series of readings—sections from Charles Payne, passages of Howard Zinn's on-the-ground reporting *SNCC: The New Abolitionist,*[8] and speeches and letters from Dr. King—I tried to help students see the Civil Rights Movement as a coalition of multiple groups who had competing understandings about the root causes of racism and the best strategies for uprooting it. We investigated the relationship between these foundational understandings of the world as it is, the world as it should be, and the strategies for pressuring governmental agencies at local and federal levels. Charles Stewart's "The Evolution of a Revolution: Stokeley Carmichael and the Rhetoric of Black Power" was a particularly useful text for introducing democracy and social change as rhetorical concepts.[9]

I began thinking about incorporating service-learning into my classes after I revamped the course to include contemporary social movements. Using the same approach I had taken in the Civil Rights Movement class, my students and I identified the worldviews undergirding groups like ACT-UP, Greenpeace, the Guerilla Girls, Reclaim Public Space, and others, and evaluated how their definitions of democracy shaped their methods of social protest. Who did the organizations identify as having power to create change? Which organizations rooted their critiques in rational deliberation? Which grounded their actions in transforming the experiences of space? How did groups try to circulate their messages? What genres of writing and protest did organizations use, and how did those forms advance or constrain them? I introduced students to the words of activists by using Benjamin Shepherd and Roy Hayduck's 2002 anthology *From ACT-UP to the WTO, Urban Protest and Community Building in the Era of Globalization.*[10] I introduced the theories of elite and direct democracy by asking students to read the short and pithy *The Manufacture of Consent,* Noam Chomsky's searing critique of Walter Lippmann's theory that democracy cannot be left to the "bewildered herd" of "the people" because they are too emotional and self-centered to be entrusted such an important task.[11] I placed Lippman alongside chapters from Craig Rimmerman's *The New Citizenship,* which lays out a case for participatory democracy, the belief that citizens should be responsible for the decisions that most affect them, and that through the very process of learning to work together, people grow into their roles as citizens.[12] We watched *The Democratic Promise*[13] to learn about Saul Alinsky's philosophy of community organizing, and we read firsthand accounts of contemporary Industrial Area Foundation work, like Michael Gecan's *Going Public: An Organizer's Guide to Citizen Action*[14] and Ed Chamber's *Roots for Radicals: Organizing for Power, Action and Justice.*[15] We looked at how contemporary social protest movements defined the public's roles within a democracy, and we evaluated how well they enacted these principles in the models of action they used.

Public Writing and Social Protest

Although my writing courses about social protest were heady places for investigating the power of rhetoric and the rhetorics of power, I was concerned about a disconnect in the course. Students were learning about public rhetoric, but the only kind of writing that I asked of them was academic. They wrote about publics, but they never wrote for or with publics.

My first attempt to resolve this was to ask students to write proposals that they could potentially send to the organizations they studied. The proposals would map out a set of actions that the student felt would be aligned with the organizations' philosophies of social change. A student studying the Guerilla Girls, for example, might study the exhibits at the National Gallery and suggest what kind of protest (if any) would be appropriate for that museum. The approach seemed like a good idea at the time, but now I see it was fraught with problems. Predictably (though I didn't predict it then), students felt out of place writing such proposals. I positioned them as consultants to organizations whose staff had been on the ground doing social protest for much longer than any of us. They knew that college students on the periphery of these organizations had little authority. There was no exigency for the proposals—no one at the organization had asked for their advice. The task felt like an exercise in thinking, as something for the class; it did not bridge the divide between academic and public writing.

My second attempt was to ask students to propose an action that would advance the goals of the social protest organizations they were studying but that could take place at the university. I attempted to return to the students a sense of their own authority and expertise. As university insiders, they had knowledge that the social protest organizations did not. We did not presume to tell the organizations what to do generally, but now offered insight about how to do their work in this particular location. This setup was better, I felt, but it did not resolve the problem of the students' tangential relationship to the organization they were now asked to endorse publicly on campus.

Social Protest and Service Learning

So, I turned to service learning. Now, I wanted a course in which students, working with local organizations, could study the public rhetoric of those organizations and, by the end of the semester, have enough expertise to complete a small public writing task that would benefit the organization. I met volunteer coordinators of several local nonprofits at a local service-learning conference. I met with the Office of Community Service at my school. Once I chose six potential nonprofits to work with, I met with staff at each of them to map out mutually-agreeable partnerships. I offered to place my students as volunteers with their organization for twenty hours over the semester, and we brainstormed together about writing tasks that students could produce at the end of the semester that might be of some use to the organization. Some asked for brochures, some asked for volunteer manuals, some asked for volunteer evaluations of lesson plans, and some asked for newsletter articles.

The first time I taught the service-learning class, the basic structure of the course still focused on the rhetorics of social protest. We looked at models of social movements in class, we read the same texts about elite and participatory democracy, and students supplemented this with their work at community organizations. Some met in a morning literature discussion group with guests at Miriam's Kitchen, a nonprofit that serves meals and provides counseling and community for homeless men and women. Others tutored middle school children at Higher Achievement Program (HAP), a nonprofit where motivated middle school students are encouraged to take on the mantles of scholars.

These are great organizations, places that attend carefully and thoughtfully to the communities in which they work, and I continue to place students with many of them today. But none of these organizations would define itself as doing social protest as we had defined it in the course. While I can see, now, that they resist the discourses of individualism that lays the blame for poverty or illiteracy at the feet of those they serve, what was most visible to my students that first semester, given the framework of the course, was that these organizations did not define the root causes of the issues in the same way our class readings did. The nonprofits did not define civic action or social change the same way. None staged rallies or picketed. None organized their constituents to march on city hall or to demand change at a DC school board meeting. Not surprisingly, my students wrote that the organizations with which they worked over the semester were well-meaning but misguided. Students completed the work of the course, but they left feeling disillusioned about the potential of community-based organizations to make change.

Public Writing with Community Organizations

My response to my first missteps has been to set aside the framework of direct democracy and social protest that had guided my earlier approaches and to begin with the community organizations themselves. What kind of work do they actually do? Why is it valuable? What challenges do they face? How do they draw people into their vision? How do they persuade people that change is needed and possible?

This book is structured around the course that I have devised—a one-semester seminar in which students partner with community organizations and study the rhetorics of public formation. I have ongoing relationships with dozens of nonprofits in DC. I require students to spend twenty hours a week working at those organizations, and we spend our class time investigating how physical spaces and community discourses shape those communities, reviewing different philosophies about how to create democratic change, and examining the specific historical and cultural contexts that influence how people might get things done in DC. At the end of the semester, students write materials for their community partners. By collaborating with experts in the community and writing within the supportive structure of our class, they practice inventing a public in their writing.

I have not abandoned my passion for grassroots community activism, and I haven't set aside a vision of democracy where everyday people can speak back to governments, institutions, and corporations that have tried to shut them out. In fact, I see my approach as well attuned to that philosophy because I want to begin on the ground with the people who are doing this work day-in and day-out. I want to listen and invite my students to listen to how people create the world they want to live in and how they find the words and actions to live out that vision. I understand the ideal public I would strive for as one along a continuum of choices that every public organization must make as it responds to the particular exigency that has called it into being. I recognize that as people come together to make change, they have to contend every moment with shifting conditions and with competing visions about the best public responses to those conditions. My argument in this book is that when people write (or speak or perform) public texts, they invent the public they wish to address—a complicated but powerful rhetorical move. My argument is that to best study and teach the complexities of public writing, we should partner with multiple community nonprofits. To fully experience the challenge of inventing publics, those who study public writing should write with our community partners.

OUTLINE OF THE BOOK

I write this book for people who seek a useful theory of how people come together to form publics and the rhetorical moves they draw on in their public writing (defined broadly to include speeches, photos, written documents, and public actions). I write it also for people who wish to teach others how to do such writing. While my own field is rhetoric and composition, and while I teach this course as a first-year writing seminar, I have drawn on the scholarship and pedagogy of people in many fields, in and out of the academy, to develop my theory and pedagogy. Many people teach service-learning courses with the goal of revitalizing civic engagement, helping students see the joys and rewards of working together with others to make real and meaningful change. This book is for all of those people.

I begin the book by pursuing a question I posed in this introduction: how do we decide which kinds of groups are the best models to draw on as we investigate the very question of what a public is and how it forms? In chapter 2, I argue that we need to think critically about the frameworks we use to evaluate public organizations so that we can more fully understand the range and complexity of their arguments. I begin with a common and persuasive claim among many who study public theory and community organizing that some nonprofits are too privatized and hierarchical to serve as models of how publics work. Human services nonprofits, they argue, are too service-oriented and do not help community members recognize their power as citizens who can fight back to change the conditions that have brought those service providers to the community in the first place. In response, I locate this dichotomy of real public vs. private service within a matrix of theories of democracy with three main axes: what is the purpose of government (for the people), who has power to make decisions (of the people), and what kinds of actions are appropriate for the public (by the people.) When composing a public text, one takes a stand on a particular point in each of these three axes and implicitly or overtly rejects the others. This move of claiming one set of goals, actors, and actions as truly public is the central, powerful move of public writing. Because of that, I caution that those of us studying and teaching how publics form need to be very self-conscious about how we, ourselves, make this move. Instead of setting out a single ideal against which all other publics should be judged, I argue that we should examine each public as a moment of struggle.

To illustrate that point more fully, I consider the history of nonprofits in this country, looking particularly at the human services sector. Within an ever-evolving context of "smaller government" and capitalist emphasis on individualism and efficiency, nonprofits are now more than ever responsible for those who suffer from the structural inequities in that system. If we then dismiss such organizations for doing the once-public work that has been relegated to them, we overlook how many nonprofits resist that system even as they work within it.

I end that chapter with a paradigm for "public work" that goes beyond those actions that are often held up as the epitome of social change, such as marches and sit-ins and other tactics that force government or corporate responses. I show instead how actions including charities and projects can be evaluated as meaningful and profound aspects of public formation. Using Life Pieces to Masterpieces as a case study, I illustrate how nonprofits that might at first appear to reinforce private, neoliberal values are, on closer inspection, performing much more radical cultural work.

In chapter 3, I offer a closer look at how specific public ideals are embedded in the rhetorical structures of public writing, using examples from the texts of local community organizations. I identify how different organizations define public agency, how they structure their words and interactions so that people see each other as necessary partners, and how they draw on local history and geography to shape a public identity. I also briefly introduce the challenge of circulation—how a particular public vision is broadcast so that others will also imagine and talk about the public in those terms. The challenges of both setting out a particular public ideal and circulating it become evident when comparing multiple organizations working on similar issues and multiple organizations working in close geographical proximity. I end the chapter with a pedagogical framework for partnering with community organizations to highlight these components of public writing.

Chapters 4–6 look more deeply at three critical components of public rhetoric: the idealized singular public sphere, the counterpublics who reject that normative ideal, and the role of the traditional media in circulating the normative and counterpublic ideals. The most dominant conception of democracy is that citizens deliberate and come to rational conclusions about the right course of action and that the media help by circulating those conversations and allowing the citizens' deliberations to rise to the attention of the representatives who make decisions. In chapter 4, I analyze how the public norms of the idealized public sphere are carried forward through specific rhetorical constructions and are built into the infrastructures of the traditional media. Using as an example an essay from *Harper's* along with a kind of manifesto from the Committee of Concerned Journalists, I show how the traditional media forwards the norms of the idealized public sphere. Not surprisingly, the role offered to citizens in this vision reifies the act of reading and contemplating, with the media responsible for facilitating these deliberative conversations.

Chapter 5 takes apart some of the assumptions undergirding the idealized model by considering American counterpublics. I illustrate how alternate conceptions of the public sphere manifest in the rhetorical structures of counterpublic texts. Drawing on scholarship by and about African-American, Native-American, and Latino rhetors, I show how they reject the idealized public sphere's conceptions about the purpose of government, the role of experts, and the priority of disembodied reason and how their counterpublic visions are manifested rhetorically in the public interactions they forward.

In chapter 4, I explain how the traditional media forwards the model of the idealized public sphere, and in chapter 5, I note how counterpublic rhetoric rejects that idealized sphere. In chapter 6, I consider the challenge that this raises: if the traditional media constrains the kind of public imagination that can circulate there, how do counterpublics spread their public visions? To answer this question, I look at four case studies of counterpublic rhetoric and show how they work with and against traditional media.

In chapter 7, I turn my attention to how publics form online. Scholars who look for publics online fall into the same habit I observed in my own teaching and scholarship: they have delineated as "real public spaces" those online spaces where a diverse group of people comes together to decide what should be done and to carry out that action. In this chapter, I resist this move and instead examine how a particular community organization uses its online space to build a public. I study the social networking of a local soup kitchen, Miriam's Kitchen. Though the organization does a fine job of bringing donors and volunteers and staff together as a community, the online space does not include homeless people. By looking more closely at their philosophy for working with chronically homeless people, I argue that their choices are appropriate and well-aligned with the publics they seek to create. Through this investigation, I show how critical it is to examine public formation within the context of multiple venues of circulation: the rhetorical work of the online Miriam's Kitchen is deeply influenced by the public formation that happens within their walls.

Because I teach public writing within a university setting and because such relationships are often fraught with tensions, I conclude the book with a reflection on the relationships between university and public writing. In chapter 8, I argue that as we teach both public and university writing, we should clarify how academia is positioned within theories of democracy and how the writing we teach here likewise promotes a certain conception of how democracy works. The university is deeply embedded in a vision of democracy closely aligned with the idealized public sphere I lay out in chapter 4: a place of constant reading, writing, and deliberating to arrive at progressively more complex and accurate understandings of how the world works. Like it or not, we are also linked with elite democracy; the university is a place where people go to become experts who can provide services and direction to nonexperts.

I also find that the vocabulary I have developed to talk about public writing is helpful for understanding academic writing. Academics writing for their disciplines must, as Bartholomae notes, invent their university audience each time they write, invoking the values and underlying assumptions of that relationship through their rhetorical choices. Just as public writers must consider the exigency that brings their public together, the capacity that they have to meet that need, and the relationships they must foster to get the work done, so the academic writer must attend to exigency, capacity, and relationships. Just as public writers lay out their visions within a context of competing and clashing public visions, so academics write in a context of constant struggle—struggles with and across disciplines about the values of particular methodologies and movements and struggles within and outside of academia about the very nature and purpose of universities. Teaching public writing, then, can provide a helpful lens through which to look at the university and the demands of university writing.

I follow the final chapter with three appendicies that offer practical guidelines for how to negotiate university-community partnerships within a course on public writing.

NOTES

1. Susan Kameraad-Campbell, *Doc: The Story of Dennis Littky and His Fight for a Better School*. (Alexandria, VA: Association for Supervision and Curriculum Development, 1989, 2005).

2. Dennis Littky continues as an educational reformer, now heading up Big Pictures Learning, an organization that promotes radically student-centered teaching at both the high school and college levels. www.bigpicture.org.

3. Terence H. Hull, "Introduction to Indonesia's Population from 1950–2000: Carving Out New Futures," in *People, Population, and Policy in Indonesia*, ed. Terence H. Hull (Jakarta: Equinox, 2005), xviii.

4. Terence H. Hull and Valerie J. Hull, "From Family Planning to Reproductive Health Care: A Brief History," in *People, Population, and Policy in Indonesia*, ed. Terence H. Hull (Jakarta: Equinox, 2005), 1–70.

5. Myles Horton, Herbert R. Kohl, and Judith Kohl, *The Long Haul: An Autobiography*. (New York: Teachers College Press, 1998), ix.

6. David Bartholomae, "Inventing the University," in *When a Writer can't Write: Studies in Writer's Block and Other Composing-Process Problems,* ed. Mike Rose (New York: Guilford, 1985), 135–165.

7. Charles M. Payne, *I've Got the Light of Freedom: The Organizing Tradition and the Mississippi Freedom Struggle.* (Berkeley: University of California Press, 1996).

8. Howard Zinn, *SNCC, the New Abolitionists.* (Boston: Beacon Press, 1964).

9. Charles J. Stewart, "The Evolution of a Revolution: Stokely Carmichael and the Rhetoric of Black Power." *Quarterly Journal of Speech* 83, no. 4 (1997): 429–446.

10. Ronald Hayduk, and Benjamin Heim Shepard, *From ACT UP to the WTO: Urban Protest and Community Building in the Era of Globalization.* (London; New York: Verso, 2002).

11. Noam Chomsky, *The Manufacture of Consent.* (Minneapolis, Minn.: Silha Center for the Study of Media Ethics and Law, School of Journalism and Mass Communication, University of Minnesota, 1986).

12. Craig A. Rimmerman, *The New Citizenship: Unconventional Politics, Activism, and Service.* (Boulder: Westview Press, 2005).

13. Alec Baldwin et al. *The Democratic Promise.* (Seattle: Indieflix, 2007).

14. Michael Gecan, *Going Public.* (Boston: Beacon Press, 2002).

15. Edward T. Chambers, and Michael A. Cowan, *Roots for Radicals: Organizing for Power, Action, and Justice.* (New York: Continuum, 2003).

Chapter 2

Publics Worth Studying

Effective advocacy does not begin with the principals of good argument, but with an analysis of those historical and material conditions that have made some arguments more viable than others.

—David Coogan[1]

I argue that we need to build, or take part in building, such a public sphere: that the public is always constructed and that it cannot, in our society, be unitary.

—Susan Wells[2]

Not surprisingly, a common ancestor claimed in much of the scholarship on civic engagement and service-learning is philosopher, educator, and public intellectual John Dewey. This is true across many academic disciplines. American studies professor Keith Morton and sociologist Sandra Enos hark back to Dewey in an article published in *Public Affairs*.[3] Public policy professor Phillip Levine uses Dewey as an anchor as he proposes how to engage young people in his book, *The Future of Democracy: Developing the Next Generation of American Citizens*.[4] Composition and rhetoric scholars Thomas Deans and Linda Flower each explain Dewey's strong impact in their field's scholarship on civic engagement in *Writing Partnerships* and *Community Literacy*, respectively.[5] Troy Murphy sides with Dewey as he reviews the influence on communication studies of the famous debate between Walter Lippmann and John Dewey.[6]

Dewey's theory of democracy places great trust in the power of ordinary people to govern themselves; he sees democracy as an ongoing process of learning through which people discover their capacity for governing as they work out the issues that impact their daily lives. In this process, deliberation among citizens is perhaps their most important action. As Levine puts it,

> Dewey's theory . . . provides a response to those who would say that deliberation is "just talk," that it lacks sufficient impact on votes and policies. Dewey would reply that the heart of democracy is not an election or the passage of a law, but personal growth through communication.[7]

I admire Dewey's approach, and his work has influenced my ideas about democracy a great deal. However, I worry that too often scholars who study and teach about the public sphere or public writing begin with their commitment to a Deweyan approach and, in the process of describing and promoting this democratic ideal, either ignore or vilify those actually-existing publics that do not readily fit within Dewey's approach.

The consequence of such a move is twofold. For one thing, if we only count one kind of deliberative process as truly public, we end up with disdain or cynicism about actually-existing publics that might draw on different ideals. Troy Murphy makes this point well in his critique of some of the common programs for educating citizens and students about deliberative democracy.[8] Such dismissals lead to the second and related problem: we give up an opportunity to study how those other publics form—to learn how those publics persuade people to come together with a different sense of capacity and interrelationship and how their discourse reinforces a different understanding of government, publics, and communication. Ultimately, we lose track of the larger context in which these publics regularly clash, intermingle, and negotiate their relationships to each other. Additionally, we lose the opportunity to discover how each public, depending on the rhetorical situation, may position itself in different places along the continuums of public identity—sometimes making more elitist appeals for a particular kind of expertise, sometimes promoting a more populist view in response to another public's controlling expertise, and so on. Publics are never fixed or unitary; they always maneuver and reconfigure in the constantly changing contexts in which they circulate.

I'm not saying that we should treat all publics as equal, as if it's all the same if a public promotes bigotry or multiculturalism. I am saying—as I said in the introduction—that we are sometimes too quick to label some groups democratic and some not, some kinds of behavior appropriately public and some not. Naming how the world works, what aspects of that world are appropriate for public action, and what public action should look like— these are all fundamental moments in calling people together as a public. As scholars and teachers of public writing, we would do better to look at how our ideals fit within a broader framework, a full scope of how people delineate "public-ness." We must account for the many ways people experience their roles as members of the public. As is true for any public text, any claims we make will always scrape against these alternate ideals. Public writing is the place where these competing visions clash, both overtly and through rhetorical choices that signal such affiliations.

THE CASE AGAINST PRIVATE NONPROFITS

To illustrate how smart and well-meaning scholars may reduce the scope of study with too narrow a definition of public, I offer as an example an article by Public Service and American studies professor Keith Morton and sociologist Sandra Enos, "Building Deeper Civic Relationships and New and Improved Citizens."[9] Morton and Enos argue that faculty who wish to teach students to engage in public work should avoid partnerships with human-service sector nonprofits, which are too privatized, hierarchical, and corporate-minded to offer students opportunities to experience what it means to create a public. Instead, they propose working with more community-oriented groups that teach citizens how to come together to rally for political change. I'll review this article in detail because the authors make a series of significant moves that I'd like to unpack to illustrate how their focus on one ideal of public shuts out a more complex understanding of publics.

In "Building Deeper Civic Relationships and New and Improved Citizens," as they do elsewhere,[10] Morton and Enos trace the legacy of service-learning to John Dewey (*The Public and Its Problems* 1927), Jane Addams, founder of the U.S. Settlement House movements ("The Subtle Problems of Charity" *Atlantic Monthly* 1899), and Stanford sociologist and educator Paul Hanna (*Youth Serve the Community* 1936). Both Hanna and Dewey were concerned that people needed to learn from each other how to come together and shape the world they lived in. Hanna, in particular, felt that the rise of industrial capitalism had narrowed opportunities for young people to "make a direct contribution to the working of democracy."[11] Drawing on Dewey, Hanna argue that youth need the opportunity to practice acting as citizens.

Morton and Enos then jump to the present to explore the challenges of implementing this vision. One challenge is defining specific characteristics of active citizenship that a Deweyan-inspired service-learning course might try to promote. Morton and Enos are concerned that proponents of service-learning have become so focused on teaching the processes of "active citizenship" that they have stopped asking whether "the political and cultural landscape in which those students live" is itself democratic.[12] They argue that we need to "shift our focus from preparing students to be active citizens to preparing our students to join in creating democratic culture."[13] The argument seems to align with Susan Wells' call to scholars in composition and rhetoric: "If we want more for our students than the ability to defend themselves in bureaucratic settings, we are imagining them in a public role, imagining a public space they could enter . . . [W]e need to build, or take part in building, such a public sphere."[14] The laudatory goal is a return to Dewey's broader message, to influence students toward a more robust public-mindedness.

The second part of the article offers two lessons. First, Morton and Enos share a specific in-class exercise that Enos uses, and it's an exercise that I have come across from multiple service-learning advocates. Students read a scenario in which two passers-by give a poor, hungry man money. The first passer-by gives him five dollars because she feels compassionate after hearing about his experiences. A second passer-by gives the man one hundred dollars, not because he cares more, but because his religion requires it of him. In discussing this scenario, some students value the first person's actions, and some prefer the second. Enos then asks the students, "Is this the way we would want to feed hungry people, relying on momentary bursts of charity or relying on membership in voluntary organizations, like churches or other nonprofit organizations?"[15] The very wording of this question ("momentary bursts of charity," for example) argues that providing direct service through nonprofits is less valuable than working to address the root causes of the poor man's condition. "Naming the problem and learning how to uncover its origins introduces the students to a process of active deliberation and careful social analysis," Morton and Enos write.[16]

Second, Morton and Enos interview students who have graduated from "one of the few programs in the United States offering a major and minor in Public and Community Service Studies," the Feinstein Institute in Providence College, where Morton works. They note with disappointment that the number of program graduates who have undertaken "explicitly 'public' work upon graduating (in local and state or federal government, public policy research, or community organizing) . . . do not seem to have done so in greater numbers than students from" other departments at the college.[17] Instead, more than 75 percent of their program's graduates end up working in "non-profit and education sectors, helping to run human- and community-service organizations or becoming teachers through alternative schools or programs."[18] Morton and Enos note that the students don't identify their work as public work, but rather as "helping" work. Students value the skills they've learned about how to work with "diverse groups of people" and "engage conflict constructively."[19] They note that students identify more with the professionals managing the community organizations than with the constituents they are serving.[20]

In response to these findings, Morton and Enos examine the choice to place students with partners in the nonprofit sector (They also review the constraints of the university; I'll take up that argument later in a later chapter.) Morton and Enos lay out important critiques of nonprofit human service sector, which (1) "mutes and masks the political and public dimensions of its work"; (2) "focuses primarily on helping individual clients, with a generic goal of upward mobility, thereby acting as a conservator of the values and beliefs of the dominant culture"; (3) sets its agenda "through dialog between the staff of the nonprofit organization and the staff of the funders" rather than through dialog with community constituents; and (4) "has increasingly adopted a corporate management model" based on efficiency rather than relationships."[21] They argue that students working with such organizations are "learn[ing] to mute criticism of government policy and funders, to focus on individual clients, are learning to communicate with and emulate the people who control the resources, and are learning to value rational, expert-based models of service."[22] These lessons, Morton and Enos argue, undermine the program's broader goal of creating public-minded graduates.

The authors close with a few suggestions: that we teach students to critique their own interests through such processes as "power mapping" and that we choose organizations that "emphasize building relationships with people who are connected to places and to the networks of relationship that define place."[23] They suggest building on the work of community organizations like the Asset-based Community Development Institute at Northwestern (run by John McKnight and John Kretzmann) or the Industrial Areas Foundation (founded by Saul Alinsky). These groups help communities build citizen-led organizations that in turn force government and corporate powers to attend to the needs that the community organization has defined. They enact many of the arguments that Dewey espoused, highlighting the capacity of everyday citizens to direct government to appropriate action and insisting that community organizers work with community members, building on their assets and local knowledge while teaching them strategies for analyzing and fighting power. Such community-oriented groups are set in direct contrast to the more individual-oriented human-service sector nonprofits, which Morton and Enos suggest are not working as publics or conducting public work.

Ultimately, I agree with Morton and Enos that we can find productive relationships with community-based organizations, but I resist their easy characterization of human-service sector non-profits as having been co-opted by the values of private corporations and patronizing charities. I have seen many nonprofits that work on issues of poverty and homelessness critique the status quo, even if their methods of doing so are not oriented toward changing public policy. Similarly, I have seen education nonprofits critique the public schools, even if they still work with students to help them meet the imposed educational standards. Rather than group nonprofits into two categories—privatized, corporate, human-services non-publics and community-based, grassroots, social movement publics—we need to look carefully at the historical trajectory of the relationship of governments and nonprofits, as well as at the local and material conditions of each nonprofit itself. While some may align smoothly with the corporate, individualized ideology that Morton and Enos decry, many might use this rhetoric tactically for some purposes (such as funding) even as they struggle against the discourse in other places. Extending the points that David Coogan has made in his analysis of the rhetorics of nonprofit and service-learning, I argue that our analysis should originate within the local and material histories of the organizations themselves.[24] In the process, we may find frameworks that operate in a space other than the dichotomy of private-corporate-individualism and public-government-structuralism.

A MATRIX OF DEMOCRACY: FOR THE PEOPLE, OF THE PEOPLE, BY THE PEOPLE

Morton and Enos acknowledge that "any definition of democratic citizenship is itself an ideological expression located in this history [of contested definitions of democracy]."[25] When anyone makes a claim, even implicitly, about some democratic ideal (the purpose of government, say, or whether people can effect change, or how citizens should interact), all the opposing ideals of democracy threaten to erupt and assert their different interpretation of the situation. Public writing is a constant battle to make one view seem inevitable in hopes that the audience will set aside the other possibilities.

It is also the case that no matter how much we profess to value one spot over another, we are influenced by the whole matrix of democratic ideals. We are surrounded by all the competing discourses of democracy, and we have internalized their logic. We can deploy the rhetoric of any democratic ideal at any moment to explain what is happening around us, and we are not always consistent. For example, while I like to think of myself as trusting people to govern well, I fall easily into using the rhetorics of elite democracy. I have ranted after certain elections about the idiocy of the people who were manipulated into voting for narrow self-interest or who let passion overcome reason. When 9th District Court Judge Walker ruled in the summer of 2010 that California's ban on gay marriage was unconstitutional (Proposition 8), I praised a system that ensured equal protection by having an expert check the wisdom of the referendum voters. We are all of us immersed in the rhetorics of multiple visions of democracy, and it's important to acknowledge the complexity and fluidity of our own ideals.

I'd like to start, then, by making more explicit how the arguments that Morton and Enos make about what counts as public map onto the competing theories of democracy. I'll first trace out a matrix of democratic ideals, noting how different publics manifest as points within that multi-dimensional matrix. With that as a background, I'll then return to Morton's and Enos's argument that privatized social services nonprofits are inadequate sites for studying publics. I'll show how these competing theories of democracy have played out historically and why we would do well to move beyond dichotomies that limit our understandings of how actually-existing publics work. Then I'll offer an alternative way to conceptualize the human services nonprofits as doing public work.

Sociologist and philosopher Jürgen Habermas explains in "Does Democracy Still Enjoy an Epistemic Dimension?" that we can categorize theories of democracy according to "the different weighting that citizens . . . assign to rights and liberties, inclusion and equality, or to public deliberation and problem-solving."[26] The combination of these components "determines how they see themselves as members of the political community."[27] Imagine a diagram with three axes: one traces assumptions about the purpose of government, one traces assumptions about who makes political decisions, and one traces assumptions about the appropriate actions that citizens might take to effect change.

For the People (The Purpose of Government)

Let's imagine that the horizontal axis traces assumptions about the purpose of government. Is government's purpose primarily to protect privacy and individual rights or is it there to structure the interdependence among people? The ends of this axis could be labeled individualist and communitarian. At right end, government is there to protect individuals and their property from the harm and intrusion of other individuals; here, we find a rhetoric of "rights and liberties." In *individualist* theory of democracy, citizens operate as watchdogs, ready to call government or each other to task for encroaching on their rights. Many people refer to what I'm calling the individualist position as *liberal.* I'm avoiding that term because its common use has expanded beyond the focus on personal rights, and I don't want those additional connotations to muddle the explanation. This view of the purpose of government is pervasive:

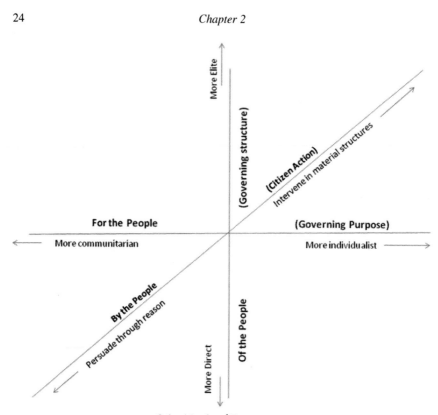

2.1   Matrix of Democracy

Liberalism is one of those things that seem to be "in the air" as people go about their everyday activities. It is evident in the fact that political movements from all points in the political spectrum are more likely to frame their claims in terms of the language of rights than any other discourse (such as, say, appeals to religion or the social good). And it is also evident in the fact that American culture is still, to a large degree, if not exclusively, a culture of business, a culture that believes in entrepreneurialism.[28]

The link that Thomas Streeter makes between liberal individualism and business is significant here; it is one of the center pins of Morton and Enos' argument.

At the left end of the "purpose of government" axis, a more socialist or communitarian perspective argues that because people are not isolated, solitary creatures, the government must go beyond protecting people from each other. It must instead bring people in relation to each other to shape an interdependent identity. In a communitarian democracy, the role of the government is to work out systems through which people take care of each other:

contributing taxes or labor to build infrastructure, staff firehouses, mediate disputes, and so on. The rhetoric here focuses on our responsibilities to each other as members of the same community. It is the rhetoric of patriotic sacrifice and "it takes a village."

Of the People (The Structure of Government)

The vertical axis accounts for who is trusted to lead. On it, we can set out a variety of government systems based on degree of citizen participation, moving from the least citizen participation (on the top) to the most citizen participation (on the bottom). Traditionally, this axis has three main sections: elite, representative, and direct. The elite theory of democracy is often associated with Walter Lippmann—Dewey's notorious adversary, who in the years following World War I, felt that democracy was too precious to be put in the hands of the uneducated masses because they were too self-interested and too excitable. Instead, he argued that democracy required that the masses be led and educated by experts so that they could be guided to endorse the best action for the state.[29] A somewhat more contemporary argument in favor of elite democracy is laid out in Thomas Dye and Harmon Zeigler's *The Irony of Democracy:*

> If the survival of the American system depended upon an active, informed and enlightened citizenry, then democracy in America would have disappeared long ago; for the masses of America are apathetic and ill-informed about politics and public policy, and they have a surprisingly weak commitment to democratic values—individual dignity, equality of opportunity, the right to dissent, freedom of speech and of the press, religious toleration, due process of law. But fortunately for these values and for American society, the American masses do not lead, they follow.[30]

A second view, in the middle of the axis, is a republican democracy, which emphasizes political participation through representatives who listen to people's opinions and then negotiate with each other to find a best solution for the people. The masses contribute to those negotiations by making their preferences heard; these preferences are manifest in "public opinion." The rhetorical work in republican democracy takes place both in the deliberations among the representatives and also in the ways that citizens convey their public opinion, from letters to congressional representatives to working for political campaigns or parties to voting people in or out of office. Citizens work out public opinion by talking about public issues in all sorts of places. In a common model of republican democracy—one which does not fully account for the complexities of the system but that nevertheless dominates in many everyday practices and pedagogies—the media plays a neutral and vital role; it circulates these public conversations so that other citizens and leaders can understand where the public stands.

In direct democracy, the bottom section of the axis, people are entrusted with the power to directly govern themselves. They are sovereign; they can and do control their situations through the mechanisms of direct democracy: referendums (an individualist model structured so that people vote for their own interests and majority rules) or places like town hall meetings (a more communitarian model, where people are expected to deliberate and then enact policy that will benefit the whole group).

By the People (The Actions of Citizens)

Along this axis, we might lay out the tactics people use to persuade those in power (whether government, institutions, or "society" as a whole) to change. The tactics account for what one believes is necessary to create change and range from deliberating and reasoning with other citizens—whose individual actions will yield the needed change; to collectively agitating in order to transform the very institutions that perpetuate the problem the people want to change.

When an issue is understood as a problem that resides in individuals— their misunderstandings of a situation, or their personal biases and weak- nesses—then the method for enacting social change is based on individual and personal transformation. People are educated; people are given tools for self-improvement. Within this model, social and political transformation is a matter of individual choice and behavior. One might try to change a com- munity's racist or sexist attitudes by meeting with residents, sharing personal stories, probing some of their misconceptions and stereotypes, and offering new paradigms for understanding their own experiences. This individualist model, which is heavily influenced by the philosophies of the Enlightenment, locates the power to change in individual choice—we act because of what we believe; therefore, to change people's actions, we should first persuade them to adopt a new belief.

If the power to create change is located not in individual action but with representatives who might influence policy, then one has to deter- mine whether the representatives will be receptive to reasoned argument. Depending on who has the power to create change, the target for persuasion and deliberation will change; it might be an elected representative, a school principal, the CEO of a local company, or any number of others who have the power to act on this issue. Tactics for influencing those people might include trusting the media to convey public opinion to those in power (the most passive and trusting approach) or writing reasonable and persuasive letters or meeting with them in person to deliberate and work out solutions. Also influenced by the Enlightenment, such an approach privileges the power of reason and sees those with whom one will deliberate as well-meaning and benevolent.

If an Enlightenment model assumes that people act because they believe, a more materialist understanding of belief flips this around: we believe because we act.[31] No matter what we consciously identify as our beliefs and intentions, as this thinking goes, the structures of our daily actions reinforce particular underlying ideologies about the proper relations among people. Take, for example, that Enlightenment belief in individual choice. Especially in a capitalist country where our buying power is sold to us as a mark of our individual identity, our sense of control over our behaviors and attitudes is reinforced hundreds of times a day. If we have enough money, we experience daily that we can choose Kix or Cheerios, Gap or Abercrombie and Fitch. We may not pause to question why these are the choices available, or what it is that leads us and millions of others to desire this particular style and color of sweater this year. We may not pause to consider how this "individualist" consumer identity is not available to people without wealth, and, therefore, how our belief in "individual" choice is intricately linked with our economic class.

Rather than see our beliefs as the products of internal rational debates, a materialist view says that we desire certain things and adopt certain behaviors because of the daily actions we perform. Schools, families, religious communities, neighborhoods, and other institutions to which we belong teach us "proper" behaviors and "proper" relationships to people and things. We are shown what to see and what to ignore, what identities to adopt, and what to value. By watching and responding to others, we learn how to enter a friend's house and admire its expanses of windows, its deep luxurious carpets, its walls of bookshelves—to admire the products there, the collection of material objects. Or, by watching and listening to others, we learn to enter that space and wonder who built it, how much labor it took, who cleans it—to populate it with workers. We learn about gendered space from the architecture of our houses: does the father have a desk, a study, and walls of books, while the mother collects her materials on a kitchen counter? From this, we learn who deserves autonomy and who does not.[32]

When belief is understood as a culmination of material experiences, then a public that wishes to effect change will try to change behavior without first trying to appeal to reason. This approach might involve pressuring them through coordinated campaigns that capture media attention, such as mass boycotts and strikes, marches, or large-scale civil disobedience marches.

By the People in Elite, Direct, and Republican Democracy

Ideals about the best tactics for influencing change vary as people assess which purposes of government (individualist or communitarian) and which structures of government (elite, republican, or direct) apply at a given moment.

In an elite democracy in which people arrive at their positions through rational choice, the elite would deliberate about the best course of action and then persuade the masses of its virtues through well-reasoned communications. Conversely, elite democracy might not be rooted in a model of rational choice; the elite might secure its power by maintaining those everyday institutional structures—family, religion, schooling, business models—that influence the masses to behave and believe in a certain manner.[33]

To consider another government structure, a direct democracy might operate with all decisions made through reasoned deliberation, or one might see the citizens' choices in a deliberative democracy as influenced at a more unconscious level by their daily actions and experiences; the strategy for mobilizing public change in this direct democracy would have to include strategies for intervening with those everyday experiences—redesigning public spaces, interrupting everyday actions, and so on.

Within a republican structure, one might reason with one's representatives, or one might see those in power as unreceptive to reason. When representatives and fellow citizens are seen as receptive to reason, citizens deliberate about matters of importance and, through ongoing conversations with diverse groups of people, they arrive at new knowledge which suggests the right course of action; their work as citizens is epistemic. Their public opinion becomes clear to the representatives because the discourse is prevalent in the media and because they communicate to their representatives in letters and in person, laying out rational and clear arguments for that public opinion.[34]

On the other end of the republican continuum are those who consider elected representatives to have the power to effect change but who don't see them as responding to reason. The tactic here is to show those in power that they must take action to retain their power to govern. Earth First!, the radical environmental group, sees the government as thoroughly seeped in for-profit, capitalist understanding of land value. Deliberation is unproductive in such an ideologically closed space, so they choose instead to force developers to contend with their physical actions. They occupy the land (living in trees so they cannot be cut down) and destroy the property they believe is destroying the earth (by vandalizing bulldozers and other construction equipment).

This view can also be found in Malcolm X's rejection of Dr. King's tactics in the Civil Rights Movement. Both Malcolm X and Dr. King recognized that racism was much more than an individual belief rooted in ignorance (an all-too-common characterization of racism today and one which suggests that personal education alone would be an adequate solution.) Both shared an understanding that racism was (and, I would argue, still is) lived out daily in the schools where children learned, in the buses people rode to and from work, and in the businesses where they purchased their family groceries. Both shared an understanding that these systems needed to be confronted and exposed, that African Americans needed to refuse the roles they had been asked to take and, in so doing, reveal how much the system depended on their compliance with such racism. But they advocated very different means for confronting this racism, means grounded in different understandings of the power and ability of the dominant group to yield to a cause of fairness. For Dr. King, agitation would lead both individuals and those in power to recognize the profound inequities of the system; once the violence of the current system was exposed, those who benefited from it would work to dismantle it. For Malcolm X, extending such benevolence to those who benefited from the system was naïve. He argued for more direct action so that the government would act, not because they were persuaded of the righteousness of the position, but because they felt the action necessary to maintain their power to govern.

There's a middle ground as well: those who favor a republican democracy but are skeptical about how representatives learn about or respond to public opinion. They take steps to make sure their views are heard. They also do not presume that the representative is entirely benevolent; they see those in power as choosing not necessarily the best action for all of the constituents, but rather the actions they hear the most about, understand the best, or find the most expedient. Citizens working under this model take steps to pressure representatives to take action on their behalf. Instead of allowing the media to determine what ideas have risen to the level of public opinion, they communicate directly to their representatives through letters, e-mails, and personal visits. They stage events to influence media coverage, organizing a march of such size that the media will attend, or they saturate the talk show circuit so that their view is widely distributed. They might use combination of the two, like staging a sit-in at a government office and bringing the media to cover it. The goal here is not necessarily epistemic; they are not working with other citizen groups or with the representative to identify the most reasonable and comprehensive action. Rather, they understand their own needs as competing with all of the other representative's constituents, and they understand the process as one of analyzing and demonstrating power.

THE WORLD AS IT IS AND THE WORLD AS IT SHOULD BE

Identifying the right kind of actions that the people should take for a well-functioning democracy means staking out a place along all three axes—the purpose of government, the form of government, and the tactics for influencing government. Yet, arguments about democracy are actually located on two spots of the matrix, simultaneously. In a call for public action, we'll find implicit or explicit arguments about where the "ideal" democracy sits on the matrix and where the actually-existing democracy sits on the matrix. Lippman emphasized this distinction as he made his case for elite democracy; he dedicated a chapter of *Public Opinion* to "The World Outside and the Pictures in Our Heads."[35] Saul Alinsky, the father of radical community organizing, emphasized this distinction as he trained organizers to agitate people toward a more direct democracy. Even today, the Industrial Areas Foundation training program includes a careful reflection of "The World As it Is, and the World as It Should Be."[36]

Michelle Obama talked about this concept in her address to the Democratic National Convention in 2008. As she kicked off the Convention, she recounted watching Barack lead a community meeting in Chicago:

> Barack stood up that day, and spoke words that have stayed with me ever since. He talked about "the world as it is" and "the world as it should be." And he said that all too often, we accept the distance between the two, and settle for the world as it is—even when it doesn't reflect our values and aspirations. But he reminded us that we know what our world should look like. We know what fairness and justice and opportunity look like. And he urged us to believe in ourselves—to find the strength within ourselves to strive for the world as it should be. And isn't that the great American story?[37]

The power of public writing, I would argue, is located in precisely this moment: the ability to rally others to agree with a specific characterization of "the world as it is" and "the world as it should be," and to agree about the power of those in that world to effect this transformation. As both scholars and creators of public writing, we should be mindful of how we make the case for what world exists and what world is desirable.

MORTON AND ENOS IN THE MATRIX OF DEMOCRACY

How does Morton's and Enos's argument fit into this matrix of democracy? Morton and Enos define "the world as it should be" as a "genuinely democratic culture," "a sustainable, community-based culture in which people participate directly in maintaining a healthy public sphere."[38] Their position, which I would name "participatory democracy,"[39] sits on the left, communitarian end of the purpose-of-government axis. They urge a critical look at organizations that employ elitist structures where service-professionals position themselves as the experts, providing for the community without consulting that community, and they are rightfully concerned when students identify as the "helpers" without establishing meaningful, reciprocal relationships with their fellow citizens.

While Morton and Enos see the ideal democratic structure as a republic (middle of the structure-of-government axis), they criticize the dominant manifestation of the current, republican system for acting as if individuals can effect change through rational exchanges with their representatives. Thus, along the third axis, they argue that citizens need to learn how to mobilize communities to pressure representatives—strategies of community organizing that position those in power as neither benevolent nor particularly receptive to reason. Change happens through structural transformations, which are accomplished when many people collaborate and challenge the root causes of social problems. They write,

> All definitions of "citizenship" as a bundle of cognitive, affective, and behavioral attributes adhering to an individual person will ultimately fail to solve the problem of how to engage youth in civic life. These definitions all presume that the terrain in which the new "citizens" act is neutral territory, wide open to their energy and presence. We do not see public space as much available or open . . . . Service learning . . . [should concentrate] on democratizing the political and cultural landscape in which those students live.[40]

I agree with how Morton and Enos define the actually-existing and ideal democracies on the matrix, and I, too, wish to go beyond the rhetoric of "service" and "helping" that dominates much nonprofit work and investigate (and teach students to investigate) the wide range of tactics that publics can use to effect change. As explained with my narrative in the previous chapter about my initial missteps in designing service-learning courses, I agree that we need to be very mindful about how the democratic visions we promote in our classes coincide with those in the community organizations we study or with whom we partner for service-learning classes.

Morton and Enos add an additional layer to the matrix of democracy, as well, a critical one that examines political systems within the context of economic forces. They examine how capitalist economic ideals have become enmeshed with theories of democracy. This additional layer, I believe, complicates their dichtomoy of private-corporate individualist nonprofits and public-government structuralist nonprofits.

NEOLIBERALISM: CAPITALISM AS DEMOCRACY

As an economic system that relies on consumption, the accumulation of private property, and a workforce acclimated to managerial hierarchy, capitalism is not neutral to any of these axes of democracy. As Morton and Enos explain, capitalism works by rendering political and social connections in the language of individualism and consumption. It relies on

> [a] separation of economic decisions making from particular places and from the lives of those most directly affected, the rendition of all objects and relationships as active or potential commodities, the fragmentation of human experience across unconnected spheres of activity, and the substitution of the marketplace for the public sphere.[41]

Capitalism is built on cultural and social values that align readily with the individualist, elitist, and passive democratic ideals. The term often used to describe democracy that has been redefined in terms of the goals of capitalism is "neoliberalism." The purpose of government is individualist: to protect private property and to facilitate business. "Citizenship is portrayed as an utterly privatized affair whose aim is to produce competitive, self-interested individuals vying for their own material and ideological gain."[42] The structure of neoliberal government trends toward elitism because it is a more efficient model for getting the business of government accomplished. Direct democracy is too long and involved a process; moreover, direct democracy where citizens influence business, government, and each other through collective action does not fit within a free-market paradigm. CEOs need to make decisions based on profit-margins for shareholders, rather than demands of labor or community members. Within capitalism, power is rightfully accrued with capital, and capital is the tool for political influence. Citizens play their best role as consumers who direct business and government action through their purchasing power. Their choice of products affects the bottom line, which motivates appropriate change within the free-market system.

Capitalism lays out its own its own democratic logic by pronouncing that everyone (citizens and representatives) best serves the public good by endorsing those activities and attitudes which serve the economic good. Citizens are responsible for safeguarding the space for capitalism, but within that space, economic decisions are rendered as private. Extending the individualist purpose of government, capitalism argues that governments and citizens should protect individual rights and private property, including those of businesses. In free-market capitalism, businesses should be free to govern themselves by their own (economic) principles, such as supply and demand and the profit motive. Corporations should be beyond the reach of governments and citizens who might try to insert nonmarket-related concerns into the economic equation.

An implicit warning in Morton's and Enos's article is that those who study and teach civic engagement must be on the lookout for how capitalism can co-opt both the rhetoric of democracy and the practice of nonprofit, public work. The trends toward more elitist, hierarchical nonprofits in which professionals provide service "products" that community members "consume" aligns well with a capitalist rhetoric through which citizens are further socialized into their roles as consumers and have a very limited power to influence the public market. They are right to warn about the growing privatization of public responsibilities and public actions.

In response to this concern, Morton and Enos propose that teachers who want students to learn the practices and disposition of more communitarian, more direct democracy, should place them in community-centered nonprofits whose goals and practices are more visibly in line with these public ideals. My quibble with Morton and Enos is not with their desire to define real public work as more direct or communitarian, but with their recommendation to avoid human-service sector nonprofits and other privatized organizations like them. By extension, I hear them arguing, as well, that scholars who wish to study public formation should avoid those nonpublic nonprofits as well. I argue, in contrast, that we need to attend to these kinds of nonprofits because they are manifestations of an ongoing struggle to define what is public. We shouldn't engage with them naively or uncritically, of course, but neither should we ignore them altogether. Instead, we should consider how they negotiate the complex challenge of doing nonprofit work within the pervasive for-profit capitalist context that currently envelopes public space.

A HISTORY OF PRIVATE GOVERNMENT RESPONSIBILITY

When Morton and Enos suggest that the nonprofits within the human-services sector are not doing public work, they set as fixed what is more accurately understood as an ongoing struggle to define the causes of social ills such as poverty, to name the best methods for addressing those problems, and to identify the people most responsible for carrying out those methods. They are right to expose the rhetoric of elite, docile individualism in the human-services sector, but I wish that they had considered this discourse as a problem against which many nonprofits struggle, rather than as an ideal that those nonprofits have embraced. The privatized human-services sector is one point in a long trajectory of arguments about the role of government in welfare. It is not a fixed position, and it is not an entirely solidified position. It is, however, the political and economic structure in which many nonprofits work. While some nonprofits may value this kind of industrial efficiency, many resist it, even as they gesture toward it in grant proposals and annual reports for their donors.

Nonprofits are confronted with multiple definitions of public work regularly. They navigate the ramifications of being a tax-exempt 501(c)3 (a tax bracket that revokes some rights to petition government) alongside policy wonks who believe real change happens when government programs are revised or overturned. They navigate the expectations of many funding foundations that nonprofits should operate as efficient experts to fix problems in any area, alongside the rhetoric of grassroots community movements, which presume all nonprofits should be run by community leaders. These struggles are not new, but rather reflect nonprofits' historical location in a long line of such struggles.

The tension about ideal management styles and ideal relationships with constituents—the tensions about what makes up public work—are never settled, and we would do well to examine the democratic rhetorics of nonprofits within this struggle.

Democracy, Industrialization, and the Rhetoric of Efficiency and Expertise

Though many often reference Dewey without situating his argument within the rising industrial capitalism of the early twentieth century, that context is significant, and I'm glad that Morton and Enos discuss it. I think they could go farther with that historical and economic analysis, though, because from the industrial revolution to the latter half of the twentieth century, the U.S. government and dominant culture significantly redefined the concepts of public, private, government, and nonprofit. Philanthropic work, once assumed to be the moral duty of the wealthy, was first absorbed into the government and later outsourced to nonprofits. Contemporary human-service nonprofits are the result of historically competing definitions of whether conditions such as poverty are public or private.

In the article, service-learning is linked to Dewey and Paul Hanna. In the early twentieth century, amid the Industrial Era celebration of consumerism and vocationalism, Dewey and Hanna promoted an educational model in which students would learn how to create alternative, democratic culture.[43] Their model was designed to help young citizens resist the nonpublic messages of an industrialized market economy. In the Deweyan model, people gained a sense of agency, power, and public-mindedness by coming together to learn and work together on social problems. They found meaning in creating their world rather than in consuming; they found meaning in reinserting the human faces and relationships onto what were presented as commodities and fragments. This active response to the dehumanizing effects of industrial capitalism seems to be in line with the goals of many public-minded teachers and intellectuals, such as Cornel West, who wish to fight off the nihilism and loss of agency that are perpetuated in a capitalist, consumerist culture.

Still, the Industrial Era backdrop offered a less communitarian model for the relationship of capital and the public, as well, one that Morton and Enos do not mention: the idea of philanthropy. As Robert Egger explains in *Begging for Change: The Dollars and Sense of Making Nonprofits Responsive,* the captains of industry who grew wealthy from the labor of factory workers, miners, and oil riggers were themselves caught up in the discourses of social gospel and social Darwinism.[44] They felt a moral and religious duty to address society's worst problems. Inspired also by Jane Addams' Settlement House movement, where people studied social problems as they lived and worked with the country's immigrants and poor, the wealthy felt obligated to fund studies and set up organizations to address the terrible public health conditions and poverty around them. In 1907, Margaret Sage, heir to wealth from the railroads, started the Russell Sage Foundation.[45] Oil tycoon John D. Rockefeller set up his foundation in 1910, followed by steel magnate Andrew Carnegie in 1911.[46] Not surprisingly, these foundations' analysis of poverty was not rooted in any critique of capitalism. Rather, like the Industrial Revolution itself, their analysis was grounded in an unyielding belief in the power of science and American exceptionalism. If anyone could get at the root of these social problems, they believed, it would be Americans, working in the traditions of Enlightenment.[47] Dewey's arguments were set against this Industrial-Era version of *noblesse oblige.*

I think it's important to keep this context in mind when considering Dewey's famous debates with Walter Lippman. Just as Ford transformed industrial production by shifting from a focus on craft (where a worker makes a product from beginning to end) to the assembly line (where a worker's duties are limited to a small part in a complex system), Lippman argued that the work of government was now too complex to be left in the hands of individual citizens. Ordinary citizens were not capable of understanding or making wise decisions; instead, "Lippman advocated bureaus of experts that would organize issues into more manageable frames."[48] The role of the media would be to transmit the experts' conclusions to the masses. This theory of democratic elitism, combined with a great optimism about science, fit smoothly with the new economic environment of the time, where managers controlled decision making in factories in the name of "efficiency" and where citizens were simultaneously disconnected from any control of production as workers, even as their increased power as consumers was celebrated. They weren't able make an entire car, but they could now afford to buy one. Efficiency is the hallmark of wealth, in this scenario, and it followed that the duty of the wealthy was to increase efficiency in the arena of government as well as industry.

While Dewey vehemently opposed the rhetoric of efficiency as a guiding value of democracy, we have to admit that any argument against efficiency today still struggles against a sea of proefficiency, procapitalist, proelitist discourse. Dewey challenged Lippmann's view that expertise and knowledge were qualities of an individual mind rather than the result of deliberation with others, Dewey argued that all people could be knowledgeable if such interactions were encouraged and promoted within democratic culture. Dewey challenged Lippmann's conception of a managerial sort of government transmitted to the masses. In both his arguments about schooling and his argument about government,

> Dewey replaced the notion of the spectator with the participant, and thus contrasted the metaphor of vision with that of hearing. The result was an understanding that citizens do not simply observe a world, but rather actively participate in the construction of that world through interaction and communication.[49]

My point here is that this argument between Dewey and Lippmann, often characterized as a battle of ideas about government, was imbued with the transformation of work and everyday life at many levels. As much as contemporary scholars or community activists uphold Dewey as their predecessor and the source of the ideals of schooling and community relationships they wish to promote, we must recognize his battle as one staged in an era where these ideals were hotly contested. Moreover, it's hard to say that Dewey won out; the struggle remains ongoing and intense. Lippmann's vision of democracy, Ford's vision of industry, and the rhetoric of expertise and efficiency pack a heavy punch in these fights about democracy. Any public that operates through time-consuming deliberation or delegates agency to citizens fights against the capitalist pressure for efficiency, the expected tradeoff between cheap consumption and any meaningful role in production. Measurable outcomes too often trump the squishy values of process even today, almost a century after Lippmann and Dewey debated. When Morton and Enos report that "the human-service sector has increasingly adopted a corporate management model: breaking larger problems into their constituent elements and assigning the resolution of these problems to specialized organizations and people with technical expertise,"[50] they reveal the power that the corporate mindset has had on public work: it "caused the human-services system to adopt an efficiency-based model of performances."[51] Such a model is not surprising, of course, if we consider that the philanthropic foundations to which such nonprofits apply for funding are themselves derived from the wealth of the captains of industry. But the funding stream is not the only or even the main force that pressures organizations toward this capitalist discourse of efficiency. As we have seen, capitalist ideals for the public align smoothly with the logic of liberal individualism and spectator-level political activity.

Morton and Enos argue that if students are placed in nonprofits that have come down on the side of the more privatized, corporate model of efficiency, they will only learn how to model themselves after service provider elites. Perhaps they will accrue some discrete civic abilities, but they will not understand how to challenge the corporate model of democracy. I wonder, though, if Morton and Enos have written off these nonprofits too quickly. Instead of avoiding such organizations, I'd ask if they might better be approached as a space of ongoing struggle. Where does the dominant, corporate-efficiency public circulate its worldview—both discursively and materially—and what strategies might resistant publics use to fight it? I'll first trace out another historical argument about the responsibilities of public welfare, and then I'll offer some alternatives for how we might evaluate whether or not certain nonprofits are productive models for teaching and engaging in public work.

Welfare, Local Government, and the Rhetorics of "Dependency" and "Empowerment"

Just as we can map out the discourse of efficiency as an ongoing struggle through history, so can we map out a historical struggle to locate welfare as an individual problem rather than as a systemic one. Morton and Enos consider the human service nonprofits as not truly public because the focus on individuals undercuts an emphasis on the root causes of poverty, illiteracy, and other social issues. When they describe their hopes for their Public Services graduates, Morton and Enos define public work as working "in local and state or federal government, public policy research, or community organizing."[52] They set this in contrast to "working in nonprofit and education sectors, helping to run human and community-service organizations."[53] Yet when we look at the history of nonprofits, we find that this distinction between the public sector and the human services sector is the continuation of ongoing debates about social welfare, federalism, and local control. To say that human services are not public work is to ignore how public welfare has been explicitly outsourced and funded by the government. The government itself is ambivalent here; it claims it is not responsible for welfare, even as it provides direct and indirect funding. Many in the nonprofit sector regularly push back against this presumption that welfare and human services are not public work.

One thing to keep in mind is that it wasn't until the Great Depression that the federal government played a role in funding social services at all. Before then, responsibility for social service lay squarely with individuals and local governments. But when local communities saw their private funds dry up in the Depression, they welcomed the influx of services within Roosevelt's New Deal, including the Social Security Administration, the Civil Conservation Corps (to fund people working on public infrastructure projects), and other allocations of monies to farmers and even industry.[54] The federal government also facilitated businesses' contributions to nonprofits. In 1935, faced with a loss of tariff revenue, the federal government began taxing corporations, and it provided a tax incentive for companies to set up philanthropic nonprofits as tax shelters.[55] When Roosevelt began taxing citizen's income at the start of World War II, he again offered incentives for tax payers to give money to nonprofits. In the process, Roosevelt's administration leveraged the philanthropic ideals of the industrial era millionaires into a set of tax incentives meant to encourage private citizens and businesses to fund the public service workers. Businesses and millionaires alike sought out these tax loopholes, and "philanthropy became a means to conserve wealth."[56] This new system of government-incentivized donations from businesses and private citizens often distributed through foundations created one of the funding streams responsible for distributing monies to nonprofits today.

A second money stream began with presidents Kennedy and Johnson, who devoted part of their administrations' budgets to social services. Whereas the New Deal programs, such as Social Security and Aid for Dependent Children, provided direct income to those in need, Kennedy instead began offering programs that provided indirect assistance, such as skills training and other noncash support.[57] The root causes of dependency had been redefined. The problem for the poor was no longer understood as a matter of not having money (as was argued in the Depression, when so many people from all ranks of society were without work); rather, the problem was understood as having inadequate training or inappropriate dispositions. The system was not responsible for poverty. The barriers to employment and social integration into the middle-class could be best addressed with social services.

Starting in 1962, the funding for social services came from the federal government but was administered by the states, but within a few years, the federal government agreed to contract with nonprofit vendors in addition to state agencies.[58] As a result of these changes, the face of compassion in the

United States was not the federal government or even the local government, but rather nonprofits.[59]

During President Reagan's administration, the arguments about government funding for nonprofits met with another of the ideals of corporate liberalism: the wisdom of the local market. For one thing, Reagan continued the practice began under President Nixon of giving social service money to states in block grants with fewer federal mandates about which kinds of needs the money should address. Both Nixon and Reagan argued that big government at the federal level was inefficient because it was too big to respond to citizens' needs. The better way to ensure a good response to citizens' needs was to keep money local and to subject it to market-style competition. Nonprofits would compete against each other for the outsourced government funds. Such a model fit well with the economic ideals flourishing under Reagan's administration. "In the private sector, competition would presumably produce the optimum outcome: the 'best practices' for treating social ills." Reagan applied "market logic to social services."[60]

At the same time, and unlike Nixon, Reagan cut the amount of federal money that was distributed. Concurrent with the arguments about the inefficiency and wastefulness of big government, Reagan mounted a critique of the inefficiency and wastefulness of those people who did not thrive under the national economic and political structures that were supposed to bring freedom and prosperity to all. During his 1976 presidential campaign, Reagan described—as a prototypical example—a "welfare queen" who bilked the system through numerous schemes and who received undeserved handouts. His was a tough love, meant to pressure lazy people into taking responsibility for themselves. As president, Reagan reduced funding to programs such as Food Stamps and Medicare, arguing that such programs enabled people's dependency on government handouts.

What we see, beginning with Kennedy but developing most powerfully under Reagan, is a rhetoric about welfare that locates the root causes of poverty in people's inability or unwillingness to work within what they see as an essentially fair economic system; it's based on a belief that people who apply themselves can find jobs and support themselves. This position was reinforced yet again under President Clinton, who set limits on the number of years a person could receive government aid. From this perspective, those in need were—and still are—shunted into two categories: "those who were just receiving a check became the unworthy poor, while those who were actively trying to escape welfare deserved job training, day care, and other government-sponsored services."[61]

The characterization of welfare recipients as a people who lack initiative and drain government resources exemplifies an ideology about the role of government that George Lakoff explores in some depth in his book, *Moral Politics*, and its smaller version, *Don't Think of an Elephant.*[62] A sociolinguist, Lakoff examines the metaphors underlying the rhetoric of liberal and conservative American pundits and politicians. After a careful analysis of conservative powerhouse James Dobson and his influential Focus on the Family, Lakoff identifies a metaphorical framework he calls the "strict father morality." Within this system, self-discipline is a primary moral value, one that intersects smoothly with free-market capitalism. Those who are self-disciplined will work hard and fight for their self-interest; they understand that they must compete to get what they need, and they understand that in a competitive world, there will be winners and losers. Good parents, and by extension, good governments, reward and punish their children/citizens so that they learn how to live and survive in this competitive world. Within this model, social welfare programs that give away services are damaging and immoral because they encourage dependency.[63] By extension, compassionate conservatism demands that government withhold handouts and incentivize people to "take responsibility" and be "self-reliant." Ascribing the roots of poverty to systemic problems within capitalism or the inequities of a pluralist democracy doesn't fit within this model, as it suggests that the person has agreed to see him or herself as a victim, as someone willing to cede power to this larger system rather than take responsibility to work hard, figure things out, and succeed.

Beginning with Kennedy, revitalized by Reagan, and reinforced by Clinton, the federal government has undergone a political recharacterization of its responsibility for supporting the poor. Whereas government aid policies were once grounded in providing direct assistance to people deprived of work during what was understood as a systemic crisis in the Great Depression, they are now grounded in providing limited noncash aid through skills development programs so people can find work within what is understood as a functioning economic and political system. Of course, there's some tension here. By funding such programs indirectly through local nonprofits, the government buries the critique of systemic causes and locates solutions at the local, even individual level. However, by funding such programs at all, the government acknowledges a responsibility to do something and acknowledges obliquely that the current economic, social, and political system is not functioning at its ideal. Arguments in Congress and in statehouses across the country regularly return to this tension. The current recession has raised this debate to the fore again. Those who side with President Obama and call for stimulus packages and extending unemployment benefits see the loss of jobs as part of a systemic problem, brought on by financial speculators and the government's failure to oversee the economic infrastructure. Those who call for the end of unemployment payments or government support for struggling businesses locate the problem squarely on the shoulders of individuals (including individual businesses) whose poor choices led to their current conditions. The recession is the result of the necessary correction of market forces, including shedding of over-regulated labor and eliminating badly managed businesses; interfering in this correction, even to make lives easier for those affected, will prohibit the necessary recovery, they say. As is quite clear from listening to the news pundits today, arguments about the government's role in either the economy or the public welfare is certainly not fixed and final.

Given this long debate, I return to Morton's and Enos's argument that the nonprofit human services sector is not a good place to learn about democracy. Their argument is bolstered by many progressive organizations that refuse foundation and government funding because that funding comes with too many strings and too many expectations that the organization will carry forward an individualist, corporate discourse and management style. For example, the progressive community organization Incite!, which sees their work to end violence against women of color as revolutionary, has published an anthology of radical critiques of the kind of control that foundations and government organizations maintain through their funding. The anthology is provocatively titled *The Revolution Will Not Be Funded: Beyond the Non-Profit Industrial Complex* and details stories of how foundations seek to dull any systemic critiques by the organizations they fund.[64] While I agree with the observations of Morton, Enos, and Incite! that the funding streams of capitalist foundations and the federal government, along with the constraints of the 501(c)3 status, inundate human services nonprofits with individualist, conservative ideologies, I would again argue that we should not presume that these structural constraints control everything. As was true for the corporate rhetoric of efficiency, the rhetoric of individualism and "self-help" has long been contested. We should consider whether the rhetoric is also resisted within nonprofits.

When Morton and Enos suggest that the human-services sector is only about helping and not about truly public activity, they seem to yield the whole sector to those who characterize social services as private. Instead, we can investigate how the dominant message that the root cause is individualistic is constantly reinforced, circulated, and maintained through government policies and economic systems but also resisted by people who work within and outside those systems. If we look closely, we can see that resistance. Jeffrey Berry outlines such strategies in *A Voice for Nonprofits*.[65] Despite the constraints of a 501(c)3 tax-exempt status, many nonprofits work closely with government officials, providing information at representatives' requests and working side-by-side with them to shape policy. They often provide amicus briefs or help draft "Dear Colleagues" letters in which representatives lay out a line of thinking about an issue for their fellow congressmen or senators. Nonprofits also may educate their constituents about how to lobby representatives. If you ask them directly, though, the nonprofits may not call this public work. At the same time that they advise government on behalf of their constituents, the nonprofit directors in Berry's study understand that they have to characterize their work as apolitical to retain their tax status. Berry's book is an interesting analysis of how nonprofits negotiate this tricky space. Nonprofits that seek federal funding and operate in a culture saturated with the rhetoric of capitalism have to negotiate all of these competing definitions.

I also argue that nonprofits that do not direct their energies toward trying to effect change through government still do public work. Though they may not lobby for changes in policy, many still define the issues their programs address as public rather than private concerns. Many direct-aid charities refuse to judge their constituents but instead witness to the conditions that have forced those individuals into poverty. They define the issues as part of bigger systems of interactions, rather than as the result of laziness, addiction, or other personal failures; they work to meet the needs of their constituents and to try to change the larger cultural understanding about poverty, education, or whatever the issue is. If nonprofits do not lobby for government change or teach their constituents how to agitate for change, their choice of alternate modes of service should not be seen as tacit support for the current system or as agreeing with those who blame the poor for their predicament. Rather, we should consider their stance within the material and ideological constraints of their work, constraints that the organization may embrace or resist. Nonprofits may see themselves as working against the status quo in ways that don't fit with the kind of community organizing or government decision-making that Morton and Enos suggest is the real hallmark of public work.

The terms we use to stake out our visions of democracy—private vs. public, elite vs. direct—try to pin down concepts that are fluid. No nonprofit and no public is ever fully and only in one category. A nonprofit, as a kind of public, must work within the avenues of circulation it has available. It must negotiate the constraints of genre, working with and against the rhetorical assumptions of each mode of circulation. A nonprofit must work with and against competing public discourses. That is why I am uncomfortable following Morton and Enos in dismissing the whole nonprofit human services sector as private.

Instead, I think it's worth looking at nonprofits as organizations that advance multiple arguments, arguments that come into focus when we look at them within historical, cultural, and local contexts, and especially when we compare them to the arguments advanced by similar organizations and by organizations that are working in similar communities. We'll gain a much richer understanding about how publics form and circulate when we can look at community organizations without imposing one ideal about what is public action and what is not. That's a tall order, of course. Ironically, the person who helped me figure out how to get past this binary in my own thinking was Keith Morton.

BEYOND THE CHARITY-TO-CHANGE CONTINUUM

I found a new way to think about how the nonprofit service might be understood as public work in an article recommended to me by Thomas Deans, whose own book, *Writing Partnerships: Service-Learning in Composition*, influenced my approach a great deal. The article that Professor Deans recommended is from Keith Morton—the same Keith Morton with whom I have agreed and disagreed so much in this chapter. In "The Irony of Service: Charity, Project, and Social Change," which Morton published earlier in *The Michigan Journal of Community Service Learning*, Morton offers a more expansive way to understand nonprofit service organizations.[66]

Morton writes to faculty across the disciplines who teach service-learning courses. He begins by reviewing a trend he sees in the scholarship and practices of those who use service-learning to advance democratic values. Such faculty (and he counts himself as initially being part of this group) evaluate community organizations according to a continuum. The continuum begins with charities as its starting point, organizations described disparagingly as places where people of means help other people and where the service is usually conducted according to the needs of the giver. Next, he lists projects, programs with measurable outcomes and fixed timelines, which are focused on specific, immediate actions. Finally, he names the pinnacle: social change organizations.[67] These are the modes that service-learning faculty like best, he says; they are seen as the most mature form of compassion.[68] Social change organizations tackle the root causes of the problems, and in the process of challenging the appropriate targets, they teach everyone how to take action. Social change organizations treat all of their participants as part of the solution; they bring people together to deliberate for common ground. Indeed, the real goal here is not so much the particular action but rather the transformation of a community into a public. You can hear the rhetoric of Deweyan participatory democracy through and through.

Morton takes this continuum and shakes it up. After interviewing people who work and volunteer at all three kinds of service organizations, he goes back and separates each category of service into two parts: the kinds of work it does and the relationships it builds with its community. I've created a visual chart for this argument (see Figure 2.2).

Morton argues that the relationship building we value in social change is tied to central qualities that he calls "thick" service: qualities of respect and dignity, of starting where people are, and neither judging nor seeking to control them. It is profoundly nonelitist. Thick service acknowledges broader systemic causes for the concerns that mobilize us and requires we approach each other as equals. But thick service does not require that we take action by marching on city hall or boycotting stores; thick service does not have to be oriented toward government. He sees the possibility of thick service within charities and projects, as well.

Thick charity, Morton explains, is spiritually-based service, outside of time and place, and bears witness to the worth of other people."[69] Within thick charity, those who have suffered because of the inequities of government, capitalism, or other systems are received as whole people. They are not judged as having failed to assimilate. Their situation is seen as a consequence of a failed system. Recognizing that living in a society that rarely acknowledges how individual lives are held hostage to the consequences of systemic inequities, charities provide space where those individuals can rest and gather strength away from harsh judgment and disdain. In a later chapter, when I discuss the philosophy of DC nonprofit Miriam's Kitchen, I provide a concrete example of a "thick charity" organization.

In contrast, thick projects operate within time: they are grounded in timelines of measurable outcomes. Nevertheless, they are still committed to working with their constituents to understand the best activities to undertake. Their activities evolve through regular reflections on their work and the changing conditions of their work. "The logic of the project approach assumes that no solutions are ultimate, and that thoughtful reasoned approaches leading to measurable action—doing something—is the appropriate response to community needs."[70] Leaders ground their work in an ethic of listening, surviving over time, and encouraging the participation of the people who are served.[71] Life Pieces to Masterpieces, a program I described at the beginning of the introduction, is an example of a thick project. I'll spend more time examining the democratic theory undergirding Life Pieces to Masterpieces' thick project approach in the next section of this chapter.

Once we separate out the thick and thin relationships from the mode of service, we have new ways to evaluate organizations that do not take on social advocacy. Thin charities are still those who work in patronizing and elitist ways, speaking for others rather than with them and focusing on their deficits rather than their assets. But thick charity—which Morton acknowledges is espoused in many different religions—witnesses to the experiences

	Charity providing direct aid to people; immediate; works outside of time.	Project developing specific, measurable programs that will redistribute resources; works within time.	Social Change identifying and addressing the root causes of problems by working to change gov't/corporate/cultural policies or behaviors; on-going.
Thick working with people as equals, treating them with dignity and respect and honoring the experience and knowledge that they bring; deeply aware of the injustices that permeate society, and an understanding of power dynamics; asset-based	Witnessing, a profound attentiveness that shows they are worthy. Aid is given not because people are needy but because they have a right to it. Done with a clear sense that their conditions are symptoms of a bigger problem.	Developing programs in partnership with the people the program is meant to benefit; regularly assessing and adjusting to new information; programs are designed with an attentiveness to the injustices, not simply at level of fixing the behavior of individuals	Works with community members to identify community concerns and desires—often deals with multiple issues; works with community members to give them the tools & experience to challenge those institutions (gov't/business/cultural) to effect change
Thin conducting work for others, without consultation or without fully involving them in the decisions that will affect them; deficit-based	Providing help to others in a manner that accounts more for the giver's needs than the receiver; may be patronizing or inadequate.	Programs are developed without consultation with community members; they may operate through a deficit model, highlighting the lack in others. May treat only individual behavior with no acknowledgement of systemic injustices	Attacks community problems by challenging appropriate targets, but does not organize community members in planning those interventions.

Figure 2.2   Morton's Paradigms of Service

and knowledge of those served. Thin projects are run by outsiders who consider themselves to be the experts and who do not adjust their activities to the unique needs and contexts of their location. Thin social advocacy, by the same token, works for a community instead of with it.

On the matrix of democracy, thick forms of service lie closer to communitarianism than individualism because they understand individual conditions as part of a broader web of human interdependence. Thick service organizations are grounded in a belief that people are responsible for each other. Thick service organizations strive for direct democracy in their internal structures, listening to and working with those who are most affected by their decisions. Grassroots organizations, with community leaders and nonhierarchical structures, are easiest to understand as direct democracies; other organizations might shade closer to republican democracies in their structures, but if they are thick models, they will have many mechanisms through which the voices of the constituents can direct the organization's agenda.

From my experience, Morton is a little too rigid about one point: he insists that people who do community work operate primarily within one paradigm and that they only occasionally move from one mode of service, such as charity, to another, such as social change. I would argue instead that nonprofits have to operate within a culture where all of these different paradigms of service circulate and that they adopt the rhetoric of different service paradigms at different moments. Funders, as we saw in the first part of this chapter, often pressure organizations to define their missions according to distinct, measurable outcomes (How many people ate breakfast this year? How many of those people found permanent jobs and housing? How many trails did you make in the park?) rather than the less tangible experiences of hope and respect that a thick charity organization might wish to foreground. Volunteers often expect to have profound personal experiences of witnessing or to feel their own capacity for significant social change. They may expect organizations to go after root causes rather than only providing direct services. Depending on the audience and the occasion, and depending on the goal of an interaction, an organization might use the rhetorics of thick charity, projects, or social change.

What is most helpful in Morton's paradigm is that he provides a more robust understanding of the third axis of the democratic matrix, the tactics of democratic change. His paradigm of thick service suggests that we cannot assume that all non-confrontative tactics are evidence that an organization has acquiesced to the status quo: charities that welcome the homeless man and offer respite from the harsh glare of the streets or after-school programs that teach young boys how to succeed in school may still critique the root causes of poverty and the inequities in the school system. But instead of choosing to fight for policy changes or to regulate business practices, these organizations choose to counter those inequities at a more local level by bringing together people who can spread a different vision of public relationships. In other words, individualist-seeming tactics for change do not necessarily reinforce the liberal, individualist purpose for government. Recognizing this profound difference gives us a way to conceptualize a new category of public work.

I recognize that my claim here—that individualist-seeming tactics do not necessarily endorse a liberal, individualist philosophy—is a risky one: it threatens to wrench apart the two axes of democracy and pretend that they operate separately and independently, rather than as part of a complex and deeply-intertwined set of democratic ideals. It almost sounds like the kind of move that makes it easier to feel like one is challenging the inequities of a system without really fighting to change it, just creating a space where we can pat ourselves on the back as we tell each other the system is inequitable. But I think the distinction I am making here is critical for understanding how actually-existing community organizations do this work. To help me explain how such an approach works, I turn now to a close study of Life Pieces to Masterpieces, the nonprofit I described at the beginning of this book, to find some answers.

AGENCY IN THE AGE OF NIHILISM: LIFE PIECES TO MASTERPIECES

In my critique of private-corporate nonprofits, in the premises of the continuum of service, and in the history of nonprofits in the United States, I forwarded a common pattern in discussions of social issues: the dichotomy of behavioralism and structuralism. Each of these perspectives locates agency in a different place. Behavioralists see agency as solidly within individuals who control their lives by learning appropriate knowledge and actions and by acting on a belief in their own power to effect change. The root causes of success or failure are internal. Structuralists, on the other hand, locate the root causes within broader social systems, such as social norms that are so embedded within institutional structures that people don't recognize how they are being shaped through their daily actions. Agency comes from carefully analyzing the power dynamics of that system and working collectively with others to amend, counter, or dismantle it. In his critique of this dichotomy, Cornel West argues that we need to create space for a third option, one which acknowledges the interrelationship between structural and behavioral root causes and one which allows for an agency that is neither only individual nor only about collective action against institutions of power.[72] West's approach offers a new way to understand seemingly individualist nonprofit work as public work.

Life Pieces to Masterpieces (LPTM), a program dedicated to creating a safe and hopeful space for young African-American boys, is housed in a former middle school in the Deanwood area of Northeast Washington, DC. Part of the District's seventh ward, Deanwood has a rich history as a predominantly African-American neighborhood. Along with its active historical foundation, the neighborhood celebrates its history in the names of public spaces: a major boulevard is named for Nannie Hellen Burroughs, a prominent activist and founder of a teaching college for black women; a newly-renovated city park is named for Motown singer Marvin Gaye, who grew up there and played gigs in a lounge that is now a parks center; a nearby high school is named for civil engineer and civic leader Howard D. Woodson, who helped design many of Washington's famous buildings along with many of the single family homes in Deanwood.[73]

But this proud history is unknown to many outside the neighborhood for whom Deanwood and the whole of Ward 7 is clouded in a reputation of high crime rates, poor schools, and poverty. Crime rates in Ward 7 are significantly higher than other areas of the city (though comparable to Ward 8, a predominantly African-American neighborhood just to the south, also with a rich history). In 2008, 150 homicides took place in this stretch of the city east of the Anacostia River, more than in the rest of the District combined.[74] LPTM observes that in DC, "African American young men are statically more likely to go to jail than to college."[75] Overall, DC public school students graduated at a rate of 72.3 percent in 2009,[76] but four of the high schools that serve Wards 7 and 8 have been labeled "persistently failing," according to the No Child Left Behind standards. Springarn High School, which serves the Deanwood neighborhood, is one of them; it is known as a "long troubled" school.[77] The poverty rate in Ward 7 was 25 percent at the time of the 2000 census. Local bloggers and newspaper reporters capture an aura of resignation: the District government devotes most of its attention to the more central, more powerful parts of the city, neglecting the needs of the predominantly African-American wards east of the river. The neighborhoods are underserved.

In 1996, Life Pieces to Masterpieces opened its doors. Every day after school, LPTM welcomes over 100 "apprentices" through its doors. The boys, ages 3 to 21, come here to "connect, create, contribute, and celebrate" together. The program, began in 1996 by current Executive Director Mary Brown and cofounder and artist Larry Quick, provides a structure and a vision for the boys to channel their life experiences through creative expression. They also practice responsible decision making, as evidenced in the button all apprentices, staff, and volunteers wear daily: the "Shield of Faith." This color-wheel serves as "a representation of [the program's] artistic and spiritual values, The Shield of Faith focuses on spirituality, meditation, loving, giving, language, arts, discipline, and leadership."[78]

Life Pieces is a space where boys learn to resist and talk back to some of the dominant messages sent to young African-American males. For one thing, the boys learn to resist the messages of a capitalist media that markets consumption, what Cornel West calls the "intensification of pleasure" over all other activities, a disposition that "stigmatizes others as objects for personal pleasure or bodily stimulation."[79] Such messages are particularly damaging for people in underserved neighborhoods such as the one surrounding Life Pieces. West explains, "The predominance of this [consumerist] way of life among those living in poverty-ridden conditions, with a limited capacity to ward off self-contempt and self-hatred, results in the possible triumph of the nihilistic threat in black America."[80]

They are brought together in an atmosphere that celebrates the power of African-American men, offering an alternative to the messages about black masculinity that come to them through the media and in their daily lives. They are held in a safe place, away from the violence and despair on the streets and, for some, in their homes. The boys, called apprentices, learn multiple avenues of expression, including a signature sewn canvas arts style that is explained on their website as "painting fabric, cutting it into various shapes, and sewing the pieces together into visually powerful canvases that tell their inspiring stories." On the website homepage, the word "pieces" in "Life Pieces to Masterpieces" includes this poetic description: "the good, the bad, the unspoken/ the joy, the pain, the broken/ frag-ments of some-thing once whole." The term "masterpieces" is explained "our lives in living color/ our blood through a kaleidoscope/ OUR EXPRESSIONS OF HOPE" (hyphenation and capitalization in the original). Along with meditation, a value system, and a decision-making tool, artist expression is one of the strategies the boys learn for coping with the pieces of their lives. Life Pieces' slogan is "Creating Art . . . Changing Lives."

By experiencing the power and pleasure of creating art about their lives, boys learn to resist not only the consumerist message, but also an equally devastating message sent through the media, the schools, and other public institutions: the message that the lives and experiences of white Americans are front and center in the United States. that the lives and experiences of people of color are not. "These beliefs and images," writes West, "attack black intelligence, black ability, black beauty, and black character daily in subtle and not-so-subtle ways."[81] Sonia Nieto documents the how the predominantly Eurocentric curricula taught in schools undermines the capacity of minority students to find meaning and worth in their education.[82] In Northeast DC,

weak curricula are combined with dangerous school conditions, like those
Ron Suskind documented as he shadowed a young African-American high
school student in nearby Ballou High School. Kids are regularly beat up in the
hallways, and students have to choose whether to compete academically or fit
in socially.[83] The message students repeatedly receive from both teachers and
each other is that they cannot escape the brutal lives their families endure.

Life Pieces rejects these messages, creating a space where young boys have
strong male role models. Their mentors are African-American men who have
chosen an affirmative identity. In acknowledging the systemic challenges
that confront young men in areas like Northeast DC, they offer hope through
education and community engagement. LPTM offers the boys opportunities
to critique the systems that would hold them down and to talk back to power
structures through their artwork, poetry, and life choices. The program, which
draws on Afrocentric kinship traditions (every boy is given a "soul name")
and some traces of Buddhism (they learn to meditate), projects a hopefulness
and faith in the boys that counters much of the rhetoric that surrounds them.

LPTM boasts that, as a result of their program, "95% of our apprentices are
never involved in the juvenile justice system. Through our arts-based curriculum, apprentices learn how to express and process their emotions in a positive, non-violent way. As a result, our apprentices consistently improve their
school attendance and performance; improve their social and life skills; and
avoid involvement with gangs, the juvenile system, and teen pregnancy."[84]
Through the uplifting programming and the visual arts on display in the
building and in galleries throughout town, LPTM challenges nihilism through
a discourse of hope and creativity.

The rhetoric and programmatic structure of Life Pieces to Masterpieces
appears, at first glance, to fit neatly into the category of individualist, behavior-
oriented nonprofits, which aim to bring potentially delinquent outsiders back
into a working social and political system by teaching them the habits of mind
and demeanor they need to fit in. The problems that the boys must overcome
are defined as being rooted in dysfunctional families and neighborhoods, rather
than in larger political and institutional systems that discriminate against African Americans, or capitalist systems that exploit the poor. The tools of change
are education and individual empowerment, not collective, political organizing.
Agency comes from making a good choice, not from taking action as a citizen.
How can we expand our definition of public and civic to account for the profound kind of transformation that happens in places like this?

In *Race Matters,* Cornel West wants to break the standoff between the two
major trends of thought about how to address issues of poverty and racial
inequality. He writes, "The predictable pitting of liberals against conservatives, Great Society Democrats against self-help Republicans, reinforces

intellectual parochialism and political paralysis."[85] He accuses structuralists and behavioralists of ignoring how their theories overlap. The structures of systemic racism combine with a sense of individual powerlessness, he says, and lead to a bigger problem that he calls nihilism—a sense of despair and meaninglessness. He defines nihilism this way:

> Nihilism is to be understood here not as a philosophic doctrine that there are no rational grounds for legitimate standards or authority; it is, far more, the lived experience of coping with a life of horrifying meaningless, hopelessness, and (most important) lovelessness. The frightening result is a numbing detachment from others and a self-destructive disposition toward the world. Life without meaning, hope, and love breeds a coldhearted, mean-spirited outlook that destroys both the individual and others.[86]

Nihilism, he is careful to point out, is an attitude and set of behaviors that are derived from a profound hopelessness in the face of systemic institutional racism and a culture of consumerism. It derives from the living in the space of disconnection, where the stories of rugged individualism are shredded by the realities of a people bereft of resources. All that's left in the face of cutthroat market morality is hopelessness; all that's left in the face of a persistent rhetoric of meritocracy is cynicism. The behavior is one response to a very real understanding of systemic conditions.

West offers some advice as to how communities and leaders can respond to this nihilism. Looking back at the strong African-American cultural and religious institutions that bolstered African Americans as slaves and during Reconstruction, West argues for building strong community institutions that reaffirm a sense of capacity through a network of support. He wants that network to be built on a profound sort of love, a love that acknowledges the devastation of institutional racism and consumerism yet holds people accountable to resist it. He wants institutions that attend to people's whole selves in this process. Intellectual analysis of systemic inequality are necessary, he acknowledges, but not sufficient.

> Nihilism is not overcome by arguments or analysis [alone]; it is tamed by love and care. Any disease of the soul must be conquered by a turning of one's soul. This turning is done through one's own affirmation of one's worth—an affirmation fueled by the concern of others. A love ethic must be at the center of a politics of conversion.[87]

A love ethic, he says, "is a last attempt at generating a sense of agency among a downtrodden people."[88] West's "politics of conversion" is about making space for people to believe their choices can make a difference, both individually and toward larger transformations. As David Coogan puts it, West's goal is "not to change the entire social structure or wipe out years of learned behavior but to engage [a downtrodden people] in an analysis of those choices and actions that perpetuate despair."[89] The goal is to "establish a cultural context within which life choices become meaningful public choices."[90]

When we look at the work of nonprofit organizations like Life Pieces to Masterpieces alongside West's framework for attacking nihilism, then we can push past the paralyzing dichotomy of structuralism and individualism and look, instead, at how it offers the young apprentices choices that are meaningful, deliberate, and hopeful acts in the face of nihilism. LPTM directs their attention to the choices they make every day, asking them to consider those choices deliberately, to make choices that will affirm their own sense of agency. Cofounder and Executive Director Mary Brown puts it this way:

> We help define for the boys something that so often is not defined. . . . Kids hear "just do it" or "you have the power" but nobody's ever really defined what their power is. We tell them exactly what their power is. We say, "Your power lies in your thoughts, your words, and your actions." Over time they really begin to ask "what am I listening to? What am I, what are my eyes taking in? How is that being translated in terms of how I'm acting? Is it making me a better person?"[91]

LPTM's artistic focus is also offering the apprentices meaningful choices, as is embodied in the slogan "Love + Security + Expression = Life." Within the security of the program, the apprentices can express their reactions to community and family tragedies by stitching what was fragmented onto canvases, letting out the anger and fear through art instead of enacting revenge or self-destruction.

The focus on good choices is one of the central components of the LPTM model, their "Shield of Faith." Everyone in the program—the boys, the staff, the volunteers—wears a pin over his or her heart that includes a colored octagon stamped with core values. Like an artist's color wheel, each segment of the octagon has a different color and value and is positioned opposite its complementary color and value. The Shield is explained this way:

> Red is the color representing spiritual principles, complementing green, which represents meditation.
> Orange which represents loving, complements blue, which represents giving.
> Yellow which stands for language, complements violet, which represents the arts.
> By mixing a few colors, we get brown, which represents discipline.
> By mixing all the colors, we get black, which represents leadership.

Throughout the day, staff and volunteers refer to the Shield as they work with apprentices, asking them to reflect about which value should (or did) guide an everyday decision. It is no accident, of course, that in this African-American organization, the most significant values—the ones that serve as the culmination of the others—are brown and black. The message, again, is that choices matter, that people can make a difference in their lives by consciously living a value system based on spirituality, community, and creativity.

Personal behavior does matter; through our actions and our reflections on our actions, we can shape the world we are in, in some small way. It's a romantic notion, to be sure, but it's not necessarily acquiescing to a liberal, individualist status quo. The act of seeing and reflecting is an act of critique; the act of choosing is an act of resistance.

If the rhetoric of "choice" can be reclaimed from the private-public dichotomy, so, too, can the rhetoric about what is "grassroots." Life Pieces offers us some new ways to think about some traditional community-organizing concepts. A fundamental principle here is that thick community action begins from the values and practices within the community. In his book *Going Public,* which outlines the Industrial Areas Foundation's practices, Michael Gecan spends a long time talking about the importance of getting to know a community, finding its organic leaders, and listening to them.[92] The goal of the organizer is to cultivate leaders but to do so in a way that elicits the strengths of the community. John McKnight emphasizes the strategy of "asset mapping," where organizers get to know a community according to the whole range of different skills and knowledge that people from the area already know. Grassroots organizing works from this foundation, beginning with what is local.[93]

But sometimes, I'd argue, a generic call to celebrate the local can get in the way. The local is always a construct, always a site of conflicting and clashing ideals. The attitudes and practices most apparent in a community may not be embraced by everyone. And, as we might expect, the battle over what is local is often couched in terms of what is authentic: competing public identities are celebrated and vilified by calling some "the real thing" and linking the others to "outsiders."

Here's an example particularly relevant to the work of Life Pieces. In some areas of DC, as is true in many African-American communities, the question of community authenticity is tied to one's attitude about education. Kids who seem to care too much about academics may be dismissed as "acting white," and they might be ostracized.[94] More than just name-calling, the label accuses the academically-oriented student of buying into the dominant logic that all it takes to get out of a cycle of poverty is hard work and a good education. The flipside of that logic, of course, is that those who have not "made it" simply didn't want it enough. Acting white in this construction means one has assimilated a mainstream ideology and no longer acknowledges the persistent racism and other structural inequalities that defy the supposed meritocracy of democracy and capitalism. Sociological studies of "bad" students confirm that their behavior is often a deliberate defiance of what they see as an unfair system.[95]

What is the appropriate response from a community organizer who recognizes the merit of this local critique of external, mainstream ideologies? One way, of course, would be to mobilize the community around actions and goals tied to exposing the flaws of mainstream discourse. When you dig down beneath the antischooling attitudes of disenfranchised black students, there is a profound logic to rejecting an educational system that suggests that America runs as a meritocracy. The holes in the ideals of meritocracy begin with a school system that is so glaringly underserved that the students know that doing well there will not level the playing field. Following the community organizing models such as the Industrial Areas Foundation (Alinsky) or Asset-based Community Development (McKnight and Kretzmann), we could seek out community leaders and agitate to bring parents, students, and educators together to fight against all those barriers that continue to keep many African-American high school graduates from getting jobs or leadership positions. At the level of education, we could follow the model of civil rights leaders Bob Moses and Charles Cobb. Their book, *Radical Equations,* argues that algebra is a "gatekeeper" course, and they propose a whole-school approach that teaches young students how to agitate to ensure meaningful education rooted in their everyday lives.[96] We could fight to bring in more jobs and lower the devastating unemployment rate: what's the good of an education if you look around and see so many high school and college graduate without work? We could fight to create more meaningful work for high school graduates. All of these steps would challenge the broader, root causes of educational resistance.

Such approaches would be strong examples of grassroots, participatory democracy, but they are not the only answer. Another approach—one also grounded in local knowledge—is to break down the logic of that local argument at another point, arguing that African Americans can succeed academically while remaining critical of racist and classist ideologies. Education is not the same as acting white; it is not same as presuming that the educational and political playing field is level. Plenty of African-American men and women who have earned high school or college degrees do so with eyes wide open. They recognize that American educational policy, structure, and history have served the interests of the dominant group—white, middle-class—more than others. Like Mary Brown and the staff and many of the volunteers at Life Pieces, they have sought out the mentors and the texts, the theories and the strategies with which they can anchor their identities, recognizing the inequities without letting those inequities grind them down.

In Life Pieces, the young apprentices are surrounded by black male mentors, role models who have stayed in school and for whom black masculinity is tied to being scholars, artists, athletes, and gentlemen. The program is deeply rooted in a celebration of African and African-American culture. The boys have "soul names"; they chant "We are Black History"; they learn to articulate what they value about themselves and what they aspire to as black men. They are offered a way to strive in their education, to believe in their capacity to shape their lives, and to celebrate their creative powers. The apprentices in Life Pieces to Masterpieces are the philosophical descendants of those proud and hopeful civic leaders who founded Deanwood over a century ago.

This approach to fighting nihilism is not unique to Life Pieces or to programs that center on youth and education. In "Counterpublics in Public Housing: Reframing the Politics of Service-Learning," David Coogan offers an excellent analysis of how activists within Chicago public housing projects drew on a "politics of conversion" to "engage residents in an analysis of those choices and actions that perpetuate despair."[97] We need to seek out those the public arguments that challenge the behavioralist vs. structuralist dichotomy, arguments that critique the status quo while offering a broader range of both tactical and strategic actions. We need to begin with the rhetorics of community organizations and allow them to help us build more robust and accurate theories about what public work looks like.

WHAT DOES THIS MEAN FOR A PUBLIC WRITING COURSE?

Public writing, as I see it, refers to all the actions people do in the name of "the public good" and to the rhetorical work it takes to carry out those actions. In "Service Learning and Social Change: The Case for Materialist Rhetoric," David Coogan argues that public writers succeed when they consider the arguments inherent in the community they would invoke as well as within the institutional structures of power that surround that community. Within this framework, we need to recognize that naming what are rightfully public and private has long been a rhetorical move within the context of capitalism. It is not only a move of neoliberals—those who see a seamless link between capitalism and individualist, passive democracy—but also a move of those who try to reclaim public space and public ideals from the neoliberal grasp.

I'm all for laying out principles to guide our public interactions, and I ultimately agree with those who advocate for participatory democracy. But as scholars and activists regularly discover, the world is usually more complicated than we can capture in our theories and terminologies. The actions we might sequester as private might still do public work; the behaviors we might celebrate as participatory might in fact serve democratic ideals we disagree with. It is vital, therefore, that we expand our theories by taking into account what happens on the ground and looking at how each public ideal clashes with, borrows from, or merges with other public ideals.

As we study and teach public writing, then, we should bring these multiple and clashing ideals about democracy to the foreground and identify how public writers have responded. By understanding how people on the ground, in community organizations of all types, work within this fraught context to invent a public, we can start to develop a repertoire of rhetorical moves of public writing. Those rhetorical moves are not discreet, isolated techniques that writers can dip into at will, but are complex responses to competing pressures of any public rhetorical situation. In the next chapter, I look more closely at the rhetorical challenges that community organizations face as they work to invoke publics. I'm particularly interested in those public-making moves that are not overt but that are built into the rhetorical structures of the writing: the implied audiences and the subtle cues that invoke a worldview or a belief in public capacity. Using examples of some local Washington, DC community organizations, I offer the rhetorical tools that public writers use to respond to the rhetorical challenges of building publics. In the process, I also offer some strategies for how to design a public writing course in which students, working with community organizations, can identify similar rhetorical tools and build their repertoires as well.

NOTES

1. David Coogan, "Service Learning and Social Change: The Case for Materialist Rhetoric." *College Composition and Communication* 57, no. 4 (Jun 2006): 668.

2. Susan Wells, "Rogue Cops and Health Care: What do we Want from Public Writing?" *College Composition and Communication* 47, no. 3 (1996): 326.

3. Keith Morton and Sandra Enos, "Building Deeper Civic Relationships and New and Improved Citizens." *Journal of Public Affairs* 6, (2002): 83–102.

4. Peter Levine, *The Future of Democracy: Developing the Next Generation of American Citizens.* (Medford, Mass.: Tufts U P, 2007).

5. Thomas Deans, *Writing Partnerships: Service-Learning in Composition.* (Urbana, Ill.: National Council of Teachers of English, 2000); Linda Flower,

Community Literacy and the Rhetoric of Public Engagement. (Carbondale: Southern Illinois University Press, 2008).

6. Troy A. Murphy, "Deliberative Civic Education and Civil Society: A Consideration of Ideals and Actualities in Democracy and Communication Education." *Communication Education* 53, no. 1 (2004): 74–91.

7. Peter Levine, *The Future of Democracy,* 44.

8. Murphy, "Deliberative Civic Education," 74–91.

9. Morton and Enos, "Building."

10. Keith Morton, and Sandra Enos, "Developing a Theory and Practice of Community-Campus Partnerships," in *Building Partnerships for Service-Learning,* ed. Barbara Jacoby (San Francisco, CA: Jossey-Bass, 2003), 20–41.

11. Morton and Enos, "Building," 85.

12. Morton and Enos, "Building," 97.

13. Morton and Enos, "Building," 97.

14. Wells, "Rogue," 326.

15. Morton and Enos, "Building," 89.

16. Morton and Enos, "Building," 90.

17. Morton and Enos, "Building," 90.

18. Morton and Enos, "Building," 90.

19. Morton and Enos, "Building," 90.

20. Morton and Enos, "Building," 90.

21. Morton and Enos, "Building," 94.

22. Morton and Enos, "Building," 95.

23. Morton and Enos, "Building," 98.

24. David Coogan, "Service Learning and Social Change: The Case for Materialist Rhetoric." *College Composition and Communication* 57, no. 4 (Jun 2006): 667–693; David Coogan, "Counterpublics in Public Housing: Reframing the Politics of Service-Learning." *College English* 67, no. 5 (2005): 461–482.

25. Morton and Enos, "Building," 84.

26. Jurgen Habermas, "Political Communication in Media Society: Does Democracy Still Enjoy an Epistemic Dimension? The Impact of Normative Theory on Empirical Research." *Communication Theory* 16 (2006), 412.

27. Habermas, "Political Communication," 412.

28. Thomas Streeter, *Selling the Air: A Critique of the Policy of Commercial Broadcasting in the United States.* (Chicago: University of Chicago Press, 1996), 28.

29. Noam Chomsky rants about Lippman in his book *The Manufacture of Consent* (Minneapolis, Minn.: Silha Center for the Study of Media Ethics and Law, School of Journalism and Mass Communication, University of Minnesota, 1986). Chomsky pushes particularly hard on Lippmann's depiction of the "masses" as "the bewildered herd." Another good summary of Lippman vs. Dewey is in Nathan Crick, "The Search for a Purveyor of News: The Dewey/Lippman Debate in an Internet Age." *Critical Studies in Mass Communication* 26, no. 5 (Dec. 2009): 480–497.

30. Thomas R. Dye, and L. Harmon Zeigler, *The Irony of Democracy: An Uncommon Introduction to American Politics.* 2d ed. (Belmont, Calif.: Duxbury Press, 1972), 2.

31. I laid out this individualist/material distinction previously in "In(ter)Ventions of Global Democracy: An Analysis of the Rhetorics of the A-16 World Bank/IMF Protests in Washington, DC." *Rhetoric Review* 25, no. 4 (2006): 408–426.

32. This way of talking about belief is often associated with Marxist philosopher Louis Althusser; a good explanation of his argument can be found in Kathleen Weiler, *Women Teaching for Change : Gender, Class & Power.* (South Hadley, Mass.: Bergin & Garvey Publishers, 1988).

33. Louis Althusser takes this view and calls these structures the "ideological state apparatus"; see Louis Althusser, "Ideology and Ideological State Apparatus," in *Lenin and Philosophy and Other Essays,* ed. Louis Althusser (New York: Monthly Review Press, 1970), 121–176. Chomsky argues that elite democracy maintains its power by manipulating the media in order to "manufacture consent"; see Noam Chomsky, *The Manufacture of Consent.*

34. I would argue that this perspective is one of the most prevalent in actually-existing understandings, even though it does not accurately describe how democracy really works. The theory is laid out and analyzed by Habermas, who calls it the "bourgeois public sphere." Jürgen Habermas, *The Structural Transformation of the Public Sphere: An Inquiry into a Category of Bourgeois Society.* (Cambridge, Mass.: MIT Press, 2000; 1989). I call it the "idealized public sphere," and I discuss how the traditional media perpetuates this ideal more fully in chapter 4.

35. Walter Lippmann, *Public Opinion.* (New York: Free Press, 1965).

36. You can find this logic spelled out in the works of two contemporary IAF organizers, Ed Chambers, who directed the IAF until 2009, and Michael Gecan, who was a lead organizer in Brooklyn, NY. Edward T. Chambers, and Michael A. Cowan, *Roots for Radicals : Organizing for Power, Action, and Justice.* (New York: Continuum, 2003). Michael Gecan, *Going Public.* (Boston: Beacon Press, 2002);

37. Michelle Obama, "Michelle Obama's Democratic Convention Speech," *Huffington Post* 25 Aug. 2008, www.huffingtonpost.com/2008/08/25/michelle-obamas-democrati_n_121310.html (20 July 2010).

38. Morton and Enos, "Building," 88.

39. Others who endorse this position have different names for it: Benjamin Barber calls it "strong democracy"—Benjamin R. Barber, *Strong Democracy: Participatory Politics for a New Age.* (Berkeley: University of California Press, 1983, 2003). Craig Rimmerman calls it "the new citizenship"—Craig A. Rimmerman, *The New Citizenship: Unconventional Politics, Activism, and Service.* 3rd ed. (Boulder: Westview Press, 2005). Those who focus primarily on the epistemic function, where citizens gather to figure out how to best understand the world, often call it "deliberative democracy" (among this camp we can find Habermas and Murphy). I choose "participatory" over "deliberative" to insist that there are other modes of participation beyond deliberation.

40. Morton and Enos, "Building," 87.

41. Morton and Enos, "Building," 85–86.

42. Henry A. Giroux, "Neoliberalism, Corporate Culture, and the Promise of Higher Education: The University as a Democratic Public Sphere." *Harvard Educational Review* 72, no. 4 (2002), 429.

43. Morton and Enos, "Building," 84.

44. Robert Egger and Howard Yoon, *Begging for Change: The Dollars and Sense of Making Nonprofits Responsive, Efficient, and Rewarding for all.* (New York: Harper Business, 2004).

45. Incite! Women of Color Against Violence, *The Revolution Will Not be Funded: Beyond the Non-Profit Industrial Complex.* (Cambridge, Mass.: South End Press, 2007), 4.

46. Incite!, *Revolution,* 4; see also Egger and Yoon, *Begging.*

47. Egger and Yoon, *Begging,* 3.

48. Troy A. Murphy, "Deliberative," 76.

49. Troy A. Murphy, "Deliberative," 77.

50. Morton and Enos, "Building," 94.

51. Morton and Enos, "Building," 94.

52. Morton and Enos, "Building," 90.

53. Morton and Enos, "Building," 90.

54. Eggers and Yoon, *Begging,* 10.

55. Eggers and Yoon, *Begging,* 10.

56. Eggers and Yoon, *Begging,* 10.

57. Jeffrey M. Berry and David F. Arons. *A Voice for Nonprofits.* (Washington, D.C., Brookings Institutions Press, 2003), 10.

58. Berry and Arons, *Voice,* 12–13.

59. Berry and Arons, *Voice,* 15.

60. Berry and Arons, *Voice,* 18–19.

61. Berry and Arons, *Voice,* 12.

62. George Lakoff, *Moral Politics: How Liberals and Conservatives Think.* 2nd ed. (Chicago, IL: University of Chicago Press, 2002); George Lakoff, *Don't Think of an Elephant! Know Your Values and Frame the Debate: The Essential Guide for Progressives.* (White River Junction, VT.: Chelsea Green Pub. Co., 2004).

63. George Lakoff, *Elephant,* 9.

64. Incite! Women of Color Against Violence, *The Revolution Will Not be Funded: Beyond the Non-Profit Industrial Complex.* (Cambridge, Mass.: South End Press, 2007

65. Berry and Arons. *Voice.*

66. Keith Morton, "The Irony of Service: Charity, Project and Social Change in Service-Learning." *Michigan Journal of Community Service Learning* Fall (1995): 19–32.

67. Morton, "Irony," p. 21–23.

68. Morton, "Irony," p. 20.

69. Morton, "Irony," p. 26.

70. Morton, "Irony," p. 27.

71. Morton, "Irony," p. 27.

72. Cornel West, *Race Matters*. (New York: Vintage Books, 1994).

73. Deanwood Historical Society. *Deanwood 1880–1950: A Model of Self-Sufficiency in Far Northeast Washington, DC*. (Washington, DC: Deanwood History Project, 2005).

74. Metropolitan Police Department (DC), "Citywide Crime Statistics: Annual Totals, 1993–2009" mpdc.dc.gov/mpdc/cwp/view,a,1239,q,547256,mpdcNav_GID,1556.asp.

75. Pieces to Masterpieces, "Contact," n.d. www.lifepieces.org (Aug. 2010).

76. District of Columbia Public Schools, "DCPS Graduation Rate Continues to Climb," District of Columbia Public Schools: Press Releases 2010 dcps.dc.gov/DCPS/About+DCPS/Press+Releases+and+Announcements/DCPS+Graduation+Rate+Continues+to+Climb (Jan. 8, 2010).

77. Leah Fabel, "25 Area Schools are Labeled Persistently Failing," *Washington Examiner* 2010, www.washingtonexaminer.com/local/25-area-schools-labeled-persistently-failing-87406677.html (Aug. 2010).

78. Life Pieces to Masterpieces, "Our Model," n.d. www.lifepieces.org (Aug. 2010).

79. Cornel West, *Race Matters*. 26.

80. Cornel West, *Race Matters*, 26.

81. Cornel West, *Race Matters*, 27.

82. Sonia Nieto, *Affirming Diversity: The Sociopolitical Context of Multicultural Education*. (White Plains, N.Y.: Longman, 1992).

83. Ron Suskind, *A Hope in the Unseen: An American Odyssey from the Inner City to the Ivy League*. (New York: Broadway Books, 1998).

84. Pieces to Masterpieces, "Contact," n.d. www.lifepieces.org (Aug. 2010).

85. Cornel West, *Race Matters*. 4.

86. Cornel West, *Race Matters*. 22.

87. Cornel West, *Race Matters*. 29.

88. Cornel West, *Race Matters*. 29.

89. David Coogan, "Counterpublics, "463.

90. David Coogan, "Counterpublics," 464.

91. Rosetta Thurman, "28 Days of Black, Nonprofit Leadership: Mary Brown," Feb. 4, 2010 www.rosettathurman.com/2010/02/28-days-of-black-nonprofit-leaders-mary-brown (Aug. 2010).

92. Michael Gecan, *Going Public*. (Boston: Beacon Press, 2002).

93. John P. Kretzmann, and John L. McKnight, *Building Communities from the Inside Out: A Path Toward Finding and Mobilizing a Community's Assets*. (Evanston, IL: Asset-Based Community Development Institute, 1993).

94. See Ron Suskind for evidence of this trend in DC schools, and John Ogbu for sociological studies of this trend in other American cities. John U. Ogbu, *Black American Students in an Affluent Suburb: A Study of Academic Disengagement*. (Mahwah, N.J.: L. Erlbaum Associates, 2003); John U. Ogbu, *Minority Status, Oppositional Culture, and Schooling*. (New York: Routledge, 2008).

95. See for example, Paul E. Willis, *Learning to Labor: How Working Class Kids Get Working Class Jobs.* (New York: Columbia University Press, 1977), or for an autobiographical account, Mike Rose, *Lives on the Boundary: A Moving Account of the Struggles and Achievements of America's Educational Underclass.* (New York, N.Y.: Penguin Books, 1989). A good overview of theories of education and resistance is available in Kathleen Weiler, *Women Teaching for Change.*

96. Robert Parris Moses and Charles E. Cobb, *Radical Equations: Civil Rights from Mississippi to the Algebra Project.* (Boston: Beacon Press, 2001).

97. David Coogan, "Counterpublics," 463.

Chapter 3

Public Writing with Community Organizations

When I consider the broad scope of what it means to study and teach public writing, I find it helpful to lay out four central premises:

1. Public writing is a site of rhetorical struggle located within ideological, historical, and material spaces. Successful public writing draws on a repertoire of rhetorical strategies that attend to these struggles as they invoke the desired public.
2. A full repertoire for public writing goes beyond the genre of the traditional persuasive essay or letters and includes the tools of community building (such as affirmation, exploring mutuality, and listening), the tools of resistance (such as confrontation, silence, or material interventions), and nondominant ideals of public relationships.
3. The theory and practice of public writing has to include repertoires of circulation as well as composition. Venues of circulation reinforce particular public ideals, and public writers have to work with and against those ideals to be heard.
4. Academics (including students) who study public writing must account for how academia is also a public. Academic writing is one genre through which higher education stakes out its purpose within the broader matrix of democracies.

I introduced a way of thinking about the first premise in the previous chapter, in which I traced some of the ideological, historical, economic, and material conditions that are ever-present in public texts. In the process of creating a framework for understanding the many competing democratic ideals that impinge on public texts, I argued that we can view much nonprofit work as public work.

In this chapter, I'll continue to explore the first and second premises. I analyze the public writing of local nonprofit organizations to identify some of the rhetorical tools they use to build their publics. As I do so, I hope to offer a method for working with the rhetoric of community organizations so that others, partnered with different organizations in different locations, can discover more of the rhetoric of public writing. At the end of the chapter, I'll offer a way to structure a first-year writing course so that a class of students, working with multiple community organizations, can discover some of these rhetorical tools themselves.

I'll touch only briefly (in this chapter) on the third and fourth premises; a fuller discussion of those can be found in the remaining chapters.

Nonprofits are valuable sites for analyzing public rhetoric because their texts are so visible. Their mission statements and genesis stories often are readily accessible on their websites. They circulate annual reports. They regularly send out flyers and announcements, calling for funds or volunteers or touting their activities and successes. Most have newsletters and volunteer manuals. Some will share grant proposals. I approach organizations' materials not as master texts that lay out coherent and thorough overviews of the public ideal the organization forwards, but as fragments that work together over time to build a public.

Community organizations build their power through internal work (such as agenda-setting with their constituents, training volunteers, and developing organizational infrastructures), and they project their public ideals through both cyclical and opportunistic publications (those tied to particular calendar events and those that arise from current events). Scholars (including students) who immerse themselves within community organizations have opportunities to learn from those people who engage in the struggle of public-making every day.

Academic scholarship is not ignorant to the rhetoric of community organizations, of course, and the theories introduced by sociologists, linguists, cultural geographers, political scientists, cultural studies scholars, and rhetoricians can provide helpful frameworks for considering the rhetoric of community organizations. However, as I've cautioned in the previous chapter, we must not be so seduced by the academic terminology and premises that we overlook the material, historical, and ideological contexts that everyday public writers have to negotiate.

I find it valuable to investigate community texts not according to how well they mesh with one theory or another, but as moments of often profound rhetorical conflicts in which public writers have to attend to the pressures of multiple, often conflicting needs. The theories can often help explain those multiple pressures, but the writing itself shows how those pressures are accommodated or rejected or circumscribed in the moment of public making. In the next section, I offer case studies of some of the specific rhetorical challenges that I've observed among the nonprofits with whom my students and I have partnered, and I explain the rhetorical choices they make to create a sense of agency and interdependence within their publics while responding to geographical, historical, and ideological contexts.

RHETORICS OF AGENCY AND CAPACITY

Lloyd Bitzer writes that what turns any situation into a rhetorical situation is rhetorical exigency: the situation must be seen as "capable of positive modification," and where the desired change "requires discourse or can be assisted by discourse."[1] To extend his argument, in a *public* rhetorical situation, the rhetor posits that the malleable situation requires people to work together to make that "positive modification"; moreover, the rhetor has some way to reach those change-agents. Part of the rhetorical task, then, is to make the audience believe that, by coming together, they are capable of making change. Except in the most extreme libertarian-individualist democracies, the sense of agency invoked in public texts insists on the interdependence of the audience members who orient toward each other to gain this agency. The public comes to feel their collective power among not only those who are immediately present or known, but by feeling as if they are among strangers who lurk at the edges of the known spaces and who share this approach. The strangers' affirmative presence is regularly signaled in the discourse. Finally, publics coalesce through the circulation of discourse: a public solidifies as a social entity when people see the discourse in multiple places, from multiple speakers, over the course of time.[2]

Public Agency beyond the Power of the Vote

The most commonplace rhetoric of public agency, I would argue, is about the power of the vote. This rhetoric is deployed during any election, of course, but also in any march or rally where "the people" display their ability to vote someone in or out of office. The size of a movement is a red flag for elected representatives, announcing the people's power to change direction by installing a new leader.

On January 20, 2009, Master of Ceremonies Senator Diane Feinstein reinforced the sovereign role for the American public when she began the Obama Presidential inauguration by declaring, "The freedom of a people to choose its leaders is the root of liberty."[3] Not just the power to create change, but also an identity as "free people" is rooted in the vote. The physical setting reinforced how each voter was one among many. Like the Obama campaign, which staged rallies and even his election-night acceptance speech in locations where tens of thousands of people could gather and participate, the Inauguration committee gave "everyday people" unprecedented access by opening the entire National Mall for public viewing. A sea of people stretched all the way down the National Mall, from the steps of the Capitol building to the marble feet of Abraham Lincoln.

Celebratory or protest events on the National Mall use that physical space to highlight the symbolic target of their actions: the Capitol and the White House. The size of the crowd is hailed as evidence of the power a movement has to pressure its representative government, the power of voters to hold their representatives accountable to public opinion. Historians attribute President Kennedy's willingness to move forward with civil rights legislation to the pressure of the estimated 200,000 people who gathered in 1963 for the March on Washington for Jobs and Freedom.[4] The numbers reported for such events is so significant that the National Parks Service, charged by Congress since the seventies to estimate crowds at DC events, stopped doing so in 1995 after the organizers of the Million Man March threatened to sue them for undercounting their crowds. The *New York Times* reports that "most sponsoring organizations of events that draw hundreds of thousands of people complain that Park Service estimates are too low."[5] Roger Kennedy, who was Federal Parks Chief at the time, told *The New York Times* that "It happens every time . . . Right-to-lifers want more people than pro-choice people, and vice versa. It's always so competitive."

As one of the thousands of people on the Mall that day, I can attest to the heady sense of power that came from watching President Obama take his oath. More precisely, my family, friends, and I watched him on a big screen positioned about one hundred yards away from us, and we heard his solemn words echo off the marble walls of the Washington Monument. We would have seen better at home; we would have been warmer and more comfortable (as my young boys regularly reminded us that frigid day). But I wanted to be with the crowds. I wanted to be among the people who spilled across the Mall and chanted and sang and cheered. Standing there on the National Mall among such a diverse group of people, united in a sense of power and hope, celebrating the peaceful transfer of government from President Bush to President Obama, from the forty-third white man to our first African-American president, witnessing a culmination of years of campaigning and centuries of cultural transformation, I felt myself one of the American people. I was "We the people." I was "the people have spoken."

Whatever one feels about President Obama's accomplishments in office, the election of our first African-American president was, as Senator Feinstein reminded us, a testament to people's voting power. A great number of people from all across the political spectrum came to believe in their power as voters. In 2008, the estimated voter turnout for the Presidential election was exceptionally high for U.S. standards—somewhere between 61.7 percent and 63 percent of the eligible voting population. This high rate of voter turnout was an anomaly in the larger trend, which had been declining since 1968. People's faith in the power of their vote to effect change waxes and wanes.

The power of the vote, when it is seen as an individual, isolated act, is sometimes considered one of the weakest powers in democracy. In his classic text, *Political Participation,* political scientist Lester Milbrath puts voting in the category of "spectator activities," along with exposing oneself to political stimuli, initiating a political discussion, attempting to talk another into voting a certain way, wearing a button, and putting a sticker on the car.[6] The next layer of civic activities, which he calls "transitional activities," provides a greater sense of agency: contacting a public official or a political leader, making a monetary contribution to a party or candidate, and attending a political meeting or rally. Finally, "gladiator activities" are at the top of the pyramid: fewer people engage in them, but those who do feel their power to effect change most fully: in this category, people contribute time to a political campaign, become an active member of a political party, attend a caucus or a strategy meeting, solicit political funds, and run for or hold public or party office. Milbrath argues that people who engage in transitional or gladiator activities gain greater confidence in their ability to work the system and offer greater commitment to that system.

As a candidate, President Obama accounted for the limitation of the individual vote by invoking citizens not merely as voters, but also as *civic organizers.* On February 5th, the "Super Tuesday" of the campaign, he described a swelling chorus of voices and urged others to feel the power of "ordinary people":

And today, on this Tuesday in February, in states North and South, East and West, what began as a whisper in Springfield has swelled to a chorus of millions calling for change. A chorus that cannot be ignored. That cannot be deterred. This time can be different because this campaign for the presidency is different. It's different not because of me, but because of you. . . . Tonight I want to speak directly to all those Americans who have yet to join this movement but still hunger for change—we need you. We need you to stand with us, and work with us, and help us prove that together, ordinary people can still do extraordinary things.[7]

Obama addressed his audience as organizers, as people who would work at the grassroots level to engage others and help them become involved. His campaign was especially successful at mobilizing and deploying the hundreds of thousands of volunteers who came to canvas neighborhoods, staff phone banks, host house parties, and drive people to the polls on Election Day. The campaign website exhorted viewers to organize themselves, to host or attend neighborhood gatherings, and to engage with others in their community through a quick "Neighbor-to-Neighbor" link.

Just as Milbrath's hierarchy of political participation focuses on civic power within the confines of a republican government structure and political party systems, so did Obama's civic organizers stay within the hierarchy of this system. While they drew on the tools of community organizing, their ultimate power would be to elect their new leader. Not all organizations or movements locate the power of change within the voting booth or the elected officials. Indeed, most nonprofits, as we saw in the last chapter, are constrained from overt political endorsements, though they may effect change within the political system more indirectly.

The voter-to-elected official model that Milbrath laid out is one of the most common ways that people imagine civic power, so publics that define agency within other models have the additional task of demonstrating how their conception of agency works. Numbers still matter here: such publics signal the power of their vision by showing that their convictions are shared by more people than might be immediately apparent in a room or as signatures on a petition. Websites count the number of "hits"; groups broadcast the number of their "fans" or "followers" on Facebook or Twitter. Local community organizations tout the numbers of volunteers who have served food or tutored students.

Life Pieces to Masterpieces, as we saw in the last chapter, locates the target of their work not in terms of pressuring city or national government to change the laws or funds to their community, but rather by confronting a different cultural power—the messages circulating through media, economic structures, and everyday lives that would interpolate their apprentices into a disempowering role. Their methods for resisting that interpolation include close, interpersonal engagement, critical analysis of cultural messages, and a space to work out alternative, empowering personal and community responses. This approach is not isolated from the more traditional civic roles—the apprentices occasionally attend the DC City Council meetings—but it does not confine itself to a republican definition of civic power. Their repertoire of agency is not about organizing their neighbors to vote but about working to redefine societal roles.

Other local organizations work at the intersection of these modes of agency: they define citizen power both in terms of their ability to mobilize elected officials to take action and in terms of the citizen's power to make things happen themselves, outside of government structures, by taking charge of public space.

Agency, Reconstitution and Liberating Memory

A close look at a DC nonprofit illustrates some of the rhetorical challenges and possibilities of invoking a sense of agency. Washington Parks and People

(WPP) "lead greening initiatives across the city . . . to help revitalize once-for-gotten communities."[8] Their goal is to empower communities by focusing on the green public spaces of those communities. These dual goals are reflected in their name and in the language of their mission: "Parks & People is working to revitalize Washington by reconnecting two of its greatest but most forgotten assets: its vast network of public lands and waterways—comprising one of the highest percentages of park land of any city in the world—and its core of dedicated community leaders and organizations."[9] The language here affirms the power inherent in the community: the nonprofit is not bringing a new experience to the communities but "revitalizing them," returning them to a past vitality. They are not forging new alliances, but "reconnecting" the "assets" that are already there.

How were the connections and vitality lost? WPP defines the problem as one of neglect—these communities were "forgotten," and they are "underserved." Here, they name the same conditions for potential nihilism that Life Pieces to Masterpieces confronts: a resignation to helplessness because the community does not have the attention of those in political power and a yielding to the fatalistic narratives about the community that are circulated with the media, popular culture, and everyday institutions. No one can get out, no one can make a difference, and no one cares. The police are part of this neglect, not only when they allow crime to continue, but also when they treat the whole community as criminal. In an article in *East of the River,* a longtime resident reminisces about a local park. He says, "Once the dealers took over, the cops came and they took everything out"—all the recreation equipment, benches, and the like. In trying to make the area inhospitable to drug dealers, the police made it inhospitable to everyone.[10]

Communities can be revitalized, according to the logic of WPP, when residents reclaim their roles as activists, pressuring both city officials and unofficial neighborhood attitudes. Washington Parks and People focuses on the visible green spaces in a community as a way to illustrate and motivate community agency. The organization's leader, Steve Coleman, explains, "So often, people are fatalistic about these forgotten green spaces. You need to do the surprising, visible thing on the ground to get people energized about what's possible."[11] The process includes not just changing the physical space, but also making visible the "invisible landscape" by "researching the history of the park, talking to locals about their memories of the park's past, and forming alliances with local institutions—from the police precinct to performing arts groups."[12]

Nonprofits emerge and evolve; their visions and their methods adapt to new needs and new areas. The evolution of Washington Parks and People shows how the rhetorical tools for invoking agency and defining the capacity of a community also evolve and grow. While the organization's fundamental principles do not change as it shifts from its first project (Meridian Hill Park, in the multicultural neighborhood of Adams Morgan, DC,) to its later one (Watts Branch Park, in the predominantly African-American neighborhood of Ward 7), as WPP transitions, it works within the unique histories and exigencies of each place and, in turn, draws on different rhetorical tools to invoke the agency of the community members.

An article published in *Landscape Architecture Magazine* recounts the nonprofit's beginnings.[13] In 1990, a young boy was shot in Meridian Hill Park, a small enclave in the middle of the city; he died in the arms of a man whose housemate, Steve Coleman, was neighborhood association chair. Coleman called a meeting. Fifty people showed up. They decided to try to reclaim the park from the drug dealers and criminals, the people responsible for the boy's death. Some knew stories about people in Southeast DC who had successfully reclaimed public space, so they looked them up and talked to them. They derived a plan and a set of principles for working in their diverse neighborhood: "Always say hello. Never carry a weapon or anything that can be perceived as such. . . . Always travel in multiracial groups."[14]

Working against the advice of the police, the group began interacting with everyone who used the park or wanted to use the park. Eventually, they grew to pressure police, city park offices, garbage collectors, and neighbors to create the park they wanted. Working with the government bureaucracy and also working to change how everyday people saw and used the park, the group transformed the space back into a beautiful, vibrant place. These days (as I mentioned in the introduction), residents gather in Meridian Hill Park for drum circles, dance performances, and all manner of community activities. The park has been identified as one of the safest in DC.

The group's evolution is clear in its changing name—first in 1990, they were Friends of Adam's Morgan (a specific neighborhood); then, in 1994, they were Friends of Meridian Hill (a larger geographical area); in 1998, they became Washington Parks and People (which encompasses the whole city.) The group's changing sense of itself happened not through isolated self reflection, but in response to the coverage it received in local and national venues. As the *Landscape Architecture* article explains the 1994 renaming:

> Friends of Meridian Hill was born . . . after a letter to the *Washington Post* noted the sudden growth of local interest in the place and warned that this effort, like so many before it, was doomed to failure unless the broader, social issues of the neighborhood were addressed. "That's why we became Friends of Meridian Hill—not Friends of Meridian Hill Park or Friends of Meridian Hill/Malcolm X Park," Coleman says. "We recognized that it had to be the whole historic hilltop. We didn't have the luxury of a part that is a complete world unto itself."[15]

That same year, Friends of Meridian Hill received the National Park Foundation Leadership Award, the National Parks Service's highest honor for community parks partnerships. President Clinton called the park's revitalization "a shining example for our nation."[16]

In the coverage of President Clinton's Earth Day ceremony in Meridian Hill Park, Coleman reinforces the possibility for community-led change: "There wasn't anything miraculous that we did here. . . . We didn't do anything that couldn't be done by anyone else and that's the message I want to get out."[17] Word did get out, and the organization received requests from all over the city to help revitalize their parks. And they did. In 2001, WPP embarked on its next major project, the Watts Branch Park in Ward 7. As WPP transitioned into a city-wide organization, its new name reflected both its broader geographical identity and its philosophy: Washington Parks and People.

The organization felt its power and identity reflected back to it in awards, Letters to the Editors, community discourses, and magazine articles; this allowed it to grow its vision geographically. All the while, it focused on defining the community around the parks as an agent of change. John Hammerback and Richard Jensen have argued that the rhetorical task of social movements is one of reconstitution: people who do not identify themselves as agents are reconstituted as people who believe in their own capacity to make a difference.[18] Hammerback and Jensen studied the United Farm Workers and noted how Cesar Chavez's own position as a farm worker, along with his use of Mexican-American rhetorical moves and themes, led migrant farm workers to identify with him. By embodying the life-experience of those in whom he wished to affirm capacity, Chavez's own success as a leader became part of his reconstitutive power.

Coleman's position as the leader of the award-winning Washington Parks and People has potential reconstitutive power. In the genesis story that was printed in *Landscape Architecture Magazine,* Coleman is held up as an ordinary citizen who decided to take action. Residents in the neighborhood surrounding Meridian Hill Park might see the possibility of their own transformation in his story and in his claim, during Clinton's Earth day celebration at the park, that "we didn't do anything that couldn't be done by anyone else." But the identification may be complicated by race: can Coleman, as a white man, stand in as "anyone else?" His white privilege may make it harder for people of color to see themselves as having equal access to the relationships and resources he has. While the rhetorical challenge of reconstitutive leadership was certainly present through the genesis of WPP in the diverse neighborhood of Adams Morgan, it became even more apparent when the organization began working with the Watts Branch Park.

In a 2007 article about WPP's role in helping transform Watts Branch Park, we can see one way that the organization addressed the challenge of reconstitutive leadership in a multicultural organization: they highlight the contributions of multiple leaders and share genesis stories based on their multiple stories. Dennis Chestnut, a community leader from the Hillbrook neighborhood of Ward 7, was a WPP staff member in 2007 when he was interviewed by a reporter of the local paper *East of the River*. Chestnut links the beginnings of Washington Parks and People to African-American environmental activist Josephine Butler. In the same way that the *Language Architecture* article told the story of Coleman's drive to change Meridian Hill Park, Chestnut tells Butler's story.

> The organization began with Josephine Butler, an average citizen living in Northwest who tried by herself to clean up the [Meridian Hill] park . . . She attracted attention and support from fellow citizens who together managed to gather support from police, leading to a mass cleanup of the area that had been overrun by drug activity and crime. This massive effort led to the creation of the nonprofit.[19]

Both of the genesis stories are true. Butler had begun an effort to clean up Meridian Hill Park years earlier and had been a committed community activist throughout. Butler led WPP at the time of her death in 1997. WPP highlights its association with Butler prominently: its headquarter building next to Meridian Hill Park is named the Josephine Butler Parks Center. The website refers to her as "our inspiration."[20]

Additional strategies for reconstitution work by focusing not on current leaders but by highlighting the historical agency in the community itself. In *Teachers as Intellectuals,* cultural studies scholar Henry Giroux calls this move "liberating memory."[21] For Giroux, the purpose of looking back at history is not just to highlight those figures whose charismatic power and circumstances may have led them to fight for justice; he also recovers the "forms of historical and popular knowledge that [have] been suppressed or ignored and through which we once again discover the 'ruptural effects of conflict and struggle.'"[22] The pedagogical moment, for Giroux, highlights both the suffering and the resistance; it will not allow either aspect of the history to be erased.

Washington Parks and People embraces this liberatory memory by calling up the history of the neighborhoods surrounding the park. WPP worked with community leaders to rename the Watts Branch Parkway "Marvin Gaye Park," in honor of the singer who grew up there. The building where Gaye first played is now a WPP park center: the Riverside Center. Along the walls inside the Riverside Center, WPP has posted huge timelines, dating back to the 1700s, that list major figures in the neighborhood's past and recount both suffering and resistance. The timeline includes the Bennings, who were white slaveholders and their slaves (Benning Road is a major road in the area), and Levi Sherriff, another white slaveholder whose land was apportioned to his daughters, including Mary Dean, after whom Deanwood is named. The timeline also includes Nannie Helen Burroughs, an African-American activist and abolitionist who founded a training school for African-American girls in 1909 (a DC school and major road in the area are named after her), and dozens more. They have a large reproduction of a photograph of the Suburban Gardens, a prominent amusement park for African-American families, who could watch swimming exhibitions, go on rides, and listen to famous speakers such as Clarence Darrow.[23] WPP seeks out longtime residents of the area to capture oral histories and keep alive not only a sense of the Park, but also a sense of the capacity and constant transformation of the neighborhood. (University writing students who partnered with WPP several years ago conducted these interviews, which WPP has displayed during community events.)

In addition to displaying the community history, WPP uses the historical research to guide its programming. Coleman explains, "[The park] doesn't have to be about just preserving what once was. The past can be prologue, a jumping off point."[23] If Marvin Gaye brought down the house with his music years ago, then new musicians could do the same. On what would have been Gaye's 67th birthday, in 2007, Watt's Branch Park was renamed in his honor. An annual Capital Hip-Hop Soul Festival has taken place every year since then, with lineups of national musicians and local talent. In addition, WPP drew on the park's history as a Civil War encampment to invite the actors of the film *Glory* to come to the park to meet with area children.[24]

INTERDEPENDENCE AND STRANGERS: US AND THEM

So far, my examples have focused on rhetorics of reconstitution in which people identify with contemporary or historical-change agents. While valuable, I don't think these moves capture the full picture of how a public creates a sense of interdependence, a reliance on others to build towards power. Charles Payne writes about how SNNC workers in Mississippi orchestrated their mass church meetings to create and make use of this interdependent power.[25] Within the meetings, Payne writes, church ministers, business owners, sharecroppers, and other local people found themselves so bolstered by the sense of power and capacity in the room that they would commit to take on the work of the movement. By sitting, standing, singing, and talking with that collective, they were helped to imagine whom they could be, and they were transformed publicly into those new roles. Organizers fostered the energy of the meeting by inviting local people and leaders from across the state who shared news of other locations. People felt the power of the large group in people present and also felt connected with strangers elsewhere who were also working for the cause. The power came when people could imagine themselves in solidarity with like-minded people in the room and beyond it. What creates this power of interdependence?

An Expansive Us

At WPP, the Marvin Gaye Park is described as "extending 1.5 miles through what is arguably the longest continuously African-American community in the country."[26] In this process, they link a string of distinct neighborhoods, suggesting an interconnection among neighborhoods that have had long rivalries. They also draw on ecological metaphors to stress the point: they highlight different area's effects on the watershed. Most importantly, however, they stress the vitality of the neighborhood organizations and leaders already in the area. Listen to the affirmations of community in their mission statement:

> Washington Parks & People is the capital area's *network* of *community* park *partnerships*. Parks & People is working to revitalize Washington by *reconnecting* two of its greatest but most forgotten *assets:* its vast network of public lands and waterways—comprising one of the highest percentages of park land of any city in the world—and its core of *dedicated community leaders* and *organizations*.[27] (my italics.)

Yet, in addition to highlighting the interconnections among people who actively participate, a motivating element of a public is that it is always oriented toward strangers. The power of a public is that it convincingly asserts that strangers already share its vision (even if they haven't heard of it yet). Such moves work both to convince the people already part of the public that they have agency and to convince others of that agency. The larger the sense of a public, the more power it appears to have to pressure changes from government or communities and the more power it has to get the attention of more strangers and force them to contend with the worldview. Because of this, rhetorical theories of social movements and public spheres must move beyond theories of identification—as valuable as they are—and account for the rhetorical moves of marking strangers. By examining the mark of the stranger, we can recognize both the hope and the violence in public formation.

In *The Structural Transformation of the Public Sphere,* Jürgen Habermas defines the public as the gathering of a diverse group of individuals who come together freely to talk about matters that affect them all. The gatherings are public neither because the people present are all strangers nor because everyone from the imagined public is actually participating. Rather, it is public, he says, because at any time, a stranger could walk in and join the conversation. A public is oriented toward the open door. The stranger has a place there.

I agree with public sphere critics[28] who caution that existing publics are not fully open, but it seems clear that the promise of such a stranger relationship is integral to the conception of a public.[29] Public power comes from believing that strangers out there already share this view (even if they have not heard it yet) and that a broader space exists where our discourse is circulating. To some extent, we want to be jolted with reminders that the public is bigger than we are. Cultural studies critic Michael Warner puts it this way: "Our partial non-identity with objects of address in public speech seems to be part of what it means to regard something as public speech."[30] What this means rhetorically is that people who are addressed as a public want signs that the group is larger than their own identity.

The implication here is rather liberating. When I ask students to write to a public audience, they often insist on writing with bland generality. "If I say anything too specific," they explain, "the general reader will feel left out." However, when we realize that invoking strangers can solidify the audience as a public, we are free to draw on personal narratives, describe places, refer to specific people, and use a variety of rhetorical moves that heighten pathos and urgency. To a great extent, the discourse succeeds when each participant recognizes moments when he or she is not identified as the recipient. One quick example from WPP's website can illustrate this. In describing some projects, WPP refers to a slew of unexplained acronyms and city initiatives:

> The Riverside Center at Marvin Gaye Park's Heritage Green . . . has recently won improvement grants from the HSC Foundation, DC Great Streets Initiative, Deputy Mayor for Planning and Economic Development, Local Initiatives Support Corporation, DC Department of the Environment, and Community Foundation for the National Capital Region. Now this town hall and program center for the stream valley is coming alive with new heating and air conditioning, flooring, handicapped accessibility, and kitchen/café.[31]

Most readers do not know that the HSC Foundation is a local public health institution, or what all of the various city programs entail, but knowing about their support for the transformation of Marvin Gaye Park helps convey a sense of WPP's reach and potential power.

An Exclusive Us

The mark of the stranger is not always inclusive, however, and sometimes the move sets the desired public against other groups—individuals or publics who are at odds with the worldview of the organization, who either don't see the same "world as it is" or don't define "public good" or "public behavior" in the same way. Rosalyn Deutsche makes clear in her analysis of struggles over New York City parks that public discourse naturalizes which uses of public space are deemed legitimate and, therefore, which *people* are considered legitimate public citizens. She studies the discourse surrounding Jackson Park in New York City, which was redesigned so that it would be inaccessible to homeless people. She notes that the rhetorical terms of exclusion include phrases such as "reclamation" of the park for "the community," and the determination to "keep the park a park."[32] The illegitimate are set aside as nonpublic, without rights to use that public space.

In WPP discourse, the nonredeemable park users are the drug users and criminals, and it's interesting to trace how these characters show up in the park narratives. WPP likes to share that the Marvin Gaye Park area used to be known as Needle Park. They announce among their accomplishments that they've removed 12,000 hypodermic needles. In a description of the park that is distributed by the National Recreation and Parks Service, they also celebrate that they helped shut down a Methadone clinic that had attracted drug users to the area.[33] And yet, while they make it clear that drug dealers and users make it hard for the rest of the community to use the park, they also suggest, at least briefly, that drug users are redeemable. Coleman explains that one of the first people he met in Meridian Hill Park was "a former inmate and recovering drug addict whose efforts on behalf of Meridian Hill eventually earned him recognition as Washington, D.C.'s Volunteer of the Year."[34] WPP tries to navigate the challenging intersection of creating an inclusive vision of "community"—one that recognizes the historical and contemporary context that constrains residents' own sense of agency without demonizing other community members as outside their circle.

This move works only insofar as the people who would be reconstituted as community actors value this inclusiveness. If they see the problem that they seek to change as originating in part from those other people—the homeless, say, or drug dealers—then the disconnect between their vision of "the world as it is" and WPP's vision will preclude any sense of belonging. WPP seems to try to operate right at the edge of this insider/outsider distinction. Other nonprofits are more explicit about which people they see as capable of creating change and which people are an impediment to that change.

In a promotional video about Life Pieces to Masterpieces, for example, Executive Director Mary Brown describes the welcoming, safe environment that they provide for the apprentices. As she describes how they drive the boys home in the LPTM van, Brown chokes up. The few seconds she takes to compose herself are emotionally powerful to watch. She says,

> We're driving them home [she pauses to compose herself, and the camera stays on her face] and we're dropping them off. And after they learn about love, se-curity, and acceptance, and after they learn about hope and possibility and being peaceful and "just saying no to drugs," and after we do all that, we have to bring them home. [The camera now looks out the front of a van as it moves through a city street at dusk.] And see our little guys with their Shield of Faith [a pin they all wear displaying the affirmative LPTM decision-making color wheel] have to walk through all kinds of negative elements. [The camera now follows a small child walking on the sidewalk in front of a row of attached houses, and then fades to black with the lettering: "Only 30% of African American young men in D.C. graduate from high school." This is followed by "100% of Life Pieces apprentices not only graduate, but go on to post-secondary education."][35]

The community streets and the homes the boys return to are linked to nega-tive elements and opposed to the safety and optimism of Life Pieces. Those who engage with Life Piece's vision also define the community as a place of potential danger, where young boys have to wrestle with life-changing decisions every day. Cofounder Larry Quick affirms this message in the next frame of the video: "All I want from these boys is one thing. They don't have to be college graduates. They don't have to be A Students. They have to be able to maneuver through this madness and stay alive."

The move to designate the community attitudes and members who are part of the public while naming and separating those who are not is not unique to Life Pieces. A similar example can be found on the Higher Achievement Program's website, where a former HAP "scholar" describes the communi-ties the scholars come from as a place of hopelessness:

> For many of our scholars, their environment at home and at school is the greatest obstacle to their success. Some of these students—and remember, they're only in middle school—feel people have already given up on them. Knowing people don't care makes it a lot easier to give up on yourself or quit, to stay home, to just hang out, or worse.[36]

This comment is displayed as a "Portrait of Achievement," and the link is prominent on HAP's main page.

The move to circumscribe some attitudes and actions as belonging to the group of people who can make change while setting aside those attitudes and actions that impede change is a critical one for public formation. It's a move, as I noted in the previous chapter, that challenges the common rhetoric of community work as something that an entire geographic community embraces because it illustrates that sometimes, the challenges of a community are defined as internal, and the necessary action is not to try to work with the "problem people," but to create a space where their influence will not be perpetuated. Questions of agency and capacity are always tied to the exigency that calls the public into being. The strangers who belong to the public are those who accept the public's definition of both the problem and the capacity to address it.

BRIDGING MOVEMENTS: GROUNDWORKS ANACOSTIA RIVER, DC

One final point I'd like to illustrate about the rhetoric of public formation is that for nonprofit and other community organizations, the rhetoric they must contend with is not only rooted locally but is also part of broader national and international social movements. The public arguments within the mission statement of a local environmental organization became clear to one scholar of public rhetoric, Alexandra Evarts,[37] when she looked at the competing ideals of the conservationist and the environmental justice branches of the environmental movement.

Groundwork Anacostia River DC (GWARDC) is headed up by longtime Northeast DC resident and environmental activist Dennis Chestnut. Chestnut, who at one time headed WPP's Marvin Gaye Park initiative, split from WPP in 2008 to focus more explicitly on environmentalism. Through the national organization of Groundworks USA, he founded a DC chapter that is oriented toward all of the DC wards that line the Anacostia River (Wards 5 and 6 on the west of the river, Wards 7 and 8 on the east). Officially founded in 2010, GWARDC had already embarked on multiple area parks-cleanup campaigns, water testing days, and programs to involve area youth in environmental projects.

GWARDC's slogan is "creating better, safer, and healthier neighborhoods"; its mission is "to bring about the sustained regeneration, improvement and management of the physical environment by developing community-based partnerships which empower people, businesses and organizations to promote environmental, economic and social well-being."[38]

An organization's mission statement projects its vision of how it works as a public. The text of most mission statements is quite condensed; the genre requires a compact and focused statement of purpose. As a result, the organization's position on the unstated but pervasive arguments that have shaped it are often packed into their carefully chosen terminology. Unpacking the wording of a mission statement can be a productive method for making those arguments visible and for understanding the rhetorical challenges that organizations contend with.

Most of the time, mission statements emphasize a positive, affirmative vision, and people who were not immersed in the discourse of the issue, the broader sphere of community work around that issue, or the unique context of the geographical community may find the mission statement compelling without recognizing how it speaks back to other public visions. This is no accident; part of the work of public formation is that the public's position should seem inevitable. Readers should come away thinking, "This is the right purpose for us; these are the right tasks; we are the right people to do it." Explicitly interjecting any counterarguments might constrain that sense of inevitability by revealing how the public is one perspective among many and that it might fall apart (or evolve into something new) if anyone challenges how it has set out the relationships among its members. Cultural studies theorist Michael Warner puts it this way: "It seems that in order to address a public, one must forget or ignore the fictional nature of the entity one addresses. The idea of a public is motivating, not simply instrumental. It is constitutive of a social imaginary."[39]

Evarts discovered how the GWARDC mission statement consolidates the rhetoric of both the conservationist and environmental justice strands of the broader environmental movement when she was investigating a question that at first seemed to have nothing to do with their mission statement. Her analysis helps us see how important it is to bring together multiple documents and observations to see the complexity of public rhetoric. As she attended board meetings and helped staff tables at local environmental fairs and a National Parks Service centennial celebration, Evarts could not help but notice that she and other GW student volunteers were the only white people working with GWARDC. As she investigated the relationship of race and environmental movements, she learned that most conservation-based movements are predominantly white while many environmental-justice movements are run by people of color. Tracing the genesis of these two movements revealed that each drew on fundamentally different assumptions about the relationship of people to their environments. Evarts explains:

> Historically, the Conservationists typically focus on the natural lands of the American west that the founders of the movement worked to conserve. These men represent a white, affluent ancestry of the middle to upper class constituency of the movement. Conversely, the Environmental Justice movement strives for social change that confronts environmental injustices that are consistently dealt to its predominantly African American constituency; the active leaders of the civil rights movement stand as the cultural source.[40]

Evarts traces how these foundational values led to environmental movements with fundamentally different goals and modes of action. A conservationist approach relies on its members having the leisure and wealth to
experience the awe of grand wildernesses, she writes, while ignoring the
conditions of those who do not have access to such experiences. Drawing
on Bill Lawson's concept of "racialization" and Emily Enderle's distinction
between environmental "diversity" and human "diversity," Evarts argues
that "conservationists actively value biodiversity in racialized 'white' conservation spaces of the wilderness but rarely support human diversity in
these same spaces."[41]

In contrast, the Environmental Justice movement originates not through
a relationship to wilderness but from the experience of living in environ-
mentally-degraded areas. The exigency is not conservation, but civil rights:
"Environmental organizations and civil rights groups centered in mono-cul-
tural communities banded together to address the close relationship between
social inequities and environmental degradation."[42]

Evarts writes that the broader environmental movement is beginning to
build bridges across these two conceptions of environmentalism. She sees
the mission statement of GWARDC as such a bridge. Looking back at
GWARDC through this lens, she noticed with some excitement how the
rhetoric of the organization drew from both movements, equally balancing
appeals to conservation with appeals to social justice. The mission statement,
as I explained earlier, is

> [T]o bring about the sustained regeneration, improvement and management of
> the physical environment by developing community-based partnerships, which
> empowers people, businesses and organizations to promote environmental, eco-
> nomic and social well-being.

Evarts notes how the statement encompasses both a reverence for the natural
world and an orientation toward the people who live there.

> The diction of the statement simultaneously serves the interests of both groups.
> Regenerating, improving and managing the physical environment could imply
> that the organization works to "maintain" the natural world for the justice of
> humanity; or these words could imply that the organization works to "flourish"
> the natural environment for the justice of ecology.[43]

Her analysis of GWARDC's choice of goals (such as "Return brownfields to
economically productive use while restoring blighted landscapes with healthy
environments") identifies more places where they combine the discourses of

both movements: brownfields are environmentally toxic areas, such as those usually at the center of environmental justice activities, and the goal focuses both on the economic and ecological health of the community.

Evarts was able to recognize the multiple rhetorical layers within the Groundwork Anacostia River mission by considering the GWARDC documents—the mission statement and the descriptions of individual projects—beside her own observations and the rhetorics of other environmental movements. She compared their wording to that of the Audubon Society and the Sierra Club. She reflected on the events she had attended where she saw her analysis play out.

A public vision is never manifest in a single document, but emerges from the circulation of a range of materials as the discourse spreads around. To understand the rhetorical power of public discourse, scholars must immerse themselves in it and consider it against the rhetorics of other publics. Often times, the full implications of the rhetorical moves becomes apparent only when one tries to write with and as the public.

DESIGNING A COURSE TO HIGHLIGHT THE PUBLIC FORMATION

Pedagogies of public writing should provide opportunities for students to recognize the powerful rhetorical arguments embedded within community discourse. Writing and speaking well in a community does not mean following a prescribed set of rules such as those sometimes offered to those interested in public writing. For example, in *Easy Writer,* a pocket reference similar to handbooks used in many composition courses, Andrea Lunsford asserts, "In the United States, Canada, and Great Britain, many audiences expect a writer to get to the point as directly as possible and to articulate that point efficiently and unambiguously."[44] She points out that this expectation—one which, it is fair to say, is often attributed to "good" public writing in America—is not shared by other cultures, and cautions her readers to think carefully about their readers' expectations. Throughout the small text, she includes thoughtful advice for multilingual writers about the nuances and quirks of American writing.

What I like about Lunsford's textbooks is her attention to moments like these when she situates common expectations within a broader context. At the same time, I find myself questioning the assertion that American writers are all about efficiency and directness. This move is the method by which a particular American public asserts itself as the public. To be an American, the move argues, is to be part of a group that is most comfortable speaking directly and for whom the ideal relationship among citizens is one of efficiency. As I pointed out in the previous chapter, this conception of American democratic interaction is just one among many competing ideals. Instead of presenting public writing as the discourse prescribed by a single, unified American public, a pedagogy of public writing should locate public writing as a space of multiple, competing publics that each vie to be accepted, however briefly, as *the* public. Through their discourse, publics affirm their differing beliefs about what the world is, what it can be, and the ideal relationships among citizens.

In the first part of this chapter, I've demonstrated some of the rhetorical moves that some DC nonprofits use to bring people together to work for public good. These rhetorical moves do not begin to cover the full repertoire of strategies in public writing, which is vast, extensive, and always changing. Public writing encompasses all the ideals within the matrix of democracy plus all the unique local and issue-related histories and ideologies. My goal in teaching public writing is not to provide students with the full repertoire of rhetorical moves of public writing (an impossible task), but to offer some strategies for uncovering some of the rhetorical moves within a public. In this way, I hope, students are better prepared to compose public texts.

My approach to teaching public writing is to allow the theories about the public that I introduce in this book to emerge from students' experience working with and studying the rhetorics of public organizations, rather than impose the theories as an explicit framework in the course. I send students out to work with a variety of nonprofits, ask them to reflect on what they see and are curious about, and use the classrooms as a space where we contextualize and pursue the public arguments that they observe. I design my courses as "problem-posing" places (to draw on Paulo Friere's pedagogy); my role is to facilitate a deeper exploration of the questions that arise as students compare the kinds of public work they are engaged in.

I try to design the class so that students see the writers in community organizations as experts in public writing, as people whose on-the-ground experience within a community can direct us to richer understandings of the many components of public writing. I am following David Coogan's lead here: he argues for "rhetorical scholarship in the public sphere" that will "test the limits of rhetorical theory in the laboratory of community-based writing projects in order to generate new questions for rhetorical theory, rhetorical practice, and rhetorical education."[45]

Before the start of each semester, I meet with volunteer coordinators at a variety of local nonprofits and identify meaningful activities that my students can do with them. Some students serve as academic mentors at Life Pieces to

Masterpieces, some take minutes and help run community cleanup days with Groundworks Anacostia River, some help homeless women use the computer lab at Thrive DC, and some provide educational play for young children living in transitional housing while their mothers attend tenant's meetings. I have settled on requiring my students to work at such tasks for twenty hours over the semester. In addition, we use our class time, readings, and writing assignments to investigate the challenges of community work: how do the organizations attend to local histories and cultures, how do they invoke a sense of capacity in their constituents and volunteers, and how do they accommodate the potentially competing expectations of funders and community leaders? At the end of the semester, students prepare documents that the organization has commissioned of them: brochures, volunteer manuals, evaluations of lesson plans, teaching materials, presentations for community meetings, and so on. I brainstorm potential assignments when I meet with the organizations at the beginning of the semester, and the students sometimes discover additional opportunities during their time there.

As a problem-posing pedagogy, this approach to teaching requires a willingness to let the students' experiences guide the discussion. I include some required, common readings to introduce to students some strategies to find and analyze community arguments. I try to introduce the readings based on something that they have observed, to show them how they can use their observations to explore some of the tensions within a geographical community, a nonprofit, or both. Over time, I have built up a large store of support materials to draw on, but I try to remain open to the constant changes within communities and organizations. Nonprofits are constantly evolving and experimenting, and their communities are constantly evolving. For example, within the last year, Life Pieces to Masterpieces decided to expand its volunteer base and introduce a more multicultural curriculum along with its arts and Afrocentric focus. When Thrive DC moved to a new neighborhood, it began to have more Latino clients, along with more families. These changes influence an organization's approaches; its methods and its discourse have to change, and students and I consider the implications of the changes.

I provide some of the nitty-gritty logistics for my course design in the final appendices, but I will elaborate here on how I choose community organizations with whom to partner. As I hope I made clear in the previous chapter, I do not believe the class should work with only those organizations that seem to embody an ideal of direct, communitarian democracy. In contrast, I identify organizations that define public work at different points in the matrix of democracy. My goal in choosing partners is to generate meaningful discussions within the class as students return from their experiences, compare notes, and try to understand the differences they are observing.

Work with Multiple Organizations in the Same Issue Area

One strategy I use is to work with at least two or three nonprofits that tackle the same general issue area. For example, we work with several homeless-advocacy organizations. Miriam's Kitchen provides breakfast and dinner along with case-management services and community activities for people who are usually chronically homeless (I talk more about Miriam's Kitchen's philosophy in chapter 7). Thrive DC offers services similar to Miriam's Kitchen but is located in a different area of town and has a commitment to serve only women and children in the evening hours. Known as the Dinner Program for Homeless Women until just last year, Thrive DC's approach to homelessness acknowledges the connection between domestic violence, gender, and homelessness in a way that neither Miriam's Kitchen nor *Street Sense* do. *Street Sense*, a street newspaper, provides vendors opportunities to make money as well as opportunities to write and be published. Its writers' workshops also offer a sense of community.

As my course load and number of students increased, I added opportunities for students to help in the after-school programs of two transitional housing organizations in DC. The program at Independence Place is part of a much larger, comprehensive homeless advocacy group, So Others Might Eat (SOME), while the program at the Transitional Housing Corporation is a smaller nonprofit with a more focused mission. Finally, students who are willing to devote a significantly larger amount of time can volunteer with LIFT, a student-run nonprofit that offers one-on-one consultations to connect low income and homeless people with government and nonprofit services in DC. Here, students have a chance not only to offer services but also to direct the agenda of the organization. Many of my students attend a Speakers' Bureau Panel from the National Coalition for the Homeless, and while I have not yet placed any of my students as volunteers with NCH, I regularly draw on their materials as yet another example of nonprofit advocacy for the homeless.

As I hope this list makes clear, I choose organizations whose approaches fit into and across the range of both the matrix of democracy and Morton's service paradigms. NCH is most like a social change organization, with homeless men and women serving on the board and guiding campaigns for political action. *Street Sense* uses a model of activist journalism and vendor entrepreneurism; it seems to move between the paradigms of social change and projects. LIFT involves students directly as decision makers who shape the direction of the organization, but it provides more project-like services. The others—soup kitchens and transitional housing organizations—seem to be both projects and thick charities; they are direct-service providers.

Those organizations working within the same general paradigm might define their target populations differently or talk about the effects of their projects in ways that suggest different root causes. Sometimes, these organizations compete for the same funds, as happens each fall with the Fannie Mae Help the Homeless Walkathon and with some grants. I have to be careful that the collaborative work that students do in my classes does not compromise the organization's conflicting needs during such moments. More often than not, though, the organizations are working toward the same general goals in different areas of the city and through different methods.

We use primary documents from these multiple community organizations to look at the variety of approaches and consider how each invokes a particular public ideal. I rely on common course readings to help students start to see the different ways that publics define capacity and root causes and the different ways that those conceptions might manifest in the rhetoric and structures of their programs. For this, we read articles about models of community work, such as John Kretzmann and John McKnight's "Building Communities from the Inside Out"[46] and Keith Morton's "The Irony of Service."[47] (Morton's piece is a difficult one for many freshmen, I find, and it takes us a while to unpack it. Students tend to find so convincing his characterization of the continuum model—patronizing charity building to measured projects to heroic social change—that they don't see that halfway through the article he argues against this model in favor of thick service across all three paradigms).

As part of the class, we position the academic texts and articles about the ideals of community organizing next to the materials that students gather from and about their organizations. My goal is to help students see themselves as gaining an authority to speak about community work because they are working at the intersection of these materials. The articles provide a vocabulary to name some of the approaches they see in the community organizations. Sometimes, the vocabulary offers them a way to begin talking back to these theories. Some students argue that their organizations extend or defy Morton's categories. Some students working with different documents from the same organization notice that the organization seems to move in and out of different service paradigms, writing as a thick charity in one place but as a project in another.

These readings help us start looking, but many of our discoveries about public rhetoric come from the primary documents of the organizations. To help uncover the arguments about publics—what brings them together, what capacities people have to work for change, how they circulate—we examine the organizations' mission statements, tracing the significance of key terms to understand how they might subtly project worldviews and arguments about capacity. When possible, we look at the organization's genesis stories, too, as these often reveal a lot about how the organization defines both root causes and public capacity. Students look at how the organization is covered in local newspaper and radio coverage, blogs, and other spaces, and they assess how well the organization was able to convey its vision in those contexts. You will find examples of the writing prompts I assign to push students to investigate such questions in appendix 2.

Work with Multiple Organizations in the Same Geographical Area

In discussing the capacity-invoking rhetorics of genesis stories and mission statements, I have already shown how the rhetoric of community organizations is tied to the specific locations in which those publics form. I make this attention to geographical locations a second guideline in designing my course. I choose community partners from the same geographical areas of the city. Recently, for example, three of the organizations my class worked with were located in the Deanwood area of Ward 7 (Life Pieces to Masterpieces, the Higher Achievement Program, and Groundwork Anacostia River DC); another two were not far away in Ward 7 (The Transitional Housing Corporation and SOME's Independence Place, two groups working with families transitioning out of homelessness). Two organizations operate in Columbia Heights, which is in Ward 1 (CentroNía, a multicultural, bilingual program where my students tutor after school, and Thrive DC, one of the organizations that provides food and case-management services for homeless men and women). During the semester, when my forty-five students were serving at thirteen different organizations, they were clustered so that at least two or three were located in the same wards.

My goal is to juxtapose how these organizations characterize the community in which they work and to use these distinctions, once again, to reveal how arguments about publics are built into public rhetoric. For example, consider the analysis I provided earlier in the chapter about how Life Pieces to Masterpieces, HAP, and Washington Parks and People describe the community in which they work in very different terms. In addition to asking students to work closely with the documents of community organizations, I also ask them to read articles in the national *Washington Post,* in DC papers such as the *City Paper,* and in more local publications such as *East of the River* or the *Capital Rag.* Likewise, they scour local blogs, community listservs, and other places where people might characterize their own or other neighborhoods. The goal in these assignments is to illustrate that every construction of community is a contested one and to highlight the current points of tension about those constructions.

I have discovered that it helps to introduce some concepts from linguistics and cultural geography to show students how others have identified and analyzed such struggles. Because I teach in Washington, DC, I rely on Gabrielle Modan's *Turf Wars: Discourse, Diversity, and the Politics of Place,* which provides a thorough and insightful analysis of the DC neighborhood of Mt. Pleasant. As part of the "New Directions in Ethnography" series, the book is designed to be very accessible. In form and style, the books in this series "have been written with care to allow both specialists and nonspecialists to delve into theoretically sophisticated work."[48] Multiple chapters in Modan's book demonstrate how "community members in Mt. Pleasant create and contest visions of their neighborhood through discourses of identity, both sociogeographic and personal."[49] She traces out complex networks of linguistic contrast through which residents associate people and places in the neighborhood with different moral registers based on conflicting conceptions about such things as safety, cleanliness, diversity, and social interaction. Her book moves easily between concrete examples, transcripts of conversation, and her analysis of how the discourse marks out who is or is not considered a "real" Mt. Pleasant resident. Modan explains,

> Through the use of various discourse strategies and themes, community members create alignments and oppositions among people and places. These alignments and opposition are then evaluated positively or negatively, in relation to various value and belief systems circulating in the community. In other words, through linguistic moves, community members position themselves and their neighborhoods within a kind of abstract moral "grid" that they create for the neighborhood.
> Creating a moral geography is all about showing that you fit in and how you fit in—that you and the landscape are well matched.[50]

I also appreciate how Modan carefully analyzes her own complex role as community resident and ethnographer; this section helps launch discussions about the ethics and challenges of such scholarship, questions that the students will have to wrestle with as both volunteers and writers.

Scholars from multiple fields have taken on this work of analyzing place, and there are many additional materials to draw on, depending on the kinds of communities students are working with. Ralph Cintron's *Angel's Town* offers insight into how an urban Chicano community defines itself and its relationship to literacy.[51] Samuel Delany's *Times Square Red, Times Square Blue* looks at the discourses of public "cleanliness" that redefined what was once a gathering space for public sex into a corporate, consumer-oriented public space.[52] And, as I mentioned before, Rosalyn Deutsche, in her book *Evictions,* looks at how public parks in New York City were redefined as spaces where homeless people cannot enter.[53] Don Mitchell provides similar analysis of the transformation of People's Park in Berkeley, CA; his articles include a helpful introduction to the commodification of public space by capitalist discourses, as well. Mitchell locates his critique within public sphere theory; Deutche investigates from interdisciplinary spaces of art, architecture, urban design, and politics of space.[54]

We could expand this model to look at the discursive clashes over material, public space across a national or international scene, as I have illustrated in sections of this book. But I'd argue that pedagogically, it's useful to begin this analysis in local communities because working with, writing about, and writing for community organizations provides students an opportunity to be immersed in the rhetoric and experience it at more than an intellectual level.

Writing With and For Nonprofits

In the final writing project for my Public Writing course, students produce a document for their community organization. Some semesters, this consists of a volunteer portfolio in which students reflect on their experiences offer the volunteer coordinators a glimpse at what it is like to be a volunteer at their organizations. As I explain to my students, nonprofits rely heavily on volunteers, but they rarely have the opportunity to hear from those people about the quality of that experience. Unhappy volunteers usually leave; others are so busy doing the work that they don't have the time or inclination to reflect about which parts of their experience were most fulfilling, which policies or activities confused them, or what the organization could do to ensure that the volunteer was interacting most ethically and positively with the constituents. When possible, I arrange for students to verbally present their analysis to the members of the organization, and the resulting conversation can help students see that their observations matter and can give the organization a chance to ask more questions or clarify misunderstandings.

While these interactions are valuable for the students and the organizations, and while they do give students an opportunity to practice writing to audiences outside the academy, I prefer a model where students can choose from a range of writing tasks commissioned by the organization. When different students are writing and helping each other with materials in a range of genres for a range of audiences, then they come away with a richer understanding of the variety and complexities of writing within nonprofit community organizations. Moreover, when students have to write on behalf of the organization, in a newsletter article, for example, or by creating a Powerpoint presentation for the organization to use at local community meetings, they have an opportunity to see just how complex public rhetoric is.

Before I provide an example, I want to emphasize that in my course design, I work with staff at the community organizations to identify potential writing projects my students might take on. Some are group projects, and some are individual projects. Some are written to the organization itself (such as volunteer portfolios, evaluations of lesson plans, and memos about best practices); others are for external public audiences (such as videos or Powerpoints that the organization might use to introduce its work; brochures; portions of fundraising grants, and the like.) I choose tasks that I think my first-year students will be able to tackle successfully after a semester of writing about and working with the organization. I also make it clear to the organization that the documents will be written by people who are just learning how to invent the public. I work with the students, of course, offering feedback on drafts and guiding them with models of genre and analysis of their rhetorical situation, but inventing a public is a complex rhetorical task, and the student is likely to miss some of the implications of their word choice or document design that they or their community partners use.

Because I want to ensure an ongoing partnership between my classes and the community organizations, I make sure that the reciprocity of our relationship does not depend only on my students successfully completing a commissioned task. My students study the organizations all semester, reading and learning from community documents, and perhaps interviewing staff members about how they conceptualize their public work. In return, they provide a document and twenty hours of ongoing service that meets the organizations' regular needs. Students tutor in after-school programs and staff computer labs for homeless clients; they clear trails and plant trees; they make meals, file papers, and sort food. To my mind, these are the services that the community partners rely on, and I do my part to supplement those experiences with an academic framework that allows students to understand and appreciate the complexities and opportunities of such work.

I want the commissioned tasks to be equally as valuable, and many of them are. One group of students created a Powerpoint that Dennis Chestnut took to the national Groundworks USA conference to introduce the local chapter. Another student produced a short slideshow about how Miriam's Kitchen attracts young people to volunteer and was told that with her material, the organization was awarded thousands of dollars more than they had been in previous grant cycles. These are the outcomes I strive for, but because I cannot guarantee that all of the documents my students produce will match with the vision and needs of the organizations, I ensure that the community partners benefit in other ways from our relationship.

Regardless of how well the documents serve the community organizations, though, they work well from a pedagogical perspective. An overview of one student's work with the Columbia Heights-based organization CentroNía illustrates how commissioned tasks can provide students with opportunities to practice public making.

A many-faceted program, CentroNía's mission is to educate children and strengthen families in a bilingual, multicultural community. Began as an attempt to revitalize a local church childcare program, it has evolved in response to a perceived ongoing need to support multilingual communities in the broader DC area. CentroNía is headquartered in the Columbia Heights neighborhood where the population in 2000 was 31.7 percent white, 45.7 percent African American, and 24.7 percent Hispanic and Latino.[55] CentroNía has a multilingual daycare center, a DC Bilingual Public Charter School, professional and vocational training for adults, and a center for family and community development.

Several of my students volunteered with CentroNía by working closely with the Communications Manager. She designated a variety of writing and research tasks for them. Some were research reports to educate CentroNía staff about best practices in multilingual education or nonprofit, multicultural management; these would be distributed internally. Others were public relations pieces about various facets of the program; these would be published in the newsletter or used in fundraising reports.

In my course, students studied CentroNía's website, pamphlets, annual reports, and other documents to become familiar with its discourse. They compared these to government documents (such as census data), news reports, and DC cultural tourism documents. The goal in this analysis was to help them recognize how the discourse conveyed particular worldviews. In some ways, this was obvious: CentroNía publishes its documents in both Spanish and English. In other ways, the distinctions required close readings and awareness of some of the trends in community organizing. For example, the CentroNía materials highlight community assets; they refrain from characterizing community members as lacking or in need. Rather, they highlight the abilities they offer and the possibilities to which they aspire. More than a public-relations strategy, this rhetoric coincides with John Kretzmann and John McKnight's philosophy of asset mapping.[56]

Writing about an organization and writing with and for that organization demand that students pay close attention to such rhetorical indicators of worldviews. One student, who had presented her detailed analysis of CentroNía's bilingual educational philosophy at a student academic conference earlier in the semester, remarked that she was struck by the challenge of writing a newsletter article using the voice of the organization. She recognized that she would need to embody the worldview that she has just analyzed; furthermore, she recognized that for her piece to be successful, it would need to convey the ethos of the organization to continue its public-making function. For her final project, she interviewed faculty, parents, and students in CentroNía's Pre-K program, selected a specific anecdote about a four-year-old who added Spanish to her already fluent Russian and English after a year in the program, and wove in information about how CentroNía's program has been chosen by the DC government as a model for Pre-K education. At the same time, she gained a greater awareness of the multiple and divergent audiences of such public writing—the families who participate in CentroNía and the families who have not yet become part of it; the current funding organizations and the potential future ones; the employees and the managers; the longtime volunteers and the brand-new ones. Although the newsletter article is just a small piece of the extensive and multi-faceted methods CentroNía uses to create and reinforce its public, the project required the student to wrestle with many of the components of public making—her process and final project evidenced rhetorics of mutuality, affiliation, affection, and an orientation toward those strangers who might "show up and salute."

SOME LIMITATIONS OF WORKING WITH NONPROFITS

This pedagogy of public writing provides a more complex introduction than models that limit the definition of public writing to one vision, whether that be the participatory, deliberative model endorsed by Morton and Enos or the dominant, efficient one suggested by Lunsford. But it is not without its limitations, and as we work within this model, we must keep these limitations in mind and find ways to fill in what is missing. For example, a point that Morton and Enos raise about nonprofits is quite applicable here: it's hard to find community organizations that employ more confrontational methods. My solution has been to take note of the historical allusions to such confrontations that are raised in the present moment. Students working in the Columbia Heights and Shaw neighborhoods of DC, for example, often encounter narratives that explain the current need for redevelopment by referring back to the riots that exploded in those areas after Dr. King was assassinated. Though often described as foolish acts that caused the downfall of historical African-American neighborhoods, the riots can also be understood as dramatic acts of revolution and resistance by men who felt that there was no other way to confront systemic racism. This view was documented at the time by *Washington Post* reporter Ben Gilbert, who interviewed arsonists responsible for much of the destruction. Reading their observations and arguments provides a glimpse at a much more radical, revolutionary vision of social and political transformation.[57]

Another challenge is that within some well-established organizations, students and scholars are rarely invited into internal, agenda-setting deliberations. I do not wish to suggest that we should have easy access to such spaces, as those who participate have established themselves as trustworthy and committed. Such spaces are vulnerable spaces where people hash out disagreements that they do not wish to share with outsiders. Neither scholars nor students should presume to be welcome there. Paula Matthieu makes this point with a dramatic anecdote about a student who writes to the editor of a Chicago street paper.[58] The student has been required by her professor to offer advice to the nonprofit (the professor never asked if they needed such advice—they didn't). The student also asked the editor to send her a slew of materials and to let her know when the next staff meetings were so that she could attend. The editor was not interested. It would have taken a great deal of time to work with this student and provide her what she needed for her class, and the result would not have benefited the newspaper.

While I don't expect community organizations to invite students into the inner workings of their organization right away, I have found that after students have shown their commitment over a semester, many organizations are very eager to learn from the students about their experiences. Students provide a perspective on an organization that an organization doesn't often have a chance to hear, and after a semester of regular activities with an organization, students often can provide very helpful recommendations about the effectiveness of those activities. The work of composing those recommendations into memos that the organization will take seriously is not insignificant for a writer who is venturing into public writing: the task has to balance both an emphasis on commitment and understanding of the community values while offering suggestions about how to improve particular activities. In a small way, I consider activities such as these to provide students a glimpse into the important internal work of an organization.

I also like to find at least one organization a semester where students have access to board meetings or other high-level deliberations. These students' reports back to the class give us a way to talk about this layer of community work. Among my community partners, for example, Groundwork Anacostia River DC has invited students to their board meetings, and LIFT is deliberately conceptualized as a student-run organization; students engage in regular reflective debriefings that guide the organization.

ADDITIONAL CONSIDERATIONS ABOUT PUBLIC WRITING (OR, WHY READ THE REST OF THE BOOK?)

So far, my analysis of the community nonprofits has focused on how their discourse invokes particular visions of public work. I've laid out some methods for identifying and analyzing those visions whose arguments become most visible when they are set next to the discourse of groups working with similar issues or in similar geographic areas.

Pedagogies of public writing must account not only for how publics form but also how they circulate. As you can see from the kinds of documents I have used in this analysis, the work of public formation takes place in many different venues, including everything from mission statements, websites, and brochures to online videos, magazine and newspaper articles, and Letters to the Editor. I have not yet accounted for how these particular venues might shape the public ideals that they forward. As John Trimbur warns in "Composition and the Circulation of Writing," it matters whether something is published in *The Wall Street Journal* or the *National Enquirer*.[59] It's not just that one publication is delivered to you and the other is sold at the checkout counter of a supermarket. Rather, at a more fundamental level, the forum conveys arguments about expertise. I'd extend his point, noting that the traditional newspapers and national magazines are businesses that are literally invested in a specific public ideal. In the next chapter, I explain this connection further, demonstrating how both national magazines and traditional newspapers perpetuate an ideal of democracy in which citizens' main role is to read, talk, and allow the media to circulate their public opinions to each other and those in power. This model reifies particular kinds of expertise and particular dispositions towards fellow citizens. In the course I've laid out, students turn to magazine and newspaper articles about their communities and their community organizations. Chapter 4 shows how those venues of circulation may forward or counter some of the public ideals that an organization would put forward. Chapters 5 and 6 look more closely at the rhetoric of groups that oppose the dominant media characterization of the public and show some of their techniques for getting heard. In chapter 7, I look at online social networking as a potential space of public formation. In chapter 8, I return more explicitly to the university public writing class and investigate how these theories of publics might apply to the academy itself.

NOTES

1. Lloyd Bitzer, "The Rhetorical Situation." *Philosophy and Rhetoric* 1, (Jan. 1968), 6.

2. Warner, Michael. *Publics and Counterpublics*. (Cambridge: Zone Books, 2005), 90–97.

3. Diane Feinstein, "Opening Welcome Remarks at the 2009 Presidential Election," *American Rhetoric: Online Speech Bank*, 2009 www.americanrhetoric.com/speeches/ dianefeinsteinpresidentialinauguration.htm (Aug. 16 2009).

4. M. L. King Jr. Research and Education Center, "March on Washington for Jobs and Freedom," mlk-kpp01.stanford.edu/index.php/encyclopedia/encyclopedia/enc_march_on_washington_for _jobs_and_freedom (20 May 2009).

5. Michael Janofsky, "Federal Parks Chief Calls 'Million Man' Count Low," *New York Times* 1995, www.nytimes.com/1995/10/21/us/federal-parks-chief-calls-million-man-count-low.html (19 July, 2010).

6. Lester W. Milbrath, *Political Participation: How and Why do People Get Involved in Politics?* (Chicago: Rand McNally, 1965).

7. Barack Obama, "Remarks of Senator Barack Obama: Super Tuesday," Feb 05, 2008 www.barackobama.com/2008/02/05/remarks_of_senator_barack_obam_46.php (19 July, 2010).

8. Washington Parks and People, "Welcome," 2007 www.washingtonparks.net (5 Aug. 2010).

9. Washington Parks and People, "Accomplishments." (5 Aug. 2010)

10. Gabriel Pacyniak, "Lincoln Heights: Future Beacon on a Hill?" *East of the River,* May 2006, n.p.

11. Susan Hines, "Shared Wisdom: Stone Soup." *Landscape Architecture,* (June 2005), 131.

12. Coleman, quoted in Hines, "Stone Soup," 127.

13. Hines, "Stone Soup," 124–134.

14. Hines, "Stone Soup," 126.

15. Hines, "Stone Soup," 126.

16. Linda Wheeler, "President Stops to Smell the Flowers; Clinton Lauds Revival of Stately District Park," *The Washington Post* April 22 1994, A3.

17. Sean Piccoli, "Urban Renewal Jewel: Meridian Park Gets Presidential Salute," *The Washington Times* April 22 1994, C4.

18. John C. Hammerback, and Richard J. Jensen, *The Rhetorical Career of César Chávez.* 1st ed. (College Station: Texas A & M University Press, 1998).

19. Khadijah Ali-Coleman. "Marvin Gaye Park: Spawning a Change in the Neighborhood." *East of the River* April 2007, 58–59.

20. Washington Parks and People, "Josephine Buttler" www.washingtonparks.net/Josephine_Butler (5 Aug. 2010)

21. Henry A. Giroux, *Teachers as Intellectuals: Toward a Critical Pedagogy of Learning.* (New York: Bergin & Garvey, 1988), xxxv.

21. Giroux, Public Intellectuals, xxxv.

22. Patricia Sullivan, "Getting its Groove Back," *Washington Post* April 2, 2007,

23. www.washingtonpost.com/wp-dyn/content/article/2006/04/01AR2006040101105.html (15 August, 2010).

Hines, "Stone Soup," 127.

24. Hines, "Stone Soup," 127.

25. Charles M. Payne, *I've Got the Light of Freedom: The Organizing Tradition and the Mississippi Freedom Struggle.* (Berkeley: University of California Press, 1996).

26. Washington Parks and People, "Watts Branch Photos." www.washingtonparks.net/wattsbrphotos.html. (15 Aug. 2010).

27. Washington Parks and People, "Accomplishments." My Italics.

28. Nancy Fraser, "Rethinking the Public Sphere: A Contribution to the Critique of Actually Existing Democracy," in *Habermas and the Public Sphere,* ed. Craig J. Calhoun (Cambridge, Mass.: MIT Press, 1992), 89–110.

29. Christian R. Weisser, *Moving Beyond Academic Discourse: Composition Studies and the Public Sphere.* (Carbondale: Southern Illinois University Press, 2002), 70–72.

30. Michael Warner, *Publics and Counterpublics,* 78.

31. Washington Parks and People. "What's going on? Summer 2009." www.washingtonparks.net/newseltter_. (3 Nov. 2010).

32. Rosalyn Deutsche, *Evictions: Art and Spatial Politics.* (Cambridge, Mass.: MIT Press, 1998).

33. National Recreation and Park Service. *Marvin Gaye Park Backgrounder.* www.nrpa.org, n.d., (Aug 16, 2010).

34. Hines, "Stone Soup," 126.

35. Stone Soup Films. *Life Pieces to Masterpieces—8 Min. Version.,*2009. <vimeo.com/5143977> (Aug 16, 2010).

36. Higher Achievement Program. "Portraits of Achievement: Erica Pitts."www.higherachievement.org. (10 Aug. 2010)

37. Evarts volunteered with GWARDC in Spring 2010 and worked with the Lawrence, MA Groundworks chapter that summer.

38. DC Groundwork Anacostia River, "Facebook: GWARDC Information," www.facebook.com/pages/GWARDC-Groundwork-Anacostia-River-DC (Aug 13, 2010).

39. Warner, Publics and Counterpublics, 11–12.

40. Alexandra Evarts, "Reframing the Environmental Movement" Unpublished article. Washington, DC, George Washington University, 2010, 2.

41. Evarts, "Reframing," 5.

42. Evarts, "Reframing," 5.

43. Evarts, "Reframing," 9.

44. Andrea A. Lunsford, and Franklin E. Horowitz, *Easy Writer: A Pocket Reference.* 3rd ed. (Boston: Bedford/St. Martin's, 2006), 139.

45. David Coogan, "Service Learning and Social Change: The Case for Materialist Rhetoric." *College Composition and Communication* 57, no. 4 (Jun 2006): 670.

46. John P. Kretzmann, and John L. McKnight, *Building Communities from the Inside Out: A Path Toward Finding and Mobilizing a Community's Assets.* (Evanston, IL: Asset-Based Community Development Institute, 1993).

47. Keith Morton, "The Irony of Service: Charity, Project and Social Change in Service-Learning." *Michigan Journal of Community Service Learning* Fall (1995): 19–32.

48. Gabriella Gahlia Modan, *Turf Wars : Discourse, Diversity, and the Politics of Place.* (Malden, MA: Blackwell, 2007), frontmatter.

49. Modan, *Turf Wars,* 6.

50. Modan, *Turf Wars,* 90.

51. Ralph Cintron. *Immigration, Minutemen, and the Subject of Democracy.*(Paper presented at the Western States Rhetoric and Literacy Conference, Salt Lake City, Utah, Oct. 2009.)

52. Samuel R. Delany, *Times Square Red, Times Square Blue.* (New York: New York University Press, 1999).

53. Rosalyn Deutsche, *Evictions.*

54. Don Mitchell, "The End of Public Space? People's Park, Definitions of the Public, and Democracy." *Annals of the Association of American Geographers* 85, no. 1 (Mar. 1995): 108–133.

55. DC Government, "Office of Planning: DC Census by Ward," 2002 www.planning.dc.gov/planning/cwp/view,a,3,q,570104.asp (2010).

56. Kretzmann and McKnight, *Building Communities.*

57. Ben W. Gilbert, Ten Blocks from the White House: Anatomy of the Washington Riots of 1968. (New York: Praeger, 1968).

58. Paula Mathieu, *Tactics of Hope: The Public Turn in English Composition.* (Heinemann, 2005).

59. John Trimbur, "Composition and the Circulation of Writing." *College Composition and Communication* 52, no. 2 (2000): 188–219.

Chapter 4

The Public of Traditional Media: Circulating Deliberative Conversations

In his important article, "Composition and the Circulation of Writing," John Trimbur notes that if those who study public formation and public writing continue to ignore the question of circulation, they risk reinforcing the dominant—and simplistic—economic logic about distribution: that something will find an audience if its message is worthy enough, that distribution will take care of itself because things of use find a market, and that markets find the things that they need.[1] Such a view treats the sites of circulation as neutral and universally accessible. It ignores how competitive market forces restrict access for profit. Moreover, it ignores how those who control the means of distribution can dictate the rhetorical form of any texts that they will forward, thus controlling what kind of public is invoked in those texts.

Some scholars who wish to address questions of access to public discourse work backward from prominent national publications to develop an image of what "public discourse" looks like. In turn, they coach "outsiders" about the "insider language" they need to know. E.D. Hirsch, Jr. took on such a project in his best-selling 1986 book *Cultural Literacy,* followed soon after with the 1993 *Dictionary of Cultural Literacy: What Every American Should Know,* and more recently, *The Knowledge Deficit.*[2] Working from a select series of common public texts, including national newspapers and magazines such as *Newsweek* and *The Atlantic,* Hirsch and his colleagues developed an extensive list of concepts and idioms that are used regularly in such publications. Hirsch seeks to give more students access to all sites of public deliberation by teaching these concepts. He rightly notes that children of more affluent and more educated parents are more likely to encounter these concepts than other children, and he seeks to overcome that gap. His Core of Knowledge curricula, adopted widely across the United States, sets out to do just that.

I admire Hirsch's project here and agree that gaining access to current sites of public deliberation—both as readers and as writers—can be powerful. But I want to push farther to examine what kind of power is offered there. Trimbur cautions that people won't necessarily be able to influence public discourse by adopting a particular way of talking or, to use Hirsch's terms, by using "the lexicon of the culture." Trimbur writes

> The matter is not so simple . . . that by changing one's prose style . . . one can therefore take on a new identity as a "public intellectual." If anything, this wish for transformation . . . amounts . . . to what I've already mentioned as the "one-sided" view of production that Marx critiques—the fallacy that by changing the manner of writing, one can somehow solve the problem of circulation. Instead, as Marx points out, to understand and, potentially, to change the way knowledge circulates, requires thinking about how the means of production are distributed in the first place.[3]

What is distributed, Trimbur argues, is nothing less than "the productive means to name the world":

> [T]he distribution of the *Wall Street Journal* and the distribution of the *National Enquirer* no longer fit simply into equivalent moments in the circulation of commodities, guided by the law of supply and demand. Instead, what gets distributed by these quite different types of reading matter is the productive means to name the world, to give it shape and coherent meaning.[4]

Like Trimbur, I argue that the real question for those who study and teach public writing is not how we might fit our ideas in the expectations of current, dominant media outlets. Instead, the question is what kind of public do we wish to invoke in our writing, and how do these modes of circulation enhance or inhibit our ability to "name the world." When scholars and teachers point to magazines like *Harper's* or *The Atlantic Monthly* as examples of the kind of public writing that student-citizens should learn to emulate, they miss an opportunity to interrogate what kind of democratic relationship the publication endorses through its common style, its manner of marshalling evidence, and the role it offers to the public reader.

For Trimbur, the pinnacle of this rhetorical "naming of the world" lies with the way such publications produce and circulate particular kinds of expertise: "the hierarchy of knowledge and information that is tied to the cultural authorization of expertise, professionalism, and respectability."[5] If we wish to intervene in the circulation of hierarchies of expertise, he suggests, we need to do more than figure out how to get ourselves published in these places; we also need to intervene earlier in the production line to redirect the way they create expertise. His example includes the National Breast Cancer Coalition, which

> [h]as trained lay breast cancer activists to sit on study sections that rank grant proposals at the federal and local levels and on institutional review boards in hospitals and universities that oversee research on human subjects. . . . As the women learn about the biology of cancer and the design of epidemiological studies, there is also a redistribution of expertise taking place that has changed the production and circulation of scientific knowledge.[6]

Jeff Grabill offers another example of intervening in the production of expertise as he studies the knowledge-production and information-gathering practices of a community group in the town he calls "Harbor."[7] He observes how the group intervenes in civic locations that privilege the expertise of academics and professionals over that of the community. In response to venues where professionals come and lecture to the community groups, Grabill and the community members redesign community meetings so that professionals send their texts ahead of time. The community groups meet to review the material, circulate their responses and questions, and then use the meeting with the professional for detailed question-and-answer sessions. The community group's ability to have its knowledge heard and respected depends not only on its ability to contextualize the "expert's" report with its own alternate knowledge, but also in its ability to circulate its findings throughout the community. This not only grants it a role of knowledge-maker within the community, but it also gives it power in talking to and with the outside "experts." Again, expertise is rooted not only in the invention and composing processes, but also in the mode and extent of circulation.

Ultimately, what the issue of circulation makes plain is that public-formation is ongoing and constant. A public is a social relation that is invoked through discourse; to understand that a particular way of talking or describing the world goes beyond an individual writer or beyond a unique moment in time, one needs to encounter that discourse multiple times. Supposing what one wants to say could be conveyed in *Harper's* article, that publication could not be the end-goal if the broader hope is to create some kind of public movement. The *Harper's* issue will be published, read, and put away. The formation of the public will falter if someone else does not pick it up and carry it forward. The challenge of public-formation, then, is to understand how broadly the public discourse needs to circulate (what it will take to empower the capacity of that public) and to understand what channels one can use or create for that circulation.

PUBLICS, SUBPUBLICS, AND COUNTERPUBLICS:
SOME TERMINOLOGY

In this chapter, I'll explore how circulation affects public formation. Different modes of circulation carry predetermined assumptions about how they contribute to public deliberation. An article in a monthly magazine, a blog from a nonprofit website and a "join this cause" invitation on Facebook each operate within a rhetorical framework that projects its idea of how a public works. Therefore, it is harder for publics with alternative democratic visions to form within those modes of circulation.

It will be helpful, at this point, to introduce some terms that scholars of public sphere theory often use to describe different conceptions of how a public operates. The public is most commonly understood as a singular thing, that entity of democracy that encompasses all citizens. In this model, citizens work out public opinion in the public sphere, which includes all those spaces where people gather to consider a range of perspectives. The public sphere is thought to be open to all, and people are expected to engage in thoughtful, logical deliberation to resolve conflicts for the good of all. When enough people come to consensus about the issue, that public opinion legitimates state action. In addition, public opinion holds representatives accountable and ensures that the state acts for the public good. I call this model the *idealized public sphere*.

The characteristics of this idealized public sphere and its role in democracy are deeply ingrained in our understanding of public work and, at the same time, deeply contested. Indeed, many public sphere theorists argue there really is no single public sphere, but rather a multitude of smaller *subpublics*. Many subpublics struggle to stand in as the public: think how one political party will argue that "the American people demand this" while another party pronounces that "the American people will never stand for that!" As part of such contestations, subpublics often rely on the characteristics of the idealized public sphere, accusing each other of being elitist and not listening to a plurality of positions, of not reasoning well, or of not truly accounting for public good. Through such moves, a pluralist democracy may hover in this space between subpublics and the public.

A third category of publics is *counterpublics*, which reject some of the underlying values that are insinuated in the dominant idea of the public. Rather than trying to stand in for the public, they challenge the centrality of those characteristics. For this reason, many politicians and scholars consider counterpublics to be fundamental threats to democracy. Political scientist Craig Rimmerman, for example, praises King's approach in the Civil Rights Movement because it sought to bring people into republican democracy, but he sees groups like Earth First! as dangerous because they use nondeliberative means to expose and challenge the government's acquiescence to capitalist definitions of property and natural resources. As I explained in chapter 2, things look different from the perspective of those counterpublics, whose understandings of how democracy works are fundamentally different. Their goal is not antidemocratic; rather, they seek to perfect the democratic model by radically altering it. Other counterpublics challenge what they see as an individualist foundation in the idealized model of democracy.

I recount the theories of publics, subpublics, and counterpublics to look more carefully at two components. First, if a subpublic and a counterpublic have fundamentally different democratic ideals, then how are those ideals manifest in the rhetorical moves of each kind of public? Second, how do subpublics and counterpublics circulate? If no public can exist unless its discourse is spoken, written, and repeated in enough venues that others recognize it as a distinct way of thinking and acting, then where does subpublic and counterpublic circulation happen? Do those venues have any the effects on the public discourse? As I'll show in this chapter, some media, such as a popular magazine like *Harper's Magazine,* are structured around an idea of the singular public sphere and privilege dispassionate reason, bracket difference, and highlight individualism.

THE PUBLIC IDEAL OF *HARPER'S* AND HABERMAS: DELIBERATIVE CONVERSATION

I begin with an article about homelessness that was published in a national news magazine. I find the focus on homelessness to be productive because the issue itself raises the question of who is and is not part of public life, whose voices are shared, and how those voices are authorized. The rhetorical moves of inclusion and exclusion and the definitions of such concepts as "productive citizen" and "contributing member of society" stand out more sharply as normative terms when we see them deployed in this context. What I want to study, though, is not just how the author situates homeless men and women as part of the public, but also how the public he invokes for his readers meshes with the public that *Harper's* itself perpetuates through its circulation: the ideal of a singular public sphere whose members are at their most responsible when they are reading and learning about others in this public.

Peter Marin originally published "Helping and Hating the Homeless" in *Harper's Magazine* in 1987. The article invites readers to understand homelessness as a central component of our society and to take a more compassionate view toward those who are homeless. I argue that this text—as is true for most pieces by *Harper's* or *The Atlantic Monthly*, or similar magazines that come across as both popular and intellectual—circulates an image of its public audience as concerned about a vaguely defined common good and as people interested in learning about experiences they, themselves, have not confronted. In the end, the action Marin wishes them to take is to similar to the actions expected of most readers of such articles: that they think more deeply about the issues presented, imagine a new relationship with folks they may otherwise have overlooked, and keep on reading so as to expand their circle of public relationships further. Such a characteristic of the public is both valuable and insufficient.

Marin is a contributing editor to *Harper's* and publishes regularly in similar magazines, such as *Nation, The New Republic,* and *Utne Reader* (Indeed, some of his pieces in *Utne Reader* and *Nation* extend many of the lines of argument he introduces in the *Harper's* piece.) The piece is also reprinted in Thomas Dean's composition textbook *Writing and Community Action,* where it is held up as a model of public writing.[8] I am using Marin's work here much in the same way that E.D. Hirsch, Jr. and his colleagues use articles in the popular presses to develop their theory in *Cultural Literacy: What Every American Should Know:* I examine the rhetorical implications of a representative text in a nationally-distributed popular magazine to better understand this genre of writing, using it as a clue into the commonplace image of the general reader in national, American publications. However, I don't presume that these magazines accurately project the American reader or that they encompass all of the discourse of the nation. Rather, I would agree with Hirsch that these are sites where dominant cultural ideals and discourse circulate. I think it's worth studying the rhetorical moves of such texts to understand how they set out a particular vision of democracy. Though I will later question many of the presumptions that frame this public, I nevertheless find that this version is so prominent and so much a part of the affective and cultural power of the concept of democracy that we need to study it closely.

Marin's 7000-word essay challenges *Harper's* readers to consider their obligations to homeless people. He looks closely into the "catch basin" of the term *homelessness* and lists many different kinds of people who end up there: veterans, mentally ill people, elderly on fixed incomes, those who are unemployed, and people so abused by their families or society that they run away. He makes the common "there but for the grace of God" move, noting how "many of the homeless, before they were homeless, were people more or less like ourselves"[9] and he clarifies that there are two main groups of homeless people: "those who have had homelessness forced upon them and want nothing more than to escape it; and those who have at least in part chosen it for themselves, and now accept, or in some cases, embrace it."[10] Through a series of anecdotes about his own hobo years and appealing descriptions of the communities where homeless men and women gather, Marin weaves together moving pictures of both kinds of homeless people.

But Marin is not primarily interested in creating empathy—though he does this well. He also provokes his readers to examine their complicity, tracing the root causes of homelessness back to "various policies, events, and ways of life for which some of us are responsible and from which some of us actually prosper."[11] In a series of abrupt paragraphs, he makes everyone—including himself—responsible:

> We decide, as a people, to go to war, we ask our children to kill and die, and the result, years later, is grown men homeless on the street.
> We change, with the best of intentions, the laws pertaining to the mentally ill, and then, without intention, neglect to provide them with services; and the result, in our streets, drives some of us crazy with rage.
> We cut taxes and prune budgets, we modernize industry and shift the balance of trade, and the result of all of these actions and errors can be read, sleeping form by sleeping form, on our city streets.[12]

After such pointed admonitions, the main question of the essay becomes "What do we owe them?" Before arriving at his answer, Marin analyzes more changes in social and governmental structure and elaborates on the history of Western attitudes towards homelessness. Finally, he makes his case: for those homeless who do not choose to be on the margins, he argues, "a society owes its members whatever it takes for them to regain their places in the social order."[13] For those who reject the social order and choose to remain outside it, he says we have an "existential obligation" to provide them "a place to exist, a way to exist" because "a society needs its margins as much as it needs art and literature."[14] He ends on this philosophical note, linking his readers to those on the margins and demanding that his readers continue to struggle between "the magnanimity we owe to life and the darker tending of the human psyche: our fear of strangeness, our hatred of deviance, our love of order and control."[15] Marin's essay explicitly calls for soul-searching: such an internal, moral struggle "will determine not only the destinies of the homeless but also something crucial about the nation and perhaps—let me say it—about our own souls."[16]

Marin's critical essay is a remarkable piece in that he tackles a very difficult question head on. He could have chosen, as many do, to include only the "unwilling homeless" in his analysis, a group for whom it is easier to create empathy. But instead, he proposes our moral obligation even to those who have chosen to reject society: he highlights the interconnections among readers and others (including homeless people) who make up public life. He is willing to provoke his readers, to implicate them as creators of the problem that he wishes would be addressed.

Marin meets this rhetorical challenge by adopting a particularly likeable ethos. Even as he challenges his readers to see themselves unfavorably, he comes across as pleasant, earnest, and interesting. He seems to move easily among the groups he brings together in his piece: he is himself a former hobo, writing "I felt at home on the road, perhaps because I felt at home nowhere else,"[17] and he is someone who still returns to missions and shelters to break bread with the poor who go there. He is compassionate in his descriptions of their lives. At the same time, he has moved back into "society," now (he alludes to his work as a college professor), and he aligns himself to some extent with his audience of people who keep a distance from homeless people, admitting that when he walks through a park where people are "bedding down for the night, [his] first reaction, if not fear, is a sense of annoyance and intrusion, of worry and alarm."[18]

But Marin is not compassionate toward everyone, and his ability to weave back and forth between outrage and compassion is a key to the essay's success. He is righteously dismissive of fellow Santa Barbara citizens who have defended town ordinances that make it illegal for people to sleep in public parks. At a city council meeting, he writes, "one by one, they filed to the microphone to castigate the homeless"; he derides the "mindlessness of [their] fear, the vengefulness of [their] fury."[19] He calls the laws they are defending "foolish" and "mean."[20] He's not writing directly to those "foolish" and "mean" Santa Barbara citizens, but we meet them quickly at the beginning of the article, and they serve as the exigency for us to keep reading: we don't want to be like those people. He doesn't allow his national *Harper's* readers to feel smug that their own towns have not had such spectacle: "If I write about Santa Barbara, it's not because I think the attitudes at work here are unique. They are not. You find them everywhere in America" (306). He gets away with such accusations because he still addresses his readers as if they are redeemable. They will learn a broader range of perspectives.

Marin points to a range of public activities in his piece. On the one hand, his readers are responsible for sending a generation off to war and for deinstitutionalizing mentally ill people without providing new kinds of support. Presumably, the readers accomplished this through the vague responsibility of the public, whose leaders made decisions in its name. While Marin might believe that some of his reader actively sought such changes, he doesn't name any kinds of direct involvement, so their responsibility seems to come from what they did *not* do: they did *not* watch government actions carefully and critically, and they did *not* hold government accountable on behalf of those who are homeless. Indeed, they may have stayed silent because they benefited from the policies in some way.

The public readers in "Helping and Hating the Homeless" are those for whom the call to "soul-searching" at the end of the piece seems an appropriate public action. They are people who read *Harper's* to be pushed to think about issues and ideas they have not encountered much, and they are interested in being guided in their response by writers who have had time to dwell and reflect and arrive at new perspectives. A good *Harper's* article is one that pushes such a reader to look at the world in a new way, at least for a while; the writer often models such reflection in the text, considering multiple views and mulling them over out loud. Reading *Harper's* or the *Atlantic* is a way to listen in on a conversation among smart, well-intentioned, reasonable people. In this way, the magazine performs an important function in democratic deliberation, but it does not go far enough. Like the public imagined as part of the singular public sphere, *Harper's* readers can be content to read and learn, but have no real space for action.

FROM *HARPER'S* TO HABERMAS

We might think of articles in *Harper's* and similar popular magazines as examples of the public conversations that are central to "the public sphere" as that concept is laid out in Jürgen Habermas' seminal analysis, *The Structural Transformation of the Public Sphere.* To understand how public opinion becomes an authority for state action, Habermas studies the rise of capitalism in the middle seventeenth and early eighteenth century, when the increased economic power among the middle-class merchants provided them both the ability and the need to pressure the state, which controlled the infrastructures of commerce. With this economic backdrop, he observes, "private people [came] together to form a public, [and] readied themselves to compel public authority to legitimate itself before public opinion."[21] And in this historical place, he locates what he sees as the model for democratic decision-making: the *bourgeois public sphere.* In this book, I refer to this model as the *idealized singular public sphere* because it is the model most pervasive and admired in dominant American media; it is a vision of how publics work that many subpublics seek to emulate and many counterpublics work to resist.

Habermas concludes that for deliberation to rise to the status of public opinion, people need to be able to discuss matters "free from any coercive constraint so that through these discussions [they] can determine matters of general interest and common good."[22] He finds such conversations in a variety of physical places—coffee houses, pubs, public squares—and in the ongoing conversation that extends through many literary journals and small newspapers. Habermas writes,

> Citizens behave as a public body when they confer in an unrestricted fashion— that is, with the guarantee of freedom of assembly and association and the freedom to express and publish their opinions—about matters of general interest.

In a large public body this kind of communication requires specific means for transmitting information and influencing those who receive it. Today, newspapers and magazines, radio and TV are the media of the public sphere.[23]

Habermas identifies 450 clubs and over 250 journals established in Paris within four months in 1848, and he sees these publications as evidence of the unconstrained public deliberation of the period: "the appearance of a political newspaper meant joining the struggle for freedom and public opinion, and thus for the public sphere as a principle."[24] As people read and discussed public issues, Habermas theorized, they reasoned through a variety of perspectives so as to arrive at the best course of action, which then arose to the level of public opinion and could pressure the state to action.

As Habermas delineates the components of deliberation in the bourgeois public sphere, he provides a productive vocabulary to describe the commonplace experience of democracy that thoroughly saturates our usual use of the term. However, it's important to note that Habermas' model remains unfulfilled. Rather, as communication scholar Gerard Hauser notes, "It serves as a template against which actually existing discursive conditions and practices may be measured and assessed in terms of the structural and ideological distortions that define any given actually existing public sphere."[25] To gain legitimacy within a culture that aspires to this model, a public must represent itself as closely as possible to this ideal, an argument I'll explore more fully when I talk in chapter 6 about how counterpublics circulate. First, though, I'll identify the components of the public sphere and how the public sphere finds an easy mode of circulation through sites such as *Harper's*.

According to Habermas, deliberations that rise to the level of public opinion are defined by these key elements:

- The site for the deliberations is open, neutral and equal, such that elements of social status or individual identity do not influence either who has access or whose positions will be received more favorably.
- The power of the deliberations in the public sphere comes from the wit of the exchange—that is, from critical-rational discourse.
- Anything is open for discussion in the public sphere, so long as everyone generally agrees that it is of concern to all and not a private matter.[26]

Within this model, the interlocutors can deliberate dispassionately, having set aside self-interest or ideology so as to listen openly to a variety of views and sort through them reasonably. To accomplish this, the participants are seen not only as equals, but also as equally benevolent toward the common good.

The self-reflexive soul-searching in Marin's essay, along with his general treatment of his audience as well-intentioned (if uninformed), matches well with the kind of exchange Habermas defines. Although Marin draws on personal experience and describes scenes in emotionally gripping ways, he does so in a context of reasoning out the responsibilities of the public through careful consideration of a history of public responsibility. He lambastes those in the Santa Barbara city council meeting because their participation is not based on thoughtful, reasoned analysis but rather on fear and ignorance and meanness. Readers are addressed as people concerned for the common good and interested to hear views about fellow citizens they may not have met before.

The usual length of the articles in such magazines fits in with this model of the public as well. Consider how Andrew Sullivan describes the value of publishing essay-length pieces. Sullivan blogs for *The Atlantic Monthly,* once edited *The New Republic,* and contributes to numerous similar publications. He published an essay in *The Atlantic Monthly* reflecting on the differences between writing longer essays and writing blog entries:

> The points of this essay . . . have appeared in shards and fragments on my blog for years. But being forced to order them in my head and think about them for a longer stretch has helped me understand them better, and perhaps express them more clearly. Each week, after a few hundred posts, I also write an actual newspaper column. It invariably turns out to be more considered, balanced, and evenhanded than the blog.[27]

The essay-length article has room, both in its actual length and in the composing process, for the kind of careful analysis, source-checking, and reflection that is expected in the idealized public sphere.

Another way that "Helping and Hating the Homeless" aligns with the idealized, singular public sphere is that Marin does not call on his readers to take any particular action. He does not ask them to write Letters to the Editor or donate to nonprofit organizations working to end homelessness. On the other hand, he implicates his readers as having allowed some public actions to be done in their name: wars, public policy about the mentally ill, and free trade. Like the authors of many public texts, Marin hovers between asking his audience to *think* and asking them to *do.* One reason for this is to maintain his credibility as someone who has considered the issue at hand without any *a priori* interest in the outcome: while he clearly makes an argument about how we should treat those who are homeless, he is careful to seem fair-minded and reasonable, to seem like someone who would have changed his perspective had his research and reasoning led him in another direction. This, too, enacts a tenet of Habermas' idealized public deliberation: interlocutors are expected to enter the public sphere "receptive to alternate modes of expression, [willing to] engage in active interpretation to understand what is being said and how it relates to them [and to be] open to change."[28] Marin's range of examples and his self-conscious admission that he, too, has harbored the very thoughts he would have his readers expel, all contribute to their confidence that he worked dispassionately through his material to arrive at a compassionate conclusion.

All of this careful attention to a dispassionate *ethos* betrays the individualist nature of the Habermasian public sphere: it is a gathering of *individuals* who each will sort out what he or she believes. For Habermas, the deliberation in the public sphere should not slip into purposive rationality, which is "concern[ed] with finding suitable means to preordained ends."[29] Rather, public deliberation should happen prior to choosing specific action as "people . . . read[y] themselves to compel public authority to legitimate itself before public opinion."[30] Individuals deliberate first to figure out how they later might act. There is a distrust that anyone who identifies as part of larger group—as a woman, for example, or as an African American—may be blinded by that identification and therefore be unreceptive to the logical persuasion of public deliberation. We can see somewhat recent examples of this anxiety in the emphasis during the hearings for Supreme Court justice Sonya Sotomayor (would she reason differently because she is Latina) and in concerns about President Obama (would he put his Black identity ahead of his American one). In both cases, the concern is that the identification would preclude the person from considering logical arguments that countered something about that identification. Bracketing identification markers before entering the discussion, then, is seen not only as a way to ensure that others do not prejudge a speaker's position (by, for example, dismissing the views of a Latina before listening to her argument); it is also seen as a way to ensure that the speaker herself does not use that identity to prejudge outcomes.

Just as the interlocutor must demonstrate that he or she is not beginning from preconceived stances, so must he or she remain in the space of deliberation throughout the exchange. Any shift away from readying oneself for action and toward actually compelling the state to take action is a violation of this purpose: it suggests that the conversation is over, that the author or speaker has had the final word. The goal, rather, is to set out a generous yet assertive perspective and get more and more people to agree with you.

I want to dwell on this distinction a little more, however, because too often I think the expectation that public discourse remain in this open-ended space of deliberation is interpreted to mean that the authors should not offer a distinct perspective. The discourse of the idealized public sphere is not neutral. It must take a stance; its goal is to persuade. Marin provides a clear and provocative argument for how we should understand the place of homelessness within society. He argues for our responsibility toward homeless men and women. He does not simply provide information and expect his readers to come to their own conclusions; rather, he provides an argument that he believes his readers should adopt. Habermas argues that at the height of the Enlightenment public sphere, hundreds of publications circulated, each overtly affiliated with particular political parties or identities; they existed to put forward particular perspectives and encourage discourse about them. As Hauser explains, these publications were "more likely to develop associations and community among their readers than they are today . . . Insofar as the press encouraged discourses among its readership, it promoted stability among the intersubjective meanings they shared."[31] For Habermas, part of the decline of the public sphere came when newspapers shifted from this assertive public function to a more commercial one and traded deliberative rhetoric for blander, neutral information targeted to a broader range of consumers.

Today, an article in *Harper's,* more so than an informationally-oriented article in a newspaper, is designed to give its readers a glimpse into a way of thinking about an idea. While I acknowledge that newspapers inevitably frame the information they provide, their commercial interests in reaching broader audiences mean that they bury these frames under layers of apparent journalistic neutrality. *Harper's,* on the other hand, invites its authors to lay out perspectives and arguments, to walk readers through the logic of their positions in a way that provides not just information but a logical perspective. Rather than present information without interpretation and rather than delineating the right action, public discourse in Habermas' model is an invitation to shared conversation, one that takes place in published essays as well as in face-to-face deliberation, where people work to arrive at new knowledge and new ways to think about and understand the conditions of the world around them. The citizen's role in this public sphere is to keep thinking, reading, reasoning, talking, and actively engaging with ideas and with fellow citizens.

Yet, if the goal is not to talk tactics or strategy but to reason out what the best solutions are, how will public authority recognize what public opinion has emerged? How is that view communicated to the state authority? Consider, again, the matrix of democracy I described in the second chapter, where democracy operates along three axes: the purpose of government, ranging from protecting individual property to affirming the interdependence among citizens; the structure of government, where decisions are left to elites or entrusted to citizens; and the kind of action expected to effect change, which depends on how receptive one believes the decision-makers are. The idealized public sphere that Habermas presents sits towards the center of the matrix; democracy is seen as a republican system that shades towards a communitarian, direct democracy. In Habermas' idealized public sphere, citizens are trusted to work out their interdependence and arrive at rich understandings of their worlds. Their main value is this epistemic one of figuring things out. Along the third axis, the idealized public sphere presumes that this new knowledge can make its way to the representatives within a benevolent context. The deliberations of public opinion gain power when they are part of a spiraling vortex of discourse: as various people gather and deliberate, more and more people adopt a particular way of thinking and talking about an issue. That discourse spreads through personal conversations, is voiced in community forums, is reported in newspaper accounts of those community meetings, is explored in magazine articles like Marin's, and is eventually expressed in so many different venues that those in state authority recognize it as public opinion. This is why, in the idealized public sphere, it's important to keep talking, and to keep talking with lots of people; the ideas will gain more complexity through this ongoing reasoning, and a broad consensus will rise to the foreground, made visible through its pervasive circulation. The citizens' responsibility is to keep the conversation going in as many places as possible.

Within this model of the public sphere, much attention is paid to how well the media as a whole perpetuates such deliberation: much is made of questions of access, qualities of reason, and so on. Habermas, himself, argues that this idealized sphere fell apart because of problems with capitalist media. What I'd like to stress, though, is that these very deliberations about how well the media is working all rely on the foundational assumptions of this idealized model. Arguments about who has been heard or silenced within a particular news show or whether an editor has an *a priori* bias toward some political party reinforce the commonplace assumption that publications should strive toward this idealized public sphere and should keep working to correct any impediments to its realization.

Harper's Publics

I hope it is clear from the above analysis that *Harper's* and magazines like it are well-suited to perpetuate this idealized version of the public sphere. Indeed, the commercial success of a magazine like *Harper's* depends on our understanding its public function in this way: as a source of disinterested but compassionate perspectives about public issues that we should know about and as a voice in public conversations about such issues. The magazine describes itself this way:

> Harper's Magazine, the oldest general interest monthly in America, explores the
> issues that drive our national conversation through such celebrated features as

Readings, Annotation, and Findings, as well as the iconic Harper's Index. With its emphasis on fine writing and original thought Harper's Magazine provides readers with a unique perspective on politics, society, the environment, and culture.[32]

Popular-intellectual magazines depend on our belief that public issues can be worked out through ongoing cycles of rational conversation. They also depend on our belief that we as public readers must always ready ourselves for our public work by reading the views of others. The voice that predominates in these articles presumes that we are all equal to the task of such deliberation; it treats us as benevolent interlocutors, willing to push past our own perspectives to consider the greater good. While many would argue—with some cause—that magazines like *Harper's* and *The Atlantic Monthly* more often than not approach an issue from a liberal perspective, the magazine promotes the ideal that logic trumps ideology. To be published in *Harper's,* one needs to write in a manner that conveys the role of author and reader as disinterested public intellectuals engaged with public issues.

The magazine cues its readers to their roles as well. Letters to the Editor reveal readers as engaged interlocutors who hold the writers accountable: the readers write in to correct facts, to query a logical progression, and to provide additional perspectives. The letters, like the articles, are written calmly and dispassionately. The authors respond to them, further justifying their positions or, on some occasions, conceding an error. Again, this is the model of the ongoing public conversation among equals. And yet, as Andrew Sullivan again reveals, the real impact of Letters to the Editor is not as direct as the forum might imply. He writes that in his role as an essayist, the letters would not influence him. "Yes, letters to the editor would arrive in due course and subscriptions would be canceled. But reporters and columnists tended to operate in a relative sanctuary, answerable mainly to their editors, not readers. For a long time, columns were essentially monologues published to applause, muffled murmurs, silence, or a distant heckle."[33] What we see in the Letters to the Editor section, then, is a performance of the reader role alongside the actual the role of the editor, who facilitates the conversation from reader to author and from author to reader. The editor, after all, decides which writers will make it into the pages of the public conversation.

It might seem contradictory to the goal of equal access to allow the editor to play such a controlling role: we might assume that this barrier makes *Harper's* an inadequate space for the idealized public discourse. In fact, the idealized public sphere itself sets out a set of restrictions that justify the editors' control: to count as legitimate members of the public dialog, speakers must set aside *a priori* outcomes, must reason logically through their positions, must attend to public good, and must orient toward a broad public of strangers. According to these premises, then, it is appropriate to restrict authorship to those people who have demonstrated an ability to engage in such discourse and to shield authors from feedback that doesn't follow those premises. Moreover, recognizing that it takes time to reason out and explain truly public positions, it is appropriate to pay people to do so. That thoughtful deliberation requires the luxury of time explains why aristocrats were once considered the best suited to attend to the public good. Within capitalism, some people now are paid to serve that function. Finally, magazines hire fact-checkers and editors who oversee the writing, ensuring that it conforms to the expectations of honesty, open-mindedness, and public interest. All of this attention to the necessary components of idealized public discourse is built into the business model of the magazine.

As John Trimbur notes, public texts market a logic of expertise that is bound up in their modes of circulation. He writes, "We cannot understand what is entailed when people encounter written texts without taking into account how the labor power embodied in the commodity form articulates a mode of production and its prevailing social relations."[34] For Trimbur, the interesting question of circulation is not so much where do readers pick up the magazine (e.g., is it delivered to your business, or do you buy it at the supermarket). Rather, the interesting question is how does that mode of delivery reinforce something earlier in the cycle: access to the site of knowledge production. As we can see in the example of *Harper's,* the magazine circulates not only its messages about "politics, society, the environment, and culture," but also messages about who can best think through issues of national importance, whose voices we should trust during those exchanges, and what our role is as citizen-readers: to engage in soul-searching and then to perpetuate the discourse so that it can rise to the level of public opinion. Not surprisingly, other venues circulate different and competing images of what a public is and what discourse conventions should be recognized as legitimate in conducting public work. Before I examine those counterpublic rhetorics and how they circulate, I'll extend the argument I made here about *Harper's* and show how the broader field of traditional journalism also forwards this idealized public sphere.

THE PUBLIC IN TRADITIONAL JOURNALISM: DELIBERATIVE CONVERSATIONS

[A]t its best, journalism is a high public calling, and all those who practice it have a deeper obligation to their readers and views than to the demands of the market.

—David Talbot, Editor in Chief, Salon.com[35]

To consider the values inherent in the business model and genre expectations of traditional journalism, I draw on the work of the Committee of Concerned Journalists, whose findings were presented by Bill Kovach and Tom Rosenstiel in *The Elements of Journalism: What Newspeople Should Know and the Public Should Expect*. The book lays out a theory of journalism that Kovach and Rosenstiel understand to be a consensus in the field. They place the purpose of traditional journalism squarely within the idealized public sphere: journalists, they say, are responsible to create a public forum for conversation, to represent the public accurately and proportionally in their materials, to include the voices of those who have been barred from public conversation because of imbalances of power, and, through all this, to amplify public conversation so that it rises to the level of public opinion and influences the public's decision-makers.

The business ethos of many news publications—whether in print, on-air, or online—draws on the publication's ability to invoke in its readers a civic duty to be "well-read" and to share what they've heard in everyday conversations by forwarding e-mails or sharing links on social networking sites. They need audiences who want to be well-informed, who want to help build public opinion. The business model hopes that the audience will link some of its civic identity to a specific media outlet—to begin conversations with "I heard on NPR that . . ." or "I read recently in *Newsweek* . . ." or "an editorial in the *Post* explained that . . . ." In the process, the audience helps to circulate not only the content and the brand recognition but also the public ideal of citizens staying informed by consuming and circulating these media products.

While I recognize that the business model of the traditional news media is undergoing a great change, with pressure coming both from their location as one entity of larger, international corporations and from the apparently unmediated, grassroots explosion of news through the blogosphere and social networking, I still see the traditional news media as the central venue for public circulation. Those who criticize media consolidation do so by advancing again the ideals of the traditional media. Far from being isolated from the traditional media, the new for-profit media model and the blogosphere both work in a symbiotic relationship with the traditional media, reacting to and amplifying the reporting of traditional news sources and gaining another layer of credibility when their stories are picked up, verified, and circulated within traditional news sources.

Kovach and Rosenstiel's *Elements of Journalism* synthesizes the perspectives of thousands of American journalists. Conducted over two years, the study held public forums in which more than three hundred journalists gave testimony. With university researchers, they delved deeper, conducting lengthy three-and-a-half-hour interviews with one hundred journalists. They studied the content of actual news reporting, and they surveyed journalists twice about their principles. They reviewed books, histories, journalism seminars, and other materials from and about the profession. *Elements of Journalism* is full of direct quotes from these materials, with remarks from past and current editors and reporters of prominent national papers, such as the *Wall Street Journal,* the *New York Times,* and the *Washington Post,* as well as online news outlets, such as the *Huffington Post* and *Salon.com.* The study includes journalists who locate their values all across the political spectrum and with those who refused to name any affiliation.

At a time when Kovach and Rosenstiel worry that traditional journalism has strayed too far from its purpose, they set out to capture what that purpose is and to create a theory that they believe has functioned as the backbone of the industry for years without being named. Now that this purpose is being challenged, they write, they feel bound to extricate it, name it, and hold it up so that it is not trampled by the new economic conditions of the news business or lost in the wash of alternative, nonjournalistic discourse proliferating online. I don't suggest that this is the only theory of journalism operating, only that—as is true for the idealized singular public sphere upon which it draws—this theory of how journalism works is a dominant model, *a* perspective that regularly gets asserted as *the* perspective.

Kovach and Rosenstiel identify a single purpose for traditional journalism: "the purpose of journalism is to provide people with the information they need to be free and self-governing" and they identify nine elements of journalism that allow it to achieve this goal:

> Journalism's first obligation is to the truth.
> Its first loyalty is to citizens.
> Its essence is a discipline of verification.
> Its practitioners must maintain an independence from those they cover.
> It must serve as an independent monitor of power.
> It must provide a forum for public criticism and compromise.
> It must strive to make the significant interesting and relevant.
> It must keep the news comprehensive and proportional.
> Its practitioners must be allowed to exercise their personal conscience.[36]

Each of these elements is explored in a chapter of the book; the authors explain not only why an element is important to a functioning democracy but also how the element may be threatened as news companies are bought up by international corporations and by what they consider the new "media of assertion" that is a result of both a capitalist desire to increase market-share and the ability of pundits and propagandists to circulate their discourse online.

As they report about American journalists' commitment to "giving the public the information it needs to govern itself," Kovach and Rosenstiel clarify the journalists' conception of the public. What's particularly interesting is that the journalists in this study simultaneously recognize their role in creating a (sub)public that their readers will identify with, even as they talk about the public as a single, externalized thing. They understand that part of the marketing of a news outlet is tied to its ability to set out a particular way of viewing the world, the particular people that the reporters and editors include in that world, and their style of writing about it.

At the same time, Kovach and Rosenstiel assert that that the journalist's role is to amplify the conversation that is already going on in the public, to reflect back what is out there, to be true to the facts and reality, and to try to shed any biases that might influence how they report the news about the public. News media provide a shared purpose and a sense of unity not by constructing some public, but by creating a forum in which the public can see itself, "a common language and common knowledge rooted in reality."[37] The value of the traditional news rests on its allegiance to depicting "reality" and verifying and reporting "the facts." A journalist's first allegiance must be to verification and facts, Kovach and Rosenstiel write. The public comes together when it can point to the same set of facts and share information. In these assertions, the public seems fixed, unitary, and external to the newspaper—so while journalists are "creating" something, it is "rooted in reality."

Subpublics and counterpublics that wish to circulate their discourse through the traditional media can begin by leveraging this opening: journalists' simultaneous acknowledgement of and discomfort with their role in creating a public by reporting about the public, their recognition that what they've created might not match with what is actually out there.

Journalism as Citizen Conversations

One way that journalists' vision of the public sphere aligns well with the idealized, singular public sphere comes through in the metaphor of the public conversation. Kovach and Rosenstiel describe the duty of journalists in terms of three different kinds of conversations: first, the conversations that citizens will have among themselves, drawing from the information that they can gather from newspapers; second, the conversation that is displayed in the newspaper itself, the newspaper's attempt to provide a forum for that first kind of conversation; and third, a conversation between citizens and journalists in which citizens can help correct any misinformation that the journalists may have presented.

The first kind of conversation—the citizen conversation—is foundational to the journalistic enterprise. The main premise of *The Elements of*

Journalism is that the thousands of journalists Kovach and Rosenstiel surveyed, interviewed, and read agree that first and foremost, "the purpose of
journalism is to provide people with the information they need to be free
and self-governing."[38] They need to be informed about "changing events,
issues and characters in the world outside"[39] and they need information about
their government from a nongovernmental source so that as citizens they
can maintain a check on government. All of this information needs to come
from sources that citizens trust, sources that do not appear to have *a priori*
ties to any particular outcome, party, or corporation: if citizens are to use this
information to direct government, they need to believe that the information
is complete and accurate.

According to Kovach and Rosenstiel, citizen conversations have to begin
with a shared understanding of the facts of a situation. A journalist must investigate and verify facts first and foremost. From these shared facts, then, citizens
can develop a common set of knowledge and a common language.[40] This does
not mean, however, that journalists never provide more than facts. Kovach
and Rosenstiel emphasize that journalists are responsible for making sense of
those facts, providing an interpretive framework to help the public understand
the significance and relevance of the facts. What they stress, though, is that
the facts have to come first: "the first task . . . is to verify what information is
reliable and then order it so people can grasp it efficiently."[41] This language of
"facts" shares an epistemological core with the emphasis on reason in the idealized singular public sphere, a point I will explore more below.

Journalism as Conversational Forum

The second conception of "conversation" that undergirds traditional journalism is that the news provides a forum where that citizen conversation is carried out. This forum is essential for public formation: a public cannot form
unless people see their conversations as bigger than the exchange in their
immediate circle. Participants come to believe that people they don't know
share their way of talking and thinking and that this common approach has the
possibility of rising to the level of public opinion. By providing a forum for
citizen conversation, Kovach and Rosenstiel explain, journalists report back
what has been said. In the process, they shape the way participants imagine
each other. In talking about this public forum, Kovach and Rosenstiel reveal
an inherent tension in traditional journalism, journalism that wants to operate within the idealized, singular public sphere, something external and out
there, even as it acknowledges its role in creating a specific public. Though
they acknowledge both aspects, Kovach and Rosenstiel don't fully resolve
the contradiction.

On the one hand, Kovach and Rosenstiel seem to suggest that newspapers merely put into words the conversations already circulating so that other people can also read them. As Habermas does, they link the advent of journalism to the coffee shops and saloons of the seventeenth century:

> What we might consider modern journalism began to emerge in the early seventeenth century literally out of conversation, especially in public places like coffeehouses in England, and later in pubs, or 'publick houses,' in America. Here, the bar owners, called publicans, hosted spirited conversations about information from travelers who often recorded what they had seen and heard in log books kept at the end of the bar. In England, coffee houses specialized in specific kinds of information. The first newspapers evolved out of these coffeehouses in 1609, when enterprising printers began to collect the shipping news, gossip, and political argument from the coffeehouses and print it on paper.[42]

This event, they argue, led politicians in the eighteenth century to begin talking about public opinion and to formulate ideals of free speech and free press. James Carey of the Committee of Concerned Journalists puts it this way: "Perhaps in the end, journalism simply means carrying on and amplifying the conversation of people themselves." [43]

Within this model, the press has a responsibility to capture the conversation accurately. Journalists have "a primary commitment to citizens, to providing a public forum, to engaging and inspiring debate—not in having one side or another win in the public square."[44] This means not only that journalists must be independent of any political party, but also that they must represent the discussions they hear accurately, comprehensively, and proportionally.[44] The discussion should be "inclusive and nuanced, and an accurate reflection of where the debate in society actually exists, as well as where the points of agreement are."[45] In a particularly apt metaphor, Kovach and Rosenstiel write, "Journalism is our modern cartography. It creates a map for citizens to navigate society. That is its utility and its economic reason for being."[47]

At the same time, even in the historical example of the coffeehouses and pubs, Kovach and Rosenstiel recognize that people chose to visit one establishment over another because they were interested in the specific kinds of conversations happening there. "In England, coffeehouses specialized in specific kinds of information."[48] And just as each pub or coffeehouse cultivated its own ambience, newspapers and news outlets recognize that the differences in their coverage is part of what draws their audience to them. The journalist-cartographers measure different conversations and report about and cultivate different arguments about what the public looks like and how it operates. Each news outlet has different news values, even if they don't make those explicit anymore. "Publishers a century ago routinely championed their news values in front-page editorials, opinion-pages, and company slogans, and just as often publicly assailed the journalistic values of their rivals. This was marketing. Citizens chose which publications to read based on their style and their approach to the news."[49]

News outlets wrestle with their responsibility to both report and create publics as they put together their news coverage. Editors have to imagine a public and then use their idea of a public to create a public that comes together as people engage with their news coverage. The audience gains a sense of itself as a public when people repeatedly see themselves in relation to the audiences discussed and addressed in the news. Kovach and Rosenstiel write, "Whenever an editor lays out a page or a website she is guessing at what readers want or need to know. However unconscious, every journalist operates by some theory of democracy."[50]

Kovach and Rosenstiel position the publics that editors imagine as an extension of the famous 1920s debate between journalist Walter Lippmann and philosopher John Dewey. As I explained in chapter 2, Lippmann was pessimistic about the potential for citizens to engage in meaningful discourse and arrive at useful public opinion; he feared that their knowledge was too limited, their personal prejudice and self-interest too great. The process of working out political decisions through democracy was inefficient and flawed. Within his theory, a public could be the recipient of information but never an expert and rarely a part of the conversation. Newspapers would communicate the thoughtful, reasoned analysis of experts; it would be a medium about and for this elite group. Dewey, in contrast, placed the blame for weak citizen participation not in the people themselves, but within a system that did not provide people with experiences and opportunities to develop to their full potential. For Dewey, efficient government was not the goal; rather, fully engaged citizens, supported by a free press and participatory education, was the goal. Democracy was the process of learning and developing together; a means, not an ends.

Kovach and Rosenstiel suggest that the journalists in their study have sided with Dewey: editors consider their readers/viewers as experts in something, some of the time. Kovach and Rosenstiel explain that when designing a newspaper or website page, editors follow a theory they attribute to Dave Burgin, "the theory of the interlocking public." According to this theory, an editor should create a page "with a sufficient variety of stories that every member of the audience would want to read one of them."[51] Because only 15 percent of readers will be interested in any single story, the job of the editor is to provide enough variety that each reader will see his or her interests reflected back somewhere on the page. Burgin lays out three levels of interest for readers:

they might respond as an *involved public*, that is, with "a personal stake and strong understanding" of the issue, or as an *interested public*, that is, a public with "no direct role in the issue but [which] is affected and responds with some first-hand experience," or finally as an *uninterested public*, "which pays little attention and will join, if at all, after the contours of the discourse have been laid out by others"[52] Within this model, each reader is thought to be part of an involved or interested public for at least some of the time, and Kovach and Rosenstiel observe, "everyone is interested and even an expert in something."[53] According to this study, then, journalists are working within a theory of the public in which citizens are capable of understanding and contributing to meaningful public deliberation.

The importance of this model, however, is not just that individual citizen's capacities are affirmed; it is also that the layout of the page (or website or broadcast) juxtaposes the imagined citizens with each other. Skimming the page, the reader sees the broader set of public issues that others in the public are engaging. The editor has to have enough of a sense of the public to capture all of those various interests and reflect them back on the page. Readers who rarely see themselves in the pages will stop purchasing the paper; viewers who rarely see their concerns described in a broadcast will flip the channel. Online viewers will click away. And this loss of audience is more than simply a problem of reduced sales. The missing public will no longer write Letters to the Editor to correct an editor's myopia. As that public disappears from the editorial imagination and from the pages of the paper, for example, they will no longer be visible to the other readers of the paper, whose concept of the public will become narrower. Thus, the journalists' responsibility is to reflect back to the public the full spectrum of its interests and to keep everyone aware of the multiple conversations and concerns. This aligns with Kovach and Rosenstiel's eighth element of journalism: "it must keep the news comprehensive and proportional."

Another way that journalists seek to keep the members of their imagined public in relationship with each other is by assuming a responsibility to make news "relevant and engaging"—the seventh element of journalism. Here, Kovach and Rosenstiel argue that making the news "engaging" does not mean slipping into "infotainment"; instead, they offer a series of strategies for telling a news story so that its relevance and significance become clear. To figure out what is significant, they suggest that journalists focus on the audience and ask, "Who is the audience for this story? What different sorts of people have an interest in this subject, however passing? What do these people need to know about this to make up their own minds on the subject?"[54] Again, the goal of the journalist is to keep different parts of the public in relation to others: the uninterested public can be shown the significance of something whose value is already clear to an involved public. Indeed, Kovach and Rosenstiel argue that journalists see an important role for themselves in finding voices that have been silenced in some way and providing them a way to speak back to power and to examine the "unseen corners of society."[55]

Journalism's Conversational Feedback Loop

The third metaphor of public conversation that is central to traditional journalism is the feedback loop between journalists and the public, a conversation that is critical to the public's trust that journalists can get the facts straight. This feedback loop fits within the epistemological foundation of the idealized public sphere because it relies on people with a diversity of perspectives sorting out which elements of a report are facts and which have been invented because of the reporters' biases and limitations. The public plays an important role in this process: "the audience becomes not consumers but 'pro-sumers,' a hybrid of consumer and producer."[56] When a member of the public critiques the inaccuracy of a report or the bias of a reporter, the reporter then takes that into account and may make a correction. The next story about the issue will include this revised perspective, which itself might be challenged by another public reader/viewer, and so the cycle continues. In this theory, the public respondents help provide a more robust level of functional truth by helping reporters recognize their potential limits. Functional truth is "a sorting out process that develops between the initial story and the interaction among the public, newsmakers, and journalists over time."[57]

The feedback loop is one of a number of ambiguous but central methods of verification, a goal central to the journalistic enterprise. And, as is true for the theory of the idealized, singular public sphere, the roots of this method are tied back to the seventeenth and eighteenth century Enlightenment and the goals of the scientific method. Although there is no method parallel to the scientific method that serves to verify the facts for news, journalists are supposed to devise their own ways to meet the goal of shedding their biases. And, just as scientists are expected to explain all of their steps and assumptions so that their experiments can be independently verified, journalists are expected to be fully transparent about "what they know and don't know," how they found their information, and why they came to the conclusions they did. "Only by explaining how we [journalists] know what we know can we approximate this idea of people being able, if they were of a mind to, to replicate the reporting. This is what is meant by objectivity of method in science, or in journalism."[58]

When Kovach and Rosenstiel insist that the journalist's first duty is to facts, they don't mean that journalists only report facts, but that any interpretation or analysis must happen after the facts have been determined. Just as the expected behavior of citizens in the idealized public sphere is not to allow one's preferences or ideologies to get in the way of following a reasonable argument to its conclusion, so journalists are expected to set aside any personal biases. Yet, as we can see from attempts to recruit growing numbers of minority journalists, the news field understands that people from different backgrounds and experiences will define news differently. Kovach and Rosenstiel write, "There is already ample evidence that newsrooms lacking diversity are unable to do their jobs properly. They miss news. Their coverage has holes. . . . The myopia of traditional definitions of news is proof enough that personal perspective colors journalism."[59] Operating within the model of the idealized public sphere, journalists wrestle with the same question: how "to be a journalist without either denying the influence of personal experience or being hostage to it."[60] Their solution is the same: journalists should be journalists first, so that "racial, ethnic, religious, class, and ideological backgrounds inform their work, but do not dictate it."[61] As I'll explain more fully in the next chapter, this anxiety about the potential epistemic influence of identity is not universal. The counterpublic rhetoric of many oppressed groups challenges the idea that people should always keep their race or gender at arm's length, lest it contaminate their thinking. Nevertheless, this fear of identity-intrusion is a key component of the idealized public sphere.

That fear brings us back to the feedback loop. To keep their identities in check, journalists depend on their editors' skeptical review of their work, on a culture of collaboration in the newsroom (an ideal that Kovach and Rosenstiel acknowledge is not always present), and on feedback from their public audience. These respondents must regularly evaluate how well they have been able to isolate the facts and how well their interpretations have proceeded from the facts rather than from other influences. And, therefore, the respondents themselves must be from a diverse enough background to help journalists recognize when their assumptions have not begun with the facts or followed reason. Some of this diversity comes from the mix of the interlocking publics—the interested and uninterested publics may provide a check on the involved public, for example.[62] For this feedback loop to work, the engaged, responding public needs to be as diverse as possible, which means that the public invoked in the news outlet needs to include this breadth. As long as traditional journalism relies on this system of verification, then they are obligated to pursue a diverse public and to provide access to that diverse public both within their pages and through their feedback loop, such as Letters to the Editor.

The feedback loop is both an opportunity and a challenge for counterpublics that wish to engage traditional journalism: on the one hand, the model has a built-in place for public critique, but on the other hand, the journalists must be able to hear and understand the critique. As I mentioned earlier,

journalist Andrew Sullivan says that some critiques never reach the reporters because editors filter out those that they consider to be less worthwhile.
For the critique to have an impact, then the discourse of the critique must
match well enough with both the public ideal that the editor has put forward
(the imagined public already invoked and addressed in *The Washington Post*
or *Wall Street Journal,* for example) and with the broader discourse of the
idealized public sphere—one that sees the public and representatives as open
to persuasion through reason, one that considers that proper citizens work to
keep a conversation going, and one that works to mitigate the potential inter-
ference of personal identity.

If we recognize the traditional public sphere as one model that guides
traditional media but does not fully account for the actually existing sphere
of multiple kinds of publics and public discourse and if we recognize that
journalism still is a prominent and powerful venue for circulation, then the
question becomes whether counterpublics can leverage the public ideals of
the traditional news media so that their own ideas and discursive models can
circulate through the traditional media. If so, how? And how does the recon-
figuration of traditional media under new corporate, economic structures
reinforce or transform the public image that is circulated?

JOURNALISM UNDER CAPITALISM

The Elements of Journalism argues that when news organizations are subsumed into larger, corporate structures, traditional journalistic ideals are
threatened. Kovach and Rosenstiel outline well many of the dangers of the
changing economic news system even as they promote the old system that
is, it must be noted, still a capitalist model. The difference, they suggest, is
that under the old system, for-profit news outlets could compete based on the
values of journalism, whereas now they are expected to compete against other
kinds of businesses. In the old model, news outlets competed for the opportunity to represent the public to itself and to create strong public forums for
democracy; in the new model, they argue, the goal is simply profit.

The traditional model of journalism asserts its value by claiming to accurately depict and engage with the public sphere in the singular, idealized
model. And yet, as we've seen, the business model of traditional journalism
recognizes that each news source projects a different image of that public
and calls up a different public through its audience: competing news sources
circulate different and often clashing publics, and their own marketing relies
on this difference as they distinguish the news values and world view of their
own approach from those of their competitors. And yet there is slipperiness
here because even as each outlet admits to projecting a particular vision of

the public and a particular set of news values, it argues that its own values are most aligned with the real world. This seeming disconnect is fundamental to how a public works.[63]

Journalists—as is true for all who create public texts—have to act as if their understanding of the public is accurate; they have to believe that their vision of the public is the best representation of the public. They set aside the awareness that they are invoking a public in order to create the address that will call it into being. A growing audience confirms that this invocation is accurate and gives the news outlet more legitimacy. In this sense, the corporate goals and the journalism goals of the newspaper both seem to converge on gaining a bigger, broader audience.

In the traditional business model, news media make a profit by selling advertisements, though advertising is not supposed to influence the content or tenor of the news coverage. Kovach and Rosenstiel argue that this model does not compromise journalistic integrity because what is being sold to the audience is not the content of a news story, but rather the broader relationship and trust that comes from the transparent, reflective, thorough work of a reporter. "Rather than selling customers content, newspeople are building a relationship with their audience based on their values, judgment, authority, courage, professionalism, and commitment to community. Providing this creates a bond with the public that the news organization then rents to advertisers."[64] The advertisers are the consumers, here—they buy the product, which is access to the space where a public comes together.

Kovach and Rosenstiel suggest that this model worked well until news outlets were bought up and bundled into larger, for-profit conglomerates, but their critiques of the for-profit pressures on journalism seem to apply equally well to the traditional for-profit model: the inability to serve as a true watchdog because of the pressure not to undermine the profit motive of the larger company and the push to conceptualize audience as consumers rather than as a public.

In the traditional economic news model, the tension is supposed to be between advertisers and journalists. The process of verification that is the foundation of traditional journalism requires that journalists disclose any conflict of interest and, ideally, refuse to cover any story where such a conflict might exist. Should news outlets foreground the desires of the advertiser over the news goals, then reporters sacrifice their independent judgment in order to promote (or refrain from critiquing) an advertiser's product. Kovach and Rosenstiel suggest that the problems with this arrangement show up most forcefully within the new economic structures, where news companies are one component of a larger corporation. Such arrangements are more and more common. In 2001, "ABC represent[ed] less than two percent of the profits at Disney. News once accounted for most of the revenue of Times, Inc., but it is just a fraction of that inside AOL. News is less than two percent of the profits of General Electric."[65] When the reporter is part of a larger company that makes many different products or a company that has business relationships with multiple other corporations and policy makers, then the journalists are constrained because their potential conflicts of interest have expanded exponentially. All of this means that journalists have a harder time serving as a watchdog of corporate power or as a check on the politicians and policies that might benefit those corporations.

Moreover, as news becomes just one more product in an array of for-profit corporate divisions, news divisions are pressured to adopt the same kind of market-driven management as the other divisions. The process of verifying and reporting the news is a time-consuming and expensive process; it is not an efficient business model. Other kinds of news-like products are cheaper to produce: talk shows, which mimic a deliberative exchange among experts without investing in fact-checking, can seem like a good alternative. News pundits replace reporters. The new media model does away with any attempt at cartography: no one works to ensure that the public has a comprehensive and proportional sense of itself. Instead, the more entertaining components of the public are given a chance to speak in bursts that are shaped and managed to play up their dramatic appeal. Deborah Tannen provides many examples of such staging in *Argument Culture,* her sociolinguist analysis of American politics and media. She recalls being invited as a Holocaust scholar to debate Holocaust deniers on a talk show; the purpose was to watch the sparks fly.[66] The goal in an entertaining argument culture is not to arrive at stasis—not to sift out what facts are verifiable so that people can have a common ground upon which to begin a discussion. The only conversation the for-profit media promotes in marketing is "Did you see that show?"

Kovach and Rosenstiel admit that the new economic model of the news industry poses problems for their ideals about traditional journalism, and they recognize that one of the dangers of the corporate model is that the public has been transformed into the consumer. Their point coincides well with a position that sociologist Thomas Streeter makes in *Selling the Air,* his review of American broadcasting. He writes that the constraints on journalists come rarely from owners imposing top-down censorship, but rather comes through "managers and managerial consciousness . . . who censor according to the dictates of bureaucratic formulas."[67] News managers, who are expected to post profits alongside the managers of other divisions of the corporation, have an incentive to promote an audience identity as consumers rather than as publics. Kovach and Rosenstiel note some of the means for this transformation, such as choosing stories that highlight the viewer/reader role as consumer rather than as citizen: investigative reports about products (Which soap works best? Which banks have undisclosed fees?) rather than reports about abuses of corporate power or neglect in public office. Worse, the editors might begin to manipulate the page layout/broadcast sequence so it is more attractive to a particular, desired market category of viewers. While the targeted audience might wonder if the quality of the coverage has also been compromised to deliver them to the advertiser, the bigger loss is that only one part of the population will see itself in those news stories; the image of the public has been diminished. At the extreme, Kovach and Rosenstiel write, news outlets limit their audience to "the most affluent or efficient audience"—the audience that will buy the most and therefore bring in the best advertising monies. "In television, that mean[s] designing the news for women age 18–49 who make most household buying decisions. In newspapers, that mean[s] limiting circulation to the more affluent zip code areas."[68] Within this structure, journalists' pretense to evoke the public and provide a public forum manipulates the elite audience into believing its own views and perspectives represent the whole. What is actually isolation is marketed as public engagement.

Kovach and Rosenstiel rightly point out the dangers of employing corporate mindset within a news industry that locates its identity firmly within the model of the idealized public sphere, and yet they seem content to locate the problem only with the transformation to a corporate economic model. Their economic news model—the news industry as a marketplace of news outlets selling competing images of the public—is not questioned. Their model, as they see it, simply transposes upward the conversations happening in the public all the time, enhancing them by offering a more comprehensive forum for the deliberation. The "marketplace of ideas" is understood as a neutral place in which individual citizens can sort things out reasonably, but the very metaphor here is telling. Embedded in the structures of capitalism, this exchange of ideas is never neutral; it advances the discourse of capitalism. The marketplace is understood as a benevolent, advantageous system, one that works in favor of the individuals who participate in it. Those who produce materials for the marketplace are seen as also working for public good, providing an array of options for the citizen-consumer to consider. Control appears to rest with the citizen-consumer. The metaphor relies on a liberal, individualist model, in which, as Streeter explains, "thought is understood to be prior to and radically autonomous from society" and from the marketplace in which it is exchanged.[69] This way of conceptualizing the public sphere is clearly to the advantage of capitalism, as it has been from the start. As Habermas notes in his description of its beginning, the public sphere, which he tellingly calls the "bourgeois public sphere," was a forum through which middle-class business owners were able to put pressure on the state to set conditions favorable for profit. When the discourse of benevolent capitalism circulates within the public ideal the mass media uses to justify its role, the image of benevolent capitalism maintains a strong hold in the public imagination. Consequently, any anticapitalist counterpublics have an extra barrier to circulation. The "free market," after all, is rather hostile to those who question whether it is free.

The capitalist, consumerist bent of the news industry is ongoing, and as more news outlets are expected to operate as a division within bigger corporations, a more blatantly for-profit approach is likely to transform the dominant modes of public circulation. And while many argue that the Internet will serve as a check on corporate power because it allows more grassroots and independent verification, the Internet itself is developing rapidly in the service of a consumer economy. Sites for public discourse and engagement (such as Facebook) are also corporate for-profit enterprises whose motives are not always in line with the public goals of some of their users. Recent outcries about Google's proposal to allow companies to buy into faster server delivery or about how much Facebook can redesign its site to make user information available to public marketers speak to the corporatization of the Internet.

But, while I acknowledge that we are in the midst of a transformation that is putting pressure on the traditional news industry's ability to serve the idealized public function it has ascribed to itself, I also argue that the news industry remains dominant as a site for public circulation. Compromised as they might be, traditional news sources—national newspapers like *The New York Times,* national news magazines like *Harper's* and *The National Review,* in both their print and online versions, and their equivalents in local communities—remain a central mechanism through which publics can circulate. They can direct a great deal of traffic and interest to certain people, events, and organizations; they can pick up and carry forward certain ways of talking, either by including direct quotes or by inserting links that direct their audience's attention to various sections of the public that they have invoked. And they do all this based on a professed ideal of a singular public sphere that they are supposed to both reflect and manage. This professed ideal, while never actualized, nevertheless serves as a normative force.

WHAT DOES THIS MEAN FOR A PUBLIC WRITING COURSE?

In order to gain a deeper understanding of any community or community group, we need to rely on a wide range of resources: our own experiences, conversations with people there, publications produced within the community, and also materials created about that community. The competing definitions of purpose, structure, and mode of interaction become apparent when these are juxtaposed and we can begin to tease out the arguments that are embedded in the rhetorical choices. As we engage in such analysis, we need to be mindful of how we draw on materials from different kinds of sources, paying particular attention to how we draw on the traditional media.

In my first-year course, I do not provide the overview about journalistic publics that I've offered here, but I do construct class activities and choose sources so that traditional news articles are treated as specific and not necessarily universal voices. I also acknowledge the close ties between the idealized public sphere I've described here and the values embedded in academic writing.

Looking for Journalistic Publics

One way that I organize my course so that students come to see news publications as presenting particular public ideals is to assign them to write a discourse analysis of the community where they will serve during the semester (I have also used an assignment where they do a discourse analysis of their community organization more specifically). The assignment prompt is available in appendix 2.

Students begin their community discourse analysis by researching how people talk about the community. They have to consult a range of materials. Since I teach in Washington, DC, we draw regularly on the *Washington Post* and its archives, but I also direct students to local publications, such as the Kojo Nnambi talk show on the local National Public Radio station and neighborhood newspapers such as *East of the River* and the (Capitol) *Hill Rag*. I encourage students to find publications through the Ethnic News Watch database, which catalogs many alternative papers, as well. We consider whose voices show up in which venues. We consider what kinds of audiences are presumed in which venues.

We also look at how a certain wording gets translated as it shows up in different places. Many community organizations have a standard paragraph that they use to describe themselves, and this wording is included in their press releases. We look for whether a reporter includes the wording verbatim or whether it is modified. This makes for an interesting discussion about plagiarism as well: while copying the language might seem like a violation, it serves in this case to advance the interests of the group that wrote the original copy because their specific rhetorical moves will be forwarded intact.

Sometimes, specific historical or contemporary events are mentioned so often in the materials that students encounter that the materials provide good opportunities to investigate how traditional news coverage might differ from more local accounts. In these moments, it can be helpful to bring in the theory of the interlocking publics and examine how an article is pitched within the broader scope of a page or paper layout. Can we identify which readers are presented as the interested, involved, or uninterested publics? Does the piece approach the incident seriously, or is it a fluff, entertainment moment?

Finally, we can pay attention to how things circulate: who picks up a story first? What about the story allows it to jump from one kind of publication to another? Do the stories "with legs" present a particular public ideal? Do they allow a newspaper or community to perform its conversational ideals?

Later in the course, students write materials commissioned by their community organizations. As they do so, I ask them to pay attention to how that document will circulate. If it is an internal memo, who will forward it to others in the organization, and what criteria might he or she use in deciding whether to do so? If the document is a brochure or a promotional piece, we talk about how it will be distributed: in what context? By whom? In upcoming semesters, I plan to work with a local newspaper, *Street Sense,* and ask all of my students to create press releases about their organizations; the student interns working with *Street Sense* will assess the press releases and report back on how well the students were able to anticipate the audience of that publication. In all of these commissioned tasks, I press students to consider how public writers work with and against the traditional media in order to be heard.

What I want first-year students to recognize as they work closely with such texts is simple: venues of circulation are not neutral. In upper division courses or graduate courses, I would spend more time with students examining specific articles—as I did with the Marin piece—to identify how different publications offer up different ideal public actions. For example, which publications address readers as *Harper's* does: as a reading, talking public? Which address them as activists who will take more explicit actions? How do these invoked publics fit into the matrix of democracy?

Writing Academic Publics

As much as I love teaching public writing, I have to acknowledge that I do so as a university professor in a first-year writing class in which I am charged to prepare students for academic writing. I will explore the many challenges of working at this intersection in the final chapter, but I want to stress here that academic writing is very much aligned with the idealized public sphere. In some ways, academic writing simply takes that model and ramps it up: the idealized public sphere on steroids. We don't just insinuate, as journalists do, that we should engage in ongoing conversations and deliberations to figure out the best way to understand the world we are a part of. We make those conversations visible in our texts through our fastidious attention to citations and bibliographic trails. We are the epitome of the "reading, readying" public. Academia as a whole is made very anxious when university scholars venture outside of rendering a description of the world and start making arguments about how to change it. The political professor, like the predisposed journalist, is accused of not being open to other potential explanations about their world.

Composition and communications professors are at the front lines of teaching the habits of thinking and manners of writing, everything embodied in academic discourse. I recognize that, and I don't resist it. But I do think we are especially obligated to point out how the academic approach is one of many. The academic approach, like the idealized public sphere, sits on a particular point in the matrix of democracy. We should not pretend otherwise.

In a short but interesting passage early in his *Rewriting: How to do Things with Texts,* Joseph Harris makes the claim that the academic writing he discusses is not particularly "academic," but is, in fact, the stuff of good writing anywhere, the stuff indeed of "public writing."[70] He asserts that good writing—both academic and public—conveys a "generous and assertive" voice, one that works thoughtfully and fairly with the works of those who have come before. He specifically identifies good public writing as the kind of intellectual prose found in magazines like *"Harper's* or the *Atlantic* and the *Nation,* or in *Rolling Stone* and *McSweeny's* and *Salon,* as well as in independent weeklies, little magazines, student journals, some political and cultural blogs and websites, and the like."[71] I agree that his model of academic writing transposes easily onto the kinds of magazines Harris mentions, but these are not the only (and certainly not the most common) modes of circulation. Hinging academic and public writing this way paints the public sphere as singular and unitary, rather than multiple and contested. Moreover, this public ideal does not acknowledge that, within a sphere of constantly clashing publics, truly vulnerable sorting-things-out has to take place offstage, offline, within safe houses where publics can be more honest without fear that these reflections will be stockpiled in an arsenal against them.

I don't want students to look for only this kind of deliberative exchange in public spaces—they won't find it in online community forums, in blogs, or even in city council meetings. They might find semblances of it in an organization's annual reports or newsletters, but the genres will be different. Any academic analysis of public writing—any pedagogy for teaching public writing—has to self-consciously examine this intersection for academic and community work.

I try to set up my classes as a place where we look at the writing of academic public and other publics. I think it's appropriate and responsible to position the service-learning class in this space; knowing it's never entirely possible, I try to privilege neither community writing/expertise nor academic writing/expertise. Course readings and writing assignments need to come from and are directed to both public and academic sites, even as the interdependence of such work is made clear.

NOTES

1. John Trimbur, "Composition and the Circulation of Writing." *College Composition and Communication* 52, no. 2 (2000): 188–219.

2. The project is carried on through the Core of Knowledge Foundation, begun by Hirsch in 1986, which provides curricula and training to schools nationwide who incorporate this theory of learning—and of the American Public—into classrooms from Kindergarten to 8th grade. E. D. Hirsch Jr., Joseph F. Kett, and James S. Trefil, *Cultural Literacy: What Every American Needs to Know.* (New York: Vintage Books, 1988); E. D. Hirsch, Jr., Joseph F. Kett, and James S. Trefil, *The New Dictionary of Cultural Literacy.* 3 ed. (Boston: Houghton Mifflin, 2002); E. D. Hirsch, Jr., *The Knowledge Deficit: Closing the Shocking Education Gap for American Children.* (Boston: Houghton Mifflin, 2007).

3. Trimbur, "Circulation," 212.

4. Trimbur, "Circulation," 209.

5. Trimbur, "Circulation," 210.

6. Trimbur, "Circulation," 215.

7. Jeffrey T. Grabill, *Writing Community Change: Designing Technologies for Citizen Action.* (Cresskill, N.J.: Hampton Press, 2007).

8. Thomas Deans, *Writing and Community Action.* (Boston: Longman, 2003).

9. Peter Marin, "Helping and Hating the Homeless," in *Writing and Community Action,* ed. Thomas Deans (Boston: Longman, 2003), 306–307.

10. Marin, "Helping," 307.

11. Marin, "Helping," 307.

12. Marin, "Helping," 307.

13. Marin, "Helping," 315–16.

14. Marin, "Helping," 317.

15. Marin, "Helping," 318.

16. Marin, "Helping," 318.

17. Marin, "Helping," 305.

18. Marin, "Helping," 312.

19. Marin, "Helping," 306.

20. Marin, "Helping," 305.

21. Christian R. Weisser, *Moving Beyond Academic Discourse: Composition Studies and the Public Sphere.* (Carbondale: Southern Illinois University Press, 2002), 68.

22. Weisser, *Moving,* 65.

23. Jürgen Habermas, *The Structural Transformation of the Public Sphere: An Inquiry into a Category of Bourgeois Society.* (Cambridge, Mass.: MIT Press, 1989), 49.

24. Habermas *Structural Transformation,* 53.

25. Gerard A. Hauser, *Vernacular Voices: The Rhetoric of Publics and Public Spheres.* (Columbia: University of South Carolina Press, 1999), 44.

26. Hauser, *Vernacular,* 41–44; Weisser, *Moving Beyond,* 69–70.

27. Andrew Sullivan. "Why I Blog," *Atlantic Monthly* [Electronic], (Nov. 2008): 4.

28. Hauser, *Vernacular,* 33.

29. Hauser, *Vernacular,* 51.

30. Weisser, *Moving Beyond,* 68.

31. Hauser, *Vernacular,* 68.

32. Harper's Magazine Foundation. "About Harper's Magazine." *Harper's Magazine* [Electronic]. http://www.harpers.org/harpers/about (Aug 2010), para. 1.

33. Sullivan, "Why I Blog," 2.

34. Trimbur, "Circulation," 210.

35. Bill Kovach, and Tom Rosenstiel, *The Elements of Journalism: What Newspeople should Know and the Public should Expect.* (New York: Crown Publishers, 2001), [back cover].

36. Kovach and Rosenstiel, *Elements of Journalism,* 12–13.

37. Kovach and Rosenstiel, *Elements of Journalism,* 17.

38. Kovach and Rosenstiel, *Elements of Journalism,* 12.

39. Kovach and Rosenstiel, *Elements of Journalism,* 21.

40. Kovach and Rosenstiel, *Elements of Journalism,* 17.

41. Kovach and Rosenstiel, *Elements of Journalism,* 24.

42. Kovach and Rosenstiel, *Elements of Journalism,* 22.

43. Kovach and Rosenstiel, *Elements of Journalism,* 18.

44. Kovach and Rosenstiel, *Elements of Journalism,* 96.

45. Kovach and Rosenstiel, *Elements of Journalism,* 163.

46. Kovach and Rosenstiel, *Elements of Journalism,* 143

47. Kovach and Rosenstiel, *Elements of Journalism,* 164.

48. Kovach and Rosenstiel, *Elements of Journalism,* 22.

49. Kovach and Rosenstiel, *Elements of Journalism,* 19.

50. Kovach and Rosenstiel, *Elements of Journalism,* 27.

51. Kovach and Rosenstiel, *Elements of Journalism,* 27.

52. Kovach and Rosenstiel, *Elements of Journalism,* 28.

53. Kovach and Rosenstiel, *Elements of Journalism,* 27.

54. Kovach and Rosenstiel, *Elements of Journalism,* 156.

55. Kovach and Rosenstiel, *Elements of Journalism,* 114.

56. Kovach and Rosenstiel, *Elements of Journalism,* 24.

57. Kovach and Rosenstiel, *Elements of Journalism,* 42.

58. Kovach and Rosenstiel, *Elements of Journalism,* 81.

59. Kovach and Rosenstiel, *Elements of Journalism,* 106.

60. Kovach and Rosenstiel, *Elements of Journalism,* 107.

61. Kovach and Rosenstiel, *Elements of Journalism,* 107.

62. Kovach and Rosenstiel, *Elements of Journalism,* 29.

63. Michael Warner, *Publics and Counterpublics.* (Cambridge: Zone Books, 2005), 11–12.

64. Kovach and Rosenstiel, *Elements of Journalism,* 61.

65. Kovach and Rosenstiel, *Elements of Journalism,* 32.

66. Deborah Tannen, *The Argument Culture: Moving from Debate to Dialogue.* (New York: Random House, 1998).

67. Thomas Streeter, *Selling the Air: A Critique of the Policy of Commercial Broadcasting in the United States.* (Chicago: University of Chicago Press, 1996), 38.

68. Kovach and Rosenstiel, *Elements of Journalism,* 57.

69. Streeter, *Selling the Air,* 28.

70. Joseph Harris, *Rewriting: How to do Things with Texts.* (Logan, Utah: Utah State University Press, 2006), 10.

71. Joseph Harris, *Rewriting,* 10.

Chapter 5

Counterpublics: Beyond Deliberative Conversation

An individual's language is intricately bound up in his sense of identity and group consciousness.

—Geneva Smitherman-Donaldson[1]

Rhetorical sovereignty is the inherent right and ability of peoples to determine their own communicative needs and desires in this pursuit, to decide for themselves the goals, modes, styles, and languages of public discourse.

—Scott Lyons[2]

Years ago, I was lucky enough to be in the audience when Gloria Anzaldúa spoke to a crowd at the University of Arizona. Some of her discussion centered on *Borderlands,* her bilingual, multi-genre analysis of language, religion, culture, gender, and sexuality. During the question and answer period, a young man made a comment that began along the lines of "Why do you want to alienate white men?" The gist of his question was that her blunt criticism and blatant anger had alienated him, and that this alienation was a problem since she had not persuaded white men to join her Chicana, queer, feminist causes. The speaker didn't see a place for himself in the public reader that she was calling up in her writing, and he wanted to hold her accountable for this absence. In response to this question, another person—not Anzaldúa, but a white woman—came to the microphone and asked the man, "Do you remember the sections of her book where Gloria talks about the small group of men whom she sees as her allies? Why don't you identify with them?"

It was a remarkable moment in many ways: the respondent noted the range of potential reader positions offered in the book and called the young man on his choice. As I see it now, it was a moment about *publics.* The man in the audience sought to name and solidify a particular public, a particular body of stranger-reader-citizens who might pick up Anzaldúa's book, and he wanted to point out a gap between the public she had invoked and a "real" American public: the people who are responsible to create social change, he claimed, were white-identified and male-identified. But the woman who intervened did not accept either of those premises; instead, she called upon the young man to take responsibility for aligning himself with that version of "the public." Since that kind of redirection of public identity is what *Borderlands* is all about, I am certain that Anzaldúa could have responded to this man herself. But the intervention of the white woman was a critical performance as well. The white man had invoked a particular, racialized public in his question, and he was calling on a woman of color to justify her desire and authority to invoke an alternative, mixed-race public. When the white woman responded, she transgressed the white solidarity implied in that question.

One way to read this exchange is to understand it as a rift between a conception of "the public" in terms of the idealized, single public sphere and the public as constituted by multiple, conflicting sub- and counter-publics. Like the idealized public sphere, a model of subpublics posits that smaller publics come into being when people come together to deliberate; unlike that model, however, the new model does not presume that all they come together *in the same manner.* Nancy Fraser and many other scholars insist that there isn't and never was a singular public sphere where diverse individuals circulated their reasons until the right idea emerged as *the* public opinion. "Not only were there always a plurality of competing publics," Fraser notes, "but the relations between bourgeois publics and other publics were always conflictual."[3]

Once we let go of the idea of a unified public sphere, where everyone agrees to the "proper" modes of deliberation and the "proper" topics of public debate, we get to a space where deliberation happens at multiple levels—*within* the smaller publics, as people come together through particular ways of viewing and talking about the world, and *across* those smaller publics, as each seeks to join with, contain, or sometimes eradicate the perspectives that other publics circulate. The different ways of reasoning, different ways of conceptualizing "proper" public discussion, and different access to modes of circulating these public identities all clatter together in a raucous struggle. Public interaction, then, becomes less about learning to speak and engage in a single "proper" manner, and more about how to speak and be heard across differences.

Publics form when readers accept particular visions of themselves in texts and the rhetorical structures of those texts are critical in laying out the kind of relationships that the public imagines for itself. Sometimes a smaller public's ideals align with the idealized public sphere; I call those *sub*publics. When their expectations about "proper" democratic communication conflict with the idealized public sphere, I call them *counter*publics. Anzaldúa's book is part of a counterpublic. She pushes against conventional and dominant ideas about how people should come together; she is angry, she is emotional, she moves in and out of academic discourse and storytelling; she writes poems; she writes in multiple languages. These rhetorical choices are significant in her argument; through them she challenges her readers—like the young man in the audience—to meet her on her terms, in her language, through her ways of knowing. It's not surprising that the young man did not recognize himself in her book, not because he was not there (as the woman respondent made clear), but because like many of us, he has been trained to expect a more traditional form of exchange, the form most commonly delineated in American national magazines and newspapers.

In this chapter, I'll trace some of the rhetorical moves of counterpublics to show how they challenge the assumptions embedded in the idealized public sphere and invoke alternative ways for people to come together. I begin with the question of identity, expertise, and knowledge-making, and provide examples of counterpublics who insist on the epistemic value of thinking through identity rather than bracketing it and setting it aside during public discussions. I then turn to questions of tone (such as Anzaldúa's insistence that her anger and even blame come through in her book) and the rhetorical moves of publics where public speakers are not positioned as individuals, but where the modes of exchange highlight a more integrated role.

Those who compose public texts need to have a rich understanding of how rhetorical structures convey specific ideals about public relations. Those for whom the idealized public sphere is most familiar and "natural" would do well to learn how to read and respond to the ideals projected in other rhetorics. Those for whom counterpublic rhetoric is the most familiar and "natural" have probably experienced how the sharp edge of the idealized public sphere can slice away at the alternative vision they offer. As I saw at Anzaldúa's reading, in a battle of publics, people challenge and dismiss each other because their public invocations conflict.

NATIONAL COALITION FOR THE HOMELESS: REDEFINING "PUBLIC EXPERTISE"

In late summer 2009, John H., Penny, and Steve, three members of the National Coalition of Homelessness "Faces of Homelessness Speakers' Bureau," spoke to a packed room of incoming George Washington University students about their experiences living on the streets of D.C. The three speakers were invited to GWU as part of the university's "community building community" program, during which incoming freshmen work with community organizations across the city for three days and attend programs about community organizing or community issues in the evening. The three speakers shared their personal experiences: for John, a college graduate from a well-adjusted, white, middle-class home, a combination of debilitating events—health costs, along with losing his job and his girlfriend—put him on the streets. Penny, a middle-aged white woman, traced the roots of her homelessness to being raped at fourteen and said the psychological impact led her to make poor relationship choices; she had four children by the time she was twenty-five, "lost" them all to foster care by twenty-nine, and then lived on the streets. Steve, a middle-aged African American man, spoke about how he was fired from well-paying, prestigious jobs because he was addicted to crack. Like Penny, he linked his poor choices to a persistent low sense of self and "co-dependence." All three speakers praised local nonprofit organizations and fellow homeless individuals for showing them a new meaning of community and for helping them live with dignity. They thanked the National Coalition for the Homeless and reminded students that life on the streets is very lonely. "Say hello to us," John suggested.

Such panels can be seen as serving a similar function to Marin's *Harper's* essay: to push an audience to expand their vision of "public" to include homeless individuals by educating them about the causes and effects of homelessness. The Speakers' Bureau is described in the NCH materials as primarily a means of spreading "awareness" to "build the necessary bridges with the rest of society."[4] During the GWU event, all of the panelists stressed that one of the most significant acts that students could perform would be to "say hello," and "get to know our names," to make a connection. The speakers appealed through personal stories but also through data (often attributed to NCH) about the costs and persistence of homelessness. Part of the purpose is to move the student audience, with the hope that the ideas and requests presented in this space will ripple outward, as students talk to other students and begin to break down stereotypes about homelessness.

The NCH panel is an attempt of one public (homeless individuals working in alliance with NCH) to reach out to another public (GWU freshmen committed to community service) to enlist their help in circulating a particular view of a public issue. Yet, the NCH panel also introduces a fundamental epistemological challenge to the idealized public sphere: they claim their expertise not by bracketing their identity, but by emphasizing it.

The National Coalition for the Homeless, located in Washington, D.C., is an umbrella organization for hundreds of national, state, and local organizations that work to end homelessness. It bills itself as the nation's oldest and largest advocacy program for the homeless. On its website, NCH describes itself this way:

> The National Coalition for the Homeless is a national network of people who are currently experiencing or who have experienced homelessness, activists and advocates, community-based and faith-based service providers, and others committed to a single mission. That mission, our common bond, is to end homelessness.[5]

NCH works to change public attitudes about homelessness through programs such as its "Faces of Homelessness" speakers' bureau, "homelessness challenge" (which invites people to live the life of a homeless person for 24 hours), and various national awareness days (a memorial day and a National Day of Hunger Awareness). NCH is a well-organized and well-respected nonprofit that takes its cues from state and local organizations, who help set its agenda. They serve as a national resource for those organizations, providing research reports, policy proposals, and lobbying at the national level.

Both on the panel and within the hierarchy of the National Coalition for the Homeless, homeless people are positioned as experts. On their website, NCH describes the purpose of such panels: "[The event] allows . . . the general public to interact with these 'experts' through question and answer periods, and one-to-one discussions after the presentations."[6] Moreover, calling the homeless "experts" is not just a symbolic gesture; NCH relies on homeless and formerly homeless people to direct the nonprofit: "[A]t least one quarter of [NCH's 32-member] board are homeless/formerly homeless men and women; all are advocates."[7] The NCH relies on the unique perspective that this group provides as they develop policy and outreach programs.

Such overt advocacy and self-identification would be frowned upon in the idealized public sphere. As much as that model of deliberation holds itself accountable to a plurality of perspectives by insisting that deliberation should be open to all and concern all public issues, the diversity of perspectives are thought to enter the discussion through *individuals* who speak as *individuals,* not as members of any collective identity.

The idealized public sphere has to reconcile a desire that public deliberation take place among diverse individuals with the conflicting insistence that those individuals bracket their identity markers as they enter discussion. Homeless people should be involved in our public discourse, the thinking goes, but not *as the homeless;* they should come, instead, as *individuals* who have experienced homelessness and whose voice will be added to the deliberation and help everyone arrive at a good understanding of things.

Within the structure of a republic, this potential conflict is resolved by grouping individuals in geographical affiliations: the conversation is truly "public" if it involves enough people from within a government-defined civic boundary. As Ralph Cintron notes in his careful reflection on the discourse of measurement in *Angels' Town,* "ward maps represent the management of the body politic, hence, public discussion."[8] In D.C., the circles of interconnection radiate out, first from the neighborhoods (represented in Advisory Neighborhood Councils), then within and across Wards (as designated in the D.C. City Council). In other regions (which have the privilege of congressional representation that D.C. citizens are denied), the citizen-grouping extends to state-level districts and the states themselves, which deliberate through their representatives in Congress. Each state's senators and representatives are expected to account for the broad range of people in their geographical boundaries.

This framework assumes that people within a particular geographical area understand their needs better than others do, and, moreover, that their physical relationship within the same geographical and civic boundaries creates an interdependence that will ensure that they bend "public opinion" not toward individual, selfish needs but toward the broader good of civic community (ward/district/state/nation) as a whole. Civic maps delineate whose voices will count in those deliberations but does not threaten the centrality of rational expertise as the main method for introducing and evaluating proposals.

The model does *not* extend this epistemological potential to relationships other than those inscribed in ward maps and the like because collective identification is thought to run counter to the individualist nature of rational thought. The commonplace public sphere recoils when a group demands representation based on racial, gender, sexual, class, or other identity markers. The logic of one's argument should stand on its own merit; racial, ethnic, and other markers should not influence how others in the sphere respond to one's words. To ensure such equal reception, the argument goes, participants should transcend those markers. Second, as I noted earlier, "transcending" identity markers is thought to ensure that the speakers enter the deliberation without any *a priori* assumption about what the outcome of the deliberation should be.

An organization like NCH, which identifies homeless individuals as "experts" because of their experiences *as homeless people,* challenges that model considerably. First, the notion that *residential* status confers proper "interdependence" among citizens is called into question. How does the "neighborhood" boundary ensure that a community accounts for its homeless population? Is "neighborly" interdependence the best or only model for civic relationships? Who represents the homeless in government bodies?

Second, the NCH conception of "experts" challenges the assumption that collective identity interferes with people's ability to reason. In the idealized public sphere, the speaker who addresses strangers is expected to maintain a certain level of anonymity to assure that comments and discussions focus on "public," rather than personal or intimate, matters. Anything that could be interpreted as a narrowly self-interested position—something that pertains to you because of your race, gender, class, sexuality, etc.—must be presented as a *broadly* self-interested position, a position that *every* individual can recognize as pertaining to his or her own self-interests. The NCH pushes against all of these assumptions when it highlights the homeless men and women as experts. Doing so, it argues that if we bracket collective differences, our public deliberations will not be sufficiently diverse. Reflection on experience that is useful to public knowledge is *not* color- or gender- or class-blind. It sometimes requires people to *highlight* their sense of their own identity and the commonalities of experiences that they share with others in that group, including an understanding of how they are seen by other groups and an analysis of power dynamics that shape these experiences.

A WISE LATINA WOMAN, WITH THE RICHNESS OF HER EXPERIENCES?

A similar argument about the epistemic function of different lived experiences became the subject of heated discussion in Congress and around the country during the nomination hearings for Supreme Court Justice Sonia Sotomayor.

The U.S. senators who questioned her, and the media which reported about the controversy, focused on a seemingly provocative statement she had made in a speech: "I would hope that a wise Latina woman . . . would more often than not reach a better conclusion than a white male." But what is left out in those ellipses is significant. The full statement is: "I would hope that a wise Latina woman *with the richness of her experience* would more often than not reach a better conclusion than a white male *who hasn't lived that life.*"[9] And the context for their deliberation is also significant: Sotomayor is speaking at a symposium about Latino and Latina presence in the Judiciary. The speech was published in *La Raza Law Journal,* and then reprinted, during her confirmation, in *The New Republic.* The question she considers in her speech is how relevant her experiences as a Latina might be in relation to "decisions in race and sex discrimination cases." In the paper in which she made her now famous "Wise Latina" comment, Sotomayor argues that the "rich experiences" of the Latina and white male judge provide different baselines of knowledge and may influence the judges' motivation to accept and explore certain lines of thinking:

[T]o understand takes time and effort, something that not all people are willing to give. For others, their experiences limit their ability to understand the experiences of others. Others simply do not care. Hence, one must accept the proposition that a difference there will be by the presence of women and people of color on the bench. Personal experiences affect the facts that judges choose to see.[10]

The epistemological difference in how a wise Latina and a wise white male might create meaning out of the evidence in a case has less to do with their ability to reason as it has to do with which evidence they pursue and find meaningful. As feminist epistemologist Sandra Harding has argued, what we choose to see is always rooted in our identities in some way: claims to objectivity overlook the particular histories, experiences, philosophies, and ideologies that lead an observer to find certain questions and certain answers more acceptable than others.[11]

The consequence of the idealized public sphere's emphasis on bracketing difference is that such discourse conventions trample non-dominant groups coming and going: when non-dominant people develop theories out of their lived experiences, they are dismissed for not having bracketed their difference. When *only* people of color are exhorted to resist making generalizations from their experiences, bell hooks writes, such exhortations serve as

a means of exerting coercive power [that] leaves unquestioned the critical practices of other groups who employ the same strategies in different ways and whose exclusionary behavior may be firmly buttressed by institutionalized structures that do not critique or check it.[12]

We might note, for example, that during the Sotomayor hearings, only a few reporters or columnists noted that Judge Alito made a similar reference when he remarked that he thinks of his Italian family when immigration and naturalization cases are brought before him for review.

I want to stress also that this method of deflecting as "personal" those experiences that a dominant group does not recognize as relevant to a "public" conversation is not just a technique of those who identify as defenders of the status quo. It is a strategy that all who have been disciplined into the discourse strategies of the dominant public sphere can draw on. For example, Chela Sandoval exposes this deflection technique in her analysis of histories of feminism. After recounting how Allison Jaggar's typology of the feminist movement ignores the theories of women of color, Sandoval writes,

[Jaggar] claims that a specific U.S. third world feminist theory, method, and criticism "does not exist." This dismissal is based on her understanding of the written works produced by feminists of color during the 1970s and 1980s (authors such as Paula Gunn Allen, Audre Lorde, Nellie Wong, Gloria Anzaldúa, Cherrie Moraga, Toni Morrison, Mistuye Yamada, bell hooks, the third world contributors to *Sisterhood Is Powerful,* or the contributions to *This Bridge Called My Back*), which, she claims, operate "mainly at the level of description."[13]

According to Sandoval, Jaggar is unable to recognize the knowledge and theory production in the contributions of women of color because she is limited by her definition of what counts as knowledge and what counts as mere description.

Malea Powell identifies how this knowledge/experience dichotomy erases non-dominant perspectives in her analysis of academic studies of Native Americans. She writes, "When scholars convince themselves that they cannot study Indians (i.e., others) from the basis of Indian experience and existence, that they must make their efforts 'scientific' and thus distance their work from Indian 'reality,' they displace the very voices—those of Indian peoples—that they claim they want to hear."[14] When critiques rooted in personal experience are dismissed as "merely personal" unless the claims can be "objectively" verified by people outside the "self-interested" individuals who are making those claims, then the critique is effectively blocked. The conversation circles around the question of validity rather than any real engagement with the critique being offered.

As I hope I've shown here, the insistence on using personal "interested" experiences as part of one's analytical critique of dominant ideologies is not only a stylistic choice. Rather, it is the move of a *counterpublic,* a demand that the assumption about epistemology that undergirds the dominant public sphere be refigured. It is an attempt "to supply different ways of imagining stranger sociability and its reflexivity," as cultural studies scholar Michael Warner puts it.[15] In the end, the use of personal narrative by marginalized groups may not be an attempt to gain access to the dominant public sphere—not an attempt to correct an exclusion—but it may be a critique of the way the idealized public sphere imagines how knowledge-making happens among diverse strangers. The critique is offered through stylistic choices. Warner explains,

> One cannot conjure a public into being by force of will. The desire to have a different public, a more accommodating addressee, therefore confronts one with the circularity inherent in all publics: public language addresses a public as a social entity, but that entity exists only by virtue of being addressed. Its seems inevitable that the world to which one belongs, the scene of one's activity, will be determined at least in part by the way one addresses it. In modernity, therefore, an extraordinary burden of world making comes to be borne above all by style.[16]

Critiques of calm, rational, scientifically-grounded prose expose how the requirements of that form sift out alternative epistemological perspectives.

For me, this critique comes through most strongly in Anzaldúa's *Border-lands/La Frontera,* where she deliberately combines genres to help us see how traditional, academic discourse is based on a foundational belief in the Enlightenment split between "mind" and "body." By weaving brief personal narratives, images, metaphors, and poems into her book, she argues for alternate and subversive ways of arriving at and sharing knowledge. She seeks a way of defining knowledge-making as an intensely personal and physical experience. And for Anzaldúa, the intensely personal process of listening to her body is not something outside of cultural, ideological formations, but is simultaneously constructed by them and, as a site of contradictions and pain, a way of breaking out of them. So long as we pay attention to that most personal of things, our physical selves and the contradictory images and longings we have been taught to suppress, and as long as we examine the relationships among these and the dominant ways of knowing that have been passed on to us, we can arrive at new ways of viewing and talking about the world. That, I see, is the hopeful message Anzaldúa offers. She helps us recognize how tying ourselves to one form of writing means tying ourselves to one way of seeing the world; she offers an alternative.

INDIVIDUAL-CENTERED AND PEOPLE-CENTERED RHETORICS: REDEFINING "PUBLIC RELATIONS"

If *Borderlands* invokes a counterpublic with new criteria for what counts as "knowledge" in public discourse, other American counterpublics challenge the idealized public sphere's treatment of interlocutors as isolated individuals. The idealized public sphere operates on the assumption that the goal of public interaction is a particular kind of decision making, the ability to congeal public opinion so as to pressure the state to take action. The public is called up in a series of strategic, though isolated, moments of interdependence among individual citizens, whose relationship then dissipates (except in a rather vague way) until the next encounter. Michael Warner considers how the ideal of the "reading public" that is a central premise in the idealized public sphere delimits the actions that public takes on:

> Because this dominant public is called into being through the circulation of texts, the attribution of agency to publics works in most cases because of the direct transposition from private reading to the sovereignty of opinion. All of the verbs for public agency are verbs for private reading, transposed upward to the aggregate of readers. Readers may scrutinize, ask, reject, opine, decide, judge, and so on. Publics can do exactly these things. And nothing else.[17]

However, the model of democracy as a collection of individuals is not the only American model. Reading verbs are not the only actions available for publics: "Counterpublics tend to be those in which this ideology of reading does not have the same privilege."[18] We can see alternatives by examining the ideologies that undergird some Native American and African American rhetorics.

In "Language and Literature from a Pueblo Indian Perspective," Leslie Marmon Silko describes the language practices of the Laguna Pueblo. Silko challenges the Western assumptions about the relationships among rhetor and audience. She explains,

> The storytelling always includes the audience and the listeners, and in fact, a great deal of the story is believed to be inside the listener, and the storyteller's role is to draw the story out of the listeners. This kind of shared experience grows out of a strong community base. The storytelling goes on and continues from generation to generation.[19]

The stories emerge from the interaction. At the same time, the listeners trust the storyteller to guide the overall experience. Silko reminds her own audience, "As with [a spider's] web, the structure will emerge as it is made, and you must simply listen and trust, as Pueblo people do, that the meaning will be made."[20]

According to Silko, the importance of the interaction is in the relationships that are developed and maintained through the ongoing cycles of storytelling. She says, "The stories are always bringing us together, keeping this whole together, keeping this family together, keeping this clan together."[21] Anthropologists and ethnologists classified old, traditional Pueblo stories as more important than contemporary family stories; however, Silko rejects that hierarchy: the purpose of all stories is to provide a sense of location and relationship for the listeners within an ever-widening spiral of relationships—"so you can move, then, from the idea of one's identity as a tribal person, to a clan identity."[22] Allowing people to separate and isolate themselves from the group is dangerous:

> When some violent emotional experience takes place, people get the urge to run off and hide or separate themselves from others. And of course, if we do that, we are not only talking about endangering the group, we are also talking about the individual or the individual family never being able to recover or survive. Inherent in this belief is the feeling that one does not recover or get well by one's self, but it is together that we look after each other and take care of each other.[23]

The stories serve not only to bring people into the community, but also to provide for them some critical perspective on their own experiences. "Keeping track of all the stories within the community gives a certain distance, a useful perspective which brings [any new and distressing] incidents down to a level you can deal with," Silko explains.[24] The interactions of storytelling are crucial for survival, because storytelling provides both the distance to be able to understand each thing in context and the connection to be able to recognize that one is not alone in any suffering.

The interactive component of Pueblo storytelling reinforces the communal values. The conception of the "public" space that comes out of these rhetorical traditions is drastically different from the image of the collection of individuals in the idealized public sphere. The rhetorical dynamics insist on the equal importance of the storyteller and audience, and each has a role to play in maintaining the larger community. They are not *individuals* negotiating for self-interest, but a *people* guided by a commitment to the larger group.

Scott Lyons has elaborated on this concept in his essay, "Rhetorical Sovereignty: What Do American Indians Want from Writing?" He writes, "A *people* is a group of human beings united together by history, language, culture, or some combination therein—a community joined in union for a common purpose: the survival and flourishing of the people itself."[25] Drawing on examples from early Cherokee towns in Georgia, Lyons describes a national identity where "reason and rationality were deployed always with an idealistic eye toward the betterment of the people, including but not limited to the individuals which constituted it, through the practices of tradition and culture."[26] Describing the Haudenosaunee or Iroquois League, he emphasizes that their purpose in negotiating with each other and outsiders was "for the sole purpose of promoting, not suppressing, local cultures and traditions, even while united by a common political project."[27] He stresses that the democratic model offered here goes beyond self-governance; it recognizes that the group is more than self-interested individuals, but is made up of individuals who have a responsibility to promote *each other's* "local" interests and cultures, and the traditions that support them.

An additional example of rhetorical models that challenge the individualist paradigm of democracy can be found in Geneva Smitherman-Donaldson's analysis of the language of Black America. Written in 1977, *Talkin and Testifyin* challenges the presumption that Black English is merely the result of African American's laziness or simple ignorance of the rules of "proper" English. As she lays out the inherent structures and linguistic principles of Black English, Smitherman draws connections between these structures and those of the West African worldview from which they derive. One of these principles is:

> Though the universe is hierarchical, all modes of existence are necessary for the sustenance of its balance and rhythm. Harmony in nature and the universe

is provided by the complementary, interdependent synergic interaction between the spiritual and the material. . . . Similarly, communities of people are modeled after the interdependent rhythms of the universe. Individual participation is necessary for community survival. Balance in the community, as in the universe, consists of maintaining these interdependent relationships."[28]

Within the modes of discourse in Black English, this worldview is exemplified most clearly in the tradition of call and response. In the call and response exchange, the audience responds with words, gestures, or sounds to the speaker's statements. While the tradition is most often associated with the traditional Black church, it carries into secular contexts as well. As with the Native Indian rhetorical conventions described earlier, the assumption here is that if only one person is speaking, the interaction is flawed. The participation of all parties is essential, and there is a wide range of appropriate responses to any rhetor's speech: "the only *incorrect* thing you can do is not respond at all."[29] Smitherman (drawing on work by Oliver Jackson) elaborates:

> We are talking, then, about an interactive network in which the fundamental requirement is active participation of all individuals. In this kind of communicative system, "there is no sharp line between performers or communications and the audience, for virtually everyone is performing and everyone is listening." The process requires that one must give if one is to receive, and receiving is actively acknowledging another.[30]

The system is not without hierarchy: the speaker still sets the agenda and manipulates the dynamic. But the audience must provide feedback, and the speaker is expected to adjust, to play (with) the audience. "Emphasis is on group cohesiveness, cooperation, and the collective common good."[31]

I want to stress that, although I am drawing examples from the traditions of Native American and African American rhetorics, I am not claiming that the rhetorics here are essentially Native American or African American. I heed David Holmes' warning that "if one is not careful, even the expression 'African American Rhetoric' intimates a narrow perception of what constitutes African American identity and experience."[32] Rather, they are deployed as rhetorical strategies for communicating value systems that many Native Americans and African Americans have embraced.

In these examples of Native American and African American linguistic traditions, the rhetorical interactions take place in the "safe houses" of the marginalized communities. Given the history of violence against both Native Americans and African Americans, it is not surprising that their rhetorical traditions would emphasize the need for communal identity as an element of survival. The expected roles of speaker and audience serve to reinforce an interconnection and identity as well as a sense of mutual responsibility and activism: the role of both speaker and audience is to construct each experience, to shape it. To merely "receive" ideas or "give" ideas violates the interdependence needed for survival in a dominant culture.

But the dominant public sphere is not a safe house; as a public, it is in perpetual crisis, offering up its identity through the circulation of discourse and becoming reaffirmed only when someone takes up that circulation. The dominant public sphere operates at a site of contention, competing with counterpublics for that circulation. It would be misleading, naïve, and dangerous to presume that these rhetorical conventions of the counterpublic could simply be imported into the dominant public sphere. The struggle here is not a struggle for access, but a struggle for the recognition of alternate subject positions, alternative publics.

DECORUM AND ANGER IN THE CONTACT ZONE: REDEFINING "PUBLIC RELATIONS"

Recognizing the dominant public sphere as a place of contestation, some counterpublics see the dominant ideal of decorum in the idealized public sphere as one of the tools that that dominant public uses to constrain critique. As I pointed out in chapter 2, one of the main axes in conceptions of democracy has to do with how a public imagines its target audience: are those who have the power to make change receptive to reason and operating with goodwill toward everyone in the public, or are they protecting their own interests (sometimes in the name of what is good for all)? Anger is a way to call out the hypocrisy of those who profess to be working in one's best interest; one speaks in anger to break through the misguided self-perceptions of those who think they are open and benevolent.

In the idealized public sphere, interlocutors are to be treated as benevolent individuals who are hardworking and tolerant. In America, especially, a celebration of individualism floods the national culture. One of the dominant myths is the "self-made man," the typical protagonist in Horatio Alger stories. Rooted in these American stories is the ideology of individualism: that one is responsible for him or herself, and that through hard work, dedication, and willpower, a person can overcome great odds. America provides the ladder of opportunity, and any individuals who have enough desire can climb up the ladder. However, the myth also implies its opposite: if one slips down the ladder or, even worse, does not begin to climb it, then the problem lies in the individual's lack of ingenuity or drive. David Bleich describes the dangerous edge of this philosophy bluntly: it leads to "the belief that social injustice is usually the fault of the victim."[33]

Two elements of this "American" story directly impact the discourse conventions of the American idealized public sphere. First, the public sphere is made up of a collection of *individuals* who see themselves as *autonomous:* they believe they landed where they are because of their own hard work. Second, they welcome all others who have demonstrated their commitment to the same. Thus, at the same time that the American national culture values individualism, it also prides itself on its tolerance and diversity. The American story is not just about the person who rises from poverty; it is about the (legal) *immigrant* who rises from poverty. The dominant myth posits America as a culture that constantly provides the opportunities for the outsider who learns the etiquette of the national culture and then acts on the many opportunities that become available. Indeed, whenever a new person arrives with a particularly unique narrative of surmounted obstacles, his or her entrance into the group is welcomed with a round of backslapping and congratulations. It serves as proof that the literacy "ticket" into American public life is inclusive.

"Tolerant" "individualism" leads to a particular version of multiculturalism, a kind of naïve pluralism that ignores issues of power and the institutionalization of oppression. This liberal multiculturalism sees social injustices such as racism as individual problems rooted in some people's ignorance. Thus, racism is be solved by "educating" individual racists, who presumably are the way they are because they haven't had the opportunity to look around and see that their views have been based on provincial experiences. Likewise with other "social problems"—sexism, classism, homophobia, ableism, ageism, and so on. Within the framework of liberal pluralism, these injustices are to be corrected individually and can be overcome individually.

Kenneth Burke admonishes us to look carefully at those times when we claim ourselves as individuals, isolated from other systems around us. When we do so, he tells us, we blind ourselves to the larger forces we are implicitly identified with. His classic example is that of the shepherd:

> If the shepherd is guarding the sheep so they may be raised for market, though his role (considered in itself, as guardian of the sheep) concerns only their good, he is implicitly identified with their slaughter. A total stress on the autonomy of his pastoral specification here functions *rhetorically* as a mode of expression whereby we are encouraged to overlook the full implications of his office.[34]

Whatever the shepherd's intentions, his role in the larger system of animal husbandry is harmful to sheep. Thus, an emphasis on "goodwill" and "good intentions" performs the rhetorical function of pushing members of the public sphere to concentrate narrowly on people's individual behavior and expressed beliefs, and to overlook the full implications of power imbalances.

In particular, it creates a safe place where those in power—whites, for example—can expect to be treated as benevolent and well-intentioned, even when, because of their whiteness, they maintain a position of privilege.

Sharon Crowley and Debra Hawhee point out how the contemporary concept of "opinions" maintains this same rhetorical function: it keeps the emphasis on the individual and makes it very difficult to challenge people's assertions. In *Ancient Rhetoric for Contemporary Students,* Crowley and Hawhee argue that opinions are seen as part of a person's identity—views that he or she has developed individually and that, in turn express who he or she *is* individually.

> The belief that opinions belong to individuals may explain why Americans seem reluctant to challenge one another's opinions. To challenge a person's opinion is to denigrate that person's character, to imply that if he or she holds an unexamined or stupid or silly opinion, he or she is an unthinking or stupid or silly person.[35]

"Opinions" are seen as a dramatically different category than "facts." While "facts belong to everybody," "opinions are intimately tied up with an individual's thought and personality."[36] It becomes impolite, then, to challenge a person's opinions for fear of being seen as attacking her character and identity. An expected polite deference to others' "opinions" reinforces the sense that opinions and attitudes—whether racist or otherwise—come from internal and psychological places rather than from larger societal structures. The expected solution is to let it be, to attribute the opinion to that person, and to move over to create space for this opinion among the many other autonomous opinions out there.

Picture those conversations in bars or coffeehouses where one person in a group makes a racist or homophobic comment. Anyone in the group who is offended by the comment must decide how much to say in response. There is the very real possibility, in many settings, that calling the person on the offensive comment will be seen as such a breach of etiquette that the group would ostracize the person who points it out. The offended person is expected either to remain silent or to speak in such a way as not to create discomfort. Add to this picture the American belief in diversity and we have an image of the ideal public sphere where people of all races, classes, genders, etc., gather amicably, where everyone behaves with decorous politeness—where everyone agrees implicitly not to jeopardize the image of harmony and equality in the group.

bell hooks dismisses this colorblind public sphere as "the comforting 'melting pot' idea of cultural diversity, the rainbow coalition where we would all be grouped together in our difference, but everyone wearing the same have-a-nice-day smile."[37] When we are expected to "[wear] the same have-a-nice-day smile," it's hard to challenge the privilege accorded to different groups based on race, class, or gender because these are not grounded in individual intentions; they are bigger, more pervasive. To suggest that intentions are not one of the most significant aspects of a person's role in the public sphere violates a central concept of the public sphere—that the public sphere functions precisely because of the goodwill that individuals have towards each other.

Once we acknowledge an imbalance of power, the image of a public sphere comprised of autonomous individuals engaged in harmonious pluralism cannot be the foundation for truly democratic public interactions: rather, during negotiations, rhetors must constantly examine how their own positions are intertwined with others and with the larger cultural and social institutions around them. The dialog needs to be one where people are made to confront their complicity in the oppression of others. The challenge, of course, is to find a way to provide a critique within a system that stops hearing as soon as the critique challenges the hearer's sense of benevolence.

To further explore this question of decorum, anger, and the "proper" relationships among citizens, I turn to Lynn Z. Bloom's *College English* article, "Freshman English as a Middle-Class Enterprise." Bloom argues that one of the goals of freshman composition is to introduce students to the etiquette of middle-class society. As one example of this etiquette, she observes that middle-class composition teachers have clear expectations about appropriate topics for first-year writing courses. She writes,

> [N]o matter what kinds of writing assignments we give, as middle-class teachers we expect freshman papers—on whatever subject—to fall within the realm of normative discourse in subject, point of view, values implied. . . . When we receive a paper that incorporates what Mary Louise Pratt calls "unsolicited oppositional discourse, parody, resistance, critique" and—intentionally or unwittingly—transgresses these normative boundaries, we go to pieces.[38]

Bloom equates "unsolicited oppositional discourse" with papers that are "racist, misogynist, sadistic, or otherwise debased or debasing."[39] She describes offensive essays about gang violence or gay bashing, and examines the teacher's uncomfortable responses. The main taboo of these papers appears to be their rejection of the American ideal of equality. Although many teachers refuse to challenge the student's positions head-on, they express their disapproval indirectly. By refusing to accuse the students of having violated any social taboos, the professors demonstrate their goodwill (and their presumption of the students' goodwill) and model the decorum of the imagined public sphere.

While I agree that such over-careful politeness can deflect more critical responses in such moments, I want to call attention to a different move within this passage. Bloom equates the idea of "unsolicited oppositional discourse" to papers describing gang violence and gay bashing. Given her reference to Mary Louise Pratt, the leap that she has made is a telling one. In Pratt's famous "Arts of the Contact Zone" essay, rhetors who practice oppositional discourse do so in order to intervene in the stories that the dominant culture tells itself—to force the dominant culture to see how its own myths of success, tolerance, or benevolence cover over oppression.[40] While Bloom's examples depict readers who are made uncomfortable because *writers* have violated the American ideals of tolerance, what Pratt is talking about are occasions where writers point out how their *readers* have violated that American value. This is a much different interaction. It's not the situation of a self-defined "tolerant" person trying to decide how to point out politely that the comment her colleague made was offensive. Rather, a person who thinks he or she is "tolerant" is forced to hear that *he or she* has been racist. "Unsolicited oppositional discourse" is the rhetoric that is used to attack the benevolent self-image of those who are complicit in oppression.

Bloom argues that the typical middle-class response to essays that are blatantly racist or homophobic is to find a way politely and indirectly to call attention to the problem, and to do so in a way that does not cause discomfort to the listener. I would argue that the appeal to decorum is also the means by which the dominant culture shrugs off the much more pointed and discomforting challenge of "unsolicited oppositional discourse." Such a challenge is dismissed as rude precisely because it positions us in an uncomfortable position. This is especially true if the author of the oppositional discourse expresses any anger.

"Good" public writing is seen as calm, rational, and unemotional. Anger is allowed only for those issues that the group has already agreed are worth being angry about. One can rage about dead-beat dads, for instance, or terrorists, or snipers. The rhetorical effect of such anger is to rally the group to reinforce the current value system. However, what if one seeks to critique the dominant group? Then, the rhetor is expected first to establish a connection and identification with the group and second to set out a rational and deliberate argument. The calm tone is thought to demonstrate the rhetor's belief in the goodwill of the audience and the rhetor's desire to maintain a relationship with them. According to dominant discourse conventions, anger and rage make such relationships impossible. I disagree.

In celebrating a rhetoric of anger, as I do here, I do not presume that *all* anger is productive, or that *all* contexts in which a person speaks with anger include within them an invitation to enter into a relationship to learn together.

Anger can be a tool of exclusion, a tool of authority that shuts down inquiry. Anger can be a method of silencing the listener. My claim is not that *all* anger is productive, but rather that *some* anger can be productive, and that therefore we need to make sure that we do not fall into the easy habit of shutting out anger because it violates the expectations of public discourse. Banning the expression of anger is not the only possible rhetorical response.

In "The Uses of Anger," Audre Lorde writes to all women to encourage them to speak their anger about racism, and she writes to white women to encourage them to hear it. Lorde argues that anger offers both parties—the angry speaker and the person who hears it—possibilities for growth: "My fear of anger taught me nothing," she writes, and "your fear of that anger will teach you nothing, also."[41] Hearing anger offers the possibility for growth precisely because it dismantles the presumption that the only way to demonstrate goodwill is to remain calm. If a person is speaking angrily to me, then—because of the very fact that the conversation is happening—a relationship has been established between us. The angry person is speaking to me; he or she wants me to hear; he or she expects me to listen. There is, by default, an expression of goodwill in that very act.

Yet if I refuse to listen because the person is angry, then I am denying this gesture of goodwill and refusing to respond to it; I am only acknowledging that his or her anger makes me uncomfortable. The discourse conventions in the dominant culture see anger as pushing people away, and teach us, as listeners, to see only half of the interaction. If I cannot learn to hear anger as an act of goodwill—as a sign of possibility for a new kind of relationship—then I have already found a way to refuse that new relationship. Lorde writes,

> My anger is a response to racist attitudes and to the actions and presumptions that arise out of those attitudes. If your dealings with other women reflect those attitudes, then my anger and your attendant fears are spotlights that can be used for growth in the same way I have used learning to express anger for my growth.[42]

But more often what happens, she asserts, is that when people hear her anger, they say, "'Tell me how you feel but don't say it too harshly or I can't hear you.' But is it my manner that keeps [them] from hearing, or the threat of a message that [their lives] might change?"[43]

Although Pratt doesn't name it as such, I would argue that expressing righteous anger is an art of the contact zone. It is an art, like the others she names—parody, satire, humor, imagined dialog, denunciation, multilingual expression[44]—that allows people to call attention to the rules of culture that exclude them; it is a strategy that can expose how rhetorical conventions themselves create and reproduce that exclusion. But as with the other arts of the contact zone, it is rarely taught and often explicitly discouraged.

PERFORMING RHETORICS OF AMERICAN PUBLIC SPHERES

The discourse conventions of the idealized public sphere provide a particular relationship for speakers/writers and audience members: the focus is on individuals who tolerate each other, who occasionally identify with each other, who behave in ways to reaffirm a sense of goodwill and presumed generosity among members, and who present their arguments through a logic of reason that excludes certain kinds of knowing. These discourse conventions constitute a willful ignorance of the power dynamics that surround who is allowed to speak, what form that speech should take, and what value systems are inherent in the roles that one must assume in the rhetorical situations.

E. D. Hirsch, Jr., has argued that the discourse conventions of the American public sphere are neutral and universal, that "literate culture is the most democratic culture in our land" and that it "has become the common currency for social and economic exchange in our country and the only available ticket to full citizenship."[45] Through his Core of Knowledge curriculum, Hirsch wants to give everyone access to this language of social and economic power, access to full citizenship. He is especially aware that children growing up in non-white and working-class neighborhoods are less likely to absorb this literacy in their daily interactions; his laudable goal is to ensure that everyone who goes through school in the United States will come out with the cultural literacy they need to engage as equal members of the idealized public sphere. "Getting one's membership card [into literate culture] is not tied to race or class. Membership is automatic if one learns the background information and the linguistic conventions that are needed to read, write, and speak effectively."[46]

The assertion that anyone who merely learns these conventions can "buy a ticket" into the inner circle and then can have an equal chance to be heard, to be understood, and to effectively persuade others in the idealized public sphere leaps right over the privileges of race, gender, sex, class, and other dynamics that shape how people are heard. Furthermore, conventions such as the requirement to presume a goodwill among all parties denies one side the possibility of accusing others of benefiting from those privileges. These conventions serve to protect the dominant group from hearing critique, and provide them with an easy way to dismiss threatening arguments. The rhetoric of tolerant individualism shields them from the rage of those who are oppressed.

Let me be clear: it is not only that the discourse conventions of the idealized public sphere make it difficult for people to critique the oppositional views of the American myths that privilege the dominant, white power in this country. Dismissing the way ideas are presented is one mechanism for refusing to listen to them. But the refusal to entertain alternate rhetorical practices is a refusal to experience the alternative worldviews embodied in those discourses. When white Americans share in Pueblo storytelling or participate in African American call-and-response, they are forced to take on a new role as audience; they are forced to experience new stranger-relationships, new experiences of a public. The rhetorical practices force those involved to act out the values—to go beyond engaging intellectually with concepts such as communal identity and to *perform* those values in the dynamic of the rhetorical situation. When we do not allow for the alternative rhetorics of the counterpublics to circulate, when we insist that the current discourse conventions are adequate to addressing the content of all concerns that could be raised in the public sphere, we assert that the only way that people need to entertain alternative values is *intellectually,* not viscerally. The most anyone is expected to do is to *think* about things, not to change (inter)actions of the rhetorical situation in which they are thinking.

There are, of course, many, many additional values embedded in the discourse conventions of the idealized public sphere in America: an emphasis on linearity and directness ties with America's investment in progress narratives; an emphasis on efficiency and conciseness exemplifies a belief in "thrift;" a focus on moderation (in tone, development, style) coupled with an aversion to excess (seen as flashy, self-indulgent) projects a particular, value-laden aesthetic. Other scholars have explored the ways that these discourse conventions reinforce a particular and exclusive public sphere. See, for example, Gustavo Guerra's analysis of the NEH's dismissal of the "cluttered" aesthetic of Latin American artists, and the many fine essays in *Writing in Multicultural Settings* (edited by Carol Servino, Juan Guerra and Johnella Butler) and in *Race, Rhetoric, and Composition* (edited by Keith Gilyard).

I do not mean to presume to have covered all of the ways that the discourse conventions of the idealized public sphere exclude alternative values and shut down critique. But I hope that I have offered enough examples and analysis here to show the problem is not just about access. Because the discursive practices of publics require rhetors and audiences to perform certain identities—because they push rhetors and readers to see themselves and their world in different ways—we can best challenge those assumptions about the neutrality or universality of the idealized public sphere by acknowledging the wide range of counter-rhetorics available in America, by going out and experiencing them. We need to articulate how such rhetorics call up alternate public spheres.

We also need to develop a fuller understanding of how and where counterpublics circulate and how they work with and against the publics that are inherent in the most common forms of circulation, the mass media. I'll consider that question in the next chapter.

WHAT DOES THIS MEAN FOR A PUBLIC WRITING COURSE?

To introduce counterpublic rhetorics to my students, I have sometimes organized courses explicitly around American rhetorics, where we read some of the scholarship I have referenced here. I introduce Lynn Z. Bloom's "Freshman Composition as a Middle-Class Enterprise" alongside Mary Louise Pratt's "Arts of the Contact Zone" as a way to demonstrate how writing is a contested space. We investigate the ever important work of Scott Lyons, Malea Powell, Geneva Smitherman, Gloria Anzaldúa, Audre Lorde, and others who expose how different components of the idealized public sphere constrain alternative public ideals. One activity I have found particularly helpful is to ask students to analyze the conceptions of multicultural pluralism proposed by the authors in the anthology, *Writing in Multicultural Settings.* We juxtapose these conceptions with the proposal by Nathan Glazer in *We Are All Multiculturalists Now,* an exercise that allows students to look at the many layers of that term and how conceptions of democratic relationships are built into rhetorical choices.

Doing justice to the complexity of counterpublic rhetorics requires more time than is offered in a one-semester course. It's especially difficult to fit all of this complexity into a course where I am also introducing the components of public writing through community-based writing and service. My solution has been to allow discussions about counterpublic rhetorics to evolve from the experiences and observations that students make, rather than to structure them into the course as an explicit unit. In my first-year writing courses on public writing, I have noticed several consistent moments where such conversations arise. When they do arise, I make room in the class discussion and course readings so that we can pursue those questions further. (Sometimes students run with it, using these questions as the focus of their research papers; their findings filter back into the class through the peer workshops and class presentations about their work.)

The community organizations with which my students and I partner often see themselves as working in the space between dominant and counterpublic rhetorics. They value the expertise of lived experience. They recognize anger as a potentially constructive force, something that can bring people together to agitate for change. They understand that demands for decorum and anything that is tinged with assumptions that those in power are benevolent will likely be met with skepticism and distrust. At the same time, they recognize how hard it is to intervene in public discourse without accommodating the expectations of the idealized public sphere. They have seen how quickly important and critical ideas are dismissed because they are spoken in Black English or are rooted in personal stories. Many of these organizations take an approach that straddles the public and counterpublic: guiding people so that they can negotiate the expectations of the dominant public sphere, but doing so in a manner that positions that public as one kind of rhetorical space, neither ideal nor universal but nevertheless powerful.

As my students and I prepare to begin working in local communities, we read pieces, such as a helpful chapter in Thomas Dean's *Writing and Community Action*, that introduce the idea of *reciprocity*. If students are hoping to go into a community to "help" others, and if they expect their actions to be greeted with kindness and appreciation, these readings will disabuse them of those goals. Especially when students are from local universities, they come into communities as representatives of institutions and publics that may have long histories of neglecting or even exploiting the nearby neighborhoods. Within such contexts, I point out, they may be greeted with cynicism or even anger. They don't enter a community that presumes their benevolence or their sincere commitment. Students have to earn this, and they do so by recognizing the logic of the anger, by coming back again and again, by finding ways to treat expressions of anger not as rejections but as tests, as an invitation to engage at a level that acknowledges the potential imbalances of power and history.

Sometimes opportunities arise from students' observations about their own work in the community. Students who tutor African American students at places like Life Pieces to Masterpieces or the Higher Achievement Program sometimes posit that the students are held back in life because "they can't speak proper English." When moments like this arise, we take some time to explore the terms we use to describe what they've observed. Who defines "proper"? What does it look like? We explore how Black English works—it is not merely incorrect Standard English, but a language with its own structures and grammar. When pushed on this, my students recognize that a person can speak Black English wrong. They also realize that white students who try to adopt Black English tread into confusing territory, all mixed up with cultural identity and power. My goal in such conversations is to unpack the idea that English is ever one thing, and to point out how language builds community.

These kinds of conversations may not happen at the community organizations themselves. At Higher Achievement Program, the young "scholars" are expected to speak Standard English, and when they don't, they are corrected. I can understand these choices, and I caution my students to pay attention to how such corrections are offered. I also caution students to pay close attention to how and when students code-switch and to consider what rhetorical arguments they might be making by choosing to speak in Standard or Black English at any given moment. Though my students might not recognize it at first, the younger scholars and apprentices are likely quite adept at moving back and forth. Life Pieces to Masterpieces and the Higher Achievement Program ask them to be conscious about when they choose to do so.

I also have plenty of opportunities to delve into the question whether or not personal identity is epistemic. I can count on having this discussion when students begin to contemplate writing their first essays, in which they describe the neighborhood where they will work by reflecting on personal observations and analyzing how others have characterized the area in local and national publications, blogs, and the like. They struggle with whether or not they can use *I* in their papers. I point out that many of the authors we have read in our class use *I* and we talk about what that allows them to do. For most, the gesture is parallel to the *I* in Peter Marin's article, "Helping and Hating the Homeless," which I analyzed in chapter 4. The personal reflections allow him to demonstrate a certain kind of compassion and inquisitiveness; they also allow him to show how he once identified with the misconceptions he now wants to correct. This is certainly the effect of *I* in Morton's "Ironies of Service" as well.

Yet students resist because they have been taught that good academic writing avoids the personal. I explain the logic of that position, drawing from the values of the idealized public sphere: in speaking to a public, one is expected to bracket markers of difference so that the persuasiveness of one's position rests on its logical reasoning. Those differences should not affect the reason, and if they do, the author is expected to accommodate that somehow—to find ways to verify his or her perspective from a more universal position. Yet, as feminist epistemologists have long argued, and as scholarship around the university is beginning to accept, reason never takes place outside of embodied people, and the rhetorical moves we use to try to erase those identity markers often have the opposite effect: instead of writing that "I felt this way," we write, "One feels this way," or "People would feel this way"—extrapolating a universal response from our experiences. I ask students to reflect on how much of their internal understandings of their experiences might be influenced by their race or class, but the goal is not to rise above. Instead, the goal is to look at how these narratives of experience are constructed through language, and to investigate the many discourses—the public understandings—that guide those narratives. In this way, once again, we arrive at a place where we are talking about public writing not in terms of individualism or with a goal to set aside difference; instead, we are talking about public writing as something situated in a constant swirl and clash of multiple publics.

One final opportunity to talk about counterpublics arises when we talk about what it takes for a public to convey its particular ideas and values through the traditional media. As I explained at the end of chapter 3, I encourage students to look at how people describe their communities in different forums—the descriptions and quotations in national papers, which often vary from local and alternative presses, which differ again from the language in local blogs. We look at how sometimes discussion about issues is deflected into arguments about the proper modes of communicating or how people are dismissed for not using Standard English.

If, as I argued in chapter 4, the traditional media perpetuates the idealized public sphere, and if, as I have argued here, counterpublics regularly challenge that ideal, then counterpublics face an especially difficult challenge: they have to find ways to circulate their ideals that won't be compromised by the traditional media. A final opportunity for studying counterpublic rhetorics can emerge at these moments, if we know what to look for. My next chapter traces some of the strategies that counterpublics use to goad the traditional press into conveying their counterpublic ideals, and considers how those moments might be brought into a public writing classroom.

NOTES

1. Geneva Smitherman-Donaldson, *Talkin and Testifyin: The Language of Black America* (Detroit: Wayne State University Press, 1986), 171.

2. Scott Richard Lyons, "Rhetorical Sovereignty: What Do American Indians Want from Writing?" *College Composition and Communication* 51, no. 3 (February 2000): 450.

3. Nancy Fraser, "Rethinking the Public Sphere: A Contribution to the Critique of Actually Existing Democracy," in *Habermas and the Public Sphere,* ed. Craig J. Calhoun (Cambridge, Mass.: MIT Press, 1992), 61.

4. National Coalition for the Homeless, "Faces of Homelessness Speakers' Bureau," 2010 http://www.nationalhomeless.org/faces/index.html (30 July 2010).

5. National Coalition for the Homeless, "About Us," 2010 http://www.nationalhomeless.org/about_us/index.html (30 July 2010).

6. National Coalition for the Homeless, "The Presentations: Faces of Homelessness Speakers' Bureau," 2010 http://www.nationalhomeless.org/faces/presentation.html (30 July 2010).

7. National Coalition for the Homeless, "About Us," 2010 http://www.nationalhomeless.org/about_us/index.html (30 July 2010).

8. Ralph Cintron, *Angels' Town: Chero Ways, Gang Life, and Rhetorics of the Everyday* (Boston: Beacon Press, 1997), 25.

9. Sonia Sotomayor, "A Latina Judge's Voice." *Berkeley La Raza Law Journal* 13, no. 1 (2002): 92.

10. Sotomayor, "Latina Judge's Voice," 92.

11. Sandra Harding, *Whose Science? Whose Knowledge? Thinking from Women's Lives* (Ithaca, NY: Cornell University Press, 1991).

12. bell hooks, *Teaching to Transgress* (New York: Routledge, 1994), 93.

13. Chela Sandoval, *Methodologies of the Oppressed* (Minneapolis: University of Minnesota Press, 2000), 52.

14. Malea Powell, "Blood and Scholarship: One Mixed-Blood Story," in *Race, Rhetoric, and Composition,* ed. Keith Gilyard (Portsmouth, NH: Boynton, 1999), 5.

15. Michael Warner, *Publics and Counterpublics* (Cambridge: Zone Books, 2005), 122.

16. Warner, *Publics and Counterpublics,* 128–29.

17. Warner, *Publics and Counterpublics,* 123.

18. Warner, *Publics and Counterpublics,* 123.

19. Leslie Marmon Silko, "Language and Literature from a Pueblo Indian Perspective," in *Living Languages,* ed. Nancy Buffington, Marvin Diogenes, and Clyde Moneyhun (Upper Saddle River, NJ: Prentice, 1997), 436.

20. Silko, "Language and Literature," 436.

21. Silko, "Language and Literature," 437–38.

22. Silko, "Language and Literature," 437.

23. Silko, "Language and Literature," 437.

24. Silko, "Language and Literature," 437.

25. Lyons, "Rhetorical Sovereignty," 454.

26. Lyons, "Rhetorical Sovereignty," 455.

27. Lyons, "Rhetorical Sovereignty," 456.

28. Smitherman, *Talkin and Testifyin,* 75.

29. Smitherman, *Talkin and Testifyin,* 108.

30. Smitherman, *Talkin and Testifyin,* 108.

31. Smitherman, *Talkin and Testifyin,* 109.

32. David Holmes, "Fighting Back by *Writing* Black: Beyond Racially Reductive Composition Theory," in *Race, Rhetoric, and Composition,* ed. Keith Gilyard (Portsmouth, NH: Boynton, 1999), 61.

33. David Bleich, "Literacy and Citizenship: Resisting Social Issues," in *The Right to Literacy,* ed. Andrea A. Lunsford, Helen Hoglen, and James Slevin (New York: MLA, 1990), 164.

34. Kenneth Burke, *Language and Symbolic Action* (Berkeley, CA: University of California Press, 1966), 302.

35. Sharon Crowley and Debra Hawhee, *Ancient Rhetoric for Contemporary Students,* 3rd ed. (Addison-Wesley: Boston, 2003), 9.

36. Crowley and Hawhee, *Ancient Rhetoric,* 9.

37. hooks, *Teaching to Transgress,* 31.

38. Lynn Z. Bloom, "Freshman Composition as a Middle-Class Enterprise." *College English* 58, no. 6 (October 1996): 659.

39. Bloom, "Freshman English," 659.

40. Mary Louise Pratt, "Arts of the Contact Zone," in *Ways of Reading,* ed. David Bartholomae and Anthony Petrosky (Bedford: New York, 2001), 581–595.

41. Audre Lorde, "The Uses of Anger," in *Sister Outsider: Essays and Speeches* (Santa Cruz: Crossing, 1984), 124.

42. Lorde, "Uses of Anger," 124.

43. Lorde, "Uses of Anger," 125.

44. Pratt, "Arts of the Contact Zone," 509.

45. E. D. Hirsch, Joseph F. Kett, and James S. Trefil, *Cultural Literacy: What Every American Needs to Know* (New York: Vintage Books, 1988), 21.

46. Hirsch, et al. *Cultural Literacy,* 22.

Chapter 6

Circulating Counterpublic Rhetoric

He who sets the terms, sets the limits.

—Scott Lyons[1]

The contemporary emphasis on linguistic conformity to the dominant ethnic of this new twentieth-century American aristocracy has the same objective as the old: to make the rising plebeian outsiders talk and thereby think and act like the ruling-class insiders.

—Geneva Smitherman-Donaldson[2]

One of the most poignant stories I know about the uplifting power of counterpublic rhetoric and the depressing consequences of trying to use that rhetoric to talk back to the world is the story that June Jordan recounts in "Nobody Mean More to Me than You and the Future Life of Willie Jordan." Stories like this motivate me to figure out how counterpublics might surmount the barriers of trying to communicate their public identity through traditional media. In this chapter, I consider how some counterpublics have been able to break through the barrier that confronted the once-jubilant students in Jordan's story.

June Jordan points out that no single, uniform kind of English prevails; English is spoken in different ways all across the world. Nevertheless, she notes, people think of Black English[3] not as one of these many Englishes but as a "linguistic buffalo." Right from the start, in the first paragraph of her essay, she wants to rescue it from this position:

Black English is not a linguistic buffalo, but we should understand its status as an endangered species, as a perishing, irreplaceable system of community intelligence,

161

or we should expect its extinction, and along with that, the extinguishing of much that constitutes our own proud, and singular, identity.[4]

She then explains how hard it is to carry through with this rescue.

Jordan's story began as she taught a literature course called "In Search of the Invisible Black Woman." Her students were predominantly young Black women and men. On the day that they started discussing Alice Walker's *The Color Purple,* she was surprised at a "tense, resistant feeling in the room."[5] She probed. A student said "Why did she have them talk so funny. It don't sound right." Another added, "It don't look right neither. I couldn't hardly read it."[6] Jordan observed, but did not point out to them, that the students used the same Black English that they were resisting in the book. She observed, but did not point out, how they rejected the language that they used to understand the world. She proposed an exercise: she wrote the first lines of *The Color Purple* on the board and asked the class to translate them into Standard English. In the process, the students realized that Walker knew what she was doing: the Black English conveyed particular ideas, relationships, and context that could not be translated into the standard form. The process of translation was both fun and eye-opening, and soon students wanted to understand both their own, initial negative reactions and more about this way of talking that they had dismissed: what was Black English? Could they learn to value it, in the same way that they had been taught all these years to value Standard English?

The bulk of Jordan's essay traces out their discoveries about the logical grammar and syntax of Black English and their analysis of the larger social values that it conveyed. She lists three main qualities they propose: (1) that because it arises from a culture that has been threatened by annihilation or assimilation, Black English "abhors all abstraction or anything tending to obscure or delete the fact of the human being who is here and now," (2) that "a primary consequence of the person-centered values of Black English is the delivery of voice," and (3) that "one main benefit following from the person-centered values of Black English is that of *clarity*" (her italics).[7] Jordan shares some excerpts of students' literary analyses, written in Black English, of Black authors. Through this process of reflecting on the language, they rescued it from their former distaste and came to see Black English as something meaningful, something that conveyed their beliefs and values in a way that Standard English did not. They came to see Black English as a language of resistance and affirmation, a way to hold onto something that the larger culture did not understand or respect.

A second narrative is woven into this exuberant story of linguistic discovery. Jordan supervises one of the young Black men in this boisterous class, Willie Jordan, as he takes on an Independent Study. Jordan describes Willie

Jordan as serious, committed, both gentle and tough. Half way through the semester, Willie Jordan disappears. What has happened? When she finally convinces him to come by and see her, she learns:

> Brooklyn police had murdered his unarmed, twenty-five-year-old brother, Reggie Jordan. Neither Willie nor his elderly parents knew what to do about it. Nobody from the press was interested. His folks had no money. Police ran his family round and around, to no point. And Reggie was really dead. And Willie wanted to fight, but he felt helpless.[8]

June Jordan secures legal counsel and pursues other avenues; she calls newspapers herself with little result. With Willie's permission, she enlists the students from the literature-turned-Black English-class to help. The other students in the class had experienced police brutality or knew people who had; Reggie Jordan's death was neither abstract nor unusual, and they "wanted to do everything at once to avenge death."[9]

Given what they had already discovered in the course, their choices of action now were completely bound up in their new understanding of the rhetorical and cultural meanings of Black English. They decide to write letters of condolence to Willie Jordan and his family, in Black English. They decided to write letters to the police, in Black English. And they decided to write letters to the editors of all the local publications they could imagine, in Black English. The letters would be prefaced by an explanatory note. She explains,

> Now we had to make more tactical decisions. Because we wanted the messages published, and because we thought it imperative that our outrage be known by the police, the tactical question was this: Should the opening, group paragraph be written in Black English or Standard English?[10]

This decision was excruciating, painful, as it embodied all they had come to feel about the struggles over language. Jordan writes:

> I have seldom been privy to a discussion with so much heart at the dead heat of it. I will never forget the eloquence, the sudden haltings of speech, the fierce struggle against tears, the furious throwaway, and the useless explosions this question elicited.[11]

She traces out different sides of the debate for a paragraph; in the end, the students choose to write the paragraph in Black English.

> It was heartbreaking to proceed from that point. Everyone in the room realized that our decision in favor of Black English had doomed our writings, even as the

distinctive reality of our Black lives always has doomed our efforts to 'be who we been' in this country. [12]

In the final pages of her piece, Jordan shares the paragraph the class jointly wrote to preface the letters. No local papers or TV stations picked up the story or printed the letters. The article concludes with a short essay (written in Standard English) in which Willie Jordan sums up his experiences and his painful understanding of racism.

The story of Willie Jordan and the class's devotion to him, their desire to support him and rally around him, and their painful choice about what language best conveys their unwavering commitment to him and his family—the story moves me each time I read it and tell it. I offer it here as an example of that great challenge for counterpublics—how to speak publicly through media that do not recognize one's rhetoric as an option for "proper" public engagement.

I recognize that June Jordan's full-out embrace of Black English as a core embodiment of Black culture and resistance is not shared by all African Americans, even among those who value Black English. Some of the claims she makes seem almost essentialist, grouping all Blacks together and suggesting that those who do not speak Black English do not share those experiences. I recognize that there is no singular African American public. Just as is true for the broader American public, subpublics within the African American community struggle to define what it means to be "really" African American or "really" Black. Nevertheless, what I find valuable about this story is that is demonstrates how one Black public— the public that this class experiences—understands its identity as fully intertwined with a way of speaking. And this public encounters that all-too-common moment when their way of experiencing and speaking the world runs headlong into the wall of the idealized public sphere, which refuses to engage.

It's not an uncommon story. Indeed, Geneva Smitherman-Donaldson explains that when she first pitched her book, *Talkin and Testifyin,* her publishers wanted her to revise the passages where she had used nonstandard English. Her book, mind you, is an explicit academic analysis of Black English. It traces the origins in West African languages and explicates many of the cultural values embedded in the grammar and delivery. Throughout the book, Smitherman changes it up, switching between more academic, Standard prose and Black English. Her point is that she can make the same intellectually astute observations in Black English and, in the process, affirm an alternative discourse, with all its stylistic ideologies. But even writing on *this* topic, she had to fight to use Black English. She had to fight to claim that her audience would include people who used Black English themselves and others who would value the specific invocation of a multilingual audience. The gatekeepers of academic and general circulation continue to reinforce a more monolithic concept of the "American public."

Smitherman won her fight, but the students in Jordan's class did not. What alternatives did they have? What methods have counterpublics used to goad the traditional media to engage—to cover a story, to forward a way of thinking and talking about the world, to suggest modes of public action beyond the deliberative one most engrained in traditional media?

I offer four case studies in this chapter to illustrate how counterpublics maneuver with and against traditional journalism. The first three examples involve tactics employed by alternative papers that advocate around issues of homelessness. The fourth and more extensive example looks at the global convergence for fair trade capitalism (sometimes called anti-capitalists or anti-globalization protestors). These groups come together to protest global monetary institutions, like the World Bank and the International Monetary Fund.

In two of these examples, alternative newspapers leverage the ideals of traditional journalism to create space for their discourse. These examples show how a public works within the logic of the traditional media—whether or not they agree with that logic. These are tactical moves of groups that are outside of systems of power. *Spare Change,* in Boston, does this in fairly common ways: through boycotts, street protests, and press releases, the street newspaper appeals to mainstream journalists' desire to reflect back to their public the issues that are relevant and significant to at least part of that public. In the second case study, the alternative newspaper *Hospitality* goads the *Atlanta Journal-Constitution* with accusations of bias, charging that the mainstream paper distorted the facts about the public benefit of urban development. In both cases, the targeted mainstream journalists agree to cover the events. Yet the case studies are not simple moments of success: they reveal how a combination of persistence and serendipity must be in place for such tactics to work.

The third case study investigates how street newspapers challenge "public" interactions at a more material level. Street newspapers are written about issues of poverty and homelessness; many of the articles are written by homeless men and women, and the newspaper is distributed through homeless street vendors. In addition to providing coverage of an issue that it believes is regularly overlooked by the national press, the street newspaper co-opts the market economy of commodified street space when homeless vendors sell the paper. Thus, the street paper works against dominant discourses not only by providing an alternative paper, but also by intervening materially into people's experience of public space and homelessness. Again, this tactic does not obviously undercut the dominant discourse. It works with, rather than against, the capitalist appropriation of public space. However, it does so for the purpose of interjecting a counter-discourse that makes visible the negative consequences of capitalism—those who are left on the streets despite the supposedly benevolent economic system.

Finally, I consider the moves of a global, fair-trade counterpublic. During the April 16, 2000, DC protests of the IMF/World Bank (called A-16 by those involved), protestors practiced their own anarchist decision making to counter what they see as the flawed democratic structures of the international monetary organizations. They also took over and reconfigured the public space around the meetings, talking back not only through the usual avenues of press releases and websites, but also through their on-the-ground reclamations. I spend some time on this case study, because it is a counterpublic with many layers. The convergence was organized online, and across many countries, which allows me to tease out these layers as they evolved in the planning of the event, during the event, and in the reflections offered after the event. In the end, the A-16 Convergence is a productive place to see how counterpublics enact their democratic ideals.

CIRCULATING COUNTERPUBLIC RHETORIC: THE ALTERNATIVE PRESS

I consider the methods that I recount here not as "strategies" but as "tactics." In *Tactics of Hope,* Paula Mathieu draws on Michael de Certeau's terminology to talk about relationships of power. "Strategies" are actions tied to stable organizations—in this case the news industry. Strategies are the "proper" workings of those organizations, activities that bolster the discursive and material structures of that institution.

> [De Certeau] describes *strategies* as calculated actions that emanate from and depend upon 'proper' (as in 'propertied') spaces, like corporations, state agencies, and educational institutions, and relate to others via this proper space. . . . The goal of strategy is to create a stable, spatial nexus that allows for the definition of practices and knowledge that minimize temporal uncertainty. Strategic thinking accounts for and relies on measurability and rationality.[13]

Extending this argument, the strategies of the news industry are those discursive and material actions that reinforce its role as the mediator of the public sphere. When editors imagine their "publics" and design their news coverage to reflect and mediate those publics, they seek to maintain a stable, ongoing space for public circulation. They also make it clear which publics this value system has acknowledged, which publics already have access to this means of circulation.

As Michael Warner notes, those subpublics that see themselves fully aligned with the dominant idea see no contradiction; instead, they reaffirm the overlap as evidence of their rightful role in speaking as "the public."[14] Subpublics enter into cross-public space with little tolerance for deviations from the conversational model. Clashing subpublics often try to dismiss each other for falling short of "real" public interaction. "Real" public engagement, they suggest, means bracketing difference to engage in rational-critical discourse for the purpose of figuring out how to pressure the state toward some common good.

But publics that are outside of this power system—who don't have ready access and who resist the assumptions about "the public" that undergird this system—use alternative ways to interject themselves. "Tactics," Mathieu explains, "are available when we do not control the space."[15] Again, she quotes de Certeau:

> The place of a tactic belongs to the other. A tactic insinuates itself into the other's place, fragmentarily, without taking it over in its entirety, without being able to keep it at a distance. It has at its disposal no base where it can capitalize on its advantages, prepare its expansions, and secure independence with respect to circumstances. The "proper" is a victory of place over time. On the contrary, since it does not have a place, tactic depends on time—it is always on the watch for opportunities that must be seized.[16]

If newsmakers have not included them or cannot find ways to include them without marking them as outside "the public," then subpublics and counterpublics need to look for opportunities. Recognizing that they don't have the power in any single instance to overturn the ideals of the dominant public sphere, they nevertheless find moments to spring forward and shake up that structure, often using the very values of that structure to demand momentary entrance.

One tactic is to emphasize those areas of overlap and to follow as much as possible the dominant rules. For example, those who share a more critical perspective of dispassionate, disembodied "rational discourse" may nevertheless affirm a commitment to working things out through deliberation. As we have seen, Supreme Court Judge Sotomayor can speak eloquently to the question of how one's lived experience affects what facts are noticed or understood as salient—she could have advanced a critique of disembodied rationalism. However, she and her advisors in the nomination process chose instead to highlight her commitment to judging "rationally" based on the "facts of the case." She downplayed her Latina identity; she played up her identity as a rational-critical lawyer. I have no doubt that many people find the earlier epistemological argument she made to be a compelling and more accurate understanding of how publics work. Yet to promote such views in the nomination hearing, Sotomayor would have been challenging the state-sanctioned vision of deliberative democracy that permeated the Senate hearings as well as the vision that permeates the national media that covered the hearings. The safer route was to downplay the epistemological differences.

What options are there when a public does not espouse either the dominant ideal's orientation to the state or its emphasis on conversational rationalism? Warner explores such counterpublics:

> Counterpublics tend to be those in which this ideology of reading does not have the same privilege. It might be that embodied sociability is too important to them; they may not be organized by the hierarchy of faculties that elevates rational-critical reflection as the self-image of humanity; they might depend more heavily on performance spaces than on print.[17]

In rejecting these components of the dominant public ideal, counter-publics also lose access to the most prevalent forms of circulation—the national media, government and civic forums, and so on. To examine the rhetoric of interactions across publics, we must consider not only the democratic vision that a public may hold but also the tactical moves that publics may deploy within a context that refuses to recognize the forms of interaction most aligned with their perspective. Such a view helps explain why public conversations regularly become meta-conversations about the rhetorical choices that a speaker or group has made. When interlocutors come up against a clash in understandings about the rhetoric of democracy—who has a right to speak, what can count as evidence, and how such material should be presented—the response, more often than not, is to berate the "offender" for not speaking or behaving "properly" in public space. The publics then maneuver to control the definitions of "proper" speech.

The Ideal of the Comprehensive Public: Goading for Inclusiveness

In *Rules for Radicals,* the deliberately outrageous community organizer Saul Alinsky offered some key tactics for public maneuvering. He argued that the best way to force another party to react is to hold them accountable to the standards they themselves have set, exposing the gap between what they say and what they do. "Make the enemy live up to their own book of rules," he wrote in *Rules for Radicals*.[18] Along these lines, one tactic that subpublics and counterpublics can use is to hold the news media to the idealized standards of the idealized, singular public sphere (even while understanding that those standards are impossible).

Consider the news values that I discussed in chapter 4:

Newspapers should provide a comprehensive image of "the public," by writing about a variety of issues, each of which is relevant and significant to at least part of that public. In this way, the news media reflects the different parts of a public back to itself.

The public image that is reflected should be described accurately; journalists need to do everything they can to avoid affiliations with one part of the public (particularly a part of the public that the news is charged to 'watch'). If they do have affiliations, they need to be transparent about them.

Publics can work through disagreements through rational deliberation; the newspaper is a forum for that exchange. This assumption privileges discourse over other kinds of social interventions (such as non-rational discourse or physical changes in material space).

Street newspapers appear to operate within the paradigm of traditional journalism, but their very presence and business model suggests a fundamental critique of the middle-class myopia of traditional news outlets. Extending my analysis of counterpublic epistemologies from the previous chapter, I'll lay out quickly some of the discursive tactics that street papers use to present an alternative public ideal. But my main concern in this section is about circulation. Most street newspapers are small and local; their circulation is in the thousands even within cities of millions. What tactics does a nonprofit like a street newspaper use to make the mainstream media pick up and circulate their discourse?

According to the North American Street Newspaper Association, "A street newspaper is a newspaper that primarily addresses issues related to poverty and homelessness and is distributed by poor or homeless vendors."[19] The articles in a street newspaper identify and explain events, legislature, and spaces that affect those living in poverty. The vendors who sell the paper pay a small amount for a bundle of papers, which they then sell for a small profit. *Spare Change* uses this model in Boston. In Washington, DC, the street newspaper is *Street Sense,* in Chicago *StreetWise.* Vendors for the paper stake out areas by train stations and well-traveled sidewalks to sell their papers. They are a consistent presence and often have regular clients, who strike up conversations.

In the same way that the National Coalition for the Homeless reinforces the idea that people's sense of identity and lived experiences are valuable for meaning-making and deliberation, street newspapers assure that the experiences and perspectives of homeless men and women are taken seriously. There is a tension within street newspapers, though, about the best tactic for approaching the dominant, middle-class public that usually writes off homelessness and issues of poverty as not relevant to the public that they imagine.

In *Tactics of Hope,* Paula Mathieu argues that the acts of writing and intervening in public life through street newspapers are crucial activities that allow those who are homeless to find a way to talk back to a public that regularly renders them invisible. Moreover, she points out, these authors found their voice in the paper because other, more conventional venues had closed down for them: "When individual efforts at finding employment, housing, or another form of justice proved unsuccessful, writers turned to public writing out of frustration or a desire for social change."[20] She describes articles from Chicago's *StreetWise* in which vendors testify about their lives, in the hopes that readers will see the authors differently.

Within DC's *Street Sense* and on their website, homeless and poor people are consistently characterized as "regular" people who work hard to end their homelessness. The vendors identify as among those homeless people whom Peter Marin called reluctantly homeless, working to find a way back into housing, employment, and "normal" social circumstances. Vendors are regularly profiled on the back page of the paper, with a photo and responses to ordinary questions about their favorite movies or books. They are quoted on the website as setting New Year's resolutions to find housing, overcome addictions, and reconnect with family. Through both the writing and their work as vendors, street newspapers provide a way for homeless men and women to challenge some stereotypes—they are not lazy or anti-social; they are entrepreneurial and working to engage with society.

Even within this space that seeks to give a positive voice to those who have been pushed aside, the pervasive and controlling power of the dominant public is always present. As Mathieu notes, it creates a paradox for homeless writers. While they see themselves as experts who have something to say, as people who can and want to speak about their experiences being homeless in order to move others to action, some do not want to have a public identity as a homeless person. Some of the writers Mathieu worked with did not allow their faces on television or their names in an anthology because they did not want their families to know of their affiliation with a street paper.[21] These positions provide a double critique of the supposed neutrality and equality within the idealized public sphere: the homeless authors recognize the stigma that comes from their position. Even as they understand the need to draw on their insider perspectives in order to fight back against prejudices and unfair social practices, they recognize the consequences of stepping into that role publicly.

Street newspapers support homeless people who want to make their voices heard; they operate in a complicated space, as a public that wishes both to critique the narrow-mindedness of the dominant public while also securing a less hostile relationship with that public. To circulate their perspective, they not only have their own publications, they also have access to the many tactics of media intervention available to other, non-journalistic groups: protests.

We can see how a street newspaper uses both its own circulation and public protest in an account about the Boston street newspaper *Spare Change*, which Paula Mathieu and Diana George describe in their article "Not Going It Alone: Public Writing, Independent Media, and the Circulation of Homeless Advocacy." Through their actions, *Spare Change* forced cable companies, mainstream papers, and public officials to carry a story about an event that affected a marginalized group, homeless people. The process *Spare Change* used is probably the most common and most familiar; it draws on the news industry's need to be seen as accurately reflecting back the interests and concerns of "the public." Those who want to be included in the coverage, then, have to call enough attention to themselves that the media must attend to them, lest they be accused of ignoring something that the public cares about. This happens in two ways. One way is through the journalistic element of providing a comprehensive public forum. A reporter or editor becomes convinced that enough potential readers have seen or heard about the issue that they will expect it to be covered, that they will turn to the paper for a fuller understanding of an event they already know about. A second option draws on the journalistic element of monitoring power and offering a voice to the voiceless: the reporter or editor becomes convinced that the reason people are not hearing about something important to the public is because another public has worked to silence that perspective. The media then steps in to correct the problem by providing access to the voice of the silenced group. To activate either of these journalistic values, publics go through traditional channels—sending out press releases, contacting reporters directly, and staging events that the media might like to cover.

Mathieu and George explain that the Board of *Spare Change* sought to prevent the independent record chain Newbury Comics from selling what are called "Bumfight videos."[22] In these graphic videos, the videographer pays a homeless person to commit a crime or physically harm himself; the videographer then records this event, produces a video, and sells it. Some of the "actors" have come forward to say that their participation in the videos was coerced. Furthermore, homeless people and their advocates argue that such videos exacerbate a hostile environment and lead to an increase in hate crimes against homeless men and women. Mathieu and George document that *Bumfights* and *Bumhunters,* videos produced in Las Vegas by three college students, have sold over 300,000 copies on the Internet. In fall 2003, Newbury Comics was also selling copies in Boston.

Spare Change began a campaign to convince the store to stop selling the videos: they wanted to interrupt at least one avenue of circulation for the videos. To do this, they needed to make public pressure weigh heavily on Newbury Comics. And yet, because they needed to operate within the value system of the idealized public sphere, they had to find arguments that did not contradict the value of the free exchange of ideas and perspectives. To do so, as Mathieu and George point out, *Spare Change* framed the boycott around the issue of coercion. They wrote an open letter to the store explaining, "Our problem with *Bumfights* is the coercive tactics the producers used to entice the homeless men to act in the film. . . . [T]he issue here is not one of offensive content but of *coerced consent*. . . . Pulling this video will not be an act of censorship, but a bold move to say no to the exploitation of homeless people."[23] Tactically, this frame is directed more toward the larger goal of encouraging the boycott itself rather than the goal of getting media coverage: if there were big enough drama, the media would cover a story about censorship. But the frame of censorship would position the store as the entity reinforcing an ideal of "free speech" and the unfettered access of all groups to circulate even distasteful materials. *Spare Change* needed not only to secure media attention, but also to shape the story in a manner that would highlight their concerns about exploitation.

To get the word out, the nonprofit wrote "articles in the 9,000-circulation fortnightly newspaper, press releases [to Boston's mainstream media publications], small leaflets handed out to passersby on the sidewalk in front of key Newbury Comics stores, slogans for posters, and a website."[24] They kept this up for five weeks, including through the Christmas holiday season.

From this activity, the story was picked up by other small, alternative presses in Boston, and then a small mention appeared in the *Globe;* the issue also surfaced in local Boston blogs. This attention, while welcome, was not enough to pressure the store. Presumably, they were not yet convinced that they should abandon either the profit they earned from selling the videos or the principle of letting the market (not picketers) decide what to sell.

The most effective coverage came about rather serendipitously. The wife of a cable news reporter brought home a press release after working at a local homeless shelter, and the reporter took an interest. He interviewed a vendor who had experienced hate crimes as well as the volunteer at *Spare Change* who spearheaded the boycott. He contacted the manager of Newbury Comics and scheduled an interview. But before he conducted the interview, the manager called and agreed to stop selling *Bumfight* videos; he said he made his decision "in response to the media circus."[25]

The *Spare Change* example illustrates not only the kind of networking that is necessary to garner mainstream-media attention and pressure but also the randomness of such attention. Mathieu and George note:

> The circulation of the public writing in this case relied on a network of relationships among advocacy groups, people meeting on the streets, and mainstream media, as well as a certain degree of serendipity: had the television reporter not felt a personal connection to the issue of homelessness, the boycott may have ended differently.[26]

The example illustrates the wide range of rhetorical abilities that publics need to deploy to be heard—articles, press releases, catchy posters and flyers for boycotters to distribute, slogans to chant, and so on. It helps make Mathieu and George's main point: that publics don't "go it alone" to create change. Rather, change requires a coordination among different publics and different venues—the newspaper shelters, the other organizations that distributed press releases, the bloggers who spread the story online, the people who stood outside the store for weeks, the volunteers at shelters who carried the message out. Moreover, the story reinforces the point that so much lies in the question of up-take: had the cable news reporter not seen the story as worthy of public attention, all could have fizzled out with no effect on the store. I have to wonder, too, how the reporter's wife's role as a volunteer helped to facilitate the reporter's ability and willingness to give voice to the homeless vendors and activists, to provide room in the story for their ways of thinking and talking about the issue, rather than framing the story around "censorship" discourse, the alternative frame that *Spare Change* itself acknowledges was available.

Through all of these means (and some serendipity), the protest organizers were able to navigate their way into broader coverage by successfully convincing a reporter that their concerns were linked to those of a broader group of people. The message of the public was "run up the flagpole" through the cable media because the reporter (and his editor) believed that their perspective would be hailed and shared by others, as both an involved and an interested public, and that the viewers would agree that this event was significant in "the public" of which they were a part.

The Ideal of Non-Affiliation: Goading about Bias

Sometimes, though, reporters are less receptive to circulating a public's perspective. In this case, an alternative strategy can be used to publicly call the newspaper out on their neglect—critiquing the paper for not living up to the "public" ideal of including all voices fairly in "the public conversation." This is the method that the alternative paper *Hospitality* used to goad the *Atlantic Journal-Constitution* into circulating their critique of a downtown parks development project, an interaction that Mathieu and George also analyze in their article. *Hospitality* is published by the Open Door Community and operates in the tradition of papers like *Masses* and *Catholic Worker,* which is to say, it was created with the purpose of providing a radical counterpoint to dominant discourse.[27] Mathieu and George examine how Murphy Davis, the founder of Open Door, used *Hospitality* to "[force] city officials to deal directly with advocates for the homeless at each stage of their plans for what the city represents as 'improving' the downtown."[28]

The strategy Davis used was to publicly accuse the *Atlanta Journal-Constitution* of falling short of their public responsibilities because of their "near-sightedness." The opening lobby in this exchange was a front-page article in *Hospitality* in which an article from the *Journal-Constitution* is pasted in the center of the page, with Davis' critique surrounding it. The *Journal-Constitution* article, "A Make-over in Woodruff," describes a parks renovation in downtown Atlanta in generally favorable terms. Yet the article betrays what Davis sees as the real reason for the renovation—to remove homeless people from the park. The slippage is shown in several quotes which speak disparagingly of homeless people as "the winos." While the *Journal-Constitution* lauds the development as benefiting Atlanta, Davis argues that the "policy of removal" is part of a long history through which the government has removed people they found undesirable.[29] As such, Davis links this development to a discourse of radical critique, sounding back to the 1950 urban renewal projects across the nation. Then, the slogan "Urban Renewal is Negro Removal" rallied many African Americans to challenge how urban planners defined the "public good." This rhetorical connection, along with her title—"Woodruff Park and the Search for Common Ground"—pins the *Journal-Constitution* against the journalistic value of creating and managing an inclusive public forum, one where all groups have equal access to deliberate about the definition of "public good" and the uses of "public space."

This article stands in as one of many moments where *Hospitality* challenged not only how developers, public servants, and police officers defined "public good" but also how the *Journal-Constitution* uncritically circulated those perspectives. What made *Hospitality* a powerful voice in this exchange is that Davis goaded the *Journal-Constitution* into responding. A columnist for the *Journal-Constitution,* Colin Campbell, wrote dismissively of Open Door's work. Unlike the *Spare Change* example, the mainstream news source did not frame the issue in the way that the homeless advocates would have—in his column Campbell was anything but receptive to their critique. But, as Mathieu and George note, he did "name the paper [*Hospitality*] and the organization [Open Door] several times in this paper," and as a result, the arguments made in *Hospitality* were noticed. Open Door was able to use the mainstream press to forward their view—that the development was "a story about poverty, race, and the politics of public space."[30] *Hospitality* used the *Journal-Constitution* "to let the public know that oppositional voices do exist, to effect change."[31]

Street Sense: The Relational Circulation in Commodified Space

If *Hospitality* relied on a tactic of forcing a mainstream paper to defend its "proper" role in providing a forum for discursive exchange, street newspapers as a whole work to both reinforce this ideal of discursive exchange and to create change at another, more material level—by working with and against the ideals of public street space.

As I discussed above, the discursive interventions of street newspapers play out the familiar arguments I have made about asserting epistemological expertise, and they rely also on the journalistic value of interjecting more voices into the broader public conversation. Street newspapers work to correct an absence that they see within mainstream papers, which circulate an image of a middle-class public, while pretending to represent everyone. Yet what is perhaps more interesting is the way that the street newspaper model intervenes in public discourse about homelessness through a more material approach.

The business model of the street paper requires an interaction between vendor and buyer that gives a particular structure to public space. As John, Penny, and Steve explained in their presentations with the National Coalition for the Homeless Speakers' Bureau that I described in chapter 5, when people live on the street, they are often overlooked and made to feel invisible. Their purpose on the street is ambiguous; they are not consumers going in and out of stores or workers traveling to an office; they are not outside exercising or walking the streets as tourists. Instead, they occupy an ambiguous role in public space, a role that most people don't know how to engage.

Don Mitchell, in an analysis of the transformation of People's Park in Berkeley from a place where homeless people gathered into a university-regulated recreation area, explains that homelessness pinpoints a central contradiction in ideals of democracy.

> The contradiction turns on publicity: the homeless are all too visible. Although homeless people are nearly always in public, they are rarely counted as part of *the* public. Homeless people are in a double bind. For them, socially legitimated private space does not exist, and they are denied access to public space and public activity by capitalist society which is anchored in private property and privacy. For those who are *always* in the public, private activities must

necessarily be carried out publicly. When public space thus becomes a place of seemingly illegitimate behavior, our notions of what public space is supposed to be are thrown into doubt. . . . [S]ince citizenship in modern democracy (at least ideologically) rests on the foundation of *voluntary* association, and since homeless people are *involuntarily* public, homeless people cannot be, by definition, legitimate citizens.[32]

Mitchell argues that the presence of homeless people in public space—especially public parks—challenges the conventional ideologies of what public space should be. He notes that the fight in Berkeley pitted visions of "open space," "commodified public space," and "recreational space" against the vision that the homeless advocates themselves put forward, that of a space where different publics mingled and met, where differences would be worked out at a speaker's platform. In contrast, "commodified public space" is a restructuring of public space into a site to promote commerce, where images of harmonious diversity are encouraged and images that would disturb a sense of order and comfort are removed. Especially in the public parks and streets of urban settings, Mitchell writes, the homeless are seen as "something of an 'indicator species' to much of society, diagnostic of the presumed ill-health of public space, and the need to gain control, to privatize, and to rationalize public spaces in urban places."[33] In an argument parallel to Davis' critique of the news coverage in Atlanta, Mitchell notes that the press that covers such interventions against homeless people "pointedly ignore any 'public' standing that homeless people may have, just as they ignore the possibility that homeless people's usage of a park for political, social, economic, and residential purposes may constitute for them legitimate and necessary uses of public space."[34] He argues that the mainstream press reinforces a dominant and capitalist view of public space.

Within cities, the normative structures of public space isolate homeless people. But by developing a business model through which homeless people serve as vendors, street newspapers refuse to leave them invisible or treat them as signs of a contagious disorder. They give homeless men and women the recognized public role of a salesperson. Once again, the rules of interaction become clear; homeless people turned vendors become visible and approachable; they can again find some social connections.

Adopting this purpose in public space admittedly does not change the experience of public space itself. The vendor sale itself reinforces the idea that the proper use of public space is for commerce. The interaction does not make the streets more hospitable to non-vendor homeless, except that in coming to know one vendor, a person may grow more tolerant toward other homeless people, and in reading the paper, one may grow more aware of the structures that exclude homeless people from public interactions. The vendor role could be seen as a way for some homeless people to gain re-entry into the dominant definition of space, or it could be seen as a tactical point of entry, acquiescing the moment of contact in order to develop a long-term relationship that might change the ideals of public space for the broader group of homeless people.

Street newspapers seem to operate in a middle ground of sorts. The newspaper does not pretend toward neutrality: it marshals its journalism and business model to advocate for homeless men and women. At the same time, it follows journalistic ethics, researching stories according to standard guidelines. The paper pursues stories that will highlight the needs of people living in poverty. In some ways the paper is similar to *Harper's:* It seeks to educate people about a part of the population they may be unfamiliar with; it wants to help them look differently at everyday events and to understand their impact on vulnerable people. On the other hand, it is unapologetic about putting the voices of homeless men and women in the center of the paper, stressing that such voices are regularly absent from the supposedly accessible "public sphere." By highlighting their expertise and by choosing alternate modes of circulation, street newspapers challenge the commonplace assumptions that the mainstream media can stand in effectively for public deliberation.

AN (EXTENDED) EXAMPLE OF COUNTERPUBLIC RHETORIC: GLOBAL PROTEST RHETORIC

My final example of counterpublic rhetoric focuses on the protests that took place the weekend of April 16, 2000 (which organizers abbreviated A-16), when tens of thousands of international protestors converged in Washington, DC, to disrupt the annual meeting of the International Monetary Fund and World Bank. The protests are a site ripe for investigating the ways publics mobilize around discourses of morality, benevolence, and violence, and how these concepts inform counterpublics. Moreover, the protestors deployed many rhetorical moves that work outside the usual frameworks of "conversation" and "deliberation."

The traditional media and the idealized public sphere work with the idea that "public opinion" rises through ongoing discussion: this model explains both the democracy they strive for and the democracy they imagine as currently in place. For the protestors, though, the world as it is, is radically different from the world as it should be, and their tactics reflect this. They challenged the international financial organizations and the media by interfering with their everyday actions, trying to expose the hypocrisy in that model. At one level, they worked like the boycotters of Newbury Comics, trying to get the (international) mass media to acknowledge that part of the public out there does not see capitalism as benevolent or ideal. The size of the protests and their activities had to be dramatic enough to force the news industry to cover the event. At the same time, the protestors did not want to spread the idea that capitalist institutions like the media or the monetary associations could *ever* stand in for the voices that they saw being trampled by capitalism. Nor did they want to spread the idea that capitalism could be challenged through the kind of rational exchange upon which the idealized public sphere rests. The mode of protest, then, had to resist any easy appropriation by the discourses of capitalism—a risky venture, since (as was the case in some instances), such counterpublic rhetoric might be incomprehensible to the media.

As many different protest groups came together for this event, they made their decisions through elaborate networks of consensus building, using processes to ensure that a minority was not trampled by the majority and distributing decision-making power extensively through the crowds. Their organizational methods, described in detail in the online materials they posted leading up to A-16 and shared in pre-protests trainings, served as a counterpoint to the dominant, idealized public sphere: they showed us an alternative "world as it should be."

This extended example offers some examples of how counterpublics succeed despite their radical critique of the medium in which their discourse must circulate, but it also offers evidence that the task is impossible. To work through this analysis, I first outline the events of the A-16 weekend. Then, I explore how an emerging rhetoric of grassroots globalization challenges the idealized public sphere that governs supranational organizations. Finally, I consider how to assess whether or not the massive protests were successful in circulating this counterpublic discourse, and what role the traditional news media played in that circulation.

Overview of the A-16 Protests

In November 1999—five months before the events in DC—over thirty-five thousand[35] activists protested the meeting of the World Trade Organization in Seattle, and their sheer numbers and intensity surprised the monetary organizations, the city of Seattle, and the international press. These groups—environmentalists and labor unions alongside international feminist and anti-capitalist groups, among others—came together to call attention to the ways that the financial overseers exacerbate unregulated pollution, sexism, and dangerous working conditions. They came to call attention to the fallout of

WTO/IMF/World Bank policies that force developing countries to privilege exports and debt-repayment over environmental, labor, and health needs of their populations. They targeted the Seattle WTO meeting because the European Union planned to launch the "Millennium Project," an agreement that would formally eliminate the right of nations to privilege local economic development or to impose environmental or labor restrictions as part of WTO investment criteria.

In Seattle, protestors locked arms and disrupted the negotiations. Rioting and vandalism by the notorious, black-clad, self-proclaimed anarchists led to city-wide curfews. The events were covered in the national and international presses. Some studies of the economic impact of the event suggest that stock prices of firms in environmentally abusive industries declined after the protests, confirming organizers' claims that they succeeded in opening WTO policies to public scrutiny. A more immediate effect was optimism among the diverse protest groups that the movement itself was viable and growing. Some organizers quickly identified the IMF/World Bank annual meetings in DC the following April as the next event to target.

The IMF and World Bank host approximately ten thousand guests at their annual meetings. During the April 2000 meeting, thirty-five thousand protestors arrived as well, encouraged by ninety-one organizations from across the world as part of the "April 16 Nonviolent Direct Action and Organizer Convergence."[36] As was true in Seattle, the sponsors, endorsers, and protestors included a diverse range of civil groups, from labor unions to queer activists, indigenous peoples, and mothers of the "disappeared" in South America; they came from all parts of the globe—First World, Third World, Global North, and Global South. The preparation "included three months of international organizing and planning; cross-country caravans; a week of teach-ins, rallies, events; and several police incidents."[37]

Taking a cue from the events in Seattle, DC police vowed that the meetings would not be disrupted. Their numbers were supplemented by the National Guard and local suburban forces. All were outfitted with riot gear; some flew police helicopters; some drove tanks. Police spent upwards of $5 million on overtime and another $1 million on protective gear.

In the days preceding Sunday's main events, the police took steps to minimize the protestors' presence. By Friday, they had erected fences next to the IMF/World Bank headquarters buildings. By Saturday, they had barricaded approximately eighty city blocks. Saturday morning, police raided a warehouse that served as a protestor greeting center and storage facility, and they confiscated giant puppets and literature. Also on Saturday, they arrested approximately six hundred people for "parading without a permit" and took them away on waiting buses. All charges were later dropped.[38]

On Sunday, April 16, protestors engaged in three main activities: a barricade of the IMF/World Bank buildings, marches, and a rally on the Ellipse in front of the White House. Early in the morning, protestors formed a human barricade along the police perimeter fence and blocked intersections within the officially closed streets in an attempt to prevent police-escorted IMF/WB delegates from attending the meetings. Many IMF ministers and delegates slept in the IMF buildings to avoid passing through the barricade; most of the buses made it through the line. Four top ministers, representing Thailand, France, Portugal, and Brazil, were prevented from entering for six hours.

In addition to the barricade, the protestors danced and marched through the area with large puppets and banners as they headed for the rally on the Ellipse. This march was an act of civil disobedience, since the police had not issued parading permits. The atmosphere was playful seriousness, as the puppets mocked the rhetoric of globalization and capitalism. One group carried a fat, pink pig with the slogan "world bank" on the side. Another carried the large, smiling face of "Liberation" looking down on the crowds. Other puppets depicted IMF officials or "corporate evil."

The event on the Ellipse was the only government-sanctioned event, in that the Park Police had issued a permit for the rally. Endorsed by the AFL-CIO and emceed by Michael Moore, the rally drew the largest attendance of all the A-16 events—somewhere between thirty-five thousand (as the newspapers reported) and fifty thousand (as the event organizers reported).

The World as It Is: A16 Critiques of Global Democracy

The A-16 protestors sought to disrupt the annual meetings; on a larger scale, such protestors' goal is to disrupt the rhetoric of free-market global capitalism and the rhetoric of undemocratic supranational institutions. The protests, then, are not about only IMF/World Bank, WTO, G-7, and other sites of international financial decision making; they critique traditional models for decision making and envision new ones. For one thing, the protestors reject the dominant rhetoric of benevolent capitalism, in which capitalism is not seen as a separate and distinct entity vying to control public deliberation but instead is said to operate as a neutral structure that facilitates public deliberation. The international organizations that the fair trade and democratic globalization protestors target are sites where this benevolent capitalist rhetoric is perpetuated.

International organizations such as the IMF, World Bank, and WTO operate at the nexus where modern nation-states meet the globalized free market. And there, the very concept of the nation-state clashes against the logic of global capitalism. Nation-states secure social legitimacy by maintaining internal law and order, by securing their borders, and (in democratic states) through participation that binds citizens to each other. In contrast, as Jürgen Habermas notes in his 1998 assessment of the European democracy, market economies "obey a logic that escapes state control."[39]

In early modernism, the nation-state could exert control over national economies through welfare and social policies, through environmental and monopoly regulation, as well as through tariffs and other measures; taxes levied on the corporations helped to fund these measures. Within such a context, the economic dynamic of the market reinforced the modern nation-state. The current trend in free-market globalization, however, has severed this relationship, since transnational conglomerates cannot be controlled by individual nation-states.

Responses to this new relation between nation-states and global capitalism are decidedly mixed, and the rhetoric of the different sides draws on fundamentally different beliefs about the relationship between capitalism and democracy. Pro-capitalists claim that capitalism is a benevolent and a necessary (for some, the *only* necessary) precondition for democracy and the enforcement of human rights. Anti-capitalists claim that the demolition of the nation-state has catapulted global society into a frenzy of capitalist competition, the result of which is drastic economic disparity and violation of human rights.

We can hear the rhetoric of capitalist benevolence in the words of Jimmie V. Reyna, a DC international trade attorney who attended the WTO summit meeting in Seattle: "[T]he WTO has done much to expand trade and create economic development. Economic development means jobs. Jobs mean prosperity, and prosperity means a higher level of life for the everyday person."[40] As Rhoda Howard-Hassman explains, promoters of a globalized free market see multinational investment as the "engine of development" that "promotes economic rights through investment and job creation [and promotes] civil and political rights through the creation of a stable and tolerant environment" in which a democratic culture will form.[41] Such a model parallels the rise of democracy in Europe.

Overall, the standards of living—as measured through economic factors—have increased with globalization. Kemal Dervis, administrator of the U.N. Development Program, points out that "the empirical evidence is quite clear: over the last two decades a greater number of people have been able to escape extreme poverty than ever before in human history."[42] However, he is quick to point out that the world is still rife with instability and insecurity, and that conditions of employment can be quite degrading.

Those who do not subscribe to the rhetoric of capitalism do not see an increase of jobs in developing countries necessarily as a "benefit." Whereas free-market advocates assert that capitalism is a precondition for democracy and human rights, many fair trade protestors see the profit motives of capitalism as irrelevant to (and at times counter to) the goals of positive international development—equitable distribution of wealth, ecologically sustainable development, and non-exploitative social relationships. Capitalism, they argue, is structurally designed to exploit some things and people (land and laborers, for example) in order for others (shareholders) to profit. They see the very motivation to spread a free-market economy across the world as a way for corporations to ensure access to cheaper labor and material resources without the profit-inhibiting constraints that nation-states might seek to impose. This is the perspective offered by "Ron Judd, an electrician who heads the King County Labor Council, AFL-CIO, a key sponsor of the anti-WTO events in Seattle. He explains: 'The steelworker from Pittsburgh needs to understand that the exploitation of the steelworker in Indonesia is in neither of their best interest. . . . It takes food off one table, and it doesn't allow the food on the table of the other'."[43]

Ironically, the protestors and financial institutions seem to agree—to a small degree—that free-market capitalism should not be the only force governing international economic issues. The IMF/World Bank and WTO gain their legitimacy as *political* entities set up to direct and regulate a global economy; by their very existence, they counter the logic of pure capitalism. The organizations draw on a rhetoric of international democracy built through consensus and participation. They claim to provide a supranational forum for global, public deliberation. However, the organizations equivocate about the degree to which participating nations are to base their decisions on national concerns or on the logic of free-market capitalism, and the structure of the voting relationships and decision-making process makes it almost impossible for poorer countries to counter the capitalist logic. For many protestors, the organizations seem merely a front to provide apparent political legitimacy to the logic of free-market capitalism; they wish to expose this sham. Yet the concern is deeper than this: even if nation-states were given equal voting rights in this forum, could nations with such inequities of wealth deliberate rationally and arrive at consensus? The conflict over the structure of deliberations in supranational institutions is simultaneously that the current system doesn't meet the ideal it professes and that that ideal is flawed anyway.

Habermas notes in "The European Nation-State: On the Past and Future of Sovereignty and Citizenship" that when economic markets are severed from nations, one potential result is an abdication of politics, a "*postpolitical* world."[44] When nation-states compete against each other like Hobbesian individuals in isolated economic networks, they cease to act as nation-citizens within a broader, supranational forum. And the citizens within those nations fall to the same fate. "The neoliberal inspiration of this Hellenistic vision is all too clear. The autonomy of the citizen is unceremoniously stripped of the moral components of democratic self-determination and pared back to private autonomy."[45] Habermas believes that "the progressive undermining of national sovereignty will necessitate the founding and expansion of political institutions on the supranational level," of which the IMF and World Bank are but two examples.[46]

For the supranational organizations to fulfill the role that Habermas lays out for them, they need to consider issues from a primarily *political* standpoint. Habermas is concerned that such organizations "be connected to processes of democratic will-formation" if the world is to break from the "at present unfettered dynamic of globalized capitalist production."[47]*Political* organizations gain their legitimacy as each member comes "to recognize and appreciate citizen status as that which links her with the other members of the political community and makes her at the same time dependent upon and co-responsible for them."[48] Thus, following from his ideal of the bourgeois public sphere, Habermas argues that politically legitimate supranational organizations require a deliberative process that would create a sense of international citizenship. Does the IMF/World Bank create such political identity among its members?

The IMF purports that its decisions are made primarily by a process of consensus among legitimate state representatives in its annual meetings (where all member countries have voting rights) and in its Executive Board (where twenty-four countries make day-to-day decisions). However, the current structure gives greater power to wealthier nations. The voting power in the IMF and World Bank is linked to members' economic power. The "subscription quota"—the amount a country pays into the fund—is linked with the country's GDP. For voting at the annual meetings, each country receives two hundred fifty points to start and then an additional vote for every 100,000 in its subscription quota. Thus, the United States, for example, pays into the fund in vast amounts and has correspondingly vast voting power. The U.S. subscription is 37,149.3 million, while Tonga has a subscription of 6.9 million. The United States has seventeen percent of the voting power in the organization.

In the Executive Board, decisions pass with 51 percent of the vote. The 24 members of the board include the five largest shareholders (the United States, Japan, Germany, France, and the United Kingdom), which as a group control sixty-three percent of the Board vote. Their voting power is sufficient for the majority of decisions. The remaining 19 countries represent groups of other nations that rotate off the Board every two years. Their combined voting power allows them to veto the "most important decisions, for example, increasing the size of the IMF's resources or determining charges on borrowings from the Fund [which] require a 70% or 85% majority."[49]

Clearly, it is much easier for the wealthier countries to control decisions, a critique that is part of the 1994 Platform of Mobilization for Global Justice. The IMF responds to the concern by claiming its decisions are made through consensus among members:

> Is the IMF dominated by the G-7 (especially the U.S. Treasury)?
> No. It's true that the bulk of the IMF's financial resources are provided by the G-7, but decisions on policy and country matters are made by consensus among IMF shareholders.[50]

Curiously, however, the explanations that follow this statement tend to corroborate the accusation against the IMF. The explanations say that the voting power is shared, but admit that the United States controls a substantial percentage of that voting power. They emphasize that all countries have an equal opportunity to be heard (as if this were the same as equal voting power), and they admit that many decisions are made without a formal vote at all. In response to a question about distributing the voting power more equitably, the IMF explains that the imbalance of voting power is a necessary incentive to keeping the wealthy nations in the institution:

> Some have argued that the IMF's voting structure should be changed to introduce the country's population (instead of its financial contributions) in the formula that determines quotas. Would this provide for truly democratic representation? The problem is that such a system would create an imbalance between the countries' financial contributions to the IMF and their ability to influence IMF policies. This could endanger the IMF's ability to recycle financial resources, and eventually, the creditor countries might not be willing to provide resources to the Fund to lend to countries.[51]

Rather than creating a space for deliberation in which member countries come to see themselves as interdependent and co-responsible members of a larger, global community, such a structure protects the investments of the wealthier countries. The motivation for wealthy countries to participate at all, the IMF seems to admit, is not because they feel a public connection—a sense of an interdependent relationship with other world citizens—but because they want to be able to influence the decisions there.

Another critique about the deliberative process concerns the representatives. Ideally, representatives would present the collective voice of the people in their nations, but critics point out that this is not necessarily the case. "[N]on-democratic States are run by elites who act in their own interests. They are no more likely to protect their citizens' interests against foreign exploiters than they were to protect them against local exploiters."[52] Such was the case in Indonesia, for example, where the citizens bear the burden of debt that Suharto accumulated as personal wealth.[53] The process of representation and the policies in the IMF/World Bank require neither state representatives nor policy designers to consult with the local citizens whom the policies will affect most immediately. Overall, the IMF/World Bank fails to meet Habermas's conditions for a supranational democratic organization, since the structure prohibits the deliberation that would make it legitimate as a political entity.

Even so, fixing the IMF/World Bank's voting formulas or requiring representatives to be elected by their constituents might not be good enough for some of its critics. This is because the IMF/World Bank draws on a model of consensual deliberation that Habermas calls the "liberal model of the bourgeois public sphere" and what I have called the idealized, singular public sphere. We know the elements of this idealized public along with their critiques: people are supposed to be able to bracket differences, but bracketing is not possible. Status differences—in this case, wealth disparities—always influence the negotiation. The gesture to create a level playing field draws on a rhetoric of benevolence: the wealthy nations *appear* generous by considering their poorer counterparts as equals in the neutral public sphere of international deliberation, but they can act generous because the overall structure benefits the wealthy. "In the rhetoric of generosity [and benevolence], the social and economic inequalities of capitalism are not represented."[54]

We can see this best by considering a brief moment when one kind of colonialist exploitation was named and accounted for.

When the U.S. conquered Cuba in 1898 to prevent it from liberating itself from Spain (what is called "the liberation of Cuba from Spanish rule"), it cancelled Cuba's debt to Spain on the reasonable grounds that the debt had been forced on the people of Cuba without their consent. That doctrine, called "odious debt," was later upheld in international arbitration, with U.S. initiative.[55]

The concept of "odious debt" places the responsibility of the debt with the colonial power. Without this acknowledgement, the discussion of "debt" can never truly begin at an equal place. When a wealthy member state sits next to an exploited member state and pronounces the relationship even, that rhetorical move brackets past abuses and exploitation. By accepting a place as "equal," the exploited country allows that the colonialist history need *not* influence current deliberations. The two countries begin their relation with the current imbalance as a given starting point.

But what if that history will *inevitably* influence members' perceptions of logic and reason—what if this influence occurs at a much deeper level than can be rationally identified and set aside? An alternative deliberative model would account for the fact that rationality cannot always supersede ideology; it would assume instead that ideology in its material manifestations always controls rationality and, therefore, would attend to those material conditions.

To consider a rhetorical theory that might account for the power of ideology, one has first to examine some assumptions about rationality and intentionality. Debates about the IMF/World Bank often get unhinged at the question of "intent" when "intent" itself is of interest only when one believes in rational, Enlightenment models of decision-making. Such a model presumes that I can know consciously and intentionally what I believe, and that if I believe something I will act in accordance with those beliefs. Thus, the persuasive strategy is a matter of providing "ignorant" people with the right "facts" and the rest will follow. However, for people who see individual and cultural beliefs as embedded in the material conditions of our lives, the focus is not on *intent* but on *results*.

As I explained when discussing the different axes on the matrix of democracy, a materialist approach to persuasion does not try to account for intents and does not presume that people make choices rationally. Instead, the assumption is that institutional structures and rhetorics of our daily actions drive our beliefs. To create change, then, one disrupts daily activities and changes behaviors. Most importantly, the action must call attention to distortion between what one *says* and what one *does*. Furthermore, a materialist ideology also demands careful self-reflection among groups about the structures of their institutions and whether their daily activities align with the values they profess.

The World as It Should Be: The A-16 Vision of Democratic Participation

The A-16 protests sought a model of democratic participation that would account for the material conditions of belief and offer a broader vision for citizen participation. This goal was embedded in the organizational structure of the April 16 Nonviolent Direct Action and Organizer Convergence. The skepticism about the constraining nature of institutions was apparent within the protest groups. That is, given a distrust that any representative organization can hear and speak for everyone, the protestors used an organizing system that deliberately created space for multiple positions and that highlighted self-determination through active democratic participation.

The coalition operated under a system that empowered each subgroup to act in its own interests. During the weekend, activists worked together as affinity groups, which operate by creating a democratic and safe space for those five to twenty participants who agree to be in the group. According to Mobilization for Global Justice,

> Affinity groups challenge top-down decision-making and organizing, and em- power those involved to take creative direct action. Affinity groups allow people to "be" the action they want to see by giving complete freedom and decision-mak- ing power to the affinity group. Affinity groups by nature are decentralized and non-hierarchical, two important principles of anarchist organizing and action.[56]

Affinity groups empower spokespeople to attend council meetings, where once again the group as a whole must achieve consensus about policies, activities, and so on. The consensus process, it is important to recognize, goes beyond a "majority rules" voting and demands that those involved be fully persuaded of the item under discussion before action can be taken. Each person agrees *only* to the action that he or she is willing to perform. It takes just one person to block the consensus. In this manner, the interactions allow members to bring their particularities into the negotiation; they do not need to bracket them before the conversation, and they cannot be compelled to agree with decisions that have not accounted for those particularities. Thus, each member of an affinity group must engage in an intense process of listening to and persuading others. The decision-making process, while time-consuming and cumbersome, provides a greater legitimacy to the final decision.

As an example of how the affinity groups operated during the protests, consider the interaction that took place Sunday morning on G and 21st Streets. Here protestors blocked an intersection near the IMF building to prohibit police escorts from driving delegates to the meeting. (These roads were already closed to non-police traffic by police roadblocks.) Eleven people occupied the intersection, seated in a large circle. They were locked together using chain-and-pipe "lock box" devices: plastic pipes covered their out- stretched arms; inside the pipes, their wrists were chained to a carbine bolted to the pipe. In the center of the circle, the protestors were chained together with bicycle locks. While these people sat in the road, the other members of their affinity group provided food, water, and otherwise attended to them. Those in the middle had agreed to take the risk of police retaliation and arrest; those who offered water had agreed to a supportive role. While they had coor- dinated with other groups to determine what area of the designated "protest zone" to cover, they were expected to design and carry out their own protests. On the streets, the groups coordinated their actions by creating "spokescoun- cil meetings" with affinity groups nearby. Each group was therefore in charge of its own actions and creating its members' own identities as "non-violent protestors" and was not subject to an overarching definition of "proper action of civil disobedience" that came down from above.[57]

The notion of strategic cooperation runs contrary to a more common vision of social movements where the leaders and members provide a single vision, and followers join based on that vision. Not recognizing this divergent style, the national press at times characterized the A-16 movement disparagingly as lacking consensus—even though the kind of consensus implied in this critique is not something the coalition aspired to and even though, ironically, no action could be taken under the anarchist plan without the explicit consensus of the people most immediately involved in it.

The affinity group model rejects the idea of the singular public sphere and instead creates a structure for the interactions across multiple subpublics. Multiple affinity groups operate simultaneously, each working to create room for new identities, new topics, new genres. Like counterpublics, the affinity groups operate in two ways: they are "safe houses" where participants can share their perspective despite the inhospitality of the dominant culture to those beliefs, and they are places where non-dominant groups deliberate about how to intervene strategically to reshape the dominant sphere. Nancy Fraser writes about counterpublics, "It is precisely in the dialectic between these two functions that their emancipatory potential resides. This dialectic enables subaltern counterpublics partially to offset, although not wholly to eradicate, the unjust participatory privileges enjoyed by the members of dominant social groups in stratified societies."[58]

In *Methodologies of the Oppressed,* Chela Sandoval argues that it is not productive for a resistance movement to maintain a single identity. The very desire for "coherence" is a constraint; it allows the oppressed to identify only one form of oppression. In contrast, the "differential mode" of opposition involves moving between and among different kinds of opposition, and emphasizes that oppression and opposition are performative.[59] Drawing on this approach, a protest movement may rely on multiple rhetorics and multiple positions. At times, protestors might reach out to the dominant culture by working within the values of the idealized public sphere, as is the case on the websites where the discourse of democratic globalization is explained rationally and directly. At other times, protestors might resist the idea of the singular public sphere by performing an alternative identity—that of affinity groups/counterpublics who use tactics such as blocking roads, displaying satirical puppets, or weaving yarn through police barricades. Even as the protest movement seeks to theorize the interrelationships among its constituents—who themselves perform multiple, intertwined identities as laborers, women, citizens of the Global South, environmentalists—the protestors may choose to strategically present the movement as unified in some situations and multiple in others; it may choose to highlight one set of concerns in one context and a different set elsewhere.

The A-16 protests provided a larger context in which smaller affinity groups were recognized as legitimate sites for alternative rhetorics. The groups could speak back to the dominant culture (represented by the monetary institutions) using whatever rhetoric they felt could best project their own subjectivities or could best reflect back to the dominant culture the false vision it had of itself. Employing forms of intervention that are not rooted in spoken, rational discourse (such as speeches or pamphlets) but instead are rooted in alternative rhetorical moves (such as visual puppets, weaving in the fences, dressing up as Radical Cheerleaders, or inviting the World Bank members to a round of "Anarchy Soccer") reinforced the point that ideology cannot necessarily be challenged through rational discourse. While I wouldn't go so far as to claim that all of the groups understood each other fully, or that the dominant, capitalist public heard the messages directed towards it, I think it's important to recognize that each rhetorical act in the protest was simultaneously a public declaration of a subjectivity (the ethos of the group), a public declaration of a (loose) solidarity (the ethos of the larger convergence), and a public declaration that multiple perspectives and rhetorics could co-exist and feed off each other to create this larger identity. The rhetoric of the protest movement was about inclusion and celebration of difference in a way that few other public or counterpublic events are.

Defining "Successful" Protest in the Contact Zone: New Rules for Evaluating Rhetoric

Much of the media coverage focused on strategic maneuvering—What streets would the protestors block? Where did the police find reinforcements?—rather than on the competing views of globalization and public deliberation. Some editorialists, like pundit David Frum, decried the protestors as throwbacks from the sixties who sought to march simply for the sake of marching, or as naive socialists "left with nothing constructive to say about poverty and development."[60] Some newspapers, comparing the events to those in Seattle, called the protests a failure because they did not shut down this meeting. Others noted that the activists had disrupted the meetings but scolded them for not producing a coherent message for public consumption. But to whom might such a message be directed? What "successful" messages might already be evident in the protests? Those who participated in the protests, along with those who expressed solidarity with them, defined the protests' success in varying manners. Their multiple definitions of "success" reveal some steps toward a concept of global citizenship made up of multiple and divergent counterpublics, a model that accounts for power and wealth inequality, for the multiplicity of world identities.

Some supporters emphasized the goal of momentum and movement building. Well-attended A-16 protests, following on the heels of Seattle, signaled that the democratic globalization movement was gaining momentum, and the events themselves brought in new activists. Long-time environmental activist Nadine Bloch is quoted in a *Washington Post* article as saying, "A big, visual, huge evil-looking corporate puppet can be worth a thousand words. . . . This is all about building a movement. One of the ways you build a movement is to reach out to people in ways they can understand."[61]

Likewise, Colin Raja, the director of Just Act, an organization that encourages teen involvement with the movement, expresses support for the actions as momentum-building events:

> [T]hese actions were also hugely successful. Although they did not completely shut down the meetings, the actions mobilized some 20,000 participants, gathered major national and international attention, and sustained the momentum of the anti-corporate globalization movement. [62]

Accounts such as those of Walden Bello, Executive Director of Focus on the Global South in Bangkok, also describe the protests as successful because the sheer numbers created newfound enthusiasm in the movement:

> Just the mere fact that 30,000 people had come to protest the Bretton Woods twins was already a massive victory according to organizers who said that the most one could mobilize in previous protests were a few hundred people. Moreover, the focus of the media was on Washington, and the first acquaintance of hundreds of millions of viewers throughout the world with the World Bank and IMF were as controversial institutions under siege from people accusing them of inflicting poverty and misery on the developing world.[63]

Bello's analysis allows for a second definition of success as well: the protests called attention to the monetary organizations themselves. Though they did not substantially disrupt the meeting, no particular items on the agenda of the meeting were significant enough for that to matter. Rather, what was important was to bring attention to the fact that the organizations exist and that citizens around the globe feel the organizations fall well short of their benevolent goals. Kevin DeLuca and Jennifer Peeples emphasize this purpose when they argue that the Seattle protest was successful because of (not in spite of) the symbolic violence there.[64] When anarchist protestors broke the storefronts of chains representing international corporations, they argue, the police violence ramped up, as the media used the dramatic footage of the violence to introduce the story. At the same time, they increased the amount of space devoted to covering the protestors' demands. The definition of success in both of these accounts is media attention to the critique of the financial institutions.

Not all of the activists agree, however, that the movement should protest the monetary institutions generally; they prefer more strategic occasions. This is the position of Naomi Klein, a journalist for *The Guardian* whose influential anti-free trade globalization book *No Logo* came out right between the Seattle and DC events. Klein has argued that the DC site was poorly chosen because the particular agenda of the April 16 meeting was not as significant as the WTO agenda in Seattle. She argues that instead of trying to maintain momentum, activists should direct their energies into other, more productive activities. In an interview posted at the Independent Media Center, she says:

> I think part of it has to do with a fear that exists that if you don't have another big protest really soon, the whole thing is going to disappear. We're relying on protests too much. Part of it was that Seattle, it seemed to me . . . , took the Left by surprise. What were they surprised at? That they even existed. That they actually could mobilize people, and it was so thrilling. It was like whoah, we exist, but that they almost didn't believe it, so they had to keep proving it. And I think it's possible that Washington, DC was chosen too quickly as the next protest site; that perhaps that wasn't the best strategic point because it wasn't that important a meeting.[65]

A more important task for the activists, Klein writes, is "theory work," which she sees as a self-analysis of how these groups are intertwined. Rather than think of themselves as disparate affinity groups, Klein asks them to identify the interdependence among their organizations:

> I think that the theory work that needs to be done is for everyone who cares about this movement to not just say that we can all meet on the same street corner and have a protest together, but really work to identify what are the threads of this web, what do they mean, what are the real connections? What's the connection between militarization around the world and the protestor repression here at home Not just a laundry list of here's the things that we're against. But more intense intellectual work.[66]

Such theory work can be seen as "solidarity" work through which groups gain a clearer sense of their own identities and interrelationships. Because events like the A-16 Convergence begin from a radically different starting point than the democratic model of supranational organizations, such theory work can lead to a much richer definition of "global citizenship." The diverse groups' individual priorities and strategies reflect the multiplicities of their local conditions, and at the same time, their participation in and agreement to the organizing methods of the A-16 Convergence suggest that they share at least a few values. First, they share a conviction about the rights of citizens and local organizations to participate fully in their own governance: they draw on a vision of radical democratic participation. Second, they are sensitive to questions of power, and to the process by which ideologies of inequality and colonialism are embedded through material actions. Along with this, they share a skepticism about the power of rationality to bracket such ideologies. Third, they share an emerging awareness of their interdependence and co-responsibility as global citizens.

Within the A-16 Convergence, activists cooperated with each other within affinity groups and through the speakers' councils, in consensus-building systems that amplified individual voices. To this end, they served as a coalition of strong publics, which Fraser defines as "publics whose discourse encompasses both opinion formation and decision-making."[67] At the same time, however, during the events themselves, the system encouraged a kind of autonomy such that small-scale consensus and autonomy overrode large-scale consensus and purpose. Some groups' actions (leaving the barricades) made other groups' actions (trying to maintain them) ineffective. Thus, the anarchist model, while it promoted a kind of interdependent democracy in the supercouncils prior to the protests, reverted to an atomistic model during the weekend, and groups were not compelled to consider how their individual choices for action/inaction had a direct effect on others. Benjamin Barber sees this as a fundamental flaw in focusing on "perpetual consent" as the foundation of democracy:

> Perhaps the most disconcerting among the defects of liberalism that arise out of its dependence on consent is the reactivity—and thus the negativity—that consent imparts to all liberal politics. Politics becomes purely defensive, the model political act is resistance to the encroachment in the private sphere defined by the autonomous, solitary person.[68]

—or in this case, the sphere defined by the autonomous affinity group or civil organization that is participating in the protest. This is a major problem with the current structure, as it parallels the Hobbesian, individualist model of pure competition.

Klein, Habermas, Fraser and Barber all call for more theorizing about new kinds of democratic participation, a process that simultaneously celebrates the diversity of participants, recognizes that the public sphere is always a site of conflict about its own structure, and moves beyond the individualist, reactive practices of autonomy and towards the creation of circular, reciprocal, deliberative bonds among the participants. Fraser adds that we should not envision a single, deliberative process, as "that would be tantamount to filtering diverse rhetorical and stylistic norms through a single, overarching lens."[69] Rather, like Sandoval, she calls for multiple sites and tactics for intrapublic negotiation.

The participants within the democratic globalization protests surrounding the IMF/World Bank came together as optimistic, global citizens to create alternative, democratic spaces for political action. They came together as members of subaltern counterpublics, seeking to affect the public deliberations that were sanctioned within the IMF/World Bank institutions, but they also came together with each other to create an intrapublic movement. If Klein is right, then they are progressing towards increased self-reflection and collaboration, and this, in turn, will shape their intrapublic decision-making processes—the processes through which they can build coalitions that recognize both difference and interdependence. As the movement grows and develops, new models of democratic citizenship will continue to emerge. What emerges from looking closely at this example of counterpublic rhetoric is that publics have to work out their ideals at many levels. We hear in the response to the event that one of its main values was to solidify participants' identity as part of a public—as part of a large, international group of people who could work together to call attention to the flaws in a powerful economic structure. Whether or not others understood them, the power of the event can be evaluated by its ability to maintain this loose identity among the protestors. At another level, what emerges is more internal discussion and debate about that identity. The convergence organizers were able to work out a structure for their work, through the consensus-building anarchist networks, but the conversation continues among participants at all levels about whether this model best represents what they want to do, how much they see their mode of operation in terms of *tactics* or whether they should begin to come together into a more unified, coordinated group to develop *strategies*. Public formation is an ongoing and constant process, one that requires many different forums for circulation, including the forum of an event where people take action together.

At the same time, the example shows how a *counter*public is able to make use of the traditional media to circulate a message. A few reporters were willing to convey the discourse and public perspective of the protestors, in the way that the cable reporter covering the story about the *Bumfights* videos began his investigation: listening to the voice of the group considered powerless in the dynamic. More often than not, the protestors leveraged the traditional news media in the same way that the Open Door nonprofit in Atlanta goaded the *Journal-Constitution:* the media named them and gave enough publicity that viewers/readers began to seek out information directly from the counterpublic itself. As some participants explained, the event was successful because the A-16 protestors harnessed enough media attention that people around the globe understood that the benevolent rhetoric of the global monetary institutions could be challenged.

Finally, the counterpublic rhetoric at this event circulated not only through language—though it did that, in traditional and alternative news coverage, through the convergence and other organization websites—but also through a takeover of public space. Taking over the streets was not just a way to disrupt the meeting, but also a way to revise that space, populating it with mammoth puppets and crazy costumes, making the streets unfit for the vehicles of capitalism but instead transformed into a space governed by different values, different relationships among citizens—a place that celebrated its alternative identities.

WHAT DOES THIS MEAN FOR A PUBLIC WRITING COURSE?

In a pedagogy for public writing that extends across several courses, I'd recommend a course dedicated to the question of public and counterpublic circulation. I have approached such a course from both angles, sometimes beginning with careful attention to the values of the traditional media and sometimes beginning with counterpublic rhetoric.

In the section of the course on traditional media, I lay out some of the elements of journalism I explained in chapter 4, and we examine criticism that the media does not live up to those values. We then move into an analysis of those values themselves, locating them along the matrix of democracy. When *Crossfire* broadcast from our university campus, I brought my classes there and used that experience to kick off an analysis of democratic ideals, and how corporate influences move talk shows from "conversations" to "arguments." Deborah Tannen's *Argument Culture* is a useful text for helping students identify how the idealized public sphere is both desired and undercut.

In the section of the course on counterpublic rhetoric, we look at publics that circulate through different venues, such as street protests, boycotts, sit-ins, and the more lighthearted moves of parody and satire. We look at how various publics work with and against the idealized public sphere, considering the role of the alternative media, as Paula Mathieu and Diana George discuss in "Not Going It Alone." For this section of the course, I am especially attentive to current events in which the method of protest or argument is called into question. I try to hook our examinations of counterpublic tactics to current events and then work backwards, illustrating some of the historical connections to earlier activists and events. For example, it would be interesting to teach a unit about the Tea Party activists who disrupted Congressional senators' and representatives' town hall meetings in 2009. Their attitude toward the mainstream media and the elected officials is clear: neither is seen as open to hearing their ideological critique. The techniques they used in those town hall meetings were not so much different than those deployed by community organizers, Saul Alinsky, and the IAF—a point raised by the progressive research center, Media Matters,[70] among others. The uproar about whether such tactics are necessary or productive—whether they are a threat to "civility"—are not new arguments, and they are productive ways to show that people have always moved around on that third axis of the matrix of democracy, the one that suggests how "good" citizens are supposed to behave, the proper and necessary moves to petition for change.

In my first-year writing course, my goal is to introduce students to the broad concepts of public writing: that public writing is always a site of rhetorical and ideological struggle; that the repertoire of public texts goes beyond the traditional essay; that public formation relies on circulation as much as composition; and that the university and its rhetorical ideals should be understood as one of many competing publics. The question about how counterpublics are able to circulate within and outside of traditional media is a tough but important element of this broader goal. In my first-year classes, I am content if students leave with a sense that multiple publics are able to succeed at this challenge. Conversely, I am content if, when they encounter a protest or parody or other kind of intervention that they do not immediately understand, they pause before dismissing it.

Admittedly, few of my students have the opportunity to write or create truly counterpublic materials, and the risks of doing so can sometimes be surprising. Nancy Welch describes a student who had a run-in with the police after she pasted a handbill to a metal utility box: doing so is a crime.[71] Universities usually constrain such activities as well, as Rachel Riedner documents in her analysis of university response to a student sit-in which took place in the Student Center. (The University had them arrested for trespassing.)[72]

Nevertheless, I raise the question of counterpublic circulation in my first-year writing classes. When students are asked to find and create public texts, and we consider where we might look for materials that convey a particular public rhetoric, I suggest that they turn to sources outside the traditional media. We compare not only who can speak and what can be said in those places, but also how the whole venue of circulation forwards or constrains those voices. When students are asked to write public texts, we consider how those texts will make their way around, and we consider how they might circumvent the traditional media to do so.

I haven't spent much time in this chapter examining how the Internet allows publics to communicate outside the traditional media, though the A-16 protests were enabled to a huge degree because of the access that organizers had to each other online. Moreover, when the traditional media covered their protests, readers could turn to the protest groups' websites to hear in their own words and images why they were there. The online alternative newspaper *Indymedia* covered the event through the words of organizers and activists themselves. In the next chapter, I look at how public theory scholars and activists have used the Internet.

NOTES

1. Scott Richard Lyons, "Rhetorical Sovereignty: What Do American Indians Want from Writing?" *College Composition and Communication* 51, no. 3 (February 2000): 452.

2. Geneva Smitherman-Donaldson, *Talkin and Testifyin: The Language of Black America* (Detroit: Wayne State University Press, 1986), 190–91.

3. What to call this language is unsettled: some people use the term "African American vernacular;" Jordan and Smitherman use "Black English," and argue that it's not a dialect so much as a whole language, with its own grammatical structures. I've also heard "Black Dialect." Senator Harry Reid was vilified for choosing the term "Negro Dialect," though that phrase was used by linguists at various times. I have chosen to use "Black English" here because it's the term that Jordan adopts in her story.

4. June Jordan, "Nobody Mean More to Me than You and the Future Life of Willie Jordan." *Harvard Educational Review* 58, no. 3 (1988): 363.

5. June Jordan, "Nobody," 364.

6. June Jordan, "Nobody," 364.

7. June Jordan, "Nobody," 367.

8. June Jordan, "Nobody," 371.

9. June Jordan, "Nobody," 371.

10. June Jordan, "Nobody," 371.

11. June Jordan, "Nobody," 371–72.

12. June Jordan, "Nobody," 371–72.

13. Paula Mathieu, Tactics of Hope: The Public Turn in English Composition (Portsmouth, NH: Heinemann, 2005), 16.

14. Michael Warner, *Publics and Counterpublics* (Cambridge: Zone Books, 2005), 116.

15. Mathieu, *Tactics,* 16.

16. Mathieu, *Tactics,* 16.

17. Warner, Publics and Counterpublics, 123.

18. Saul David Alinsky, Rules for Radicals: A Practical Primer for Realistic Radicals (New York: Vintage Books, 1989), 128.

19. North American Street Newspaper Association, "What Is a Street Newspaper?" 2010 www.nasna.org (19 August 2010).

20. Mathieu, *Tactics,* 35.

21. Mathieu, *Tactics,* 17.

22. Paula Mathieu and Diana George, "*Not* Going It Alone: Public Writing, Independent Media, and the Circulation of Homeless Advocacy." *College Composition and Communication* 61, no. 1 (September 2009): 130–149.

23. Mathieu and George, "*Not* Going It Alone," 140–41.

24. Mathieu and George, "*Not* Going It Alone," 141.

25. Mathieu and George, "*Not* Going It Alone," 141.

26. Mathieu and George, "*Not* Going It Alone," 142.

27. Mathieu and George, "*Not* Going It Alone," 134.

28. Mathieu and George, "*Not* Going It Alone," 134.

29. Mathieu and George, "*Not* Going It Alone," 135.

30. Mathieu and George, "*Not* Going It Alone," 135.

31. Mathieu and George, "*Not* Going It Alone," 138.

32. Don Mitchell, "The End of Public Space? People's Park, Definitions of the Public, and Democracy." *Annals of the Association of American Geographers* 85, no. 1 (March 1995): 118.

33. Mitchell, "People's Park," 118.

34. Mitchell, "People's Park," 118.

35. As is the case in most protests, these numbers are disputed. Major newspapers reported 35,000, while the organizers' websites refer to "over 50,000" protesters. See, for example, www.globalexchange.org.

36. 50 Years Is Enough, "Mobilization for Global Justice," www.50years.org (22 November 2002).

37. 50 Years Is Enough, "Mobilization

38. No guilty verdicts were assessed against any of the 1,300 people arrested during the weekend. In 2004, the DC Council passed the "First Amendment Rights and Police Standards Act" (DC 15–352), designed to prevent this kind of pre-emptive arrests in future protests. In 2010, the courts ordered the city to pay damages to the wrongly arrested people.

39. Jürgen Habermas, "The European Nation-State: On the Past and Future of Sovereignty and Citizenship." *Public Culture* 10, no. 2 (1998): 400.

40. Ann LoLordo, "Protesters Say Their Mission Was Accomplished in Seattle," *Baltimore Sun* 5 December 1999, A1.

41. Rhoda E. Howard-Hassman, "The Great Transformation II: Human Rights Leap-Frogging in the Era of Globalization," 2005 www.globalautonomy.ca (25 October 2005), 7.

42. Kemal Dervis and Ceren Ozer. *A Better Globalization: Legitimacy, Governance and Reform* (Washington, D.C.: Center for Global Development, 2005), xx.

43. LoLordo, "Protesters," A1.

44. Habermas, "European Nation-State," 414.

45. Habermas, "European Nation-State," 414.

46. Habermas, "European Nation-State," 398.

47. Habermas, "European Nation-State," 413.

48. Habermas, "European Nation-State," 410.

49. International Monetary Fund, "Common Criticisms of the IMF: Some Responses," 2005 www.imf.org (27 October 2005).

50. IMF, "Common Criticisms."

51. IMF, "Common Criticisms."

52. Howard-Hassman, "Great Transformation," 7.

53. Noam Chomsky, "Noam Chomsky on the IMF/WB Debt Forgiveness," 2000 a16.monkeyfist.com (27 October 2005).

54. Rachel Riedner and Kevin Mahoney, *Democracies to Come: Rhetorical Action, Neoliberalism, and Communities of Resistance* (Lanham, MD: Lexington Books, 2008), xx.

55. Chomsky, "Chomsky on the IMF/WB."

56. Mobilization for Global Justice, "Affinity Groups, A-16, 2000," www.a16.org (22 November 2002).

57. This openness led to some consternation after the Seattle protests, where some anarchists damaged commercial property. On www.indymedia.org, protest organizers insist that most protestors believe in non-violent civic disobedience.

58. Nancy Fraser, "Rethinking the Public Sphere: A Contribution to the Critique of Actually Existing Democracy," in *Habermas and the Public Sphere,* ed. Craig J. Calhoun (Cambridge, MA: MIT Press, 1992), 124.

59. Chela Sandoval, *Methodologies of the Oppressed* (Minneapolis: University of Minnesota Press, 2000), 58.

60. David Frum, "Protesting, but Why?" *The New York Times*, 19 April 2000, A23.

61. Dan Eggen, "From All Walks of Life, They Make a Stand: Environmentalists, Feminists, Other Activists Organize DC Protests of World Bank and IMF," *Washington Post,* 8 April 2000, A1.

62. Colin Raja, "Globalism and Race at A16 in DC." *Colorlines: Race, Color, Action* 3, no. 3 (2000): xx[[AuQ: Please provide page ref.]].

63. Walden Bello, "The Year of Global Protest Against Globalization," 2001 www.focusweb.org/publications/2001/2001 (24 October 2002).

64. Kevin Michael DeLuca and Jennifer Peeples, "From Public Sphere to Public Screen: Democracy, Activism, and the 'Violence' of Seattle." *Critical Studies in Media Communication* 19, no. 2 (June 2002): 125–152.

65. Naomi Klein, "Conversation with Naomi Klein about the Anti-Corporate Movement," *Seattle Independent Media Center* http://seattle.indymedia.org (7 September 2000).

66. Klein, "Conversation."

67. Fraser, "Rethinking," 134.

68. Benjamin R. Barber, *Strong Democracy: Participatory Politics for a New Age* (Berkeley: University of California Press, 2003), 7.

69. Fraser, "Rethinking," 126.

70. Brooke Obie, "The Right Wing Media Hate Alinsky, Except When He's Shaping Their Movement," 10 February 2010 http://mediamatters.org/blog/201002010041 (20 August 2010).

71. Nancy Welch, "Living Room: Teaching Public Writing in a Post-Publicity Era," *College Composition and Communication* 56, no. 3 (February 2005): 472–473.

72. Riedner and Mahoney, *Democracies to Come*, 42–47.

Chapter 7

Publics 2.0: Public Formation through Social Networking

> Most of the people around us belong to our world not directly, as kin or comrades or in any other relation to which we could give name, but as strangers. How is it that we nevertheless recognize them as members of our world? We are related to them (and I am to you) as transient participants in common publics, potentially addressable in impersonal forms.
>
> —Michael Warner[1]

During the Fall 2009 National Coalition for the Homeless Speakers' Bureau, when homeless and formerly homeless people spoke to incoming students at George Washington University, the last speaker, Steve Thomas, closed out his personal story of living on the streets by inviting the students to friend him on Facebook, send him comments through his nonprofit's website (STREATS.org), and follow his video blog (BetterBelieveSteve.com). His invitation epitomizes the ease with which the Internet allows people to connect publicly, without the "entanglements of intimacy" that Jane Jacobs explains can make people hesitate to talk to strangers. Jacobs uses the phrase to describe the balance of relationships that city dwellers develop as they relate to each other not as friends, but as people who share the same street or the same city. A 1960s urban designer, Jacobs lays out a theory for creating safe urban streets, spaces she defines as unique because they necessarily throng with strangers and therefore can't rely on the "webs of reputation" that motivate families or small communities.[2] In small communities, "gossip, approval, disapproval and sanctions . . . are powerful [because] people know each other and word travels,"[3] but such controls don't hold among strangers. Instead, "public" interaction in urban spaces, she argues, requires a deliberate and clearly understood separation between public and private. Strangers

199

can only build a sense of community when they do not fear that once they've nodded "hello," the other person will demand money or ask to come inside to use the bathroom.[4]

The Internet, it seems, provides an excellent new space for developing such public relationships. We can "talk" to people in an online local or global forum without giving out our home addresses or other private details. We can "follow" each other through Twitter or Facebook and find out what others are doing or thinking without the pressure to respond. We can interact with strangers through blogs, e-mail, listservs, social networking sites, You-Tube, or the comment section for online news articles. When we go online, we can wander virtually down many streets, potentially bumping into millions of strangers. The scope of our public relations, it seems, is infinitely extended.

The Internet is not entirely without privacy risks, however, and the ability to reach out to strangers on the Internet does not in itself build the public relationships Jacobs advocates. Such relationships are shaped through infrastructure. For Jacobs, public relationships are structured into urban design when houses and apartments face outward to the streets (rather than inward to courtyards or backyard decks), when housing is intermixed with local stores, and when all are connected with sidewalks that lead strangers to pass by each other regularly. What's important, Jacobs notes—anticipating the argument that Robert Putnam puts forward years later in *Bowling Alone*—is that regular public interactions build up a sense of trust among strangers.

> The trust of a city street is formed over time from many, many little public sidewalk contacts. It grows out of people stopping by the bar for a beer, getting advice from the grocer and giving advice to the newsstand man, comparing opinions with other customers at the bakery . . . admonishing the children, hearing about a job from the hardware man. . . . Customs vary: in some neighborhoods people compare notes about their dogs; in others, they compare notes on their landlords.
>
> Most of it is ostensibly utterly trivial, but the sum is not trivial at all. The sum of such casual, public contact at a local level, most of it fortuitous, most of it associated with errands, all of it metered by the person concerned and not thrust upon him by anyone—is a feeling for the public identity of people, a web of public respect and trust, and a resource in time of personal or neighborhood need. The absence of this trust is a disaster to a city street.[5]

To build a sense of public identity, then, people need repeated moments of voluntary interactions with strangers.

The daily interaction builds a code of conduct within the area. People who are oriented toward public spaces become the "eyes" on the street, monitoring who comes and goes. Jacobs does not talk explicitly about the rhetorical forums through which definitions of "proper public conduct" are worked out in such areas. Rather, she highlights the role of the most visible people on the street—local merchants, women who sit on their porches or in their living rooms and watch people walk by, occasionally a homeless person who has claimed a corner and greets people day and night as they pass. The most visible and active public people, it seems, set the expectations. Jacobs' scenarios involve moments when these "eyes on the street" stop kidnapping attempts and break up assaults, moments that are unambiguously positive for the community. For Jacobs, public relationships form when people within the community understand that there is an agreed-upon code of conduct that protects them and others in that space.

Before I consider whether social contact and its corresponding positive sense of social conduct might occur online, I want to look more carefully at how such codes of conduct might develop and function in geographical communities. Jacob's scenarios, by highlighting those interventions that are likely to be seen as universally good, cover over real struggles within many communities (urban and otherwise) to define "proper public conduct." As Gabrielle G. Modan illustrates beautifully in *Turf Wars: Discourse, Diversity, and the Politics of Place,* her ethnography of a multicultural DC neighborhood, community members use a host of rhetorical tools to define codes of community conduct and to designate who has the authority to define those codes. It's interesting to consider, for example, that in the Mt. Pleasant neighborhood Modan studied, the vocal neighborhood civic association, which was predominantly run by the white homeowners, denounced the Latinos who "loitered" on city streets near the stores and restaurants. Jacobs sees "loiterers" as ideal city dwellers who maintain a public presence on the streets and therefore offer more eyes to monitor against criminal behavior. According to Modan, the Latino community in Mt. Pleasant also believes that public sidewalks are appropriate places for socializing. The civic association, in contrast, believes public socializing should take place in the restaurants, theaters, and other commercially-designated meeting places—places where safety and codes of conduct are controlled by the private establishment. They see "loitering" as creating a barrier to those public/private stores and restaurants. Two publics clash in Mt. Pleasant, with conflicting expectations for where and how public interaction should take place.

How do such disputes about codes of conduct get worked out? Modan finds that people with the most access to public resources—those who receive public grants, those who mobilize city policy makers—may be able to police a certain kind of "appropriate" public conduct, but their assumptions about "what Mt. Pleasant is" are never fixed and are regularly resisted. Within Mt. Pleasant,

factions struggled about appropriate use of public space in community meetings, on listservs, in conversations on the street, in theater performances, and
in grant applications. Significantly, not all of the engagement took place in
deliberative venues. While the civic association meetings, listservs, and grant-
writing, which were conducted primarily by those also in the civic association,
took advantage of more deliberative spaces, responses to (and resistance to)
their discourse took place in *other* everyday spaces—conversations in work-
places, conversations at parties in the neighborhood, confrontations on the
streets themselves. Modan analyzes how various sides mark out their definitions for Mt. Pleasant through a series of linked discursive contrasts, which sets
up a "moral geography" for the area. For example, when a listserv post about
"cat-calls" suggests that the police should be called in "to educate" residents
about how to properly interact with women on the street, others read this as
denigrating the Latinos who hang out on the street. In response, those who
identify with the Latinos dismiss the civic association as "suburbanites"—a
category that in turn is linked with bland homogeneity and a feminized obses-
sion with safety. "True" city dwellers, in contrast, are indexed to appreciate
racial, economic and architectural diversity and know how to read and respond
appropriately to the dangers of the city.[6] Each side in this ongoing struggle to
control the definition of Mt. Pleasant puts forward its own moral geography
through formal and informal interactions, in formal, deliberative spaces and in
informal and brief exchanges, and through their use of street space.

Much of the scholarship about the democratic possibilities of the Internet examines whether it serves as a space to work out the kinds of public
disagreements that Modan examines in *Turf Wars*. Those who celebrate the
democratic potential of the Internet greet it as an ideal space for democratic
work because it seems to break down so many barriers to participation. In
Jacob's streets, the people with the power to set the codes of conduct are
those who are most frequently around—in her case, the stay-at-home mothers and local merchants. Modan recognizes that class barriers constrain
people's participation: residents who owned their homes felt entitled to set
policy because they saw renters as transient (even if renters had lived in the
area longer than they had). The people who could show up at the community
meetings were those with the luxury of time to do so. In the ideal image of
the Internet, the possibility of working things out through asynchronous yet
ongoing online forums seems to provide more people the opportunity to participate in setting community standards. People working multiple jobs or with
childcare responsibilities could participate online at times and places that fit
their schedules. Moreover, the Internet could address some of the potential
prejudices of face-to-face deliberations: people's comments would be evaluated on their own merits, not dismissed because of their accents or whether

they were renters. Gilbert Rodman captures the heart of this utopian view of the Internet in his review of such scholarship:

> [I]f a crucial facet of a healthy democracy is the ability of ordinary people to participate actively in the public sphere as both 'speakers' and 'listeners,' then the Internet may be the only form of mass media that has the potential to be genuinely democratic.[7]

James A. Janack's analysis shows how closely such claims are tied to the notion of the idealized public sphere:

> In this scenario, the WWW would promote a vast, virtual agora where citizens could discuss and debate ideas, creating an almost limitless public sphere in the Habermasian sense (Habermas 1993). The Internet's capacity for near-instantaneous, two-way, decentralized communication has made cyberspace a potentially attractive site for extended informal political deliberation (Dahlberg 2001). Furthermore, because markers of gender, race, and class are less obvious in an online environment, some have considered the Internet a more democratic and egalitarian venue in which individuals could exchange ideas with less interference from personal prejudices.[8]

Such scholarship, having identified some of the constraints on "real" public exchange in traditional media, look to the Internet (including the WWW) as a forum which avoids those constraints.

A second wave of scholars, looking more critically at online interactions and Internet infrastructure, identifies the flaws in this utopian view. In a move that parallels Jacob's argument that the physical structures around urban public space can deeply influence how people come together in that space, scholars looking at public space on the Internet examine how its infrastructure and developing online "netiquette" constrain who has access and who controls the conversation. In virtual space, as in urban space, the goal of promoting social contact among strangers often is subordinated to consumerist goals. Just as fights over city parks place the goals of mixed-public social contact and political speech against ideals of "open space" (where we have a chance to revel in the beauty of nature), recreational space (emphasizing fitness and athletic competition), and commodified space (designed to encourage consumption)[9], so scholars examine how online spaces work with and against the corporate and entertainment-oriented online infrastructures of that space. Urban and Internet architects may favor the infrastructures of a more commodified space, which hails passersby as consumers rather than as citizens or neighbors.

What strikes me about much of the scholarship about whether the Internet can further democratic public-making is that much of it repeats the same move: it sets out an ideal for such interaction, picks a site where such exchanges might happen, doesn't find it, and so sketches out the barriers that may have prevented the ideal interaction from coming to fruition there. Susan Claire Warshauer provides a very clear example of this move in her analysis of a "community-based software" application called ExploreNet. For Warshauer, the unique quality of the software is that it allows all participants to not only contribute but also shape the structure of their interactions. The software developers "aimed to give these people the means to develop their own online 'worlds,' to break the cycle of passive viewing."[10] She likens the goals of the software developers to those who advance "participatory theater": People in the community determine the shape and substance of the (theatrical) event; the audience is not passive but is what Augusto Boal calls the "spect-actor."[11] She then makes the move that I see as so common in the scholarship: "Their success in achieving this goal will be questioned in this essay, but that they set out to achieve it is at least admirable."[12]

I would not go so far as to claim that scholars share identical visions of what an ideal online democratic interaction might be, but I do notice some interesting and significant trends. Whether they see the Internet (as a whole, or one part of it, such as the World Wide Web) as a force for or against democratic interactions, there is an underlying assumption that the ideal space would promote serious and productive discussion across diverse groups about public issues. The ideal may be either for traditional rational delibera-tion (in the Habermasian model) or for more vernacular reasoning (with the expectation that multiple publics will bring their own modes of reasoning to the exchange, as Hauser suggests). Yet in either model, the assumption is that proof of public formation will show up in examples of online *deliberation.* The scholars then look for proof of such deliberation in sites like political campaign message boards, campaign parody sites, virtual neighborhood list-servs, and other venues where cross-talk among strangers of differing views might show up. They explicate the structural barriers and the online behaviors that interfere with those goals.

In the next section, I'll provide a quick overview of some of this scholar-ship. My point in doing so is not to suggest that the findings are inaccurate, but rather to notice this recurring pattern and consider alternative methods for analyzing potential public formation on the Internet.

DELIBERATIVE EXCHANGE: POLITICAL SITES

A surprising number of articles about the effects and limitations of online interactions speak generally about the Internet without locating their analy-sis in examples of specific applications or sites, but we can develop a loose category of the places scholars seek evidence of democracy on the Internet. One focus has been on discursive exchanges in communities brought together by issues; another focus has been on communities brought together by geography.

One often-cited study in the issues-based category is Laura Gurak's *Persuasion and Privacy in Cyberspace: The Online Protests over Lotus Marketplace and the Clipper Chip.* Gurak analyzes the rhetoric of text-based discussion in listservs, newsgroups, and e-mail. Writing in the late 1990s, Gurak set out to understand "the new kind of rhetorical entity" that shows up in communities that are entirely online.[13] Looking at two groups, one a grassroots bottom-up protest and the other with top-down hierarchy coordinated by a nonprofit, she studies how participants presented and evaluated each other's credibility in online, text-only exchanges, and how the timing, anonymity, and other online structures of the communication affected their goals of online protest. She chooses her two case studies because each is engaged in social protest: one protested privacy concerns related to the software developer Lotus, and the other protested the government's proposal to insert a "clipper chip" into common devices like cell phones to intercept and decode private communication. What she discovers is that, within these issues-based communities, the glue that held the grassroots organization together was an "instant trust" along with the personal, emotional connection people felt to the cause. Recipients began trusting people in the grassroots campaign whose comments and information resonated with their own connection to the issues (even when their information was not accurate). In contrast, the campaign that was organized by the nonprofit provided more accurate information, but it did not succeed at tapping into the emotional trust and energy that motivated the grassroots community. Gurak's concern is not only about the quality of information that circulates in online public forums, but also that both forums—whether grassroots or hierarchical—were unable or unwilling to entertain alternate voices. She observes the sometimes sexist moves used to belittle and dismiss those who tried to bring another voice to the conversation.

Like Gurak, David M. Anderson looks for evidence of democratic exchanges in issues-based sites. In his own chapter of the anthology he co-edited, *The Civic Web: Online Politics and Democratic Values,* he argues that issues-based online spaces are better places than campaign websites to look for the power of the Internet for democracy. For one thing, campaign websites are too locked into their goal of electing candidates to make room for substantive discussions of issues; they are also short-lived. Issues-oriented sites, however, operate year-round and can gain a broad, geographically diverse network of followers and participants.[14]

Part of Anderson's argument focuses on the power of the campaign site moderators to regulate the exchanges on the campaign websites. However, more recent scholars have discovered that the moderators aren't the key force in setting up the codes of conduct for these sites; the users are. James Janack reveals a strong parallel with Gurak's work when he looks at how users control what can be said at a particular site. Janack analyzes the user exchanges in Howard Dean's blog and introduces many of the policing moves that we can see in all manner of online forums: labeling people "trolls," launching *ad hominem* attacks, reframing questions about issues into a discussion of campaign strategies (not "what do we think of this?" but, "is talking about this good for our candidate/issue-campaign?").[15] The "troll" label is particularly interesting, as it effectively isolates that person from conversation: people are admonished "don't feed the troll," and the goal is to ignore the "offending" person so that that thread of conversation will die out. It stops circulation. Janack rightly points out that, as with issues-based online spaces, the discussion forums on campaign sites are places that are well-regulated by the participants, who monitor each other so that they can reinforce a generally-accepted stream of comments that support the candidate or, in Gurak's case, a general line of thinking about an issue.

DELIBERATIVE EXCHANGE: COMMUNITY SITES

A second major trend in the scholarship is to look for evidence of democratic deliberation in *community-based* networks. While issues-based sites spring out of members' shared interests, community networks form because of members' shared locations. According to David Silver, community-based sites are "collection[s] of geographically based Websites, mailing lists, newsgroups, and e-mail accounts established for and around . . . particular town[s], cit[ies], or region[s]."[16] Silver is among many scholars[17] who have examined the Blacksburg Electronic Village (BEV), in Blacksburg, VA, a promising site of study because participants are linked by a geographic location; residents in the geographical community have been provided with sustained Internet access; and the local university, Virginia Tech, along with local businesses and government offices, are all linked through the BEV portal. The vision statement for BEV fits well with the idea that civic engagement is built through ongoing civic deliberation: "The goal of the project is to enhance people's lives by electronically linking the residents of the community to one another."[18] David Silver asks, "Is the BEV . . . a digital public sphere, a 'place' where users congregate, debate and discuss?"[19]

Silver finds that BEV participants use the portal as a place for consumer information—downloading coupons, reviewing movie listings, even retrieving course materials for university classes—but few people are on the listserv.

Among those who use the listserv, the predominant focus remains consumer-oriented as people ask for advice about where to find different kinds of services and products. He notes that none of the participants talk about BEV as a place of "community building" as the initial vision statement had set forth.[20] He asks why the community has not become a site for productive deliberative exchange: "[W]hy no discussion and debate?"[21]

To find clues about what might prohibit a virtual BEV community from forming, Silver turns to a particular part of BEV, the general topic BEV listserv, Bburg-L. What he finds are few participants meeting in a context that does not require them to engage with each other either by virtue of the site infrastructure or by virtue of their own felt needs to work on community issues together. The participants noted little sense of common interest and a preponderance of flame wars (often involving one "gadfly") that muted their desire to engage online with each other. Few people had a personal investment in keeping the listserv conversations going. Silver noted that they could lurk without posting, opt out of the listserv altogether, or use a "kill file" to mediate what they read. ("Kill files" filter incoming messages from designated people so that the recipient can control whose messages he or she reads.)

In attempts to control the public conduct on the listserv itself, people occasionally rallied to convince the Internet service provider to revoke account privileges for people who violated what they saw as the appropriate use of the listserv; sometimes they argued that the listserv should adopt a community "moderator" who could do the same. The main target of these protests was a specific user, whom Silver names "Harry" and who calls himself a "gadfly." On this listserv, Harry was policed in a way similar to what Janack documents on the Howard Dean blog: he was subject to *ad hominem* attacks and called a "troll," and people instructed each other not to engage with him. While Silver argues that the online discussions about how to respond to apparent breaches of community conduct are a sign that the community is working out its own issues, the participants he interviewed felt the interactions were more destructive than useful. Like many who seek evidence of community formation online, they wanted in-depth exchanges of meaningful knowledge about issues of common interest. They didn't find it on Bburg-L.

LOOKING BEYOND DELIBERATIVE EXCHANGES: INTERNET PARODY

In the articles I've reviewed above, the scholars seek out evidence for a democratic ideal that we might position near the middle of the matrix of democracy. Along the axis for the *purpose* of democracy, the goal is not only to protect individual rights but also to create a space where participants, through deliberation, come to see their interdependence. The scholars seek an online infrastructure that encourages this sense of cross-citizen deliberation. The imagined *government structure* is republican shading toward direct, where participants deliberate actively and forcefully, and may even take cyber or real-life action to influence representatives toward particular actions. On the final axis, which delineates types of public action, the scholars seem closer to the end where ideal interlocutors are understood to be rational, fair, and generous. When the scholars do not find a space where participants treat each other as benevolent partners, this lack disturbs them: the world as it *should* be, in their model, is one where public citizens engage openly and benevolently, without trying to sabotage online discussions or going down in flame wars.

As I explained in chapter 2, I am sympathetic to these democratic ideals and I probably would locate my own "world as it should be" in a similar location on the matrix of democracy. Yet I fear that when we begin our scholarship by looking for examples of such spaces, we overlook the possibility of seeing other rhetorics of democracy at work—other conceptions of the world as it is and the world as it should be, other visions for the kinds of (non-deliberative) rhetorical intervention that might move the powers that be.

Some critique, for example, may come in the form of parody, satire, and other "arts of the contact zone." Just as the A-16 protesters at the World Bank/IMF meetings carried huge, imposing puppets and dressed as "radical cheerleaders" to make fun of the supposedly democratic undertakings of those financial organizations, so many online sites use spoof and humor to poke fun at the political and community websites that fall so short of their ideals. Recognizing the many forces that police issues-based and campaign-based sites, scholars like Barbara Warnick and Erin Dietel-McLaughlin analyze how parodies critique the more serious sites. In *Critical Literacy in the Digital Era: Technology, Rhetoric and the Public Interest,* Warnick devotes a significant section of her book to the many Gore and Bush parody sites that sprung up around the 2000 elections.[22] Dietel-McLaughlin looks at the "irreverent" submissions to the CNN-YouTube debates in 2007, when citizens were invited to submit video questions for consideration as part of a presidential debate.[23] Some of the unselected questions were aired by the debate moderator Anderson Cooper prior to the debate itself, and even one of the allowed questions used an unusual format—a snowman asking a question about global warming. Dietel-McLaughlin spends more time examining the "irreverent" work of the unselected video-questions that were archived on YouTube. Both Warnick and Dietel-McLaughlin see parody and irreverence as important rhetorical tools used to help call attention to how "discursive activity has become more constrained and more highly structured because of increased regulation and commercialization of the Internet."[24] Parody, they argue, is a form that challenges not only the content of a message but also the limitations of campaign sites and debate forums. Yet, in offering critique, they nevertheless uphold the goal of an epistemic, deliberative public sphere: their point is not that such a goal is wrong, but only that we have fallen so short of it.

LOOKING BEYOND DELIBERATIVE EXCHANGES: RHETORICS OF SOCIAL NETWORKING

When we investigate Internet democracy and public formation by first looking through the lens of an idealized public sphere, the arguments are predictable: the idealized public sphere doesn't function much better online, because many of the same constraints exist there as exist in other contexts. The locations are not "unmediated" any more than traditional journalism is; they are mediated by site moderators and in many cases by the same advertising pressures to turn users into consumers.

Moreover, such *deliberative* online forums try to mimic community meetings, but without the constraints of geography—the pressure to work together that comes from passing daily on the street or drinking from the same water supply or having children in the same school. Even those who agree with the democratic ideals and methods of such places may have little incentive to stay in such places online if the discussion becomes contentious. They may abandon the difficult work of resolving differences and simply create new spaces where their own ideals of interaction and codes of conduct apply, ever fragmenting into more homogeneous units. Robert Putnam rightly warns about additional problems with limited Internet access for so many people and the tendency toward cyberbalkanization—choosing to interact only with those online folks who share your interest and world view.[25]

And there is the matter of trust. To deliberate with others—especially with strangers—requires the participants to see some sense of mutual dependence, a belief that thinking with others can yield some positive outcome. And the sense of trust comes not only through getting together to talk, but also through other kinds of social contact. If Jacobs and Putnam are right, non-political, non-deliberative social contact is just as important to public formation as that more formal discourse. What's going on in Jacobs' streets—neighbors calling out over the fence to strangers, people chatting about trivial matters to a local merchant—is not "deliberation," but is, nevertheless, an important component of public life, creating a foundation that may allow for later deliberation should that need arise. What's going on in Modan's neighborhood—people catcalling on the streets, people partying and socializing in front of stores—is as central to defining Mt. Pleasant as the formal calls to action that emanate from the civic meetings. According to Putnam, those everyday interactions build the sense of trust and mutual support and cooperation that are the foundation of civil society. Putnam worries that computer-mediated communication such as e-mails, listservs, and the like cannot convey those social cues that build interpersonal collaboration and trust in face-to-face contacts.[26] Putnam's inquiry draws on Web 1.0 examples; I propose that in some potentially hopeful ways, the structures of Web 2.0 address some of the paucities of social contact that he describes.

I would add that it's not just that we need non-deliberative contact if we are to later accomplish the other work of setting agendas and taking action together. Social contact is not only about setting up for future deliberation. Rather the multiple forms of interaction are part of constructing (and disagreeing about) a sense of communal identity and purpose. In Modan's analysis of Mt. Pleasant, people have conflicting ideals for how the "real" citizens of their community should behave. These ideals are part of the everyday contact of walking down the street and encountering people who use that street in various ways, who speak in various languages, and so on. Are there ways in which the Internet facilitates the circulation of this kind of social contact?

Instead of looking for examples of an idealized public sphere, I have begun to explore some of the components of online public formation by starting with a close analysis of a particular site. In the next section, I provide a detailed analysis of the social networking practices of a local soup kitchen, Miriam's Kitchen. I argue, in the end, that when we examine such rhetorics alongside their face-to-face contexts, we can see how non-deliberative public formation relies on the tools of engagement through circulation.

Likewise, following Rodman's example, I conduct my analysis by considering public formation in multiple kinds of online and offline spaces. The Internet itself, Rodman reminds us, is capacious. It

> can be as personal as an email note between lovers or as public as a Usenet post available to millions of readers in dozens of countries. It can be as ephemeral as a "real-time" conversation in a chatroom or as permanent as a Web-based database or archive. It can be as serious as a listserv-based support group for survivors of incest or as lighthearted as an evening of checkers in an online game room . . . All of which makes it more accurate to think of the Net as *multiple media* rather than as a single medium.[27]

People who come together as a public might use password-protected spaces to work out internal disagreements but never allude to those conversations in spaces open to competing publics. They might come together in a listserv discussion to set agendas, launch a series of blogs to reaffirm their public view, and use Facebook to circulate news clippings, photos, and blog links to friends (and, ideally, their friends' friends too) and Twitter to broadcast regular updates of their activities.

Because publics form within a milieu of multiple and competing publics, they use a range of online and physical spaces for a range of different rhetorical purposes. As I consider how Miriam's Kitchen uses social networking, I contextualize their work against other online spaces for similar public formation and against their physical site, where volunteers, staff, and homeless men and women come together as "Miriam's Kitchen."

MIRIAM'S KITCHEN AND ALTERNATE RHETORICS OF PUBLIC FORMATION

> Yes, it's another story about Twitter. But this one is not about narcissistic celebs tweeting their daily dross. This is a story about how a local charity that feeds the hungry is capitalizing on social media better than many private companies.
>
> —Jennifer Nycz-Conner[28]

In July 2009, the *Washington Business Journal* told a story that many area nonprofits already knew: Miriam's Kitchen is on the leading edge of a trend to use social networking. Because my first-year writing service-learning classes partner with Miriam's Kitchen, I have followed its transformation. I watched as Miriam's Kitchen created its first Facebook page in 2008 and then, in March 2009, with a flurry of online activity, revamped its Facebook page and launched a Twitter account. By July 2010, it had 2,775 Twitter followers; 497 people "liked" it on Facebook. And the result—celebrated frequently in updates on both sites—has been a steady stream of much-needed material donations: tea bags from Boston, socks from California, lotions, soaps, and much more.

From the perspective of many of the scholars I mentioned above, Miriam's Kitchen's social networking might seem to fall short because it is directed primarily to donors and volunteers; homeless men and women rarely post comments or make their presence known on Miriam's Kitchen's Twitter or Facebook spaces. If an ideal public space is, as geographer Don Mitchell puts it, "an unconstrained space within which political movements can organize and expand into wider arenas," then homeless people should be able to assert themselves as part of "the public" in such places—part of the "legitimate" group of people who make up our democracy.[29]

Consider that multi-vocal ideal alongside a passage from the *Washington Business Journal* article. Jennifer Roccanti, mentioned in the passage, is Miriam's Kitchen's Development Associate; she manages its social networking.

> Miriam's case workers used to say that for their guests, success was coming in for a cup of coffee. With "social media, success is now a box of tea," Roccanti says. "We got a box of tea because of Twitter, and that is successful because we have just built a relationship. It's really about building new, stronger relationships."[30]

Whereas the caseworker focused on the kitchen's relationship with a homeless person, Roccanti focuses on the kitchen's relationship with donors. Neither the caseworker's interactions nor the Twitter and Facebook interactions seem to bring the middle-class public and the homeless public together to learn from and with each other. We therefore might dismiss what's going on as reinforcing elitist public relationships, where middle-class citizens give to the poor, where "the poor" are imagined as dependent upon benefactors rather than as people who can represent themselves and speak back to social and economic inequalities. This was my first reaction: I worried that the regular updates and exchanges that Roccanti had with donors, volunteers, and other friends and followers on Twitter and Facebook reinforced an unequal, patronizing kind of charity.

But the more I have looked at what Roccanti has been doing, and the more I have considered the context in which Miriam's Kitchen carries out its work, the more I've come to see that the lens I had been using—looking for moments of an idealized public sphere—is not be the best way to understand all that's happening. For one thing, over sixty percent of the guests at Miriam's Kitchen are chronically homeless. The life conditions of homeless people upset one of the foundations of this deliberative model of public-formation: the separation of public and private. Our evaluation of Miriam's Kitchen's social networking as a public space, I argue, cannot only be based on who *enters* public space but also who can choose to leave it. Second, the theory of the idealized public sphere sees *deliberation* as the central mechanism of public formation. But after looking more carefully at how Miriam's Kitchen uses social networking, I am less convinced that *deliberation* is the key component of public formation. The non-deliberative exchanges on Twitter and Facebook create a sense of capacity and joint mission by relying on another element of public formation: circulation.

I'll begin with a review of how Miriam's Kitchen uses Facebook and Twitter. Then I'll explore in more detail how the conditions of chronic homelessness challenge the foundations of idealized public sphere. Finally,

I'll explain how Miriam's Kitchen's approach offers an alternative theory of public formation.

Social Networking at Miriam's Kitchen

Miriam's Kitchen made a big push to expand its online presence in March 2009, when First Lady Michelle Obama came to serve breakfast. With a few days' notice, Development Associate Jennifer Roccanti revamped the Facebook page and started a Twitter account. As Roccanti and Development Director Sara Gibson explained, Twitter was a way to let their supporters know about Mrs. Obama's visit in real time. The social networking was also a way to capitalize on what they knew would be a tremendous amount of media coverage. The Twitter feed that day gave access to reporters who could not be on-site. Over the course of a week from March 5, 2009 (when Mrs. Obama came to the kitchen) to March 12, the story was picked up in eight local (Washington, DC) publications, 182 national publications, and 35 international publications. Many of those reporters remained as Miriam's Kitchen Twitter "followers" after the event. A LexisNexis search reveals that the media coverage shot up from fifteen stories in 2008 to 109 in 2009.

The press' coverage of Miriam's Kitchen spawned social network connections among other people within DC and beyond. According to Roccanti, most of her 2,775 Twitter followers had not been to the kitchen before. They started following because of relationships through the media or other tweets. Her nearly 500 Facebook fans[31], she says, are more likely to have a direct relationship with the organization, such as volunteers or donors—at least in the first year. Her Twitter followers interact more than her Facebook fans.

Roccanti and Gibson reinforce two main messages about their use of social networking. First, their goal is to deepen relationships with people. Second, these relationships have landed Miriam's Kitchen donations from all over the country. Roccanti regularly repeats a story about their first success—this story shows up, for example, in the *Washington Business Journal* article[32] and in an interview with *Washington Business Tonight,*[33] and is one she repeated to me in an interview in February 2010. A California businesswoman, Kyle Smitley, had first heard about Miriam's Kitchen when she interned with First Lady Laura Bush at the White House. She began following Miriam's Kitchen on Twitter, and soon received one of Roccanti's "On our wish list today" tweets. Smitley forwarded the wish list to her business e-mail network; later Miriam's Kitchen mysteriously received boxes of socks from California and tea from Boston. The donations came from people who had had no previous connections with the nonprofit. Roccanti emphasizes that Smitley is still very involved with Miriam's Kitchen. In March 2010, she donated $1 to the kitchen for every comment on her company blog and, as Roccanti announced in a Miriam's Kitchen Facebook update, Smitley's early 2010 clothing catalog nodded to Miriam's Kitchen when one image of a young boy was captioned, "Luke wasn't afraid of anything hiding under his bed. What bothered him was that tonight, some people didn't have one."[34] In January 2010, Smitley's online catalog also included a call-out box featuring Miriam's Kitchen and inviting others to follow the nonprofit online.[35] Twitter and Facebook, says Roccanti, are about building relationships that allow people to have a direct effect and to "build relationships on *their* timeline": she allows people to "choose when and how to engage."

My own experience with the power of such social networking happened during the historic winter storms that struck DC in February 2010. In an area where average snowfall measures a few inches a year, we had two major snowstorms within a week. Snow began falling Friday night, February 5, and by Sunday morning, I measured twenty-six and a half inches on my porch. We had barely dug out when the snow began again on Tuesday. While that storm didn't bring as much snow (a total of about eight inches), Wednesday's blizzard was one of the worst I have ever experienced. The whiteouts were so severe I could not see the street a few yards from my house, and I worried all day that the hovering tree branches would tear off and jam into our roof. The storm raged at this intensity all day long on Wednesday.

What can one do in a storm like that? I checked my e-mail constantly, and I logged onto Facebook as often as I could. On Tuesday morning, between the two storms, I received an e-mail from Miriam's Kitchen (see Figure 7.1). Titled "We're There When You Need Us," the e-mail comforted its readers:

> "We know many of you are concerned about the homeless men and women you see sleeping outside or standing on street corners hungry for food and warmth. And so we hope this e-mail will help put to rest some of those concerns and assure you that Miriam's Kitchen is there when those homeless men and women need us."

The e-mail updated readers about how Miriam's Kitchen staff and volunteers made it through the snow (the chef "hosted a sleepover" for the volunteers), assured us that they had a steady stream of "emergency volunteers," and reiterated what we could do for homeless men and women, even if we could not make it to Miriam's Kitchen: We could shovel our sidewalks, call the hypothermia line if we saw people sleeping in the cold, and so on.

The day of the blizzard, Miriam's Kitchen posted this status update on Facebook around noon: "Miriam's Kitchen: Of the 62 guests we served this morning, most of them slept on the streets last night." I read this while the snow blew sideways past my window. Then a half hour later: "Miriam's Kitchen: ON OUR WISH LIST TODAY: Warm men's clothing. Our guests are coming in soaking wet from the snow & we don't have enough clothing to keep them warm. If you live near us, please help." The wind outside was fierce; the snow stung and bit.

WE'RE THERE WHEN YOU NEED US

It's been a bit of a wild ride in DC these past few days, with two feet of snow already cluttering the sidewalks and another two feet on its way tonight.

We know many of you are concerned about the homeless men and women you see sleeping outside or standing on street corners hungry for food and warmth.

And so we hope this email will help put to rest some of those concerns and assure you that Miriam's Kitchen is there when those homeless men and women need us.

We make special efforts to ensure we never have to cancel our services in inclement weather (if you can even call this week's mess 'inclement'). In fact, **in our 27 years of service to DC's homeless community, we have never once had to close our doors**. Even after blizzards in the city and fires in our dining room!

From Chef Steve Badt hosting sleepovers at Miriam's Kitchen for staff and volunteers to make sure we're here to open our doors precisely at 6:30 am each morning, to Case Managers and volunteers walking two miles in the snow to get here on time to serve our guests--the staff and volunteers at Miriam's Kitchen are dedicated to providing our guests with the best services possible--no matter the conditions.

This morning alone we served 106 homeless men and women a complete breakfast of scrambled eggs, buttermilk pancakes drizzled with warm maple syrup, roasted potatoes, stone-ground grits, garden salad, and homemade applesauce. And tonight we expect to serve just as many guests a healthy dinner of chicken & mushroom risotto, wilted cabbage with garlic, onions & peppers, garden salad, and homemade strawberry shortcakes.

But that's just one of the things we provide in these tough times.

Our Case Managers are also here to help our guests get through these cold & wet days. We have warm sleeping bags for guests who choose to stay outdoors, we have fresh socks for guests whose shoes aren't so dry anymore, and we have a space to relax for guests who have been fighting the elements and just need some time to regroup.

Many of our guests are sleeping outside, even in spite of the weather.

And many of you are probably wondering what you can do to help those guests survive in these harsh conditions.

Figure 7.1: Miriam's Kitchen Letter

I replied that I'd spread the word at George Washington University, where I work. I live miles away, but students on campus are only a few blocks from Miriam's Kitchen. I e-mailed the two Facebook updates to current and previous students. I e-mailed them to my colleagues in the writing program. I e-mailed the head of residential life.

Here are just a few ways you can get involved:

1. Donate warm socks, gloves, hats and scarves.

2. Clear your sidewalk so it's easier for people to walk (especially in the city). Many of our guests walk for miles to get to Miriam's Kitchen every day. Let's make it a little easier for them.

3. Donate warm sleeping bags, blankets and tarps-supplies our guests can use to shield themselves from the elements.

4. If you see anyone struggling or ill prepared for the weather, please call the Hypothermia Shelter Hotline at 1-800-535-7252.

And if you have questions about the services we can provide to those in need, don't hesitate to call or email us anytime.

Thank you for caring about our guests. **It's only with your help that we are able to continue to be there for the people who need us most.**

TODAY'S TOP FIVE!

Special things we do when the snow comes...

5. Activate our emergency volunteer system! All volunteers who can safely walk to MK, report for duty!**

4. Try to stock our clothing closet with as many warm items as possible from supporters like you.

3. Have Chef Steve sleep overnight at MK to ensure we can open in the morning.

2. Make cold weather foods a staple on our menus. On the menu tonight-- risotto!

1. Give special thanks to the amazing volunteers who brave the weather to make sure our guests have everything they need.**

**Because of your generosity, all of our volunteer slots for this week are currently filled!

Figure 7.1 (continued): Miriam's Kitchen Letter

On Thursday morning, the status update read: "Miriam's Kitchen: UPDATE: Thanks to all of your help, we received a LOT of warm clothing last night! We still need blankets, socks, gloves and hats though."

On Friday, Miriam's Kitchen replied to the post where I had said that I would spread the word to the GW network—"Miriam's Kitchen: Phyllis: I think your network has had an impact!"—and included a link to a GW radio

Miriam's Kitchen: Of the 62 guests we served this morning, most of them slept on the streets last night.
February 10 at 12:04 a.m.

Miriam's Kitchen: ON OUR WISH LIST TODAY: Warm men's clothing. Our guests are coming in soaking wet from the snow & we don't have enough clothing to keep them warm. If you live near us, please help.
February 10 at 11:37 a.m.

Phyllis Ryder: I will try to spread the work through the GWU network

Miriam's Kitchen: Thanks, Phyllis

- Two days pass -

Miriam's Kitchen: Phyllis—I think your network has had an impact! http://www.wrgnews.com/2010/02/community-soup-kitchen-helps-those-in.html

Phyllis Ryder: Awesome! That's heartening to hear!

Phyllis Ryder: And from another GW media source: http://blogs. gwhatchet.com/newsroom/2010/02/local-homeless-shelters-remain-open-in-blizzard-conditions/
Miriam's Kitchen: *Thanks to all of your help, we received a LOT of warm clothing last night! We still need blankets, socks, gloves and hats though.*
February 11 at 8:53a.m.

Figure 7.2: Some Wall posts (and responses) on Facebook during the February 2010 blizzard in Washington, D.C.

spot in which a GW student author shared how he discovered Miriam's Kitchen through an e-mail from a professor and met up with other students who were also on their way to deliver clothes. The GW student newspaper, the *Hatchet,* ran a similar story. GW students, teachers, and friends had rallied to the cause during the blizzard. It seems hyperbolic to say it, but those dry clothes probably saved some lives during the storm.

Both of these stories—Smitley's and mine—highlight a particular kind of capacity that Miriam's Kitchen reinforces through its social networking: the capacity of people to mobilize their networks so that others can make a material donation to the kitchen. And material donations matter to an organization that provides breakfast, dinner, case management, and a suite of community-building and therapeutic studio classes to over 4,000 homeless people, with a budget of $1.7 million. A staff member told me recently that, because of in-kind donations from area food stores, Miriam's Kitchen is able to prepare a full meal for each guest for $1.

Valuable as it is, though, collecting donations is simply the most tangible outcome of Miriam's Kitchen's social networking. The exchanges that lead to those donations are full of specific, rhetorical work that brings fans, followers, and their networks together as a public, one that adopts a particular attitude toward the conditions of homelessness, a particular understanding of their capacity to address those conditions, and a particular mode of interacting around those concerns. Recognizing that this public formation is happening among journalists, activists, online followers, and Miriam's Kitchen's staff, volunteers and donors—but without the voices of homeless men and women, a point I'll examine in more detail later—I want to use this example to unpack some of the rhetorical strategies of public formation.

Rhetorics of Public Formation: Exigency, Capacity, Circulation, and Stranger Relations

As I explained in chapter 3, extending the argument by Lloyd Bitzer, a *public* rhetorical situation is one that is seen as "capable of positive modification," where the desired change "requires discourse or can be assisted by discourse."[36] In non-elitist democratic models, where the audience is everyday citizens, the rhetor posits that people can work together to create that "positive modification." The rhetorical task of public formation is to convince people that they are *capable* of making change. Non-elitist public agency insists on the *interdependence* of the public; public rhetoric orients people toward each other to gain this agency, and it shapes their interactions so that they recognize not only their own personal power, but the power that comes from being part of a group that is bigger than they are, which includes people they know and people they don't. How does Jennifer Roccanti use the Twitter and Facebook spaces to establish public exigency, capacity, and interdependence among strangers? How does she keep the discourse circulating?

As development associate at Miriam's Kitchen, Roccanti describes her work as "building relationships" with people and "to deepen those relationships so we can meet our budget for our guests." And she quickly names what's at stake: "Our goal . . . is to raise more money so we can continue to keep our programs strong and our guests alive." As the story of the blizzard makes clear, her words are not an exaggeration: coming in out of the weather can be a matter of life and death. Moreover, as Roccanti explains, the people who come to Miriam's Kitchen are a particular subset of the broader homeless population in DC: "We have a unique community. We cater to chronically homeless people." Homeless organizations throughout DC draw different constituents: Bread for the City, for example, attracts people with very low-paying jobs whose focus is on affordable housing. DC Central Kitchen works with homeless people who seek a particular set of job skills: it employs and trains homeless men and women to work in the kitchen and as part of its catering program.[37] But Miriam's Kitchen works with chronically homeless people, many of whom "may never want to be inside," Roccanti explains. "Just coming into Miriam's Kitchen is a success for those who will stay outside." When chronically homeless people feel enough trust to come in out of the street for a small while, the choice is hardly trivial, especially during storms like the 2010 blizzard or heat waves that blast 100-degree days for weeks at a stretch.

To consider the question of social networking's public exigency, then, we have to look at two different situations. First, what exigency brings together an online community of Miriam's Kitchen followers and "fans," a group that includes many people who have never been to the kitchen or may never have talked to a homeless person, people who may not appreciate the unique challenges of living on the streets yet nevertheless sign up to receive updates about what Miriam's Kitchen is doing? Second, how does Miriam's Kitchen use social networking platforms to convince followers that their participation in this medium and with Miriam's Kitchen in general will effect change? And third—a point I'll take up later—what is the exigency for Miriam's Kitchen itself, and how does its vision of "positive modification" in the lives of chronically homeless people inform the interactions in the online community?

Roccanti imagines the online community as people who are concerned about homelessness. She invokes her audience as people who already care and want to know what to do. Her task is to help them imagine steps they can take, but to do so in a way that reinforces one of the unique aspects she sees at Miriam's Kitchen, the positive, uplifting atmosphere in which such work is done.[38] To create effective updates, Roccanti has to identify opportunities provided by current events inside and outside the kitchen that allow her to highlight this component of Miriam's Kitchen's work.

Roccanti cycles through five main types of status updates on both Twitter and Facebook. These are often tied to current events in DC or at Miriam's Kitchen. The five categories are

1. *"One thing you can do to help,"* posted every Friday
2. *Links about issues* relating to homelessness and hunger
3. *"Our wish list"* and thank-yous.
4. *"On the menu,"* posted twice a day, and
5. *Updates about events* and media coverage relating to Miriam's Kitchen

The blizzard story and the often-told story of the organization's initial forays into social networking illustrate the power of the use of the first two categories. Roccanti sends out "one thing you can do to help" every Friday, and—as with the blizzard e-mail—the advice is simple and targeted to help people identify small changes in their everyday lives and interactions that can affect homeless people. The advice might be anything from "Donate water bottles to your nearest homeless services nonprofit" (posted on a particularly steamy day in July) to "Say hello to someone on the street."

Roccanti educates people about homelessness through "links about issues," such as news articles about homeless shelters, videos about related health issues, and the like. She also regularly engages the Twitter followers in general questions, tied to some recent holiday or event, which she can then tie back to the homeless guests' experiences. For example, over Thanksgiving

---

1. "One thing you can do to help," using Twitter

*[MK Twitter]:*ONE THING YOU CAN DO TODAY TO HELP: Collect your plastic grocery bags and send them to MK! Our guests can use them to carry their belongings.
11:00 a.m. March 5, via Social Media Exchange

[MK Twitter]: ONE THING YOU CAN DO TODAY TO HELP: Do one nice thing for someone. As I heard on the vm of a donor, "make today great for someone else."
10:17 a.m. Feb. 26, via Web

2. Links about issues, using Twitter and Facebook

[MK Twitter]: Startling revelations about DC's shelter for homeless families: http://bit.ly/aeGinp
12:06 p.m. March 11, via Web
The link opens the blog page of the *Washington City Paper,* with the headline "[Mayor] Fenty's Gifts to Homeless Families: Mold, Peeling Paint, Rib Patties, and Overcrowding," posted by Jason Cherkis on March 10, 2010, at 2:45 p.m.

[MK Facebook]: Five myths about America's homeless: http://bit.ly/9gP1zW
8:04 a.m. July 12

Figure 7.3: Five Types of Status Updates from Miriam's Kitchen, using both Facebook and Twitter

[MK Facebook]: Great article about the myths of overhead expenses by the CEO of Do Something: http://bit.ly/bADBpI. It's just a numbers game, but we spent 11.8% on 'overhead' in 2008.
Do Something: Good vs. Evil | Fast Company
Overhead is seen as the devil of the not-for-profit world. Here's why that conventional wisdom is wrong.
3:18 p.m. March 23

3. "On our wish list" and thank-yous, using Facebook

[MK Facebook]: ON OUR WISH LIST TODAY: Small, unopened bottles of hand lotion. Dry skin is common among our guests, especially in the winter.
9:00 a.m. March 4, from Social Media Exchange
Anna and Frank like this.

[MK Facebook]: Thanks Mary Roccanti Meckling for sending us a huge box of toiletries for our guests. It's chock full of Burt's Bees lotions and fun international hotel goods. Almost like opening birthday presents!
8:45 a.m. March 8
Andrea likes this.

4. "On the menu," using Facebook

[MK Facebook]: ON THE MENU TONIGHT: Three bean chili, jalapeno corn bread, green bean casserole, garden salad, and fruit.
4:00 p.m. February 10

[MK Facebook]: ON THE MENU TONIGHT: Beef and barley soup, oregano mashed potatoes, tomato & cucumber drizzled with red wine vinaigrette, and fruit.
1:15 p.m. March 11

5. Updates about MK Events and Media Coverage, using Facebook

[MK Facebook]: We're presenting at the Split This Rock Poetry Festival today in DC on the benefits of poetry in community building. If you'll be there, stop by our session at 11:30!
7:39 a.m. Friday
SJ and Frank like this.

[MK Facebook]: Our Executive Director, Scott Schenkelberg, will be on the Kojo Show today at 1 pm on WAMU talking about what it's like to be homeless in a blizzard.
11:57 a.m. February 10

she tweeted "What's your favorite food at Thanksgiving?" During the snow-storm she asked "What's your favorite activity in the snow?" In May she asked, "Who do you think should control what's in your food?" accompanied by a link to a *Washington Post* story about the FDA's plan to limit salt in pro-cessed foods. These often generate some response, which she then might steer to heighten awareness about the experiences of homelessness. Occasionally, I have seen Roccanti and the leaders of other DC homeless service nonprofits banter back and forth about a particular local news story. The goal, Roccanti says, is not to make people sad or demoralized by noticing the difficulties of living on the streets, but rather to highlight that steps can be taken. In the process, she wants to convey that working with Miriam's Kitchen means working in a "bright, welcoming" place "where people aren't afraid to inter-act with homeless men and women."

The "One thing you can do today" updates encourage the readers to see themselves in some way connected to homeless individuals. In contrast, the wish lists and thank-yous encourage the readers to see themselves connected to homeless people through the work of Miriam's Kitchen. Yet they also highlight a capacity unique to the Web: the power of circula-tion through online networks. As she writes the updates, Roccanti tries to anticipate what might make her readers "re-tweet" or "share" the updates. When her thank-yous illustrate that the donations came because people for-warded the kitchen updates, she shows them how to channel this Internet power. Roccanti knows that her wish lists are re-tweeted frequently. (She learns this through a system of Google alerts and by tracking all Miriam's Kitchen–related posts on Twitter.) The cycle of requests and acknowledge-ments projects a spirit of celebration and encouragement among a group of people who may not have any other connection to the kitchen. She wants them to maintain and develop their connection as an online community that makes a difference.

The updates that receive the most comments and re-tweets are the "On the menu" updates, which are sent out twice daily. The emphasis on the kitch-en's homemade and healthy cooking reminds the online audience about the kitchen's ethos of putting the needs of its guests first. Roccanti uses the lan-guage of restaurant menus in these updates: entrees are "drizzled" with sauce; breads and desserts are "homemade," "warm," and "fresh;" grits are "stone-ground." They offer "braised cabbage with cilantro," and, as if pesto itself were not classy enough, they offer "arugula pesto." The overall message: this is not your basic soup kitchen. The menu updates dispel any stereotypical image of a dark, musty place where people line up to receive globs of gray, unappetizing food. They highlight as well how Miriam's Kitchen accounts for the most common diseases among their guests, including diabetes and hypertension. Furthermore, the updates fit well into the Twitter and Facebook model, where it's expected that we'll hear about everyday events. The "On the menu" updates call people's attention again and again to the larger work of Miriam's Kitchen.

Social networking is an especially productive medium for reminding people of ongoing urgency. Although it is possible to see Miriam's Kitchen's Twitter and Facebook posts without signing up as "followers" or "friends," most people who come across Roccanti's status updates choose to receive them. The status updates are distributed to each reader as part of an ongoing stream of updates, which they access by logging into their Twitter or Facebook accounts. The stream of updates rushes along quickly: for example, Miriam's Kitchen follows over 2,500 people on Twitter, and when Roccanti looks at one screen's worth of Twitter feed, she sees updates posted in the previous second. People check their updates randomly throughout the day, which means that anyone in the stream has a chance of being seen by anyone else, but few (if any) people are likely to see *all* the updates from all of the people they are following. At the same time, one is *expected* to post regular updates; doing so is seen as part of the contract between friends/followers. Because viewers can control how many of the new updates they will scroll through at a given time, the constant barrage of updates is not experienced the same way as a slew of e-mails piling up in an in-box or a stack of solicitation envelopes delivered to one's home. People choose to follow people or organizations and choose when to look at their updates. Usually, they scroll through the page of compiled status updates and respond to or forward any that stand out as important or amusing.

Social networking sites like these solve part of the problem of circulation by giving Roccanti steady access to a broad set of people who have indicated some interest in hearing what is going on at Miriam's Kitchen. And while she has to compete with what she calls the "clutter" and "noise" of the Twitter feed, the sites nevertheless reinforce the exigency Miriam's Kitchen wishes to circulate an exigency that says "we must pay attention" and "we can do things in our daily lives to address this," though the things we do need not be big or drastic. Roccanti is careful to manage the urgency so that it is never so overwhelming that people shut it off. Moreover, she's careful to stress the successes of the program and the ongoing enthusiasm of the staff and other volunteers. The optimistic ethos of Miriam's Kitchen combines "do it on your own timeline" and "stay tuned for more."

Stranger Relations? Chronic Homelessness, Deliberation, and Public Voice

The menu updates are *not* intended for the guests themselves, who often are in line or have already eaten when the update is sent out. As is true for links about issues relating to homelessness and hunger, and for updates about events and media coverage relating to Miriam's Kitchen, the goal of the menu updates is to build relationships directly with non-homeless people. When Roccanti describes her online audience, she is quite aware that she's appealing to volunteers and donors. In the time that I have been following Miriam's Kitchen, I have only infrequently seen a homeless person enter into the discussion, and then it's often to say "thank you" or to give a thumbs-up about a recent wish list item or donation.

Roccanti knows that many of Miriam's Kitchen's guests are on Facebook, but she does not actively reach out to friend them or invite them to chime in. She does not link to their personal blogs or other online presence; she does not specifically address Miriam's Kitchen's guests; she does not interact with them on Facebook much, since those activities would show up on Miriam's Kitchen's page in a manner that might "out" them as guests. The social networking space, then, seems to be a space where middle-class people mobilize each other to help poor people. What democratic model do these interactions reinforce?

Before I examine that further, I want to address what some may consider a barrier to guests' participation in these online social networks. We might assume that homeless people do not write on Miriam's Kitchen's Facebook wall or comment on her tweets because they lack computer access. Yet, for many in this particular population, this is not the case. According to Roccanti, guests use Miriam's Kitchen website regularly. The website includes contact information for case managers, schedules for their after-breakfast programs, and updates about their new dinner program. Many of Miriam's Kitchen's guests have their own Facebook accounts as well, have e-mail accounts, and use online resources to stay connected. The People for Fairness Coalition, an advocacy group of homeless men that meets at Miriam's Kitchen, currently is building their website. In their weekly meetings, the activists share e-mail addresses for each other, government services, nonprofit organizations, and other supporters. Homeless men and women can access computers and the Internet through the DC libraries (a situation that is not universally true; in many cities the library creates codes explicitly designed to restrict such access). And other homeless service nonprofits, such as Thrive DC, have computer labs where volunteers are on hand to assist people in setting up and retrieving e-mail, surfing the Web, and other activities. I don't mean to suggest that all homeless people have easy access to the Internet, but I do think that the active Internet use among a significant portion of Miriam's Kitchen's guests suggests that we need another explanation for why the guests choose not to participate in these social networking exchanges.

When I asked Roccanti whether she thought Miriam's Kitchen's social networking should facilitate a conversation among all followers, fans, and the homeless guests at Miriam's Kitchen, she responded, "I don't think the nonprofit has to be that link." And I think she's right.

As I noted earlier, the main people Miriam's Kitchen serves are chronically homeless men, a population potentially very resistant and distrustful of others. In "Helping or Hating the Homeless" (the *Harper's* essay I analyzed in chapter 4), Peter Marin identifies two categories of homeless people—those who have had homelessness forced upon them yet still believe in our social system enough to want to get back into it, and those for whom the conditions that led to their homelessness bespeak such a profound failure in our social system that they don't try to get back in. Marin writes of Alice, raped, traumatized, and when she eventually left the hospital, jobless and homeless:

> Everything that happened to Alice—the rape, the loss of job and apartment, the breakdown—was part and parcel of a world gone radically wrong, a world, for Alice, no longer to be counted on, no longer worth living in. Her homelessness can be seen as flight, as failure of will or nerve, even, perhaps, as disease. But it can also be seen as a mute, furious refusal, a self-imposed exile far less appealing to the rest of us than ordinary life, but better, in Alice's terms.[39]

Chronically homeless people may not want to "come back in" to relationships with others; for their own reasons, they don't buy into the promises that specific actions on their part will lead to positive, supportive responses from the social, political, and economic structures that have already rejected them. Their position poses a big challenge to those who work with them. For many, the rejection of society is coupled with—maybe caused by—mental illnesses or addictions, and the assumption is that if we could treat those symptoms, the person would be willing to rejoin, to start looking for work and housing. For some, that is true. Yet viewing their rejection as "mental illness" seems to gloss over the deeper sense of nihilism that may be based on an accurate understanding of the failures built into the capitalist, free-market, individualist structures around us.

The experience of public space for homeless people is radically different because they are not in that space voluntarily: homeless people have to interact constantly with strangers and conduct their daily lives in public view. In his analysis of the redevelopment of a Berkeley park where homeless men and women often stay, Don Mitchell writes,

> Public parks and streets . . . become places to go to the bathroom, sleep, drink, or make love—all socially legitimate activities when done in private but seemingly illegitimate when carried out in public.[40]

The presence of homeless people and their "illegitimate" uses of public space highlight the contradiction in democratic ideals: "[S]ince citizenship in modern democracy . . . rests on a foundation of *voluntary* association, and since homeless people are *involuntarily* public[,] . . . they threaten the existence of a 'legitimate'—i.e. voluntary—public."[41] People who have access to private space respond to homeless people in public space with a sense of rage, a fear sparked by the sense that their presence makes the idea of "public" unstable. Thus, whether a homeless person rejects society or tries to re-enter it, his or her very presence disturbs the "legitimate" structures of public spaces and public interactions. Homeless people feel the brunt of that disruption in their daily interactions, when they are ignored by "regular" people or when they are attacked by them. According to the National Coalition for the Homeless, "From 1999 through 2008, in 263 cities and in 46 states, Puerto Rico and Washington, DC, there have been 880 acts of violence committed by housed individuals, resulting in 244 deaths of homeless people and 636 victims of non-lethal violence."[42]

Roccanti emphasized that Miriam's Kitchen is one of the few spaces where its guests ever come indoors. For people who have learned to rely on only themselves, coming indoors can signal a willingness to trust, if only for a moment. For Miriam's Kitchen, that's enough of a step. In their main dining room, Miriam's Kitchen protects the anonymity of its guests. The expectation among volunteers and guests is that you will not engage others unless they initiate the interaction. The kitchen does not ask people to sign in to get food. No one takes pictures (and if anyone takes out a camera, staff and guests alike will remind them of this rule). Miriam's Kitchen is very aware that coming in from the streets is not the same as being willing to engage in other kinds of social or political relationships. The kitchen takes its cue from its guests.

Given this context, then, the online space honors this same intense protection of privacy—a privacy that is missing in the daily experiences of people whose every action is conducted in public and made to seem illegitimate. Inviting homeless guests into such a forum would violate the trust that the kitchen wants to build: Roccanti explains, "We wouldn't take advantage of the trust we've built with them to mention that they are guests . . . It's not that I don't want to interact with them, it's that they need to be the ones to establish that connection online." Mitchell's definition of ideal public space includes the requirement that the space be "free of coercion;" Roccanti's attitude seems to exemplify that. Mitchell's definition also requires the space to be "unmediated." Yet, for the guests, Miriam's Kitchen's social networking spaces are not unmediated spaces. Participation would take place under the gaze of Miriam's Kitchen, and participants' comments would reflect back on the organization.

Roccanti's response to my question also points out that homeless people who wish to engage in such public conversations about issues of homelessness can (and do) participate in other online spaces; they are plenti-ful. Homeless forums, such as www.homelessforum.com, are self-described as "international forums for homeless or formerly homeless people and oth-ers wanting to learn about homelessness." In video blogs such as STREATS (www.streats.tv) and YouTube channels (http://www.youtube.com/user/ToddCWiggins, for example), homeless men and women speak about the conditions of being homelessness and invite others into public conversation through the comments section. In those venues, people who choose to iden-tify themselves as homeless can, but they are not pressured to do so.

The Publics of Miriam's Kitchen

Overall, we can identify several different groups of people who interact with and around Miriam's Kitchen. The Facebook friends and Twitter followers, along with the volunteers and donors on the kitchen's e-mail distribution lists, comprise one group: a group of predominantly middle-class people who may not have much experience with people who are homeless but who have expressed some interest in being linked to an organization like Miriam's Kitchen. These people are brought together as part of a network. They don't know each other, they don't necessarily speak to each other online, but they lurk and listen and in some small way continue to engage as a collection of people who share this interest. The infrastructure of Facebook helps reinforce this idea of being among friends and strangers committed to the same idea: the Facebook application chooses six people from among the many who are "fans" or (in the more recent incarnation) who have "liked" the same page. When possible, three of those people will be among the viewers' own list of "friends," and three will be strangers.

When Roccanti thanks someone for forwarding a wish list, and thanks someone else for sending in lotion, her acknowledgement affirms the poten-tial capacity of the whole group. When she poses questions on Twitter about who should control food safety, or "what's in your fridge," she invites the group to imagine how their own lives are different from the homeless people for whom they have expressed compassion, and she does so in a forum where they can read each other's responses. The frequency and consistency of Roc-canti's online interactions and her projection of the Miriam's Kitchen ethos as a bright, fun place where people address serious issues, invites the audience to identify as people who can help make change. She forwards links and vid-eos to re-tweet and re-post, so that Miriam's Kitchen's name and philosophy of a profound respect for the experiences of homeless people will circulate. The value of social networking here is not to bring people together for delib-eration as much as to celebrate their power to circulate the Miriam's Kitchen ideal; the value of social networking is to frequently remind the group of the conditions of homelessness and of their own capacity to attenuate those conditions through their ongoing relationship with Miriam's Kitchen. Is this a "public"?

At the same time, another group comes together within the walls of Miriam's Kitchen itself. During and after meals people come together for face-to-face conversations. Some people serve food and others eat it. Some gather to read and write poetry together or to create art together. If they choose, homeless guests can meet with case managers and access additional city resources. Within this context, staff and volunteers come together with chronically homeless men (and a few women) to create a space that serves as a respite from the streets without making demands. As a low-barrier organization, the kitchen does not require guests to show ID or to present proof that they are not using drugs or alcohol. The kitchen does not require guests to show evidence of trying to get a job or a house, or of any other actions that would signal that they are trying to work to get back into the "normal" structures of society. Within this space, the group—staff, volunteers, and guests—comes together in a community that works to honor at a deep level each person's dignity. This characterization of Miriam's Kitchen aligns it with an argument Marin makes about what society owes chronically homeless people. "We owe them a place to exist," he says, and we must provide it for them with great humility, with an awareness that "those who are the inevitable casualties of modern industrial capitalism and the free market system are entitled, by right, and by the simple virtue of their participation in that system, to whatever help they need."[43]

Miriam's Kitchen's approach aligns well with the approach that Keith Morton advocates in "The Ironies of Service: Charity, Project and Social Change in Service-Learning," an article I discussed in chapter 2.[44] Morton argues that whether service is offered through direct aid (a charity model), measurable programs (a project model), or political action (a social change model), the central values that make each model "thick" and potentially worthwhile are respect and dignity, the principle of starting where people are and neither judging nor seeking to control them. Most importantly, Morton's main argument is that thick service does *not* require that we take action by marching on city hall or boycotting stores. It does *not* require that we even begin by expecting people to trust us or the larger political, economic, or social systems that we operate in. Thick service acknowledges broader systemic causes for the concerns that mobilize us, and because of this, requires that we approach each other as equals.

Within Miriam's Kitchen, guests find a space that accepts their disillusionment, a place that does not judge them for choosing to step outside of the dominant system. That space happens within the walls of Miriam's Kitchen, through the homemade meals and relationships with staff and volunteers that are steeped in a desire to offer respite from the systems that have failed them. Within this context, Miriam's Kitchen cannot and should not "friend" their guests or re-tweet guests' updates or in any way expect them into jump into online exchanges with the donors and volunteers. Doing so would cause the respite to dissolve: they'd be forced to interact with and perhaps try to educate people who believe in the very systems that have failed them.

I don't see Miriam's Kitchen's actions as a patronizing move, such as trying to protect the homeless from the potential ignorance of the public that comes together with Miriam's Kitchen on the social-networking sites. Instead, I see them respecting a desire *not* to engage in this conversation, a desire to leave that work—the work of bringing people to a place where they can imagine respectful relationships with homeless people—to the staff and volunteers.

At the same time, guests at Miriam's Kitchen who do retain some hope and trust in political and social systems are reaching out to the audiences that matter to them. The People for Fairness Coalition, begun in 2008, meets weekly at Miriam's Kitchen. Their goals are "Housing for all, safe and clean shelters for all, representation by currently or formerly homeless individuals on the city's decision-making boards, transparency in the city's decision-making through dialogue with and improved access to service providers and city officials."[45] The officers of this group are associated with particular subgroups of homeless people, including homeless women and homeless veterans, and the group as a whole conducts regular outreach on the streets, meeting with people who have given up hope and offering a connection to food, services, and other resources. The men and women sometimes refer to themselves as "caseworkers" for the chronically homeless, and they rely on their own experiences as current or formerly homeless people as part of their persuasive appeal. The other audiences the group addresses are government and service providers. The officers of the organizations testified before the DC City Council to share their stories and request funding to continue their outreach. They invite representatives from city departments to meet with them. The coalition members regularly attend meetings throughout DC to learn both more about organizing and more about the services that they can provide for each other and for the men and women who have not yet come in off the streets.

When the People for Fairness Coalition members meet, one of the kitchen's case managers usually sits with them to answer questions about what kinds of support the kitchen can lend, but the organization is run by and for homeless and formerly homeless people. Significantly, this group is not oriented toward the public of Roccanti's social networking sites; instead, it is oriented toward government and service providers as well as homeless individuals. These are the people with whom they are interested in working to improve the conditions for homeless people. They acknowledge the support that Miriam's Kitchen provides and appreciate any material support that volunteers or others might offer, but their work is not dependent on interacting with a middle-class public that has not experienced homelessness.

Miriam's Kitchen's use of social networking as a tool of public formation takes place within a much broader context of online and off-line interactions. Examining their work demonstrates that no one site or set of exchanges is adequate to show us whether and how a public comes together. The Kitchen recognizes that their online presence is not the only online space where homeless and housed people might interact. Homeless people and advocates can reach that broader audience on homeless forums, YouTube, and through other social media. Moreover, the online public work of their social networking takes place alongside the Kitchen's physical spaces—alongside groups like the People for Fairness Coalition, alongside the face-to-face relationships that build among guests, volunteers, and staff, and alongside the chronically homeless people come tentatively into the Kitchen, holding themselves apart. Miriam's Kitchen acknowledges that public space is not voluntary for those without a home; it offers some respite.

Moreover, when we understand the rhetorical moves that people use in social networking sites to create interdependence and reinforce a sense of capacity, we can see that a great deal of public formation relies on people's ability not only to generate discourse, but also to *circulate* it. Often scholars evaluate public formation according to the quality of deliberation, but in social networking, the central component seems to be that of circulation, making things happen by sharing, forwarding, re-tweeting, and getting the words out there. We need to focus on the power of circulation, that critical component of the Internet that plays such a potent role in public formation.

When we examine the kind of public spaces that congeal online, and when we try to determine what we will value as ideal public spaces, we need to examine all of these contexts and all of the components of public formation. The lenses we use to evaluate the success or failure of public spaces must carefully attend to the varied needs and contexts of their public participants and to many components of public formation, including the power of circulation.

WHAT DOES THIS MEAN FOR A PUBLIC WRITING COURSE?

Because the Internet is ever-changing, any advice for how to incorporate public formation via the Internet is likely to be quickly outdated. In its earlier incarnations, the focus was on static websites, where people could broadcast information; now it has grown more interactive. Web 2.0 applications, of which Facebook and Twitter are only two among many, have shifted the expectations for online spaces. Now groups are assessed not just for how they present information, but also for how they solicit viewer feedback and whether they facilitate conversations among users. The ethos of Web 2.0 is about user participation and control. Cade Metz at PCMag.com explains, "Web 2.0 came to describe almost any site, service, or technology that promoted sharing and collaboration right down to the Net's grass roots."[46]

There are whispers, as I write, of a new Web 3.0 incarnation, which is also dubbed the "Semantics Web." Here, applications "read" web pages, collect data, and display that data—a new generation of search engines that will concatenate huge amounts of information from across the Web. In theory, the Web 3.0 browser will learn from a user's past requests and begin to anticipate the kind of information that user will want it to gather.

Such applications are already in play, of course. Those companies who use advertising to offer particular content and online experiences to their customers already troll users' online postings and activity so that they can then provide user-specific advertising. All of my kvetching on Facebook while writing this book earned me dozens of advertising appeals from self-publishing enterprises, for example. Facebook has, over the past few years, made more and more user information public so that it can bring in more marketing revenue. Its business model, like that of many online sites, is grounded in this Web 3.0 principle.

Whether or not the Internet evolves in this manner, it will change, and democratic activists, community organizers, and nonprofits will need to adjust, looking for the best methods through which to use the technology to form and maintain public relationships. At the same time, we need to look carefully at how corporate-minded infrastructures shape the design of new applications even before they become available for more potentially public-minded uses. And we will need to adjust our scholarship and our pedagogy to suit.

For those of us who teach public writing, we need to consider how to prepare our students to draw on the multiple components of the Internet for public formation. When I began connecting my first-year public writing students with community organizations just a few years ago, the nonprofits were building their websites and working to get their content online. Now they are foraging into social networking. Since Miriam's Kitchen launched its Twitter and Facebook presence last year, many other nonprofits have done the same: nine of the twelve partners I'm working with in 2010 are on Facebook. Increasingly, my students are asked to help maintain these social networking sites. As I prepare them for the task, we can analyze how these nonprofits and other organizations have invoked public agency, capacity, and interdependence through these venues. I also must help my students balance the potentially disparate needs of the various audiences involved, considering which venues are made available to which groups for which purposes. And I can help them contextualize some of the scholarship about democracy and the Internet: while those of us who teach public writing may treasure the ideals of citizen deliberation across difference, we need to ensure that this single vision of public formation does not blind us to other methods or other places in which publics come together.

As scholars and teachers, we need to pay careful attention to how we draw on Internet materials in our analyses of public writing. We cannot treat a website as a single, definitive place where an organization projects its identity and does its public work: a website is one place and an important one, but it is surrounded by other online and physical spaces, whose infrastructures frame different kinds of relationships. Likewise, we should consider that some work of public formation will take place offline or online in a way that will not be accessible to everyone. If we consider the Internet as a site where publics circulate, where they can spread their views of "the world as it is" and "the world as it should be," then we must understand the Internet as a site of struggle. Some of the most difficult, deliberative work of a public is the kind of self-reflection and probing of core values that is too risky to make public, especially in a context where competing publics or those in power are not generous, benevolent interlocutors.

Finally, we should also reflect on our own use of online classroom spaces and the kinds of public formations that are possible there. I am mindful that classroom space is not the same as public space: the exigency that brings students together in my class is not necessarily any interest in or sense of interdependence with each other, but rather a university course requirement: first-year composition. Likewise, the exigency for their writing is not necessarily public either: the university is what compels them to write for my class, even when they are writing for community organizations. Nevertheless, I design my classes so that students have opportunities to learn from each other. I want them to have practice identifying questions and sorting though ideas together. I want them to develop the habits of mind that Harvard composition scholars Nancy Sommers and Laura Saltz describe in "The Novice as Expert": being able to "see in writing a larger purpose than fulfilling an assignment."[47] I want them to experience a public exigency: a reason to contemplate an idea fully and share their findings with others, whether their classmates, other academics, or community partners.

My reflections on the potential for online public formation have influenced how I use online course software. Just as community organizations often keep their internal deliberations out of sight of the broader public eye, I also consider how to facilitate sometimes difficult discussions about students' experiences working in DC communities without subjecting the students to scrutiny by people outside the class (and sometimes by people in the class). For this reason, I keep all of our online activity private. When we write blogs or post memos, when we share drafts, we do so within a courseware firewall that people outside our class cannot enter (GW uses the Blackboard courseware).

I use the courseware features to try to build interdependence in the classroom. For example, I ask students to post observations about their community work in class blogs (available only to the class and not to the organizations, so that students can puzzle through experiences together without feeling the gaze of the organization). Students are asked to browse each other's blogs to look for patterns and issues, which may lead to research projects or suggestions for improving volunteer support at an organization. Likewise, I have required students share their research in online bibliographic management programs (GW uses Refworks). They post annotations, read each other's annotations, and can draw on each other's resources. In this manner, I try to simulate how scholarly communities work.

Having looked at Miriam's Kitchen's online rhetoric, I have begun to incorporate more of the community-building moves that Roccanti uses. She devotes a great deal of time to maintain her connections, to affirm people's contributions and commitment, and to push them to think creatively about their capacity to effect change. For my part, I send out class updates in which I reflect back some of the insightful observations and provocative questions that students are posting in their blogs, and I give online "shout-outs" to students for special accomplishments. I point out connections or contradictions among students' observations, trying to stimulate cross-talk. Both in class and online, I try to demonstrate how students can learn from each other. I am considering delegating some of this work to students, as a way for them to practice such public-building rhetoric.

Despite all of these attempts, I do not feel that I have built the right course infrastructure for online collaboration. While other aspects of my course have created a sense of interdependence among students as they investigate questions of public writing together, the online component of the course remains useful primarily as a place to store information or for teacher-student interactions, but not for student-student joint inquiry and discussion. Part of the problem, not surprisingly, is that courseware like Blackboard is not designed with student-to-student collaboration in mind. While it can be made to accommodate this pedagogical goal, it is best suited for student-teacher and teacher-student contact. For example, when I send an e-mail through Blackboard to a group of students, they can each reply to me, but they cannot reply to each other. Indeed, they cannot even see that I sent the e-mail to multiple recipients unless I clarify that in my text.

As I continue to experiment with new course designs and new online applications (wikis, blogs, social networking, and so on), I recognize that part of what makes it difficult to sustain collaborative spaces for inquiry in my courses comes not only from the applications, but also from the larger context in which I am trying to conduct such work: my classroom is just one part of students' academic experience. In each classroom and in each bureaucratic interaction, in dorm life and in the academic rituals of convocation and commencement, students experience multiple and often conflicting assumptions about the goals of attending a university and about what it means to be a student there. In my next and final chapter, I consider what it means to teach a public writing course within an academic setting.

NOTES

1. Michael Warner, *Publics and Counterpublics* (Cambridge: Zone Books, 2005), 7–8.
2. Jane Jacobs, *The Death and Life of Great American Cities* (New York: Random House, 1961), 35.
3. Jacobs, *Death and Life,* 25.
4. Jacobs, *Death and Life,* 63.
5. Jacobs, *Death and Life,* 56.
6. Gabriella Gahlia Modan, *Turf Wars: Discourse, Diversity, and the Politics of Place* (Malden, MA: Blackwell, 2007), Chapter 3.
7. Gilbert B. Rodman, "The Net Effect: The Public's Fear and the Public Sphere," in *Virtual Publics: Policy and Community in an Electronic Age,* ed. Beth Kolko (New York: Columbia University Press, 2003), 20.
8. James A. Janack, "Mediated Citizenship and Digital Discipline: A Rhetoric of Control in a Campaign Blog." *Social Semiotics* 16, no. 2 (June 2006): 284.
9. Don Mitchell shows us these competing ideals in his analysis of the fight over the "public" identity of People's Park in Berkeley, California, in "The End of Public Space? People's Park, Definitions of the Public, and Democracy." *Annals of the Association of American Geographers* 85, no. 1 (March 1995): 108–133.
10. Susan Warshauer, "Community-Based Software, Participatory Theater: Models for Inviting Participation in Learning and Artistic Production," in *Virtual Publics: Policy and Community in an Electronic Age,* ed. Beth Kolko (New York: Columbia University Press, 2003), 288.
11. Warshauer, "Community-Based Software," 287.
12. Warshauer, "Community-Based Software," 288.
13. Laura J. Gurak, *Persuasion and Privacy in Cyberspace: The Online Protests Over Lotus MarketPlace and Clipper Chip* (New Haven: Yale University Press, 1997), 5.
14. David M. Anderson, "Cautious Optimism about Online Politics and Citizenship," in *The Civic Web: Online Politics and Democratic Values,* ed. David M. Anderson and Michael Cornfield (Lahnam, MD: Rowman and Littlefield, 2003), 29.

15. Janack, "Mediated Citizenship," 291–296.

16. David Silver, "Communication, Community, Consumption: An Ethnographic Exploration of an Online City," in *Virtual Publics: Policy and Community in an Electronic Age,* ed. Beth Kolko (New York: Columbia University Press, 2003), 328.

17. See Mark Jones for an additional look at BEV, along with seven additional community-based networks. "Can Technology Transform? Experimenting with Wired Communities," in *Virtual Publics: Policy and Community in an Electronic Age,* ed. Beth Kolko (New York: Columbia University Press, 2003), 354–383.

18. Silver, "Communication," 338.

19. Silver, "Communication," 329.

20. Silver, "Communication," 339.

21. Silver, "Communication," 339.

22. Barbara Warnick, *Critical Literacy in a Digital Era: Technology, Rhetoric, and the Public Interest* (Mahwah, NJ: Lawrence Erlbaum Associates, 2002).

23. Erin Dietel-McLaughlin "Remediating Democracy: Irreverent Composition and the Vernacular Rhetorics of Web 2.0," *Computers and Composition Online* (Spring 2009) www.bgsu.edu/cconline (24 August 2010).

24. Warnick, *Critical Literacy,* 90.

25. Robert D. Putnam, *Bowling Alone: The Collapse and Revival of American Community* (New York: Simon & Schuster, 2000), 176.

26. Putnam, *Bowling Alone,* 176.

27. Rodman, "The Net Effect," 13.

28. Jennifer Nycz-Conner, "D.C.'s Miriam's Kitchen Rides Social Media Wave," *Washington Business Journal* 2009 washington.bizjournals.com.proxygw.wrlc.org/washington/stories/2009/07/20/smallb1.html (26 July 2010).

29. Mitchell, "People's Park," 115.

30. Nycz-Conner, "D.C.'s Miriam's Kitchen."

31. In 2010, a Facebook redesign removed the option to "fan" an organization; instead, people can indicate that they "like" an organization, a celebrity, or another person.

32. Nycz-Conner, "D.C.'s Miriam's Kitchen."

33. "NonProfit Finds New Ways to Solicit," *Washington Business Tonight,* July 17, 2010 http://washingtonbusinesstonight.com/videoplayer.fm?id=2&video=mms://wjla.com/washbiztonight/wbtnonprofit0717.wmv (15 March 2010).

34. Barley & Birch, "World Changing" http://barleyandbirch.com/environmental (7 November 2010).

35. Barley & Birch, "2 truths & a lie: Miriam's Kitchen—special edition." 2010 http://barleyandbirch.com/2010/01/2-truths-and-a-lie-miriams-kitchen-special-edition (7 November 2010).

36. Lloyd Bitzer, "The Rhetorical Situation," *Philosophy and Rhetoric* 1 (January 1968): 6.

37. DC Central Kitchen's philosophy is laid out in Robert Eggar's book, *Begging for Change.*

38. In both 2009 and 2010, Miriam's Kitchen was rated one of the best places to work by the *Washington Business Journal;* in 2009, the *Washington City Paper* rated it one of the best places to volunteer.

39. Peter Marin, "Helping and Hating the Homeless," in *Writing and Community Action,* ed. Thomas Deans (Boston: Longman, 2003), 309.

40. Mitchell, "People's Park," 118.

41. Mitchell, "People's Park," 118.

42. National Coalition for the Homeless, "Hate Crimes and Violence Against People Experiencing Homelessness," August 2009 www.nationalhomeless.org/factsheets/hatecrimes.html (30 July 2010), paragraph 1.

43. Peter Marin, "Helping and Hating the Homeless," 317.

44. Keith Morton, "The Irony of Service: Charity, Project and Social Change in Service-Learning." *Michigan Journal of Community Service Learning,* no. xx[[EdQ: Add issue number.]] (Fall 1995): 19–32.

45. Todd Wiggins, "People for Fairness Coalition," June 2006 www.peopleforfairness.magnify.net/user/QD7495R46QD0GDM5 (28 July 2010).

46. Cade Metz. "Web 3.0." PCMag.com 2007 www.pcmag.com/article2/0,2817,2102852,00.asp (24 August 2010).

47. Nancy Sommers and Laura Saltz, "The Novice as Expert: Writing the Freshman Year." *College Composition and Communication* 56, no. 1 (September 2004): 124.

Chapter 8

Teaching Public Writing in Academic Settings

It is no longer clear what the place of the University is within society nor what the exact nature of that society is, and the changing institutional form of the University is something that intellectuals cannot afford to ignore.

—Bill Readings[1]

The University is not going to save the world by making the world more true, nor is the world going to save the University by making the University more real.

—Bill Readings[2]

I like to use Joseph Harris's insightful textbook *Rewriting: How to Do Things with Texts* in my first-year writing class, because his book introduces students well to the metaphor of academic writing as an ongoing conversation among scholars. Addressing himself to students, he writes,

> In the academy, you will often be asked to situate your thoughts about a text or issue in relation to what others have written about it. Indeed, I'd argue that this interplay of ideas defines academic writing—that whatever else they may do, intellectuals almost always write *in response* to the work of others. . . . The job of an intellectual is to push at and question what has been said before, to rethink and reinterpret the texts he or she is dealing with. More than anything else, then, I hope in this book to encourage you to take a stance toward the work of others that, while generous and fair, is also playful, questioning, and assertive.[3]

As I mentioned earlier in chapter 4, what I find most interesting is how Harris links this idea of good academic, intellectual writing to the broader category of public writing. A few pages later, Harris separates his notion of academic writing from disciplinary writing and links it, instead, with the writing of "public life" and prose addressed to "general readers." So much is packed into his short aside that it's worth quoting in full. In a paragraph in which he clarifies what his book is *not*, Harris writes:

> And this [book] is not a guide to the conventions that structure writing in the academic disciplines; indeed, the kind of writing that I talk about here is "academic" only in the sense that it tends to be taught in college. (If you're reading this, you are probably doing so for a course.) The sort of writing that I am drawn to strives to be part of public life. It is prose addressed not to academic specialists, but to general readers—the sort of writing you find in *Harper's* and the *Atlantic,* and the *Nation,* or in *Rolling Stone* and *McSweeney's* and *Saloon,* as well as in independent weeklies, little magazines, student journals, some political and cultural blogs and websites and the like. It's what I will often call here *intellectual prose*—with the caveat that by *intellectual* I don't mean wonkish or bohemian. I am interested in a kind of writing about texts and ideas, culture and politics, that while often associated with the academy is not confined to it, that seeks instead to address a broader and more public set of issues and readers.[4]

I find this passage revealing because Harris puts so well a common way of thinking about the value and purpose of teaching this conversational mode of writing: good general academic writing is good general public writing.

Harris marks out a space and genre for a public intellectual—someone who thinks deeply and carefully about ideas, forwarding, countering, and extending the ideas of others in a generous and assertive way. In his scenario, the public intellectual's goal is to figure out what is true by thinking with others. This public intellectual is much like the public citizen in the idealized public sphere—someone well versed in the habits of reason (which presumably he or she learns in college) and well equipped to explore complex lines of inquiry in the company of others. And, as I also argued in chapter 4, this idealized public sphere circulates quite well in the business and rhetorical structures of the monthly magazines such as those he lists—*Harper's, Atlantic,* and so on.

Edward Schiappa carries Harris's point farther, arguing that academics are especially well prepared to step into this public intellectual role. In his often-mentioned 1994 address to the Rhetorical Society of America, Schiappa admonishes academics to direct their intellectual energies not only to scholarship or classrooms, but also to newspapers, city councils, and state assemblies.[5] And he lists the kinds of intellectual abilities that he thinks will serve academics (especially cultural studies scholars, who are among his audience) as they move into these new arenas:

Most of us speak and write well. Our research skills, analytical abilities, and argumentative prowess make us formidable public intellectuals. The sort of work involved in cultural studies is particularly valuable: media criticism, the ability to trace the ideological work of texts, the ability to argue that categories taken as "natural" or "normal" are better understood as "constructed" and "historically contingent," the ability to situate an individual sign or group of signs into a larger context of meaning—these are the specific skills that cultural critics bring to bear.[6]

Schiappa describes his own foray into public life in which he successfully persuaded a local city council to approve a gay-rights initiative. He assures his readers that "when intellectuals choose to get involved, we can make a difference."[7]

I find myself in a quandary about such pronouncements. On the one hand, I do believe that the intellectual habits and genres that Harris and Schiappa describe here are valuable and worth teaching, and even that they are good tools to use in some democratic deliberations. And I wholeheartedly support the challenge that Schiappa sets out for academics—to connect with people and ideas outside the walls of the university. On the other hand, I am uncomfortable with how both Harris and Schiappa make one kind of thinking/reasoning/writing stand in for all public writing. As I hope I've shown already in this book, the kind of rhetorical training they espouse is well aligned with the idealized public sphere, but public writing in actual democracy contains many different and competing understandings of what "good" democratic interactions look like. Good public writing is *not* the same as transferring general academic discourse into new spaces; it has to account for the broader struggles about democracy and the challenges of circulation.[8]

More importantly—and this is the main point I want to explore in this chapter—we need to look at Harris's and Schiappa's claim from both sides. Those who define *public writing* as an extension of *academic writing* suggest not only that the public sphere has a unified purpose and discourse, but also that academia has a unified purpose and discourse. Harris and Schiappa argue that the purpose of the university is to prepare students for (a certain kind of) public life, but their seemingly self-evident assertion is much more contested than they let on. In this book, I've taken to talking about publics rather than the public, and the same clarification can be made for the university. We might think of *universities,* not in the sense of different disciplines or different institutions, but rather in the sense that there are multiple visions of what higher education is supposed to do, how it should carry out its work, and why its work is beneficial in the broader publics. The clash and clang among these competing Universities is especially loud in difficult economic times, when states have to justify their spending and when the tuition rises.

Much of the work of Universities, then, is to reaffirm their public value, and they do so constantly, sometimes in obvious places like strategic plans or commencement addresses or budget allocations, but also in more subtle places, like the kinds of writing faculty assign, or the design of courseware. The imagined roles and functions for the university are diverse and complex, and while they don't map directly onto the matrix of democracy, there are a number of interesting ways that they overlap. The research university ideal, grounded in a rhetoric of logic and reason, reinforces the role of experts within democracy and can dovetail rather well with elitist democracy. A second category might be dubbed the civic university, though the ideas for how to promote a national cultural identity are (not surprisingly) quite varied. In some versions, under the rubric of Civic Culture, "the University is assigned the dual task of research and teaching, respectively the production and inculcation of national self-knowledge."[9] Others, taking the Deweyan approach, define the civic university as teaching citizens the habits of mind and civic actions, so that they can actively participate in actually existing democracies.

And, finally, just as the rhetorics of democracy in the public sphere have been almost subsumed by the rhetorics of neoliberalism, so the university operates in a space saturated with neoliberal justifications for its purpose: to boost the economy, to create good workers, and to create its "products" efficiently. Henry Giroux writes, "[T]he struggle to reclaim higher education must be seen as part of a broader battle over the defense of public goods."[10] Under the same neoliberal economic forces that restructured social welfare into private nonprofits and traditional journalism into corporate media, the university is pressured to rethink the role of higher education within the discourse of capitalism. Whatever other public goals for the university are advanced—and they are put forward regularly—if the university itself is managed as a corporation, then students and faculty are interpolated into neoliberalism by everyday structures of the University's physical space and managerial hierarchies.

All of these competing conceptions of the university have implications for the project I have laid out in this book. Many pedagogical initiatives start out with the kind of intellectual inquiry I have undertaken in this book, working through theories about the world as it is and the world as it could be, and then locating in its (academic) audience the capacity to take action in the one space over which faculty have the most control: the curricular design of the classroom. But too many stop there, as if redesigning a single class will then effect broader epistemological and cultural transformations. As Rachel Riedner and Kevin Mahoney note in the first book in the Culture/Pedagogy/Activism series (of which this book is now part), too often "critical pedagogy practices . . . focus on the classroom as the primary, if not sole site of pedagogy, eschewing broader theoretical implications of such practice and de-prioritizing non-classroom cultural spaces."[11] In this chapter, I'd like to consider how the pedagogy of public writing that I have laid out in this book sits within the contested space of Universities. Students and faculty alike move in and out of the material practices and rhetorical structures through which these competing ideals circulate, and it's important to consider how those practices will contain or bolster the pedagogy.

First, I'll review briefly the competing Universities. Then, I'll take as a case study a section of the George Washington University's strategic plan, which discusses its goal of creating "community"—a metric that is simultaneously about locating the university within a broader public community and about defining its own internal community. Turning more specifically to university writing, I'll consider how these competing ideals manifest within academic discourses, and I'll argue that despite the usual rift between "academic" and "public" writing, we can speak productively about the varieties of academic writing by considering academics as members of publics, whose rhetorical moves must invoke and reinforce the public ideals of whichever university they would call into being. Finally, I'll examine how the first-year public writing course I have proposed works with and against the competing rhetorics of the university, ending with a hopeful claim for a rhetorical pedagogy that works productively at the intersection of academic and other publics.

COMPETING PUBLICS AT THE UNIVERSITY

The competing arguments about the purpose and value of the university are well known, especially to those of us who work in academic settings. Our decisions about where to work (when they are not controlled by economic and other factors) often take into account what we think higher education should be. Though I use the term *university* here to account for academia in its broadest sense, I recognize that for many who enter higher education, the real value is not embodied in a Ph.D.-granting institution, but rather in a more intimate liberal arts college or a local community college. Each makes its own case for the public value of its institutional mission and structure; each carves out a different vision about whom higher education should serve and what that service should entail. But the public arguments in favor of higher education don't align smoothly with different kinds of institutions. Like the rhetorics of democracy that I have discussed throughout the book, the rhetorics of the academy are readily available and are deployed in sometimes contradictory ways. Because these rhetorics are already familiar, my point in the following section is not to provide extensive historical or institutional analyses of them, but rather to name them quickly in order to then consider in more depth how the constant tension about these values plays out in what is taught as "academic writing."

The Research University: The Pursuit of Knowledge

In his 1987 Ryerson Lecture, a multidisciplinary event in which a professor from one part of the University of Chicago attempts to share his or her scholarship with professors from other parts of the university, Wayne Booth points out that the very notion of the Ryerson Lecture was a bit suspect. He says, "We must wonder just how much understanding can occur across our disciplinary borderlines."[12] And, in a moment that seems as if he's making a confession to those outside the university, he adds, "No one of us can understand more than a fraction of the frontline work of the rest. We are all simply shut out of almost all front parlors but our own, permitted only to do a little polite begging at the back door."[13]

Booth then sets out to rescue this "multiversity"[14] and return to it a sense of itself as a singular entity by setting aside one kind of discourse—disciplinary writing—and introducing two other kinds of rhetorical practices. "Academy rhetoric" refers to those more-general academic moves of scholarly inquiry that other scholars can identify, even if they can't fully follow the content of the work. "General rhetoric," which is shared with people "in every functioning organization or society," refers to what he sees as commonly held proofs that all people use to make sense.[15] I think it's worth noting that in this move Booth makes a distinction that Harris and Schiappa do not: for Booth, the commonplace rhetoric upon which people make reasonable public decisions is *not* equivalent to the general moves of academic rhetoric. And of course I'm skeptical about his claim that all people use the same commonsense reasoning to resolve public issues. But what interests me here is that, even as he admits that specialized academics have no way of really understanding the complex work of more than a handful of other specialized academics, he still considers the whole multidisciplinary project valuable.

Booth's goal in his lecture is *not* to suggest that academics should stop writing dense, specialized pieces. He cautions academics and general readers alike not to dismiss difficult writing as bad writing, a move he observes is often used by faculty and others who try to read across disciplines (or even across subdisciplines) and run into texts they can't make sense of. Too often, he suggests, people assume that "good" writing is the kind that follows the patterns they are most familiar with: if an anthropologist dismisses the work of a cultural studies critic as "bad writing," it might be that the anthropologist has naturalized the conventions of his own field as the qualities of "universal" good writing and is not familiar with the rhetorical conventions of cultural studies. Booth includes a particular difficult passage from Derrida as an example and asserts that "I am utterly convinced that this is *not* nonsense," even though it is opaque and hard to translate.[16]

Booth then continues with his project, which is to help academics recognize the nondisciplinary rhetorics that keep them together as a *Uni*versity. I'd like to pick up this reflection on disciplinary research where he leaves off, and ask: How do universities justify the value of such specialized research? How does the idea of the research university fit into arguments about democracy? How do other institutions of higher education fit into such arguments?

The rise of the research university in America is often attributed to the German model, where faculty were organized into research disciplines and graduate students, as their apprentices, were schooled in the methodologies that would lead to pure research. According to Bill Readings, this modern university has its predecessor in Kant and in an ideal that "reason" is the arbiter of all inquiry. Within the research university, Readings writes, "each discipline seeks its own purity—what is essential to it. And what is essential to philosophy [which, for Readings, means all disciplines other than theology, medicine, and law] is nothing other than this search for the essential itself: the faculty of critique."[17]

Academic scholarship is seen as a place for pure research, outside the pressures of the state or business, and its function is to generate new knowledge, new understandings of the way the world works, whether by understanding the physical structures of substances or the social structures of groups or the meaning structures of texts. Much as the interlocutor in the idealized public sphere learns to bracket any traces of his or her uniqueness, so the academic researcher looks for truths that are not merely particular but are useful because they can explain broader phenomena. Part of the argument for unfettered research is precisely that we can't know its later usefulness: knowledge should be pursued now because it may, at some point, generate a way of understanding that will profoundly impact the larger culture. Sometimes this is understood in terms of products—much is made, for example, of how much everyday technology can be traced back to NASA's attempts to solve problems in space travel. Sometimes the value is more ephemeral but equally potent: shifts in the ways psychologists understand "childhood" may, after a while, influence the manner in which parents raise their children.

Academics in this model generally do not see themselves as players in the broader public arena—they do not conceptualize their research as fitting within political goals or needs. Nevertheless, precisely because they are seen to be outside politics, their findings have great impact within the idealized public sphere. Having arrived at a position "independently," an academic-turned-public-intellectual may speak about it to an audience of citizens or policy makers and in this way (ideally) raise the level of public discourse to account for that expertise. The role of the State in all of this, Readings suggests, is to keep watch over the university and ensure that research is conducted according to the rules of reason. Conversely, the role of the university is to keep watch over the State and thwart its attempt to regulate university interests or ground its own governing decisions in anything other than reason.[18]

The National/Cultural University: Creating Common Culture

If the common criticism of the research university model is that professors are invested in meaningless, isolated tasks of no real "use," then the common criticism of the national university model is that professors are woefully out of touch with the "real" values of the nation. The public value of higher education in the national/cultural university is that it should bring a diverse nation together under a tent of common experiences, values, and behaviors. Princeton University's statement about its core requirements declares:

> The University requirements for graduation transcend the boundaries of specialization and provide all students with a common language and common skills. It is as important for a student . . . to engage in disciplined reflection on human conduct, character, and ways of life or to develop critical skills through the study of the history, aesthetics, and theory of literature and the arts as it is for a student . . . to understand the rigors of quantitative reasoning and to develop a basic knowledge of the capabilities and limitations of scientific inquiry and technological development.[19]

Moreover, such common experiences will provide the groundwork for personal and civic life. The President of Wesleyan University extols the civic virtues of the liberal arts education this way in an opinion piece for the *Huffington Post*:

> The development of the capacities for critical inquiry associated with liberal learning can be enormously practical because they become resources on which to draw for continual learning, for making decisions in one's life, and for making a difference in the world.[20]

The antecedents for these appeals to common culture are found in Enlightenment thinkers, such as Matthew Arnold and Cardinal John Henry Newman.[21] They are carried forward in attempts to establish national standards for course content, both in grade schools and in universities. And they are promoted by well-meaning educational advocates who recognize that there is a dominant culture, a dominant way of speaking and interacting, that gives power to those who know how to practice it. Designing education to help people move into the dominant culture is seen as liberating.

The difficulty of sustaining a national/cultural university model, though, lies in the challenge of defining just what the foundational ideas and practices are for that dominant national culture, and figuring out how to account for the perspectives that are left out. What courses are appropriate for teaching critical skills? Which materials count as providing a sufficient reflection on human character or history? Which voices will be circulated and which will be dropped out of the curriculum? Which public ideal will be advanced?

Drawing on the pluralistic, conversational model of the idealized public sphere, some people argue that what is foundational to the national/cultural university is critical thinking, defined as reviewing multiple and diverse viewpoints on every issue. In the same way that traditional journalism seeks to reflect (and create) the mixed publics of newspaper readers, so colleges and universities that root their value in the national/cultural paradigm claim a responsibility to introduce students to mixed publics.

This call to open-mindedness resonates well with the goal of investigating all sides before arriving at a position and ensuring that some louder voices don't drown out all the others. But the primacy of traditional reason asserts itself here, and there is an assumption that within the context of the classroom or the research lab, scholars will be able to sort through the multiplicity fairly and logically, and that in the process, student-citizens will acquire the kind of rational-critical thinking that is necessary to work through disagreements in the idealized public sphere. Part of the national/cultural work of the pluralistic model, then, is to offer a particular rhetorical model for public engagement, a model that continues to reinforce the ideals for public interaction that are inherent to the dominant public, even though it *appears* to be open to the full diversity of public values and discourses.

Trusting reason as a way to arrive at not just what is true but also what is beautiful and right, the national/cultural university is understood simultaneously as a place where all knowledge is up for reconsideration and a place where disciplines can arrive at some common ground. While there may not be universal consensus, professors draw on their disciplinary methodology and teach their aesthetics and critical reasoning to their students. Over time, slowly, some of those disciplinary foundations may shift, but it takes time and a great deal of persuasion to unhinge a discipline from any of its core aesthetics, methodologies and beliefs, as Thomas Kuhn has shown in his analysis of paradigm shifts in the sciences.[22] Likewise, cultural foundations can be transformed, and the best process is thought to be slow and ponderous, in the best sense of that word.

The Problem-Solving University: Creating Active Citizens

If the notion of the national/cultural university is to help students acquire the critical literacy to assimilate into the dominant culture, the goal of the problem-solving university is to teach student-citizens to read knowledge and culture with greater resistance and then to take action. In this perspective, the university should teach students how to be active, democratic citizens. This tradition—which is the one that my book connects with most closely—often draws a line back to John Dewey and his vision of democracy as a place where people grow through taking action together. Another prominent ancestor is Brazilian educator Paulo Freire. As Thomas Deans puts it, both Dewey and Freire "build their philosophies around core concepts of experience, growth, inquiry, communication, mediation, problem posing/solving, consciousness raising, ethical social action, and transformation."[23]

The goal here is to prepare students for cross-cultural deliberations, and to equip them with an ability to analyze systems of power so that they can engage in meaningful democratic actions. This public goal is understood as always being in conflict with the other visions of the university, whose purposes and practices are part of those systems of power that must be analyzed and at times resisted. One of the constraints inherited from both the research university and the national/cultural university is the focus on teaching critical thinking and literate practices, preparing people to read, write, and deliberate, rather than to intervene, protest, blockade, or offer more defiant public engagement. The problem-solving university recognizes deliberation as only one component of meaningful democratic actions. Freire cautions, "I do not suppose that education alone can solve it [socioeconomic inequity]" and "We should never take literacy as the triggering of social transformation. Literacy as a global concept is only part of the transformative triggering mechanism."[24] The place for liberatory pedagogy within systematic education is a small place, but Freire nevertheless hopes that teachers will seize it.[25]

The democratic function of the problem-solving university is more attuned with communitarian purposes of government and cultural institutions: the university is one place where student-citizens learn to see their interdependence. The ideal action for the student-citizen is not to create pure knowledge, nor to absorb cultural knowledge, but rather to create knowledge with others (including those outside of academia) in order to take action. The motivations are rooted in the ideals of social justice and equality, as they are constructed in an activist, participatory democracy.

The problem-solving university locates its mission more explicitly in bringing its resources into conversation with communities, local and global. For example, Ellen Cushman argues that by "dovetailing the traditionally separate duties of research, teaching, and service, public intellectuals can use the privilege of their positions to forward the goals of both students and local community members."[26] Unlike the research university professor, who speaks to the public as a disciplinary expert, or the national/cultural university professor, who educates the public in common aesthetics and dominant literacy, the problem-solving university professor steps off campus not to lecture but to listen, and works with communities to analyze power and imagine public actions. Pedagogy is not confined to the classroom; learning is not a one-way endeavor.

In advancing her ideal for this new kind of public intellectual, Cushman dismisses a few people she sees as public intellectuals of the wrong sort. She looks at French intellectual Pierre Bourdieu, who argues that academics need to venture into the public arena to fight to keep the right vision of "the University" in place; she considers his public move rather self-serving. Likewise, she dismisses Michael Bérubé, who says academics need to make their work more accessible to ordinary people so that those people will support the university in public fights. While I can understand why she sees their arguments about how to win favor for the university as rather self-serving, I think she overlooks how the transformation of the university, as part of the ideological apparatus that interpolates citizen-intellectuals, could preclude the kind of public intellectual that she herself would like to advocate. Bourdieu and Bérubé are worried about the way that all of these visions of the university are being subsumed by the ever-more-powerful rhetoric of the neoliberal university, with its growing control over the material conditions of research, teaching, and learning. The neoliberal university appropriates some of the language of these other ideals, and redefines education in terms of a primarily economic vision.

The Neoliberal University: Creating Citizen-Workers

Although the neoliberal university was well established in many institutions long before the current economic crisis, the loss of public funding and concerns about rising tuition have put the university under greater pressure to justify itself in terms of economic value. Consider a 2008 *Chronicle of Higher Education* article about the Ohio university system. The "here" the reporter refers to is Columbus, Ohio:

> When NetJets, a private aviation company, announced it would keep and expand its operational headquarters here, Richard T. Santulli, chairman and chief executive, didn't give credit to tax breaks or any of the other incentives states and cities typically use to woo or retain corporations.

Instead, he said the critical factor was the state's higher-education system.

Leaders of Ohio's public colleges persuaded the company that they had the breadth and depth of expertise to meet NetJets's needs, including aircraft-maintenance training at Columbus State Community College, logistics specialists at Wright State University, and a top-ranked culinary program at the University of Cincinnati—an appealing resource for a company that serves gourmet meals at 30,000 feet. And one of the world's foremost experts on seat comfort is on the faculty at Ohio State University.

So in March, after months of considering suitors like Raleigh, N.C., and Fort Worth, Tex., the private-jet service announced that it would create 800 new jobs and invest in a $200-million expansion at the international airport here.[27]

University spending is good, we hear, because it will help train workers and bring the right businesses to town.

This argument pops up to justify investment in the University of Texas system as well, as we see in this March 2010 *Chronicle* piece:

While higher-education officials in some states struggle to win support from state residents and politicians for more money, the Texas endeavor has the backing of voters, who in November approved a nearly half-billion-dollar endowment to increase research capacity at several universities in the state. The thinking goes that by creating more elite research institutions, Texas will lay the foundation for a lasting knowledge economy, attracting high-technology businesses seeking to form partnerships with universities and hire their graduates.[28]

As in the Ohio example, the value of the additional research is described in terms of the market economy: the university provides workers and serves as an incentive for businesses to resettle in Texas, bringing more jobs and money to the area.

It's not fully accurate to contrast the ideal graduates of each kind of university as fundamentally different—to suggest, for example, that the neoliberal university wants to produce *workers,* while the research university wants to produce *scholars,* the National/Cultural University wants to produce *well-rounded citizens,* and the problem-solving university wants to produce *critical citizens.* That claim is inaccurate because the neoliberal university appropriates all those previous incarnations as well. The good worker *is* a "good scholar," a "well-rounded citizen," and a "problem-solver," as those terms have been redefined under the new paradigm. The original meanings of these terms dissolve, as Henry Giroux writes, under the pressure of corporate culture, which is "an ensemble of ideological and institutional forces that functions politically and pedagogically both to govern organizational life through senior managerial control and to fashion compliant workers, depoliticized consumers, and passive citizens."[29]

The consequences of corporate culture in the university is not just the loss of certain working conditions among academics—not just the self-serving concern that Cushman presumes—but rather the loss of any public orientation at the university. Giroux sounds the caution:

> As society is defined through the culture and values of neoliberalism, the relationship between a critical education, public morality, and civic responsibility as conditions for creating thoughtful and engaged citizens is sacrificed all too willingly to the interest of financial capital and the logic of profit-making.[30]

Neoliberalism is not just an economic argument, but rather a way of promoting a market ideology in the name of democracy.

As I explained in chapter 2, we can locate neoliberalism on the matrix of democracy by identifying how it defines the purpose of government, the ideal structure of government, and the appropriate citizen action within government. Under neoliberalism, democracy takes on a nearly libertarian form. The purpose of the government is to protect the rights of individuals, including the rights of individual *corporations* to operate within free-market capitalism. Moreover, the purpose of government is to be as streamlined as possible, minimizing public expense so as to maximize the citizen-shareholder profit. Within the neoliberal model, taxing citizens and corporations means dipping into their dividend payouts. The structure of government trends toward elitism, because it is a more efficient model for getting the business of government accomplished and because it ensures that decisions will be made based on the right management goals. Citizens play their best role as consumers, who direct business and government action through their purchasing power. Their choice of products affects the bottom line, which motivates appropriate change within the free-market system.

I'd argue that, no matter which university an institution aspires to be these days, much of its infrastructure is already so immersed in neoliberalism that it becomes the dominant pedagogy of the higher education experience. Student and faculty life is governed by this ideology. Without taking up too much time here on a point that has been well articulated by other scholars, let me point out a few of the mechanisms through which neoliberalism is reinforced.

Individualism: Students' academic life is inherently individual: students choose their courses, they are graded individually on their accomplishments, and their experience renders each course distinct and isolated. Unless a course is part of a sequence in a department (and sometimes not even then), each course begins and ends on its own. There are few opportunities for students to come together to make intellectual connections between their classes. Knowledge is thus accrued individually and incrementally, and students adapt to each professor, often attributing differences in methodology or style to individual teachers' whim rather than seeing them as signaling affiliations with larger disciplinary or scholarly debates.

Likewise, faculty life is inherently individual. As a one-time writing program administrator who sought to build a sense of community and interdependence among faculty, I was once told by an exasperated dean that "[Y]ou are not a community; you are a bunch of individuals." I was required to compare faculty against each other during evaluations and to decide on merit increases myself rather than soliciting input from the group as a whole. University funding and rewards require faculty to regularly compete for internal and external grants. While many of us do find community among others who conduct similar scholarship or who teach similar classes, the university's structures do not explicitly support such relationships. We are funded for conferences when we can present—so that the university's name is advanced—but not when we will "merely" participate and engage with fellow scholars.

Marketplace of Ideas: Under neoliberalism, "the marketplace is arbiter of social destiny,"[31] and this plays out also in university structures. Students choose from a broad menu of courses. Over time, the thinking goes, the best ideas they have learned will sort to the top based on their merit. Students choose their majors based on how persuasively the departments have convinced them of the value and pleasure of their work. Learning happens by accruing and weeding out ideas, rather than by investigating the larger implications of any seeming incompatibility among those ideas.

Departments and programs are added to the university's structure as needed, with an understanding that the unnecessary additions will be weeded out over time. The response to feminist critiques of the university is to add Women's Studies, rather than restructure current departments. Similarly, the response to lack of diversity is to hire more faculty and enroll more students from underrepresented groups, without necessarily adjusting any of the infrastructures that may have contributed to their earlier exclusions. The philosophy rests on a kind of additive multiplicity based on the marketplace of ideas: the responsibility is to introduce more courses, departments, or people into the mix and see who rises to the top.

Metrics of Success: The measures of success, not surprisingly, are also market-driven: Universities decide which departments and programs to keep based on the numbers of grants they receive or the numbers of majors they graduate,[32] not based on whether their content is inherently necessary to produce scholars (as would be the criteria in a research university) or well-rounded citizens (as would be the criteria in a national/cultural university). The justification for adding upper-division Writing in the Disciplines courses at the George Washington University, for example, is described in the strategic plan as addressing the need to enhance student engagement, and, therefore, problems of retention; the justification does not refer to the values of the teaching of writing itself.

Often pedagogy is understood as the process of designing the most cost-effective ways to transfer knowledge. Such an approach dovetails well with the national/cultural university's desire to transmit the dominant culture, and so sometimes the argument is put in those terms. The ideal of efficiency is tempered by competing university ideals, and also by competing market-driven concerns, such as student retention and nationwide university rankings that take into account faculty-student ratios (such as the well-known *US News and World Report,* which causes regular consternation on our campus if GWU dips below the "top 50" mark).

The metrics of success are also consumer-driven, reinforcing the business model by positioning the student both as the consumer and as the product that the university delivers to the workforce. Student course evaluations and the exit surveys they complete when they graduate are used to evaluate the success of individual teachers, programs, and initiatives. Likewise, the graduates' employers are surveyed to assess how well the university has met their needs.

I've spent some time making a case here that the structure of the university reinforces neoliberal values. My point is not to suggest that the neoliberal university is the only one left standing, but rather that we cannot talk about any distinct university ideals without taking into account how they play out materially. We also can't talk about any of these university ideals as entirely distinct—structures and values that might seem most associated with one model are easily merged into another.

We can see this interplay of ideal universities as a university lays out a goal for "creating community" in its strategic plan. In the next section I'll look closely at such a document. Then I'll review other genres of university writing to consider how they forward (or foreclose) any of the university models I've introduced so far.

CASE STUDY: UNIVERSITY-PUBLICS IN THE STRATEGIC PLAN OF THE GEORGE WASHINGTON UNIVERSITY

One of the important lessons I take away from Wayne Booth's lecture on looking at the university as a rhetorician is that we should not reduce the term "academic writing" only to scholarly writing. Doing so not only limits the university to one model—the research university—but also considers only one kind of writer within that model. Even the research university does not run itself by circulating journal articles: professors don't write out scholarly texts in order to communicate at faculty meetings or with administrators (though they might reference such work in their memos or speeches). Nor do university presidents or public intellectuals promote the public value of a research university by trying to place scholarly articles in *Harper's* or *The New Yorker*.[33]

To investigate how arguments about the purpose of higher education play out in the everyday documents of universities, I turn to a specific section of the George Washington University's strategic plan, "Sustaining Momentum, Maximizing Strength." Published in 2003, the strategic plan lays out six major goals for the university; for each goal, it outlines a series of steps for achieving it and a series of metrics for assessing progress. While the general goals and strategies define successful GWU graduates as active, democratic citizens, those terms are then constrained by measuring the goals' success through neoliberal criteria. I'll concentrate on Goal Four as an example: "continue to develop a strong sense of community."

GOAL 4

Continue to develop a strong sense of community.

GOAL 4 METRICS

+ Diversity of faculty by gender, race/ethnicity, rank.

+ Diversity of student body by gender, race/ethnicity, nationality.

+ Rating of how well GW enhances undergraduate students' ability to "relate well to people of different races, nations, and religions" from item on GW Graduating Senior Survey.

+ Rating of how well GW enhances undergraduate students' ability to "extend my range of friendships to different kinds of people" from item on GW Graduating Senior Survey.

+ Rating of how strongly graduate students agree/disagree that "the GW environment is supportive of persons of diverse ethnic/racial backgrounds" from item on Graduate Student Graduation Survey.

+ Number of students participating in academically-based residential communities.

+ Number of faculty in residence in student residence halls.

+ Number of students involved in community service activities in the Washington metropolitan area (collected by Office of Community Service).

+ Number of active GW alumni chapters.

MAXIMIZING STRENGTH   17

ONE ESSENTIAL

element of academic excellence is a strong campus community characterized by diversity and a sense of inclusiveness. A diverse student body and faculty enrich the educational experience by exposing students to a wide range of ideas and perspectives, fostering teamwork and mutual respect, and preparing students to communicate more effectively with individuals from different backgrounds. Diversity is widely recognized as a key contributor to economic competitiveness and organizational strength. GW takes pride in the diversity of its people as well as the diversity of its disciplines, activities, and ideas. Our vision is to foster a highly supportive environment in which faculty, students, staff, and alumni interact to create a civil and caring community of great benefit to all.

Raising GW's level of academic excellence not only requires a continuing commitment to diversity but also demands that we engage in energetic efforts to build an optimal learning community. Our students must have spaces and venues in which they can interact with fellow students and faculty and explore the complex social, political, scientific, and ethical issues that challenge citizens in a democratic society. Faculty must have opportunities to collaborate with colleagues and to share their work on a regular basis.

GW's goal of developing a strong community also extends to its Foggy Bottom neighbors, the city, and the metropolitan areas of Maryland and Virginia. We will continue to provide opportunities for our students to benefit from our rich partnerships in the D.C. metropolitan area through research, service learning, internships, and volunteer activities. Such experiences foster a spirit of service and discovery and improve our students' understanding of community strengths and challenges.

STRATEGIES

❋ **Create a campus environment that values and celebrates the diversity of GW students, faculty, staff, and alumni.**

❋ **Increase the number of faculty from underrepresented minority groups to foster greater cultural diversity within the University.**

❋ **Promote and preserve a spirit of collegiality among GW faculty.**

❋ **Attract and retain students from diverse cultures, countries, and backgrounds.**

❋ **Add value to each student's educational experience by offering a breadth of intellectual, artistic, civic, leadership, athletic, fitness, and social opportunities.**

❋ **Create a vigorous community dialogue on issues of social, political, and cultural significance through public debates, forums, conferences, and media programming.**

Figure 8.1: GWU Strategic Plan Goal 4 (first page)

* Enhance the quality of the teaching and learning environment and student-faculty interaction through the construction and renovation of academic, student life, and residential facilities.

* Strengthen the sense of campus community by increasing public spaces that facilitate the exchange of ideas and by providing a campus that is well-defined, well-designed, safe, and well-maintained.

* Increase the number of academic residential communities that enable students to integrate their intellectual interests and social experiences.

* Increase the number and visibility of faculty in residence in student residence halls.

* Expand the University's service contributions to the Washington, D.C., community through the Office of Community Service, the GW Neighbors Project, and other partnerships with government, schools, businesses, and professional groups.

* Strengthen ties with GW alumni by emphasizing their value to the University community and their role as resources to faculty and students.

Figure 8.2: GWU Strategic Plan Goal 4 (second page)

In the opening section of Goal Four, the strategic plan defines the value of creating community in terms of the democratic and economic benefits of promoting "diversity" and "inclusiveness." The language here draws on the rhetoric of the national/cultural university, emphasizing the value of learning to communicate well as a *civic* responsibility:

A diverse student body and faculty enrich the educational experience by exposing students to a wide range of ideas and perspectives, fostering teamwork and mutual respect, and preparing students to communicate more effectively with individuals from different backgrounds.

This reading is further supported by the line, "Our vision is to foster a highly supportive environment in which faculty, students, staff, and alumni interact to create a civil and caring community of great benefit to all."

GWU seeks to facilitate this public interaction by bringing in a more diverse student and faculty body: it will "[i]ncrease the number of faculty from underrepresented minority groups to foster greater cultural diversity within the University" (Strategy Two) and "[a]ttract and retain students from diverse cultures, countries and backgrounds" (Strategy Four). The metrics for these goals are quantified in terms of the demographics of faculty and students; the "diversity" of these new faculty and students must be visible to be counted.

Yet the question of how this now more diverse group will come together as a "community"—rather than merely as the individuals who are quantified—is harder to get at. The plan acknowledges a need to create good spaces for such interactions, calling for a better "campus environment" (Strategy One), "vigorous community dialogue" (Strategy Six), and "increasing public spaces that facilitate the exchange of ideas by providing a campus that is well-defined, well-designed, safe, and well-maintained" (Strategy Eight).

The idea seems to be that if you can get the right (diverse) people together in a well-designed space, they will interact and become a "community." This might happen, but not necessarily. The campus redesign over the past decade has included new arches and gateways into university commons, designating these blocks of the urban campus as clearly part of the George Washington University. In Kogan Plaza, a central area of campus, vendors and student organizations regularly set up tables (after securing the permission of the university), but protesters are confined to the sidewalk. Sometimes protesters are hauled away to jail—even when those protesters are GWU students in their own student center.

Rachel Riedner recounts the story of eleven undergraduates from the university's Progressive Student Union who staged a sit-in to protest the low wages and poor treatment of adjunct faculty and service employees.[34] They took this action after trying to garner the attention of the administration in a number of more traditional ways—letters, petition drives, rallies—even while more of the workers they wanted to support were being fired. The University's response was to have the students arrested; charges were soon dropped. The give-and-take around rhetorics of inclusiveness continued at commencement that year, when the head of the Progressive Student Union was given the Student Leadership prize. The GWU president undermined her accomplishments even as he gave her the award, saying, "I think she's terrific, but I think she's wrong in some cases, and excessively idealistic in others and under-informed in others . . . but she's a great kid."[35]

Thus, despite the affirmation in the university's mission statement and promotional materials, "[t]he expectation of diversity disguises an analysis of *how* traditionally excluded voices are permitted to enter into university space and how these voices are allowed to speak, even exist, within the university community."[36] The GWU space is "well-designed" because it is well branded; the private blocks of the campus are distinct from the public of the streets. Tolerance for diversity extends only to those who will behave as if the university is benevolent. The goal is to *show* we are a caring place.

The metrics for evaluating Goal Four betray this preference for appearances as well. The metrics are based on how students rank their own experiences:

Rating of how well GW enhances undergraduate students' ability to "relate well to people of different races, nations, and religions" from item on GW Graduating Senior Survey

Rating of how well GW enhances undergraduate students' ability to "extend my range of friendships to different kinds of people" from item on GW Graduating Senior Survey

Rating of how strongly graduate students agree/disagree that "the GW environment is supportive of persons of diverse ethnic/racial backgrounds" from item on Graduate Student Graduation Survey

What is measured, then, is not how well the university succeeds in generating dialogue across difference, but how good its students feel about their experiences with others, how many friends they make who are "different kinds of people" (a category that reaffirms their difference while suggesting that the proper relationship among scholar-citizens is that of "friendship"), and how supportive the campus environment feels to the majority of graduates.

The goal of community building is reduced from its interactive elements into its individual elements: How many different individuals came, and how did individuals feel about that? In this version, multiculturalism is not about adjusting current systems to ensure the cross-pollination of ideas; nor does good knowledge making or proper decision making hinge on potentially uncomfortable interactions among a diverse group of people. Rather, the question of community and diversity is really a marketing goal: Do our student-customers report feeling good about this aspect of their experience? What else can be done to make them feel good about it?

To be fair, Goal Four does seem to tip its hat toward the ideals of the problem-solving university by extending its definition of the university community to include its relations with its geographical neighbors, from the local Foggy Bottom community, to DC as a whole, and all the way to Maryland and Virginia. The third paragraph reads:

> GW's goal of developing a strong community also extends to its Foggy Bottom neighbors, the city, and the metropolitan areas of Maryland and Virginia. We will continue to provide opportunities for our students to benefit from our rich partnerships in the D.C. metropolitan area through research, service learning, internships, and volunteer activities. Such experiences foster a spirit of service and discovery and improve our students' understanding of community strengths and challenges.

But even here, despite the gesture toward valuing a broader sense of community, the language falls short of promoting reciprocal relationships of mutual knowledge making and action. The relationship is described primarily in terms of how it will benefit the students.

It's hard to tell, from this declaration alone, if the underlying value of such partnerships is primarily the value of creating better citizens, or a more corporate one of marketing GWU as a highly networked environment. Tucked into the first paragraph, the Goal also advances a corporate advantage for diversity: "Diversity is widely recognized as a key contributor to economic competitiveness and organizational strength." When paired with other parts of the plan, the value of university-community partnerships is even more tied to a business plan, and in some of these cases the goal of reaching out to community organizations and nonprofits is dropped, while the links to corporations and government internships is highlighted. In Goal Two ("Solidify, strengthen, and strategically expand graduate professional education") GWU hopes to expand its for-profit business arm, GW Solutions; it would like more area organizations to hire its consultants. It also hopes to recruit more students into its professional programs through such partnerships. A strategy listed in Goal Two is "expand strategic alliances and partnerships with Washington-area business, government, non-profit, and K-12 educational institutions so that these agencies will turn to GW as the educator of choice for programs to benefit working professionals."

Again, to be fair, the University has secured a major grant and set up a new institution, the Center for Civic Engagement and Public Service, which offers faculty grants and support for designing and teaching service learning courses. The Center also oversees the University's volunteerism and promotes internships and careers in public service. This is an important transformation, since in the past any academic links between the University and the broader community had no real institutional support: The office responsible for volunteerism tried to help but was given no funding to do so, while administrative deans offered little guidance to faculty or chairs. I am grateful for this new trend, and I hope that the university continues to support it (which I think is quite likely so long as it continues to be funded by outside grants).

I could highlight many other ways that the strategic plan document betrays its ambivalence about the purpose of the university. In other sections, it upholds the research university model: Goal One is "GW will increase investment in those doctoral programs in which faculty members are conducting forefront research and scholarship." But even here the reasons and the metrics suggest that the motives are to enhance the business model of the university: the investment will be "at the level necessary to raise program distinction and attract and retain the very best doctoral students," and the university will pare out those "underperforming" departments and programs. The metrics here reveal the same kinds of trends that Henry Giroux has identified in his critique of the neoliberal university: volume of research grants and contracts from the private sector; percentage of faculty with external funding; productivity of research centers as measured by average sponsored funding; number of income generating licenses and patents held by faculty; number of grant proposals submitted and accepted. The university has also revised the grant procedure so as to "return a share of research revenue" to the investigators, and thus make it personally profitable for faculty to pursue their research.

Henry Giroux argues that citizens—and here I'm thinking of both students and faculty—"lose their public voice as market liberties replace civic freedoms" and that "as corporate culture extends even deeper into the basic institutions of civil and political society, . . . noncommodified public spheres [diminish]."[37] The GWU "Sustaining Momentum, Maximizing Strength" strategic plan celebrates diversity and community on one hand and measures productivity and consumer satisfaction on the other.

COMPETING UNIVERSITIES IN A PUBLIC WRITING CLASS

How might a public writing class take into account its location within the various Universities I have described? How does a class that builds bridges with community nonprofits acknowledge not only the competing definitions of the "public" that constrain and enable nonprofits (as I discussed in chapter 2), but also the competing definitions of the "University" that constrain and enable the faculty who would take on such partnerships?

In "Building Deeper Civic Relationships," an article that I used in chapter 2 as a starting point for investigating what "publics" are worth studying, Morton and Enos described some of the ways that nonprofits perpetuate a neoliberal set of values and actions. They also turn their gaze toward the university, and identify a second set of problems that "frustrate our work in moving . . . to a deeper embrace of democratic citizenship and deeper partnerships with the community."[38] The issues they name are these:

- "[T]he specialization of disciplines leaves us [faculty] inept and disempowered to build communities in which we would like to live and thrive. . . .
- "Typically, service-learning practitioners see their work as apolitical. . . . There are certain privileges that extend to us as we hold onto our neutrality and objectivity, but we may gain these at the expense of engaging in the messy work of building and creating community. . . .

- "The fact that universities are loosely coupled organizations makes it possible for members of the campus to work at cross-purposes."[39]

To some extent, the root of all three of these concerns lies with the structure of the university as a research university. The specialization that Morton and Enos decry is generated through the reward systems, where scholarly publication and scholarly affiliations are seen as the best criteria for professional advancement. The consequence is not only that we are so specialized that we may not be able to approach community issues from perspectives other than our own—for example, a rhetoric scholar who looks for community solutions in terms of opportunities for communication, rather than in terms of economic restructuring. The consequence is also that we may conceptualize the problems in terms that "fulfill our disciplinary interests but may fall far short of our civic responsibilities."[40] Both of these missteps lead to the kinds of disheartening disconnects that are often recounted among those who engage in community-based research and/or service learning: professors who try to provide services that an organization simply does not need, and students and academics who demand a lot of community time and attention so that they can conduct their scholarship but do not provide anything in return that is meaningful to the organizations. (For some specific examples, see the section on "reciprocity" in Appendix 1.)

The scholar of the research university gains his or her expertise through certain literate practices, but—as Morton and Enos point out—they are not always well equipped to translate those practices into different forums. Morton and Enos would like the Research Scholar to learn techniques for engaging in more of the generative, cooperative modes of knowledge making that the Problem-Solving Professor might bring into community spaces—a willingness to listen, to work with a community to generate questions, and to understand fully the local conditions, concerns, and knowledge. Instead, what more often happens is that the Research Scholar, transferring his or her usual literate practices into a new space, ends up not empowering the citizen-audience with new knowledge but instead positioning the citizen-audience as passive recipients, as citizen-consumers indebted to elite experts.

Such is the interaction that Elizabeth Ervin describes in her analysis of an exchange of letters to the editor between academics and nonacademics in a college-town newspaper, the *Wilmington Morning Star*. The nonacademics are much better in the exchange, Ervin observes, because they are much more willing to gesture towards an understanding of academic logic; in contrast, the academics refuse to acknowledge any form of expertise beyond that rooted in their own paradigms. Academics, Ervin observes, hold onto a traditional rationality, a "hierarchical system in which some members of a community are deemed qualified to judge and lead while others are expected to watch and follow (see, e.g. Lippmann.)"[41] Instead, Ervin argues (drawing on the words of Walter Fischer), "the proper public role of an academic expert is 'not to pronounce a story [i.e. narrative] that ends all storytelling' but to recognize that he or she is part of the public and is subject to its 'criteria for determining whose story is more coherent and reliable as a guide to belief and action.'"[42] Ervin chides academics for believing too much in their own epistemology and their own patterns for deliberation. And she notes how hard it is to give over these beliefs when they enter public spaces: we academics arrive with "the expectation that in public debate about our respective areas of expertise our ideas should count for something, maybe count a lot."[43]

A similar kind of critique can be made of a different space for public-academic interaction, the public meeting. Jeffrey Grabill works with and writes about community activists in a town he calls Harbor. The activists are dealing with the potential toxic dredging of a canal. Grabill notes that what confounds community members most when they try to work in partnership with academics is "the commonplace understanding that knowledge is produced by outside experts [read academics] and only *used* within communities."[44] Though the activists are collaborative researchers, teaching themselves and their community about the chemical and environmental impact of the proposed plans, they are not always seen as being knowledgeable. This is especially true in the "ubiquitous public meeting," which Grabill describes as

> generally a presentation on a technical issue by a recognized expert (30–60 minutes in length) followed by some questions and answers (another 30–60+ minutes). On the surface, a simple rhetorical situation. As a genre, the meeting is more complex. As an infrastructure, it is more complex still. Simply put, the public meeting is a highly standardized forum deeply shaped by the institutional practices of government bodies (that often sponsor them) and expert institutions that often supply the expertise. The meeting is fundamentally a report, delivered often by means of multiple media—voice, print documents, PowerPoint, charts, and graphs—that would be normal within expert institutions. That is, the audience is expected to ask technically appropriate and relevant questions of the expert.[45]

Grabill and community leaders redesigned the ubiquitous public meeting so that the knowledge-making capacity and active role of the citizens could come to the fore. They asked for the expert's report in advance, circulated and read it, fact-checked it, generated questions, and only *then* met with the expert. The expert gave a summary of the report (confined to fifteen minutes) and then the meeting was opened up for questions and discussion.[46] Because of this redesign, the citizens and the expert came into the meeting on much more equal footing. The research university structure does not reward such collaboration or provide much practice in it.

The second point that Morton and Enos raise—that of the apolitical scholar—also derives from the research university, where scholars are supposed
to be above the fray of politics, never influenced by the everyday lest their
reason be polluted by other motivations. For faculty and students both, the
challenge of studying and writing about people with whom you have ongoing relationships is a big one. Students often comment that they are unwilling
to criticize their community partners, even if they are uncomfortable with
something they see there: doing so seems to impose the objectives of the
university—unfettered research—into places where the power and language
of the university may have consequences. They are aware that in sharing
their observations, they cannot set aside their location as part of a privileged
institution whose modes of reason and contexts of interpretation may not be
trusted by the organizations they are working with. (Ironically, the isolated
nature of academic writing often mitigates the harmful impact of scholarly
research. In a story that Mathieu recounts from Clyde Moneyhun, a faculty
member in a mismanaged partnership is reassured that the work probably
won't do any harm because no one will read it anyway.[47])

I have felt this pressure myself, and I have worked hard to build strong
enough relationships with public organizations so that I can speak to them
directly about any concerns, working with them in person and with the
primary goal of helping an organization achieve its mission. In the process,
I may come to appreciate new contexts and constraints or even alternate
visions that I had not realized. Or I may be able to offer insights to help the
organization see a part of itself in a new manner. The primary goal is not
to create scholarly research, but to offer academic research as a potential
resource for the organization, contextualized by its needs. The research is
provided not as a scholarly report, but within the genres available to the
organization—internal memos, conversations in planning meetings, and the
like. (I have asked leaders of the community organizations I write about in
this book to help me verify the accuracy of my claims, but I do not pretend
that this book is the part of my work that will benefit them. My main contributions to the organizations comes through introducing student-volunteers
to them, helping to facilitate useful documents, and engaging in ongoing
conversations about how to best recruit and orient students [and others] to the
public missions of the organizations.) Morton and Enos describe the goals of
such university-community partnerships this way: echoing Wendell Berry,
they write: "Suppose that the ultimate standard for our work were to be, not
professionalism and profitability, but the health and durability of human and
natural communities."[48]

In response to the third problem—the potential for faculty and students to
be working at cross-purposes with other areas of their university—Morton

and Enos suggest the technique of "power mapping": "trac[ing] the economic resources that are present in their work to their sources and examin[ing] the interests of those sources and understand[ing] how the system of service in which they participate is influenced by those interests."[49] In this manner, the university is repositioned back into the public domain, as a player whose interests extend beyond any professed university purpose—creating knowledge or creating culture—and as a business-minded public.

The important move in all of this, I think, is that a public writing class needs to start treating the university itself as a kind of public, one with competing visions of its purpose and clashing goals for how to conduct its work. The university, whatever form it takes, invokes its identity just as other publics do, by doing its best to circulate its vision extensively, and in such a way that its stance seems inevitable: *This* is simply what higher education is; *this* is simply how higher education works; *this* is simply a description of reality. And, just as publics forward their ideals in public writing—embedded in the rhetorical structures of discourse that is forwarded and circulated—so universities' ideals are embedded in their literate practices. The various and competing expectations about writing at a university are evidence of the clashing expectations of what a university should do and how a university fits into the broader public sphere.

RESEARCH WRITING AND DISCIPLINARY PUBLICS

One of the challenges for a writing program is that often it is positioned as a predisciplinary space, where students should be prepared for the disciplinary writing they will be asked to write in departments throughout the university. Disciplinary writing is usually seen as antithetical to public writing, as the standards for generating knowledge are high. Whatever the discipline, scholars in the research university are thought to be apolitical, epistemic, elite. Their arguments should be derived through methods the discipline has decided can guide reasoned analysis. Their structures and formats should forward the research university's goal of transparency; they should be replicable: scholars should trace out their lines of thinking thoroughly, crediting those previous scholars who have allowed them to arrive at this new knowledge. The goal of the scholar is to create the most accurate understanding of (one piece of) the world through ongoing deliberation among experts.

Yet if we consider the components of the scholarly essay not in terms of its uniqueness, but rather as one piece of writing that sets out a particular public vision and particular role for the Scholar within that public, the moves of academic writing are not so divergent from the moves of other public writing. In chapter 3 I offered some analysis of the kinds of rhetorical moves that nonprofits use to build up a sense of exigency, capacity, and interdependence, to hail people as members of their public and reconstitute them as active participants in building their vision of the world. In chapter 4 I considered how the places where works are published affect the publics they can imagine. Here I argue that we can draw on these same analytical moves to see how the genre of academic writing invokes its public ideals.

Exigency

Public writing is required when something has to be done, when people have to come together as a public to do it, and when those people can be motivated through discourse: speeches, e-mails, letters, reports, and so on. Within the research university, the exigency for disciplinary writing is some gap in knowledge. The problem may be that some idea has been misrepresented, that some new information has put old ideas in a new light, or that new contexts or examples can extend past knowledge. Joseph Harris explains this in *Rewriting* as a need to *respond* to other academic writers. The gap is understood as something that can be addressed through disciplinary methods.

Rhetorically, research scholars name the exigency for their new work fairly explicitly. Though the declaration of the need for the research may be expressed in multiple places, it will inevitably show up in the review of scholarly literature, as the writer demonstrates how the previous works, while helpful to a point, need to be supplemented with the new knowledge.

Agency and Capacity

Just as public writers must convince themselves and each other that they have the ability to address the concern that has been raised, so disciplinary writers must lay out an argument about why their methods are adequate to the need. Public writers need to invoke the capacity of people to take action in democracy, and in the process need to convey as realities their "world as it is" and "world as it should be," along with the type of citizen response that can bridge the two. The audience—the public they would invoke—has to accept these characterizations as inevitable, as what they already knew, even if they are being introduced to the particular issue or exigency for the first time.

In disciplinary writing, scholars have to depict the state of the scholarship and the goals of the scholarship; they also must show that their methodology and materials can bridge the two. The capacity lies not so much with particular people as with the tools of reason that are the foundation of the discipline. In the process, disciplinary scholars invoke a public of other scholars who understand the field of knowledge in the same way and who would agree that the methods are adequate to the task. Here again, much of the work happens in the introduction and literature review. The scholars must account for the previous scholarship in a manner that convinces the other scholars that the exigency for this new work comes out of an accurate sense of "the (disciplinary) world as it is" and "the (disciplinary) world as it should be."

Interdependence

Public writers build capacity by demonstrating to people the power they gain from working together for a cause: the power to pressure a representative or the city bureaucracy, the power to embarrass a corporation enough that it will adjust its practices, or the power to reconstruct public space in some manner. In many disciplines outside the humanities, scholarship is conducted in research teams, and the team has to work together to get things done. But this is not the interdependence that is projected in the disciplinary writing (beyond the appreciation offered in a dedication or acknowledgement section). Rather, disciplinary scholars need each other to carry out the broader goals of the research university—to continue to create, counter, and extend knowledge. Scholarly writers and readers rely on each other to continue thinking together, through the scholarly exchange of disciplinary writing. They see the exchange as offering careful, thoughtful critique, and push each other to new levels of understanding.

Some of the tools through which public writers invoke a sense of interdependence are referencing their own past accomplishments, telling historical stories of a similar public's accomplishments, and showing how past citizens were transformed by working together. Disciplinary writing is not so different: scholars remind each other of past breakthroughs in knowledge and link their claims to those of scholars who are recognized as having made important contributions. The difference shows up in the form. For disciplinary scholars, one of the methods signaling that they value such interdependence is through the fastidious use of citations and meticulous bibliographies, where all the predecessors are given credit.

Within the line of the argument itself, all the stages and turns of the disciplinary scholar's thinking are laid out and made transparent. The move here affirms the scholar's commitment to the broader community of scholars: they are invited to follow the intellectual paths and think with the writers, and ultimately to extend or counter the piece with one of their own.

Circulation

Circulation seems easy enough to define: disciplinary scholars are published in disciplinary journals. But just as particular newspapers mark out their own versions of "the public," through which they both reflect and invoke that public, so scholarly journals mark out different visions of their disciplines. As tenure and promotion guidelines make clear, some journals are considered more "legitimate" representatives of the true rigor and scope of a field than others.

Just as in traditional media, the good arguments are presumed to rise to the top and circulate most widely, so those articles and books that are most widely cited are presumed to be the most important. Here, as in the idealized public sphere, the publishing business *as a business* is downplayed; the influence of economic market forces in the marketplace of ideas is ignored.

The idea of the academic marketplace of ideas also ignores those conditions of employment or the nature of the funding that might affect scholarship. Rewards are based on one's ability to place scholarly work with prestigious journals and prestigious presses, regardless of the varying teaching loads or the amount of intellectual work demanded in administrative duties (as the Council of Writing Program's position paper on the evaluation of writing program administrators points out).

In calls for higher education reform, critics have noted that this publication cycle is compromised by the reward structures of the research university. Scholars have to write books to be promoted, but those books are read by only a handful of people in the field. The exigency for writing in this particular genre—a monograph rather than a series of articles, for example—may stem from the promotion guidelines rather than from an exigency within the discipline itself. Academic presses, arms of many universities, are under pressure to be more profitable, so the publication opportunities for scholars are greatly limited. Other forms of circulation—open source publications, electronic books, or even publishing with nonacademic presses—are seen as less reputable. Though the ideals of disciplinary writing are supposedly advanced through its cycles of publication, the reality is much more complicated than is usually admitted.

Nondisciplinary Publics in the Research University

Though I've emphasized disciplinary writing so far in this analysis, I want to return to the point that Booth makes in his Ryerson Lecture: disciplinary writing is only one of the rhetorics that are used in the research university. Because scholars are sometimes required to evaluate people who are outside their disciplinary or subdisciplinary areas of expertise, they rely on some more-general markers of academic inquiry.

We learn how to judge whether arguments in fields beyond our full competence *somehow* track, whether the style of presentation somehow accords with the standards we recognize. We learn to sense whether a colleague, even in a quite remote field, *seems* to have mastered the tricks of the trade—and not just the trade of this or that kind of economist or philosopher, but the tricks of this whole trade, the trade of learning and teaching for the sake of learning and teaching.[50]

Booth terms this more general, nondisciplinary rhetoric "academic writing."

I agree with Booth that certain habits of disciplinary writing show up in various rhetorical conventions. I'd emphasize that what is being valued by those who review scholarship outside their disciplines in this manner is the way that the disciplinary writing invokes the research university: the way that it addresses its audience and signals its affiliation within that structure. Just as Booth admitted elsewhere in his piece that scholars are not always so generous or so able to read dense, unfamiliar writing as part of this intellectual enterprise—dismissing some complex works as so specialized as to be meaningless—I'd argue that scholars similarly may dismiss other "academic" writing that makes an appeal to a different kind of university.

Many scholars who take on a more public, activist role—imagining the university as the problem-solving university—are chastised for not being "real" professors. When bell hooks chose to write her books without footnotes, she was castigated as being less than professional, despite the complexity and rigor of the arguments. Cornel West writes that he was called out by Harvard President Lawrence Summers for not maintaining a research university focus when he devoted his energies to reinvigorating democratic life and fighting the very nihilism he had discussed in his often-cited academic books. West argues in *Democracy Matters* that what was at stake in his dispute with Summers was a fundamental difference about the purpose of the university, and he locates Summers's position as both too limited to the research university and too compromised by the neoliberal university.

Many other examples could make this same point: we can see in the general, rhetorical moves of disciplinary writing how scholars reify a particular ideal of the research university, calling up their disciplinary publics within this broader calling of the university. It's appropriate to talk about "academic writing" as doing this kind of public work. However, in our affirmation of this point, we must not forget that the research university itself is only one of the competing university models. Sometimes people dismiss a disciplinary text as nonacademic, even when the text affirms the values of the research university, because they misread the scholar's cues about scholarly exigency, capacity, and interdependence. But sometimes people dismiss scholarly texts as nonacademic because the writers have resisted the values of the research university and are promoting alternate ideals. We might consider these the counterpublic texts of the research University.

WHAT DOES THIS MEAN FOR A PUBLIC WRITING COURSE?

Part of me wants to simply declare my affiliation with the problem-solving university and declare that within such a model, a first-year writing course should be devoted to public writing and not worry about all these struggles within the academy. All writing in the curricula of a problem-solving university would help students navigate community spaces, interrogating and creating publics in the wide range of genres demanded for public work. But I recognize that the material conditions of the university, such as the funding for writing programs, derive from a commitment to the research university and the national/cultural university: first-year writing must produce students who can write in their upper-division courses and should offer the critical reasoning and cultural background appropriate to participate in (dominant) civil society. Writing programs are constrained by the expectations of the neoliberal university as well: more and more writing program administrators are charged to develop research plans and pedagogical initiatives that will bring in outside funding.

Some public writing scholars have been able to secure funding for their community-based initiatives. I'm thinking, for example, of the community literacy program that Linda Flower has helped shape between Carnegie Mellon University and the Community Literacy Center (CLC) in Pittsburgh.[51] Urban teens come to the community center with things to say and community issues that need addressing, and undergraduate and graduate students from the university partner with them. Using a process of invention and composition designed to facilitate cross-cultural communication, the university students help the teens to figure out what they want to say and to marshal their considerable rhetorical resources to say it. The teens put together sophisticated multi-genre presentations, with skits, rap songs, and essayist reflections, among other forms. They invite to the community center those other community members who are needed to resolve the issue. Through the teens' presentations and performances, they create a public space for talking productively across differences.

The CLC model is inspiring. It allows me to imagine some of the infrastructure that would be needed to create the kind of problem-solving university that I'd like to be part of. At the same time, the model is a reminder that the resources for such places don't come readily from the university. Thomas Deans reviews the CLC program in *Writing Partnerships* and concludes,

The CLC is a result of a constellation of forces which, unfortunately, are not often readily available in most university-community parings: significant commitments of senior university faculty and key community members a respected community center with which to work; a long-term, stable partnership of two institutions; funding from without (foundation grants) and within (university commitments of personnel and resources); and a companion graduate program to supply a cadre of graduate students who provide able management and research assistance.[52]

I am impressed by the confluence of forces that have brought the Carnegie Mellon/Community Literacy Center partnership into being and I admit to being daunted by the challenge of trying to replicate those forces in order to create a comparable site.

But in the end, I think it's important to keep public writing courses within the context of the research university and the national/cultural university. The CLC model would be valuable as one component of a multi-pronged department, but on its own, it does not offer all that is necessary to teach public writing. Flower is clear throughout her book that the CLC is a site where many competing publics and clashing public discourses come together: the urban teens and their university student mentors have to create a space to talk across differences, both among themselves and in the public forum they will create to discuss the issue at hand. Nevertheless, the model that students will take away as the ideal for public-making will be the process that is used there: In the collaboration, intercultural inquiry happens by a) investigating "the story behind the story," which is defined as the situated, affective, and embodied knowledge behind the speaker's words; b) seeking out "rival interpretations;" and c) working with these tools to arrive at a "joint, reconstructive negotiation with their own understandings" and then leading a community meeting at the center to work through the issue.[53]

I don't mean to suggest that this process is simple or that it's not an extremely valuable process. I have no doubt that it works well in this context. The examples Flower provides from the CLC demonstrate that through the process many urban teens have found a way to be heard and have come to see themselves as able to create the kind of public space they desire. My concern is, ironically, that the model is *so* persuasive and *so* powerful that it will come to stand in as *the* ideal of public inquiry and action. When students of public writing are brought together in such a persuasive place, they may be less receptive to seeing the potential in other processes of inquiry and public formation, in other community literacy practices.

My concern here is motivated by a compelling article by Troy Murphy, whose argument has triggered much of my thinking in this book. I read "Deliberative Civic Education and Civil Society: A Consideration of the Ideals and

Actualities of Democracy and Communication Education" years ago, as I was beginning my own thinking about the best ways to promote deliberative democracy—that node in the matrix of democracy where citizens find their agency and voice through active deliberation with each other. Scholars and public intellectuals who focus on deliberative democracy are committed to developing the infrastructures through which people can come together, in the Deweyan sense, and grow into their capacities as citizens. Murphy provides an overview of different methods that have been introduced: he reviews programs supported by nonprofits and think tanks, such as the Study Circles Resource Center, the National Issues Forum, and the Center for Deliberative Polling. He also notes how instructors carefully structure their classrooms so that students can experience this kind of citizen deliberation. The participants are carefully guided in their talk by teachers or community organizers who set the parameters that ensure their deliberation will be productive. Ideally, the infrastructures of these programs and classrooms build people's commitment to and capacity for participatory democracy.

As much as Murphy applauds the goals of such programs and pedagogies, he worries that they might backfire. He writes, "[W]eak linkages between ideal forms of deliberation and the actual practices of democracy can exacerbate student alienation and undermine the benefits of deliberative civic education."[54] He continues,

> In situating deliberation as outside of, and superior to, the realities of a public sphere marked by myriad popular appeals and robust democratic action, prototypical structured deliberation presupposes that this disciplined form of discussion must counter the unruliness of popular democratic discourse.[55]

The result is an "anti-rhetorical conception of public deliberation" (a phrase he borrows from Robert Ivie).[56]

Having juxtaposed Flower's CLC and Murphy's critique of structured, deliberative civic education, I want to hasten to say that Flower's model is much, much more aware that actual public discourse is a contested space. Her model does not suppose that real public deliberation mimics intercollegiate debate or that it *ever* takes place outside of the contested, affective, fraught clash of different literacies. And yet, despite working with many different people and despite embracing and inviting the participants to draw on a range of genres and languages in their presentations, the CLC model does promote a certain process for deciding what to say, and a certain forum for saying it. The presenters use the space of the CLC, drawing on the trust that this community institution has garnered over the years. Their desired audience comes to listen because of the already established faith, based on experience, that the interaction will be productive. These are the components of an ideal public process and product that the CLC participants are taking away. When the participants encounter other publics, where the modes of discovering knowledge are less scripted and venues for sharing their findings are less accessible, will they have a method through which to understand and evaluate those publics on their own terms?

In the end, I see a greater value in a pedagogy that brings together multiple publics, that allows students to compare their different experiences with public spaces and public rhetorics, and that offers an analytical method for understanding the multiple components of public formation, including the challenge of circulation.

Despite my first impulses to abandon the institutional space of first-year writing classes in order to create an alternative kind of space for public writing, I now see a greater value in working not just within the university, but also within the particular location of first-year writing. Public writing in this space can meet the mandates of the research university and also provide a useful way to contextualize the research university as one kind of public. I'll come at the question from the perspective of the research university to show why I think including public writing in the first-year course is productive.

Most first-year writing courses require that students be introduced to the basic frameworks of academic writing, understood in Booth's taxonomy as those general moves of disciplinary writing that signal a scholar's commitment to the research university. Within such a context, shifting the focus of the course from academic to public writing can seem like a breach, a violation of the very basis upon which the first-year course is required and funded or, at the very least, an unfair prospect for those students who will need practice in the genre of academic writing before they move on. I disagree.

Teaching students to identify and use the rhetorical tools of public formation can give them a framework through which to understand how to invoke the public that is the research university. I'd argue that it is easier to introduce the rhetorical tools of public formation by studying the rhetorics of nonprofits, because their very nature as public, nonprofit institutions requires that they continually invoke their public: their sense of exigency, capacity, and interdependence and their sense of the world as it is and as it should be. Similarly, nonprofits must regularly find ways to circulate their publics—publishing an array of documents out of their own offices, intervening in traditional media, experimenting in new media. The scope is broad and generally pretty accessible. When we design classes so that conflicting premises of these publics are juxtaposed, students can begin to isolate those values and see how they manifest rhetorically in the public discourse. And when students have to write for and with community organizations, they experience firsthand the challenges and exhilaration of public writing.

With such a foundation, I'd argue, first-year students are better prepared to see how *disciplinary* writing is not only about content but also requires rhetorical moves to invoke a public. I'm not suggesting that as first-year students they will understand all the nuances of the moves that scholars use to signal their affiliations with a discipline. But I do think they will be able to recognize the broader rhetorics that invoke the research university and to understand academic writing on that level. They can begin to write their way into this university public, drawing on their experience and practice invoking a nonprofit public.

And the flip side is important too. Because the pedagogy makes it clear that each act of public writing stakes out *one* public among many, students will be well situated to see the writing of the research university for what it is as well—academic writing that invokes *one* vision of the university. A service-learning course calls into question some of the very premises of the research university, such as the superiority of academic modes of reasoning, the role of the expert in public affairs, and the dangers of engaging politically in everyday affairs. Because of this tension, writing with and about community organizations in the context of a first-year writing class brings even more of the values of the research university out into the open.

I assign both academic and public writing in my course to help promote this inquiry. Because students work with community organizations and meet in a university writing class, they are positioned between the two. From this perspective, they talk with both communities but can also talk back to either, depending on where their own investigations lead. First-year writers who might be intimidated by academic scholarship can find a way into it through their experiences with community organization. They might begin by asking how well the academic scholarship has accounted for the historical and cultural contexts of their community organization. Likewise, academic scholarship, combined with students' experiences and commitment to the public work of their organization, might help students offer nuanced observations that can help community publics advance their own goals. By teaching public writing in a first-year writing course, I try to carve out a space where students can begin to analyze all manner of publics and to use their writing to create those publics they wish to see in the world.

A FINAL CALL FOR PUBLIC INTELLECTUALS
IN THE ACADEMY

I come back one final time to Ellen Cushman and her critique of public intellectuals. Cushman suggested that those who engaged with public audiences for the purposes of accruing public support for the university were somehow hypocritical and self-serving. I think she moved a bit too quickly in her argument. The idea of the university is a contested one, and it is not an idea or a space that we should abandon. The consequences are not just a self-serving matter of our own livelihoods. If we don't fight within and for the university as a space that resists (as much as it can) the market rhetoric of neoliberalism or the potentially elitist rhetoric of the research university, if we don't question the normative power of the national/cultural university, then we also give up on the problem-solving university, a place where student-citizens work with the publics around them to create knowledge and plan actions together. The university is not outside the public sphere; it is part of the ongoing struggle to define public space and democratic ideals. It is a powerful institution that interpolates student-citizens not only into their roles as scholars, but also into their roles within a public. Public writing—including the writing of academic publics—is a place where this struggle takes place. As scholars, teachers, and public citizens, we need to be mindful of both the consequences and the possibilities of our roles in teaching public writing.

Admittedly, this is my goal in writing this book. Though my book draws on community rhetoric and is rooted in my experiences teaching and writing with community nonprofits, my audience in this book is academics—fellow scholars at universities and colleges who value teaching and working in higher education because we define our work as public work. Recognizing that college classrooms and academic spaces are only one small part of the ongoing struggles to define public life, I nevertheless remain optimistic that such spaces matter.

The revolutionary educator Paulo Freire, mindful that the dominant forces in educational and public life tend to reinforce neoliberal and elitist democracies, nevertheless remained hopeful about the task of creating new democratic possibilities. As Thomas Deans writes,

> Still, ever hopeful, [Freire] does leave open the hope that schools can become both more democratic in their practices and more inviting of community involvement. . . . Furthermore, he offers hope to individual teachers by emphasizing that there is "a space, however small, in the practice of education, in the education system as a subsystem," that can be used for liberatory purposes and he contends, it is this "minimum space that we must use to our advantage."[57]

I offer this book in the same spirit, both hopeful and wide-eyed to the reality of the many forces that conspire to define public spaces—academic spaces, community spaces, local spaces and global—as passive and even corporate spaces. I offer this book as a way to conceptualize public writing as a space of resistance. And I offer this a pedagogy for public writing that acknowledges

its complexity, its limitations, and its possibility. May we actively write ourselves into the publics we wish to be.

NOTES

1. Bill Readings, *The University in Ruins* (Cambridge, MA: Harvard University Press, 1996), 2.
2. Readings, *University in Ruins,* 585.
3. Joseph Harris, *Rewriting: How to Do Things with Texts* (Logan, UT: Utah State University Press, 2006), 1–2.
4. Harris, *Rewriting,* 9–10.
5. Edward Schiappa, "Intellectuals and the Place of Cultural Critique," in *Rhetoric, Cultural Studies, and Literacy,* ed. Frederick Reynolds (Hillsdale, NJ: Erlbaum, 1995), 22.
6. Schiappa, "Intellectuals," 26.
7. Schiappa, "Intellectuals," 25.
8. John Trimbur, "Composition and the Circulation of Writing." *College Composition and Communication* 52, no. 2 (December 2000): 212.
9. Readings, *University in Ruins,* 15.
10. Henry A. Giroux, "Neoliberalism, Corporate Culture, and the Promise of Higher Education: The University as a Democratic Public Sphere." *Harvard Educational Review* 72, no. 4 (2002): 431–32.
11. Rachel Riedner and Kevin Mahoney, *Democracies to Come: Rhetorical Action, Neoliberalism and Communities of Resistance* (Lanham, MD: Rowman and Littlefield, 2008), 11.
12. Wayne Booth, "The Idea of a *University*—as Seen by a Rhetorician," in *Defining the New Rhetorics,* ed. Stuart C. Brown and Theresa Enos (Newbury Park, CA: Sage Publications, 1993), 230.
13. Booth, "The Idea of a *University*," 230.
14. It doesn't appear from the lecture itself that Booth is alluding here to Clark Kerr's ideal of the "multiversity" as a "knowledge factory" under an efficient hierarchical management structure, though Kerr introduced his term over a decade earlier.
15. Booth, "The Idea of a *University*," 238–39.
16. Booth, "The Idea of a *University*," 235.
17. Readings, *University in Ruins,* 57.
18. Readings, *University in Ruins,* 58.
19. Jay Matthew, "Learning the Values of Liberal Arts," *Washington Post* 2004, www.washingtonpost.com/wp-dyn/articles/A35939–2004May18.html (28 August 2010).
20. Michael Roth, "What's a Liberal Arts Education Good For?" *Huffington Post* 2009, www.huffingtonpost.com/michael-roth/whats-a-liberal-arts-educ_b_147584 .html (28 August 2010).
21. Readings, *University in Ruins,* 73–78.

22. Thomas S. Kuhn, *The Structure of Scientific Revolutions* (Chicago: University of Chicago Press, 1962).

23. Thomas Deans, *Writing Partnerships: Service-Learning in Composition.* (Urbana, IL: National Council of Teachers of English, 2000), 39.

24. Freire, quoted in Deans, *Writing Partnerships,* 45.

25. Freire, quoted in Deans, *Writing Partnerships,* 46.

26. Ellen Cushman, "The Public Intellectual, Service Learning, and Activist Research." *College English* 61, no. 3 (1999): 330.

27. Karin Fischer, "Ohio's Public Colleges Lure Businesses with the Promise of a Skilled Work Force." *Chronicle of Higher Education* 55, no. 12 (14 November 2008): A15.

28. Eric Kelderman, "Texas Push 'Em: Betting Big on Research Universities." *Chronicle of Higher Education* 56, no. 28 (26 March 2010): A1.

29. Giroux, "Neoliberalism," 429.

30. Giroux, "Neoliberalism," 427.

31. Giroux, "Neoliberalism," 429.

32. Giroux, "Neoliberalism," 432, 434.

33. Admittedly, scholars do argue about the roles of the University and the Public within scholarly texts, as is evident not only in all the citations I've included but also in the very genre of this book—an academic text written to other scholars about the rhetorics of public writing.

34. Rachel Riedner and Kevin Mahoney, *Democracies to Come: Rhetorical Action, Neoliberalism, and Communities of Resistance* (Lanham, MD: Lexington Books, 2008), 42–47.

35. Riedner and Mahoney, *Democracies to Come,* 45.

36. Riedner and Mahoney, *Democracies to Come,* 45.

37. Giroux, "Neoliberalism," 427–28.

38. Keith Morton and Sandra Enos, "Building Deeper Civic Relationships and New and Improved Citizens." *Journal of Public Affairs* 6, (2002): 92.

39. Morton and Enos, "Building," 95–97.

40. Morton and Enos, "Building," 96.

41. Elizabeth Ervin, "Academics and the Negotiation of Local Knowledge." *College English* 61, no. 4 (March 1999): 457.

42. Ervin, "Academics," 457.

43. Ervin, "Academics," 467.

44. Jeffrey T. Grabill, *Writing Community Change: Designing Technologies for Citizen Action* (Cresskill, NJ: Hampton Press, 2007), 60.

45. Grabill, *Writing Community Change,* 95.

46. Grabill, *Writing Community Change,* 97–98.

47. Paula Mathieu, *Tactics of Hope: The Public Turn in English Composition* (Portsmouth, NH: Heinemann, 2005), 120.

48. Morton and Enos, "Building," 96.

49. Morton and Enos, "Building," 98.

50. Booth, "The Idea of a University," 239–40.

51. Linda Flower, *Community Literacy and the Rhetoric of Public Engagement* (Carbondale, IL: Southern Illinois University Press, 2008).

52. Deans, *Writing Partnerships,* 140.

53. Flower, *Community Literacy,* 173.

54. Troy A. Murphy, "Deliberative Civic Education and Civil Society: A Consideration of Ideals and Actualities in Democracy and Communication Education." *Communication Education* 53, no. 1 (2004): 81.

55. Murphy, "Deliberative Civic Education," 81.

56. Murphy, "Deliberative Civic Education," 81.

57. Deans, *Writing Partnerships,* 46.

Appendix 1

Some Practical Guidelines

I offer here a few snippets of practical advice for instructors interested in partnering with community organizations to teach public writing.

FACILITATE RECIPROCITY

The idea of reciprocity should not only guide your course design but should be a key term in the course.

The scholarship about service-learning and community-based learning is full of warnings about the uneasy relationship between academics and communities, and I would be remiss not to add my own admonishments about the potential hazards and pitfalls of pursuing service-learning partnerships. The usual stories follow a narrative such as Gabriella Modan provides as she discusses how she had to negotiate university-community tensions while conducting her ethnography of Mt. Pleasant. She recalled previous academics who had come into the neighborhood to study a community. The academics intended to "give something back." Community members offered their time for interviews and surveys; they opened their space to the academics. The academics published an article or a book and left. While the academic work might be interesting, the community "may not have noticed any broad-based impact on social or economic conditions of the neighborhood at large."[1] The community members' incentive to help the next eager academic diminished.

Paula Mathieu offers similar examples of academics who establish student service opportunities with community organizations without questioning whether their expertise and that of their students will be helpful. In one incident, the executive director of *Spare Change* received an email from a student who had been told by her professor to prepare (it's not clear for whom) "media proposals/campaigns to educate people about *Spare Change* and homelessness."[2] The student requested copies of brochures and papers and access to internal meetings. As Mathieu makes clear, such out-of-the-blue requests, which present everything based on what the student/academic needs even as they demand a lot of the organization, are all too common. Too often, students and professors don't stop to ask whether the community will, in fact, benefit at all from their work. Mathieu chronicles several other variations of failed community-university partnerships: Students and professors who promise to share their products (such as videos) but don't deliver; interns who drop out after the time-consuming training; students and academics who invite people into their classes without offering to compensate them in some way; researchers whose attempts to navigate the difficult landmines of clashing public interests cause harm to a nonprofit's relationships with its everyday community partners. We need to acknowledge and take into account the clashing University ideals and identities, such as those I discussed in the final chapter. We need to be very mindful that, as we approach community organizations, we build relationships and work together to ensure that both sides are gaining meaningfully from the partnership.

Thomas Deans has a good section on reciprocity in his service-learning textbook *Writing and Community Action.* In my course, I also assign students to read passages from Gabriella Modan's ethnography of Mt. Pleasant where she reflects on the usual disconnect between academic researchers and communities.

I begin the partnership by asking students to write letters of introduction to the volunteer coordinators at their sites, and I use this process as an opportunity to begin to model rhetorics of reciprocity. The assignment requires students to research their organizations enough that their letters will be targeted and specific; they should begin to understand how each organization, even within the same issue area, has a unique approach. Their letters should speak about the students' familiarity with, experience with, and/or commitment to that particular approach. We workshop drafts with a careful attention to audience, anticipating the organizations' needs and concerns.

Reciprocity also means flexibility. Students are often constrained and concerned about academic deadlines as they conduct their work. Sometimes they expect community partners to provide them with a great deal of information or to respond to their queries immediately. I keep my deadlines as flexible as possible in those cases where big events at community organizations make it hard for them to respond to student needs, but I also caution my students that they cannot make excessive demands. The organizations' first responsibility is not to the students, but to their constituents.

FITTING IT ALL IN A SEMESTER: VOLUNTEER HOURS

Requiring students to work with community organizations as part of an academic course is challenging in many ways, not the least of which is the question of time. How can an instructor cover all the required material and still compensate students for the additional time they'll spend on the course outside of the classroom?

I require students to complete at least 20 hours of service at their organization (not including travel time). I arrived at this number after a few semesters of experimenting; some organizations require more than this time, but enough can fit within this ballpark that I consider it a fair target, both for the community organizations and for me. Students who sign up for the organizations that require more than 20 hours know this when they agree to work there.

At George Washington, the first-year writing course is a four-credit seminar, which usually meets three times a week (twice for one and half hours; once for one hour). Once students are settled in with their organizations (generally the third or fourth week of the semester), I cancel the one-hour class. I still require students to write about their experiences and submit materials online on that Friday, but we do not meet face to face.

I do not allow students to take the class and opt out of the service component. I consider it an integral part of the course. This means that students who struggle and might otherwise be eligible for an Incomplete need to finish their service hours, in addition to other required assignments, before their Incomplete will be lifted.

FITTING IT ALL IN A SEMESTER: COURSE READING AND WRITING ASSIGNMENTS

When students are working at multiple community organizations, it can sometimes be hard to fit in common course readings that will be useful to all students. At the beginning of the semester this is somewhat easier. While students are choosing their community organizations and beginning their community analysis essays, I assign course readings about reciprocity, service paradigms, and community discourse analysis.

As students move into their main, academic research analysis papers, their topics are more spread out and I do not require everyone to read the same texts. Instead, I set aside several days where the class reviews three main articles, each touching on a different aspect of a similar theme, and each providing useful concepts that students might use to frame their research analysis. I assign a third of the class to read and present on each article, and then we spend some time working out the overlaps and arguments across the pieces. While the students cannot gain a full, deep understanding of each article from these class discussions, they can gain enough understanding to decide whether or not the piece will be useful for their writing. More importantly, the exercise allows us to look at models of writing that investigate the kind of questions they are pursuing, and we can examine the rhetorical moves of academics, from multiple disciplines, who write about such issues.

The hardest part of scheduling involves the final, commissioned task. I encourage students to work in groups, as this not only makes the logistics easier but usually produces stronger, more complex documents. (Students can't make assumptions based on their own experiences; they have to account for the perspectives of the others in their group.) I ask students to map out their proposed commissioned tasks by reviewing the commissioned task on their organization's information sheet (see samples in Appendix 3), consulting with their community partners, and sending a letter of understanding to me and their community partner that explains the task and provides a schedule. They complete this just before they begin their research analysis essay, so that they can consider whether they should use that research analysis essay to prepare them for the commissioned task. I later ask them to prepare a brief genre analysis, a memo that reviews the conventions of the kind of document they are asked to produce.

MAKE CONTACT EARLY AND OFTEN

Developing a service-learning class requires that you take on the extra work of initiating and maintaining contact with community organizations. I go to all these meetings in person (rather than by email or over the phone), so that I can demonstrate my commitment, become familiar with the physical space and discourse of the organization, and create the room in our conversations to pursue the goals and concerns they express about the partnership.

I have found community organizations through several networks. First, I have attended area conferences about service learning, including one that brought faculty and community organizations together. I have also met with GWU's Office of Community Service, drawing on their knowledge of organizations that already partner with the University. Finally, I've followed up on recommendations made to me by students and by people in the community. Dennis Chestnut of Groundwork introduced me to Life Pieces, for example, because several of his grandchildren participated in that program.

Unless I have another connection, I set up my initial meetings with the nonprofits' volunteer coordinators. I bring my syllabus, a few proposed readings, and a copy of an information sheet for an organization that works with a similar population or similar issues (see Appendix 3 for some model information sheets).

At the meeting, the goal is to make sure that the experience will benefit the community partner and the students. I listen to the kinds of volunteer opportunities the organization offers and assess how meaningful the opportunities will be for students in my classes. Sometimes activities that seem tedious are still valuable if the volunteer supervisor spends the time to explain how they fit in with the larger mission of the program. I prefer activities where students will work regular hours each week, as that structure avoids a lot of legwork on my part to ensure that students are assertive enough to seek out unstructured tasks.

The main part of my meeting is to brainstorm about the commissioned tasks the organization might need, and whether or not my students will have the time and ability to do them. We try to anticipate what kinds of support students will need and who will provide it.

I use the information sheet to review logistics: How will students get to and from the site? What safety tips will be appropriate for this area? Whom will they contact each week? When will they attend orientations? Are there other special dates or special needs to consider?

I meet with each volunteer coordinator at the beginning and end of the semester. I exchange regular emails throughout the semester, alerting coordinators about who is coming, and following up to make sure a routine is established. I contact them more often near the end of the semester, to help facilitate the students' commissioned tasks. Turnover in nonprofits is high, so I sometimes have to meet with an organization more often if a new volunteer coordinator comes on board who does not know me, my students, or the class.

PROVIDE STUDENT CHOICE IN COMMUNITY PARTNERS

I introduce the variety of community organizations to my students right away, sharing pamphlets and (when possible) showing the organizations' promotional videos in class. I make sure that I talk up each one equally; I emphasize the different kinds of opportunities each site offers. I make available one-page overviews of each partnership: these include all the contact information, special dates for orientation, and the expected regular schedules for volunteering, along with descriptions of volunteer tasks and possible commissioned tasks. (Samples of some of these information sheets are included in Appendix 3.) When possible, I invite former students to come and talk about their experiences.

Within the first two weeks of the semester, students send me a memo in which they rank the top three organizations they want to work with and give me a brief reason for their choices. Some organizations limit the number of volunteers they can take; others prefer to have eight or ten. I use the rankings and the explanations to sort out who goes where. Sometimes, for example, students have listed an educational organization without specifying why they prefer that one over another. If they haven't included reasons that link them to the unique components of a particular program, and if I have some organizations with very few interested volunteers, I may ask a student to move into an organization that has openings.

MAKE ROOM FOR WORKING STUDENTS (INCLUDING THOSE ON WORK STUDY)

A good number of students coming to GWU have been awarded Federal Work Study, and they can complete that work through working with a variety of community organizations. At GWU, the Office of Community Service facilitates this placement. I have verified with them which of the community partners for my course offer Work Study, and I make this clear to students as they are selecting their organizations. If they already have a Work Study position with another nonprofit not already affiliated with my course, then I ask the student to meet with their supervisors, using the information sheet, and brainstorm about potential commissioned tasks. I then meet with the organization myself and try to accommodate.

I know that some faculty do not allow for students to complete their community service hours through their Work Study placements. I do not find the two incompatible, so long as the community organization meets the other needs for my course. In fact, I consider it an important part of ensuring that the students are able to successfully complete my course. The transition to college is difficult enough for students who are also working.

When students have very time-consuming work commitments, or if they are concerned that they cannot give time to community organizations and still concentrate on their coursework, then I meet with them to find appropriate placements. Some organizations offer Saturday hours, for example, or a few day-long events instead of regular, weekly service. However, I hold fast to the requirements of my course: students must work at least twenty hours with local nonprofits, and they must be able to complete meaningful commissioned tasks.

I use the first two weeks of my class—GWU's add/drop period—to work out service placement. This timing ensures that students who have incompatible outside commitments or who are uninterested in devoting the time to community organizations will realize the demands of the course in time to drop without penalty.

TACKLE RISK MANAGEMENT HEAD-ON

Crime happens everywhere. As an urban campus, our neighborhood is not exempt. But students quickly learn about what areas of DC are considered "sketchy" and where they should never go. Indeed, sometimes they hear admonishments from city bus drivers or taxi cab drivers, who tell them "People like you don't go to that part of town."

I have learned to make the rhetoric and realities of risk a visible part of the course. I spend a day going over standard practices for being safe in an urban environment. I make sure students program their cell phones (in class) with the contact information and emergency numbers. I let them know that yes, some of my former students have been in dangerous situations (four GW freshmen were held up at gunpoint traveling back to a metro stop at dusk). I give them choices about which organizations they want to work with, and ask them to consider travel and safety as they make their choices. They sign a university-issued waiver. Requiring students to sign a waiver to participate in class activity that is non-negotiable is problematic, to say the least. This is why I am sure to offer them choices of which organization to work with. I also make sure that we complete the process before the end of the drop period.

Check with your Office of Community Service (or, lacking that, with your chair) about the university's expectations about safety and protocols. I work with some organizations that are already associated with my university through the Office of Community Service; students are regularly directed to work there, and the OCS has worked out the protocols for transportation and safety. I also work with organizations that are not affiliated with the OCS. My supervisors know this, but I have not received any explicit direction about transportation protocols and safety risks. Instead, I follow the guidelines that the Office of Community Service uses when they set up new partnerships.

Though it is difficult to think about, be prepared for things to go wrong. Talk to your chair or community service office about the steps you should take if any student is put at risk or harmed. What kind of support can you offer to students immediately? Who at the university and at the community organizations should be contacted?

TRACKING SERVICE HOURS

At GWU, the Office of Community Service has developed a protocol for regular updates of students' service hours with various community organizations. I rely on this for some of my community partners, but not all of them are officially connected to OCS. Therefore, I have a secondary system for tracking hours. I create a wiki on the course website and require students to update it once a month, listing the dates and times they attended and keeping a running total of their hours. I also consult with the community partners a couple of times during the semester to make sure students are attending during the hours they signed up for. I tell students that at the end of the semester I will compare their posted hours with the hours the community organization has tracked. This system has worked well, because it is easy to see which students are falling behind in their hours so that we can work out concerns before it's too late.

NOTES

1. Gabriella Gahlia Modan, *Turf Wars: Discourse, Diversity, and the Politics of Place* (Malden, MA: Blackwell, 2007), 12.
2. Paula Mathieu, *Tactics of Hope: The Public Turn in English Composition* (Heinemann, 2005), 100.

Appendix 2

Sample Writing Assignments

I have included my writing prompts for the main essay assignments in my first-year public writing course. At the George Washington University, UW20 is a required, four-credit, one-seminar course. The writing faculty is encouraged to design writing courses around themes that will enhance the study of writing. Students can browse the course descriptions before registering, so they can choose their sections based on an interest in the course theme. Class size is capped at fifteen; course loads for faculty are three to four sections per semester. All UW20 students are required to complete 25–30 pages of "finished writing," which means students must submit drafts and receive feedback from instructors or peers on these pages. One assignment, at least, should include research. (For a full description of the common elements in the UW20 course design, see the "UW20 Template" at the program website, www. gwu.edu/~uwp.)

As I've explained throughout the book, and especially in chapter 3, I design the writing prompts to introduce public writing as a site of constant clash and struggle. Through the writing sequence, students consider how geographical and historical contexts affect how a community defines itself, as well as how the historical trajectories of an issue and people's ideas about democracy factor into public writing. In the end, students apply what they have learned about the rhetorics of public formation by creating a public document for their community organizations.

As a first-year writing course, UW20 must also introduce students to the moves of academic writing and the habits of scholarly research. I understand that the shift from high school to college-level writing involves moving away from report-focused writing (where the author tells what others have done) and toward more analytical writing (where the author works with and against other texts and contexts to provide a new understanding of what others have done). Therefore, the first and second assignments introduce students to the technique of using one text (or series of texts) to create an analytical framework through which to understand another text (or series of texts). At the same time, as I have argued throughout the book, a full appreciation of the complexities of a community and its rhetoric is often lost if we look only through a predetermined lens. Therefore, I encourage my students to also consider how their on-the-ground experiences might talk back to and counter the frameworks offered in the academic texts.

I have reprinted the assignments here in the form I distribute to my students, and I have supplemented them with footnotes to explain terms and activities unique to our classroom lexicon. Some of the assignments refer to our course textbooks: Thomas Deans's *Writing and Community Action* and Gabriella Modan's *Turf Wars*, Diana Hacker's *Rules for Writers*, and various assigned articles that are compiled for them in our joint Refworks account.[2]

ESSAY 1: ANALYSIS OF COMMUNITY
8 PP. INCLUDING BIBLIOGRAPHY

Your first paper, an *Analysis of Community*, is a group project, designed *to give you a close look at the neighborhood* you'll be working in and *to introduce you to a particular kind of writing:* analyzing something using a theoretical framework provided in an academic text.

The Task, Briefly

Analyze how people describe this neighborhood, looking at not only *what* is said, but also *who* is speaking and how different constituents define the area. Using a theory from our class texts about how people define community, analyze the rhetoric of community materials and help others understand some of the ongoing struggles that shape the neighborhood identity.

Audience: The primary audience for your essay is people who do public work in a community. What struggles should they know about as they enter this community?

Research Materials

Neighborhood sources: Students working in the same ward[1] but in different organizations will come together for this task. Depending on the locations of the organizations that your group members are working with, you may choose to focus in on certain neighborhoods in your ward.

To develop a solid essay, you will need to conduct and share a wide variety of research. You may end up using only a small portion of this research in the final essay, but knowing what is available will be critical to choosing the most interesting and relevant angle for your analysis.

To find contemporary descriptions and discussions of your neighborhood, your research team will use local documents. We will meet with our instructional librarian, Bill Gillis, to learn how to track down these sources.

Analytical Frameworks: Drawing on the work of other scholars who have written about community dynamics, you'll identify patterns and interpret the material you found. Choose from at least one of the texts we've read in class; choose the ones that best help you explain what you've found:

- Modan, *Turf Wars,* pp. 34–48, the section on Washington and DC
- Modan, *Turf Wars,* pp. 137–166, "The Politics of Filth"
- Modan, *Turf Wars,* pp. 88–136, "Moral Geography"
- Kretzmann and McKnight, "Building Communities from the Inside Out: A Path Toward Finding and Mobilizing a Community's Assets" (in Refworks)
- Mitchell, "The End of Public Space" (in Refworks)

OR choose frameworks derived from texts that these articles cite. You can use the Essay 1 Refworks folder to browse some of the scholarly articles that your peers have recommended as frameworks for other DC community analysis essays.

Sharing and Documenting Your Sources: Gather your research documents into a group Refworks folder so that everyone will have easy access to the same material. Refworks can also prepare the bibliography for final draft, which should be in APA format. (See Hacker, *Rules for Writers,* for more specifics on APA.)

Strategies for Collaborating

I do NOT recommend that you each research separate documents, write up your findings separately, and then try to fit those pieces together into a cohesive essay. The documents you review may paint different pictures of the neighborhood. The group needs to understand all the perspectives and how they intersect before you can develop an interesting point for your essay.

I DO recommend that you divide up the research, take copious notes, and then meet several times to share what you've found, using the meeting to identify potential patterns and to compare your observations to the theories introduced in the class readings. After several such meetings, you may converge on a way of looking at the materials and draft a rough outline. Only then should you assign people to write sections of the essay. From your conversations, each member should understand how to develop his or her section using examples from many of the research documents.

I also recommend that you have a serious conversation with your group before you get started, in which you talk about your usual writing habits, your strengths, and your past experiences with group work. Lay it all out on the table, and work together to set up a schedule and a work plan that feels fair to everyone. Acknowledge that things don't always go as we hope they will, and talk about what you think the group should do if a member skips meetings, misses deadlines, or otherwise doesn't contribute. Be explicit about this now, so that should it happen, you won't be left unsure how to respond and feeling resentful about picking up the extra work (You will submit this as a group contract).

Steps

- We will meet with our instructional librarian, Bill Gillis, to learn strategies for using our current texts as a springboard to find additional analytical sources.
- We will meet with Bill Gillis to learn strategies for finding a wide range of community documents.
- I will introduce you to Refworks, a bibliographic tool, where you will collect and share your documents.
- You will write annotations for sources that provide scholarly frameworks and for community documents.
- You will meet regularly with your collaborative writing group to
  - Share and discuss your community documents, looking for trends and potential sites of conflict about how groups define the community
  - Share and discuss framing sources that can help explicate what you see in the community documents
  - Outline the essay together, indicating which resources to use in each section
  - Divide up the work of writing each section
  - Review the document and work out any disagreements in how you might have used or interpreted your sources, and adjust your argument and structure as needed

- You will attend a workshop. Each group will read and comment on the essays of other groups. (Your group will need to complete a self-review letter before the workshop; each group member will write letters to the other groups about their essays.)
- You will meet as a group, discuss workshop comments, and revise.
- You will turn in final document and revision letter (jointly written).

ESSAY 2: ACADEMIC RESEARCH ANALYSIS
12 PP. INCLUDING BIBLIOGRAPHY

Your task in the *academic research analysis* is to review academic research related to your organization, to evaluate whether your work with your community organization affirms that research or counters it, and to consider the significance of your discoveries. You have a couple of options:

Essay 2, Option 1

You may choose *an issue that arises from your work with your community organization*—an issue directly related to its goals or methods. Study the academic scholarship about that issue to see if academics help explain some of the dynamics you see. You may find that the approach taken by your community partner is well-aligned with the academic research. If so, your analysis of the organization can serve as an intricate case study to *forward* that research. On the other hand, you may find that the organization's approach runs *counter* to the academic theories. Then your close analysis of the particular aspects of that experience will change our understanding of how things really work. You may wish to make recommendations to the organization, or you may wish to talk back to the scholars, advising them about how their scholarship has not accounted for how things really work in situations like yours.

Here are some examples:

Someone working at CentroNía might wonder: Does the 100 Books reading curricula that CentroNía just adopted serve or undermine the goals of multicultural education? How well do public schools address the needs of immigrant elementary school students?

Someone working at Groundwork Anacostia River might wonder: Do projects like the ones that GWDC endorses have an impact on the carbon footprint in the neighborhood? How are such effects calculated?

Someone working at Higher Achievement might ask: Some scholars have argued that addressing the achievement gap means not only teaching academic subjects but also preparing students to advocate for their rights within the schools (see Bob Moses, *Radical Equations*). How well does HAP's program fit with that model? Should it?

Essay 2, Option 2

Alternatively, you may investigate *the challenges that community organizations face as they seek to establish and maintain themselves.* Your questions here would be less about the particular issues and more about the challenges of persuading volunteers to work with the organizations, community members to trust them, or donors to fund them. You will need to examine philosophies of community organizing (such as McKnight's) or of writing for public audiences (such as my lecture about invoking public agency and capacity[3]). Here are some examples:

Miriam's Kitchen (a local soup kitchen) has recently begun using social networking (Facebook, Twitter, YouTube, etc.) to reach its volunteers. How does this work? Whom does it reach through this medium, and what kind of public relationship does it create among those readers/viewers? Are homeless people invoked as part of that audience? What are the implications?

Given DC's history of race relations, how does your organization respond: To what extent does the organization overtly or covertly address race? From its materials and its organizational structure, what kind of relations do you think it promotes?

Historically, have low-income neighborhoods taken up environmental causes? If so, what motivates them? If not, what are the barriers to getting involved? How have other nonprofits addressed that challenge?

As you work on this essay, keep in mind the tensions between communities and the university. Historically, many communities have found that academics treat people as objects of study, asking community members to give interviews and contribute to their scholarship without reciprocating. As you bridge between academic and community work, you will need to be mindful of this relationship, looking at the academic research with a critical community eye even as you look at the community with a critical academic eye.

Steps

1. *Research proposal:* Use Blog 5[4] to think aloud about the research questions you are considering. This will include reviewing past blogs and course readings. I will meet with students individually to review the proposals.

2. Refworks annotations for scholarly articles: After we review how to find scholarly articles in the Gelman online databases, you will gather 10 solid sources in your individual Refworks folder and print out an annotated bibliography for me. Then you'll choose your two best sources to annotate for the Essay 2 Sources folder. (See more details under Refworks Tasks 2A and 2B.) Be sure to include appropriate descriptors/tags so others can make use of these sources.

3. Draft and workshop: Prepare a draft for a team of your classmates to read and respond to during our class workshop. Include a self-review letter.

4. Revise.

5. *Turn in final draft* along with revision letter.

ESSAY 3 (OPTION ONE) VOLUNTEER PORTFOLIO
5–10 PP. INCLUDING ATTACHMENTS

Most organizations depend heavily on volunteers to complete their work, and they want to make sure their volunteers feel well-prepared and appreciated. Yet they rarely have a chance to hear a rich, rigorous reflection from those volunteers. Your final project, a *volunteer portfolio,* will provide that for them. Written from your perspective as a volunteer with your community, the portfolio provides a glimpse of what it's like to join this organization.

The Task

Prepare a *reflective letter* of 3–5 pp. in which you offer the volunteer coordinator a glimpse into your experience as a volunteer, providing concrete examples. The goal is to provide the coordinator with a candid look that conveys both the successes and the problems you encountered. You may speculate about what might have led to the successes and difficulties—whether it was because of your own expectations, because of personalities, or because of your preparation or the materials and structures you worked with. You may offer suggestions for addressing any problems; as you do so, be sure to anticipate some of the constraints or goals of the organization.

If appropriate, you may attach supporting documents to the letter. Choose those that tie in with the focus of your letter, such as

- Passages from your blogs (you may revise these from the original) and/or passages from other people's blogs (used only with their permission)
- Samples of the documents you used most frequently
- Samples of materials you might recommend that they incorporate (if any)
- Samples of articles or books that you have found most helpful (if any)

Steps

Review your activities and responses to them as the semester progressed. (Use the blogs to remind yourself).

Identify materials from the organization that you referenced most often during your work (i.e. the website, any volunteer manuals, any on-site resources, other publications, and so on). *Explain how you used them and how well they met your needs.* (Consider as you do so the other audiences the materials might address and whether the document can account for all those audiences successfully.)

Explore one or two key aspects of your experience further—providing more detail and more reflection—to explain what you took away from the experience or what additional aspects you would suggest the organization consider. To elaborate, you may wish to draw on course texts or your research for Essay 1 or 2, keeping in mind that your audience may not be familiar with the works.

Talk with other volunteers and review their blogs to see if they had similar experiences. Try to figure out what accounts for the similarities or differences.

Draft your reflection letter and your self-review letter.

Workshop: Participate in a workshop with your peers to solicit and offer feedback.

Revise based on advice from the workshop.

Attend a final meeting with your community organization. This meeting will include students from all sections who worked with your organization. At this meeting, *turn in your final letter* to me and to your community organization. The presentation should be generous and insightful and should invite a conversation with the organization. I will evaluate this interaction as part of your grade. This does not mean that the volunteer coordinators must agree with your perspectives, but rather that they should find your feedback credible and something they will think more about.

Advice on Volunteer Portfolios

Format this document as a letter to the volunteer coordinator and/or your main contact at the organization. Include a date and a salutation ["Dear xx"], and make it single-spaced. Sign your name as you would on a letter. Write the letter to the person you had the most contact with, and CC the volunteer coordinator. Don't include any tell-tale formatting that would suggest this is primarily a graded document (don't put your name or the assignment title in the top, for example). The goal of this assignment is to write a genuine letter about genuine things you've seen and experienced; if you write this as an "essay," then you're actually going against the assignment.

Acknowledge the actual relationship you have with the person you're writing to. The primary goal is to speak to the organization in the manner that is most appropriate for your relationship with it. Call people by the names that you use to talk to them. You don't need to repeat things they would already know, except when doing so assures them that you understand something that is important to them. To reaffirm your shared values, you have to name those values. If you've had previous conversations that are relevant, mention them ("I know we talked before about . . .") and use the letter as a way to extend the conversation. If you haven't had the chance to talk to them much about your experiences, then acknowledge that, too.

If you feel as if you're telling them the obvious, then pause and ask, "What about *my experience* might *not* be obvious to them?" What they *cannot* know is how well their program is working for their volunteers and why. They cannot know which aspect of their programs come through the strongest or which seem to drop away. Your reflections can help them see their organization through the eyes of volunteers like you. Try as best you can to articulate that experience, showing where you think it aligned best with their goals.

Anticipate the needs and hopes of your readers. Here are some points to consider about your potential readers:

Organizations love to hear *stories about moments or people that helped you see things in a new way, or moments that you understood to be very significant.* Telling stories about your *"aha!"* moments—those experiences where you said "Oh, now I see what this is all about!"—will be useful and rewarding for members of your organization. Such stories reinforce their sense of themselves as part of an organization where these kinds of positive things happen. Telling stories about your *"oh no!"* moments will be revealing too. These can help the organization see where something broke down, where you felt disconnected or disoriented. Reflecting on those moments—whether they were, in the end, productive, and whether they could have been anticipated by you or them—will help the organization understand your experiences better. These "aha!" and "oh no!" moments are likely to be ones that you wrote about in your blogs, so you could pull from those, revising what you said there.

How do you think your organization sees your role as a volunteer? *What ideals might it have for how volunteers might describe their relationship to the organization or the issue, and their reasons for volunteering?* LPTM offered the "mutual liberation" quote as an example[5]. That is *one* way to approach this question, if you think your organization's members also strive for this kind of relationship. If you do use the quote, then spell out with some detail what you mean by your "liberation" and its tie to theirs. If you feel as if the semester didn't really push you to see this mutuality, then talk about that. Do you think that's OK, or not?

On the other hand, your organization's members may not see "mutual liberation" as the primary thing they want their volunteers to consider. If that's the case, then what kind of relationship do you think they might want you to have with your clients/tutees/community members? Where do you get that picture from? Do you think that the organization accomplished that goal with you?

Organizations' members spend a lot of energy *recruiting volunteers,* so it could be useful for them to see what it was about their organization that drew you in. Be honest, as that can help them see what to highlight for future volunteers. Look back to the beginning of class, and think about what made you pick this organization instead of the others from the class. What materials did you look at? Which aspect of it did you respond to the most?

Organizations ideally would like *volunteers who will keep coming back.* Help your organization's members assess this aspect of their work. Have they done everything they could to inspire you to stay committed? If so, what? If not, what else was missing for you? (You might compare to what you've heard about other organizations, if that's relevant.)

If you're not planning to return, it might be valuable to explain why and to consider whether or not the organization could address those barriers. What would it take to make this organization a priority for you? You don't need to BS here; the goal is to give the organization's members a glimpse of what it takes to continue to volunteer while you're a GW student and to help them see more clearly if they can address any of those concerns. Are the barriers logistical? Concerns about whether you're really needed? Concerns about whether you're really the right person for the task? Or are they temporary barriers—like study abroad, or a class schedule that conflicts with the time, or needing to get a job? If so, would you consider returning after that, or would you look for a different kind of service? Why?

Nonprofits are always *trying to do their best with limited resources.* As you write, be careful to acknowledge this. Acknowledge the constraints that may get in the way, if any do.

ESSAY 3 (OPTION TWO) COMMISSIONED TASK
5 PP. OR EQUIVALENT

The Task

Your task in the *commissioned task* will vary depending on the needs of your community organization. Your final portfolio for the commissioned task will include the final product along with documentation of your meetings with the organization as you worked out the requirements for the document.

The task may be anything from a brochure to a walking tour to a review of a curriculum. The main audience for the commissioned task depends on the project you take on: a HAP curriculum review would be directed to the HAP curriculum director; a brochure to encourage local businesses to volunteer with Thrive DC! clients would be directed to the employees who work in Columbia Heights; and a *Hatchet* editorial about the November Help the Homeless Walkathon would be written to the GW public (or at least to the part of GW you think is most likely to join you in walking).

You can see what tasks your organization has commissioned by reviewing the community partners overview. Consider your choices early in the semester, because you may want to focus your academic research analysis on the same topic and draw on the research for both assignments.

Helpful Resources

Deans's chapter 8, "Writing for the Community," is a valuable resource for this task, as it includes

An *overview of the distinctions between "workplace" and "academic" writing,* and a useful reflection from a student about how she had to adjust her writing process to accommodate the new context of writing for a community group

Tools for thinking about your *audience,* on p. 355

Guidelines for *visual design*—important information for anyone putting together a pamphlet, brochure, slide presentation, or similar document, on p. 359

Samples of the letter of understanding (for working out your project with your community partner)

Samples of the letter of transmittal (which accompanies your document, unless the actual commissioned task is a memo going to the same person)

Steps

Review the commissioned tasks listed for your community organizations (these are included in the information sheet for each organization)[6].

Talk with the contact person at your organization about these possible tasks, and see if there are others that he or she (or you) would like to propose.

Develop a plan for how you will work on this project. Include deadlines, materials you'll need to gather, and proposals for how you will gather those materials (don't presume that your contact can quickly or easily provide them—ask and find out what the process might be).

Complete a blog (for the class and me) in which you propose possible commissioned tasks and work out a time line for completing them.

Submit a letter of understanding. See Deans, "Letter of Understanding."

Gather samples of documents that are similar to the one you must produce. Study these carefully to analyze the genre: What are the conventions of this form? What is the usual length? Voice? Kinds of examples used? What is the format? Share your findings in Blog 7.

Create a draft, write a self-review letter, and post to an appropriate time slot in the Blackboard discussion board for this workshop.

Attend a workshop: Get feedback from your classmates (in the workshop) and from your community partner (if appropriate).

Create a final draft and a letter of transmittal to accompany it. (See Deans for models of a letter of transmittal.) Turn in a copy for the organization and a second copy that I will grade.

Attend a final meeting with representatives from your community organization and other students who worked there. Make a presentation to them about your commissioned task.

NOTES

1. Within DC, wards are civic boundaries. Each ward has a councilman on the DC City Council. Because DC is not a state, it does not have corresponding districts for U.S. Representatives or U.S. Senators.

2. George Washington has a subscription to Refworks, which students can access through the Gelman library system. I set up a Refworks account for my sections, and require students to import records of scholarly articles and community documents into the database. Each collaborative group has its own folder (titled according to the ward they are analyzing); the class as a whole has an Essay 1 folder in which they post annotations of scholarly articles they feel offer appropriate frameworks for such essays. I use this system to encourage collaboration: students are required to post a certain number of unique documents to their folders and to browse what others have found. I intend to model the collaborative processes that many academics use, such

as sharing annotated bibliographies. I developed this approach in collaboration with instructional librarian Bill Gillis; we have presented about the Refworks component at the Georgia Conference on Information Literacy, Fall 2010.

3. The lecture I refer to here is a condensed version of chapter 3, in which I identify the rhetorical goals of building agency and capacity and draw on models from Washington Parks and People and other community organizations.

4. I assign students to keep regular blogs in which they reflect on their experiences at their community organizations and their responses to class readings. The blogs are part of our Blackboard site, so they are available to students in my three sections and to our instructional librarian, but not to the community organizations. Although I had hoped the blogs would create more cross-talk among students as they compared their experiences and responses, I have found that students rarely review each other's blogs. I plan to experiment with different blogging platforms and prompts. In the meantime, I ask students to report back more often during class discussions about their experiences and questions or observations they have. Ideally, students will draw on both their own reflections and conversations with their peers to identify potential research topics for their research analysis essays.

5. The Director of Education Programs at Life Pieces to Masterpieces has a quote from an "Aboriginal Elder" as her tag line: "If you are coming here to save me, you are wasting your time. If you are coming here because your liberation is tied to mine, then let us work together." At her suggestion, we used this quote as an in-class writing prompt to consider questions of reciprocity.

6. See Appendix 3 for some examples of these information sheets.

Appendix 3

Sample Community Partner Profiles

Over the years, I've created a sheet that I use to keep track of all the requests and contact information for community partners. I meet with each organization to update these forms every semester, as I often recognize that the kind of information one organization has included would be valuable for others, as well (For example, in DC, all volunteers who work in the schools or after school with youth have to have a TB test and a background check). Sometimes the writing projects I brainstorm with one organization help me think of possible tasks to suggest for others. I am clear with the community organizations that information my students write will go through a workshop process in the class.

I distribute these sheets to my students at the beginning of the semester. For many organizations, especially those that coordinate with area schools, the final details about meeting times and contact information come in at the beginning of the university's fall semester, requiring us to be somewhat flexible.

GROUNDWORK ANACOSTIA RIVER, DC, WWW.GROUNDWORKDC.ORG

Max # of UWstudents: None   Work Study option? No
TB test required? Yes   Background check required? Yes

Mission statement:
Our mission is to bring about the sustained regeneration, improvement and management of the physical environment by developing community-based partnerships that empower people, businesses and organizations to promote environmental, economic and social well-being.

Video: None yet
GW Office of Community Service Contact: [*Here I insert information about the people at GWU who help to coordinate GWU's volunteering with the community organization. The Office of Community Service does not have people designated to help coordinate with all of the organizations I work with, however. In those cases, I include the number of the Office of Community Service's main coordinator, and I send him or her a list of all the organizations I'll be working with.*]

Contact Information:
Dennis Chestnut
dennis@groundworkdc.org   Groundwork Program Coordinator: TBA
202-286-4970   SEED Green Team Leader: TBA

Address:
Main office: 3938 Benning Rd, NE   Neighborhood: Stoddert
SEED school: 4400 C Street, SE   Ward: 7

Orientation:
General Volunteer Orientation: (Monthly) @ Groundwork office
Green Team Project Orientation: To be held on a Saturday in September @ Groundwork office

Hours and Activities for Regular Service
Green Teams: Groundwork is establishing four Green Teams, which are high school after-school programs in which youth will develop leadership skills and "use a cross-cultural framework to understand their role in the global community." The high school teams focus on core environmental areas, and through field experience and field trips help "improve, maintain and manage" the physical environment. In the early fall, they prepare for a partnership with a local elementary school; in the late fall and spring the Green Team leads the younger children in an EcoKids program. Green Team volunteers will assist a Green Team leader at SEED (a local college prep high school), with 10th–12th graders; you are welcome to attend the Youth Summit as well (see below).

Hours for Green Teams: Two evenings a week and one Saturday a month. You should plan to attend at least one of the evenings each week. Groundwork will set the schedule in consultation with the DC schools, ASAP.

Event Planning: October 20–24: Groundwork is partnering with the EPA to hold a Groundwork Youth Summit as part of the EPA's 40th Anniversary celebrations. Groundwork volunteers would coordinate with Dennis to finalize plans and help them run smoothly during the weekend. In particular, you would attend the Thursday afternoon Welcome Dinner and the Friday Youth Assembly sessions, and/or the service project Friday at Kennilworth Park. You would help run the GWARDC site tour.

Writing Opportunities:

Green Team brochure: Update the brochure to reflect the current project, with a layout design that is vibrant and appropriate to the GWDC mission. Prepare a few options and make a pitch to Dennis and the GWDC project coordinator.

Ft. Mahan proposal: Research the history of Ft. Mahan in the Civil War and afterwards, documenting its transformation over time. (You may be able to track down historical photos and documents in the Library of Congress, the National Park Service, and other Washington archives.) Prepare a report about your findings, along with a proposal for appropriate programming Groundwork DC might develop.

Oral Histories: Interview elders from the Anacostia River communities and prepare a recommendation for how this information might be incorporated into Groundwork DC programming. Dennis Chestnut can arrange for the interview. To prepare for the interview, research the area so that you are familiar with landmarks and historical events, and share a draft of your questions with Dennis and Dr. Ryder. Record the interview and give a digital copy to Groundwork, along with a document that identifies the main subjects covered and when they occurred. If appropriate, make recommendations for how this information might be incorporated into the Deanwood Heritage Trail or DC Cultural Tourism.

Other ideas that spring from your experience at Groundwork DC. If you have your own idea, make a proposal to Dr. Ryder and Dennis, to make sure it's something that Groundwork will find useful.

Transportation:

To get to the main office: Go to the Minnesota Avenue Station and then walk one block south on Minnesota Avenue. Turn left on Benning Rd. The office will be on your left. (If you are going or returning after dark, a Groundwork staff member will pick you up at the station.)

To get to Green Team sites: Dennis or a Green Team leader will pick you up at the Minnesota Avenue station.

Safety Tips:
Program your cell phone with the main numbers: Dennis's and your Green Team leader's.
Program my cell number into your phone (240-xxx-xxxx) and call if you're out in the city and have a question or concern.
Plan your routes before you leave campus.
Travel in groups and follow usual safety tips for traveling in a city: Pay attention to who is around you, don't wear your earphones or allow yourself to be distracted by your phone, and if it's dark, get a ride back to the metro.

HIGHER ACHIEVEMENT PROGRAM, WWW.HIGHERACHIEVEMENT.ORG

Max # of UW students: None   Work Study option? Yes
TB test required? Yes   Background check required? Yes

Higher Achievement is a non-profit organization that provides middle school children from underserved areas year-round academic enrichment programs and preparation for top high school placement. The organization invests in talent and hard work and delivers over 650 hours annually of rigorous academic training during the most critical time in a child's development: middle school.

Mission statement:
Higher Achievement's mission is to develop academic skills, behaviors, and attitudes in academically motivated and underserved middle school children to improve their grades, test scores, attendance, and opportunities—resulting in acceptance to college preparatory high schools.

Video: YouTube, "Higher Achievement;" URL: http://www.youtube.com/watch?v=mIyEj-1dDjA

GW Office of Community Service Contact: [*Here I insert information about the people at GWU who help to coordinate GWU's volunteering with the community organization.*]

Contact Information:
Matt Thornton, Volunteer Coordinator, mthornton@higherachievement. org, 202-544-3633 x233, cell (emergencies only): 617-XXX-XXXX

Special Dates:
General Orientation for HAP volunteers will be held **September 4** from 1–3 p.m., location TBD. If you are interested in HAP, attend the orientation. (It's OK to go and change your mind afterward.)
Mentor 1.0 Orientation: at Centers, during week of September 13
Mentor 2.0 Orientation: at Centers, during week of September 20
Mentoring with your scholars starts on September 27.

Hours/Activities for Regular Service:
Seminar Mentors: 6–8 p.m. Monday, Tuesday, or Thursday: Teach a small group of 5th or 6th graders in a core academic subject: Math, Literature, or Elective Seminar.
Study Hall Aide: 5–6 p.m. Monday, Tuesday, or Thursday: Your role will be to help the middle school students complete their homework and to provide guidance and support to succeed academically.

Address	*Neighborhood*	*Ward*	*Center Director/* *Assistant Center Director*
Savoy Elementary School, 2400 Shannon Place, SE	Anacostia	8	CD: Laura Nicholson Office: 202-375-7727 Cell: 202-239-9449 ACD: Angela Booker Office: 202-375-7726 Cell: 202-239-9470
Kelly Miller Middle, 301 49th Street, NE	Hillbrook	7	CD: Martine Shorter Office: 202-375-7706 Cell: 202-239-9527 ACD: Cedric Howard/ Kenshasa Office: 202-375-7707 Cell: 202-256-2538
Brightwood Education Campus, 1300 Nicholson Street, NW	Petworth	4	CD: Mike Di Marco Office: 202-375-7705 Cell: 202-255-6540 ACD: Jenell Walton/Durya Durham Office: 202-375-7721 Cell: 202-255-6578

| Center City Public Charter School, 1503 E Capitol Street, SE | Capitol Hill | 6 | CD: Sam Dodson
Office: 202-375-7701
Cell: 202-255-7309
ACD: Moraya Seeger-Jackson
Office: 202-375-7730
Cell: 202-255-0245 |
| Adams Middle, 2020 19th St, NW | Adams Morgan | 1 | CD: Meredith Morelle
Office: 202-375-7703
Cell: 202-255-0459
ACD: Neils Ribeiro-Yemofio
Office: 202-375-7702
Cell: 202-255-2812 |

Note: If you are younger than 18, you will need a parent's signature to volunteer with HAP.

Writing Opportunities:

Alumni interviews: Interview alumni who have returned to mentor, and prepare a newsletter article and make recommendations for which parts of the interview can be used to recruit additional alumni as mentors and which parts Matt might use to prepare mentors (Contact Matt, who will introduce you to KJ, the HAP intern working on this project).

News articles: Work with the communications intern to prepare news articles about HAP; these might include interviews with Center Directors (To interview students, you need permission from HAP) (Contact Matt, who will introduce you to KJ, the HAP intern working on this project).

Ward 8 expansion: Mentors working in Ward 8 could provide a detailed volunteer reflection, describing the experience of being a mentor at this new location. This would be presented to the Assistant Center Director for Ward 8.

Webinars: Write a script proposal for a webinar that Matt could use in volunteer training. He is working on turning the orientation and mentor trainings into online resources.

Other: You may propose alternate tasks to me and Matt.

Transportation Notes:

Ward 8: Take the metro orange line to L'Enfant Plaza and switch to the Green line toward Branch Avenue. Exit at the Anacostia Station. Savoy Elementary is on that block.

Ward 7: Take the metro orange line from Foggy Bottom to Stadium Armory station. Get there by 5:45 p.m. A shuttle will take you to HAP and back. If the shuttle is not waiting for you, call your site coordinator (There may be a late pickup at Benning Road station, if you call the assistant site director at ward 7).

Ward 4: Take the metro blue or orange line to McPherson Square Station. Take the #54 bus to 14th and Nicholson Street (54 bus schedule: http://www.wmata.com/bus/timetables/dc/52–54.pdf), OR take the metro green line to Georgia Avenue station. If you choose the metro, contact your site director before you go to coordinate transportation from there.

Ward 6: Take the metro to Union Station. Walk east on F Street and then north on 7th Street.

Ward 1: Take the #42 bus from Farragut West to Columbia and 19th Street (42 bus schedule: http://www.wmata.com/bus/timetables/dc/42.pdf).

Safety Tips:
Program your cell phone with the cell #s for your Assistant Center Directors and Matt Thornton.

Program my cell number into your phone (xxx-xxx-xxxx). Call if you have a question or concern.

Travel in groups: Check with Matt T. to see who else is attending your site. Plan your routes before you leave campus. Follow usual safety tips for traveling in a city: Pay attention to who is around you, don't wear your earphones or allow yourself to be distracted by your phone, and if it's dark, get a ride back to the metro.

LIFE PIECES TO MASTERPIECES | WWW.LIFEPIECES.ORG

Max # of UW students: 4 per night   Work Study option? No
TB test required? Yes   Background check required? Yes

"Life Pieces to Masterpieces (LPTM) is a non-profit, arts-based, comprehensive youth development organization. We serve boys and young men ages 3 to 21 living in low-income and public housing east of the Anacostia River in Washington, DC."

Mission statement:
LPTM provides opportunities to discover and activate the innate and creative abilities of the members to change life challenges into possibilities.

Video: Vimeo, "Stone Soup;" URL: http://vimeo.com/5143977

GW Office of Community Service Contact: [*Here I insert information about the people at GWU who help to coordinate GWU's volunteering with the community organization.*]

Contact Information:
Tiffani Ross, Volunteer Coordinator, r_tiffani86@yahoo.com
Maurice Kie, Program Coordinator, mkei@lifepieces.org, cell: xxx-xxx-xxxx (texting is best)
Jacobi Clifton, Office Manager, jclifton@lifepieces.org, 202-399-7703
Aikta Suri, Education Coordinator, asuri@lifepieces.org

Address:
Merritt Middle School
Neighborhood: Deanwood
5002 Hayes Street, NE
Ward: 7
Washington, DC 20019

Phone Number: 202-399-7703

Special Dates:
Orientation for Life Pieces to Masterpieces. On a Saturday in September, TBD Shuttle will pick you up from Minnesota Avenue station. They will provide lunch.

Hours for Regular Service:
2:30–5:30 p.m., one or more days a week Monday–Thursday, for Academic Homework and Enrichment Time.
Extra hours (optional): You may stay until 6:30 each day; you may attend Friday afternoons (Fun Days); you may attend field trips on Saturdays.

Activities for Regular Service:
While the structured activities will focus on academics, you are encouraged to share who you are and create an environment where people welcome and learn about a diversity of cultures, practices, and beliefs.
4:00–5:00 p.m., Academic Homework time: With younger group: academic support as they complete homework.
5:00–6:00 p.m., Enrichment Time: A less structured time, where you are encouraged to help out or to lead an activity of games, songs, or other workshops based on your talents and experience. (If you want to lead an activity, see Aikta to make a proposal.)
Wednesday 4:45–5:15 p.m. is weekly Circle Time with sharing and meditation. You're encouraged to come to this at least once—and more regularly if you can—as it's the best way to understand the program beyond the academic focus.

Saturday Field Trips On the second Saturday of each month, select apprentices speak at the DC City Council during Youth Testimony Day. On the third Saturday of each month, field trips are tied to the value being taught that month. Coordinate with Tiffani if you'd like to attend.

Writing Opportunities (Coordinate with Tiffani, and she will connect you with the appropriate staff person.):
Work with the Executive Blend development team to produce specific documents (such as fundraising brochures or materials).
Prepare a series of articles for the Volunteer Corner of the newsletter, which comes out monthly. Write about your own experience and interview others to create five or more columns.
Prepare press releases for area newspapers (*East of the River, Washington Post, City Paper,* and others you identify). These should pitch a particular story idea that highlights a recent, catchy event at Life Pieces.
Write up four Apprentice Profiles that can be used on the LPTM website.

Transportation Notes:
Take the metro orange line from Foggy Bottom to Minnesota Avenue (about a 25-minute ride). *Wear your LPTM shield.* A LPTM van will *always* pick you up to take you to Merritt Middle School. If the van is not at the metro when you arrive, go back downstairs and call Maurice; ask her to call you when she arrives.

Safety Tips:
Wear your LPTM shield as you travel to and from LPTM.
Program your phones: Enter the cell #s for Maurice and the general LPTM # into your phone.
Program my cell number into your phone (xxx-xxx-xxxx) and call if you're out in the city and have a question or concern.
Follow usual safety tips for traveling in a city: Pay attention to who is around you, don't wear your earphones or allow yourself to be distracted by your phone, and if it's dark, get a ride back to the metro.
Travel in groups: If you don't know who else is traveling to your site from GW, check with Dr. Ryder or Tiffani.

MIRIAM'S KITCHEN,
HTTP://MIRIAMSKITCHEN.ORG

Max # of UW students: 2   Work Study option? No
TB Test Required? No   Background check? No

Located in Foggy Bottom, Miriam's Kitchen has provided breakfast and lunch for homeless people, along with a range of art and writing programs to recognize their creativity. They offer comprehensive case management and other services as well. Miriam's Kitchen has a regular and committed cadre of volunteers to help serve breakfast. Their greatest needs from you would be working behind the scenes helping with office tasks and working with their Wednesday lunch program, Miriam's café.

Mission statement:
Our mission is to provide individualized services that address the causes and consequences of homelessness in an atmosphere of dignity and respect, both directly and through facilitating connections in Washington, DC

Video: YouTube "Miriam's Kitchen" http://www.youtube.com/miriams kitchen#p/a/u/0/4pFlX8VQbqM

GW Office of Community Service Contact: *[Here I insert information about the people at GWU who help to coordinate GWU's volunteering with the community organization.]*

MK Contact Information:
Ashley Lawson, Volunteer & Development Coordinator, ashley@miriam-skitchen.org, (202) 452-8926
Jen Georget, Program Assistant, jengeorget@miriamskitchen.org
Chelsea Benjamin, a GW sophomore, serves as a GW liaison.

Address:
Neighborhood: Foggy Bottom
2401 Virginia Avenue NW
Ward: 2

Hours for Regular Service:
Office support: hours to be coordinated with Ashley & Jen, and Miriam's
    Café: Wednesday11:30-1:30 (You will primarily help in the office, but

should plan to work the Café several times so that you can meet and interact with MK's guests.) In addition, attend Charity Fairs, Walkathon, and other events when possible.

Activities for Regular Service:

Office support: The office needs support in preparing for grant-writing. This may include gathering data, pulling together information about the program based on the focus of particular grants, and otherwise supporting Ashley as she prepares these materials. It may also include on-going data input as Miriam's Kitchen documents their work and digitizes archives.

America's Charity Fairs: Join Ashley and/or Jen as they visit DC corporations to talk about Miriam's Kitchen and talk to workers about supporting MK through workplace giving. These usually take place in the afternoons.

Miriam's Café: In addition to greeting guests and preparing and serving food during the café, you are encouraged to offer classes during the café, such as ones based on your own hobbies (writing, beadwork, pottery, yoga).

GW Walkathon Campaign: With the Walk for the Homeless fundraiser fast approaching, one task will be to mobilize walkers. You can draw from the experiences of last year's MK volunteers & GW liaison Chelsea Benjamin and develop a campaign for GW students.

GW Supply Donation Campaign: Set up one-time or (better yet) on-going events to collect needed supplies for MK, such as toiletries, cereal, men's clothing. You might research whether leftover GWorld money can be donated to MK at the end of the school year.

Introducing yourself to Miriam's Kitchen

Miriam's Kitchen is looking for interns who are committed and reliable, who can take the initiative on tasks but aren't afraid to ask for direction, who come regularly but can be flexible, and who are willing to take on a wide range of tasks, from filing to serving food to writing grant sections. Interns should have a good sense of humor (Miriam's Kitchen prides itself on being a fun place to work.)

Writing Opportunities:

Grant writing: As you work with Ashley to prepare segments for potential grants, you may submit segments of those as your commissioned task. For example, you may document a particular aspect of Miriam's Kitchen (such as youth engagement) or highlight a particular program (such as art therapy or Miriam's Dialog.) In the past, a student created a music slide show documenting youth engagement at Miriam's Kitchen, which was submitted as part of a Fannie Mae grant. Miriam's Kitchen was awarded twice the amount they'd received the previous year, a difference that Ashley attributes to the students' document.

Walkathon: After you run your walkathon campaign, prepare an overview for the next student interns, including all of your promotion materials and reflections, recommendations.

YouTube Video: If you are creative with videography, create a video for MK to promote the Walkathon (or other events, depending on need.)

Supply Donation Campaign: After you run your supply donation campaign, prepare an overview for the next student interns, including all of your promotion materials and a cover letter in which you reflect on what worked well and make recommendations for next year.

Other options can be worked out with Ashley as the semester progresses and we gain a better understanding of the needs.

Transportation Notes:
Miriam's Kitchen is located within block from the Foggy Bottom campus, at the corner of 24th Ave and Virginia Ave, NW

Safety Tips:
Follow usual safety tips for traveling in a city: pay attention to who is around you, don't wear your earphones, and if it's dark, walk with others back to your dorm.

References

"NonProfit Finds New Ways to Solicit." *Washington Business Journal.* (July 17 2009): www.tbd.com.

50 Years is Enough. *Mobilization for Global Justice.* www.50years.org (Nov. 22 2002).

Ali-Coleman, Khadijah. "Marvin Gaye Park: Spawning a Change in the Neighborhood. " *East of the River.* (April 2007): 58–59.

Alinsky, Saul D. *Rules for Radicals: A Practical Primer for Realistic Radicals.* New York: Vintage Books, 1989.

Althusser, Louis. "Ideology and Ideological State Apparatus." Pp. 121–176 in *Lenin and Philosophy and Other Essays.* New York: Monthly Review Press, 1970.

Anderson, David M. "Cautious Optimism about on-Line Politics and Citizenship." Pp. 29–34 in *The Civic Web: Online Politics and Democratic Values,* edited by David A. Anderson and Michael Cornfield. Lanham, Md.: Rowman and Littlefield, 2003.

Anzaldúa, Gloria. *Borderlands = La Frontera.* 2nd ed. San Francisco: Aunt Lute Books, 1999.

Baldwin, Alec, Bob Hercules, and Bruce Orenstein, *The Democratic Promise.* Seattle: Independent Television Service, Media Process Educational Films, Chicago Video Project, and Indieflix, 2007

Barber, Benjamin R. *Strong Democracy: Participatory Politics for a New Age.* Berkeley: University of California Press, 2003.

———. *A Passion for Democracy: American Essays.* Princeton, N.J.: Princeton University Press, 1998.

Barley & Birch. "Two Truths and a Life: Miriam's Kitchen Special." *Barleyandbirch. com* (August 20, 2010).

Bartholomae, David. "Inventing the University." Pp. 135–165 in *When a Writer can't Write: Studies in Writer's Block and Other Composing-Process Problems,* edited by Mike Rose. New York: Guilford, 1985.

Bauder, David. "Democratic National Convention Ratings: 38 Million Watch Obama's Acceptance Speech." *Huffington Post,* August 29, 2008 2008, www .huffingtonpost.com/2008/08/29/democratic-national-conve_n_122440.html (14 Jan. 2010).

Beaufort, Anne. *Writing in the Real World: Making the Transition from School to Work.* New York; London: Teachers College Press, 1999.

Bello, Walden. The Year of Global Protest Against Globalization. *Focus on the Global South.* 2001. www.focusweb.org/publications/2001/2001 (24 Oct. 2002).

Berry, Jeffrey M., and David F. Arons. 2003. *A Voice for Nonprofits.* Washington, D.C.: Brookings Institutions Press.

Bitzer, Lloyd. "The Rhetorical Situation." *Philosophy and Rhetoric* 1 (Jan. 1968): 1–14.

Bloom, Lynn Z. "Freshman Composition as a Middle-Class Enterprise." *College English* 58, no. 6 (October 1996): 654–678.

Booth, Wayne. "The Idea of a *University*—as seen by a Rhetorician." Pp. 228–252 in *Defining the New Rhetorics,* edited by Stuart C. Brown and Theresa Enos. Newbury Park, Calif.: Sage Publications, 1993.

Butler, Johnnella E., Juan C. Guerra, and Carol Severino. *Writing in Multicultural Settings.* New York: Modern Language Association of America, 1997.

Calhoun, Craig J. *Habermas and the Public Sphere.* Cambridge, Mass.: MIT Press, 1992.

Carmichael, Stokely. "Black Power." *American Rhetoric.* October, 1966. www.american rhetoric.com/speeches/stokelycarmichaelblackpower.html (May 20 2010).

Chambers, Edward T., and Michael A. Cowan. *Roots for Radicals: Organizing for Power, Action, and Justice.* New York: Continuum, 2003.

Chomsky, Noam. Noam Chomsky on the IMF/WB Debt Forgiveness. *A16 Monkey Fist Collective.* 2000. a16.monkeyfist.com (27 Oct. 2005).

Chomsky, Noam. *The Manufacture of Consent.* Minneapolis, Minn.: Silha Center for the Study of Media Ethics and Law, School of Journalism and Mass Communication, University of Minnesota, 1986.

Cintron, Ralph. *Immigration, Minutemen, and the Subject of Democracy.* (Paper presented at the Western States Rhetoric and Literacy Conference, Salt Lake City, October 2009).

———. *Angels' Town: Chero Ways, Gang Life, and Rhetorics of the Everyday.* Boston: Beacon Press, 1997.

Coogan, David. "Service Learning and Social Change: The Case for Materialist Rhetoric." *College Composition and Communication* 57, no. 4 (June 2006): 667–693.

———. "Counterpublics in Public Housing: Reframing the Politics of Service-Learning." *College English* 67, no. 5 (May 2005): 461–482.

Crick, Nathan. "The Search for a Purveyor of News: The Dewey/Lippman Debate in an Internet Age." *Critical Studies in Mass Communication* 26, no. 5 (December 2009): 480–497.

Crowley, Sharon, and Debra Hawhee. *Ancient Rhetoric for Contemporary Students.* 3rd ed. Addison-Wesley: Boston, 2003.

DC Government. Office of Planning: DC Census by Ward. *DC Government.* Washington, D.C., 2002. www.planning.dc.gov/planning/cwp/view,a,3,q,570104.asp 2010).

Deans, Thomas. *Writing and Community Action.* Boston: Longman, 2003.

———. *Writing Partnerships: Service-Learning in Composition.* Urbana, Ill.: National Council of Teachers of English, 2000.

Deanwood Historical Society. *Deanwood 1880–1950: A Model of Self-sufficiency in far northeast Washington, DC.* Washington, D.C.: Deanwood History Project, 2005.

Delany, Samuel R. *Times Square Red, Times Square Blue.* New York: New York University Press, 1999.

DeLuca, Kevin M., and Jennifer Peeples. "From Public Sphere to Public Screen: Democracy, Activism, and the 'Violence' of Seattle." *Critical Studies in Media Communication* 19, no. 2 (June 2002): 125–152.

Dervis, Kemal, and Ceren Ozer. *A Better Globalization: Legitimacy, Governance and Reform.* Washington, D.C.: Center for Global Development, 2005.

Deutsche, Rosalyn. *Evictions: Art and Spatial Politics.* Cambridge, Mass.: MIT Press, 1998.

District of Columbia Public Schools. DCPS Graduation Rate Continues to Climb. *DCPS.* 2010. dcps.dc.gov/DCPS/About+DCPS/Press+Releases+and+Announcements/DCPS+Graduation+Rate+Continues+to+Climb (Jan. 8).

Dye, Thomas R., and L. H. Zeigler. *The Irony of Democracy: An Uncommon Introduction to American Politics.* 2d ed. Belmont, Calif.: Duxbury Press, 1972.

Eggen, Dan. "From all Walks of Life, they make a Stand: Environmentalists, Feminists, Other Activists Organize DC Protests of World Bank and IMF." *Washington Post,* 8 April 2000, A1.

Egger, Robert, and Howard Yoon. *Begging for Change: The Dollars and Sense of Making Nonprofits Responsive, Efficient, and Rewarding for all.* New York: HarperBusiness, 2004.

Ellwood, Wayne. *The no-Nonsense Guide to Globalization.* London: Verso, 2001.

Ervin, Elizabeth. "Academics and the Negotiation of Local Knowledge." *College English* 61, no. 4 (Mar. 1999): pp. 448–470.

Fabel, Leah. "25 Area Schools are Labeled Persistently Failing." *Washington Examiner,* Mar. 12 2010, www.washingtonexaminer.com/local/25-area-schools-labeled-persistently-failing-87406677.html (Aug. 2010).

Feinstein, Diane. Opening Welcome Remarks at the 2009 Presidential Election. *American Rhetoric: Online Speech Bank.* 2009. www.americanrhetoric.com/speeches/ dianefeinsteinpresidentialinauguration.htm (Aug. 16 2009).

Fischer, Karin. "Ohio's Public Colleges Lure Businesses with the Promise of a Skilled Work Force." *Chronicle of Higher Education* 55, no. 12 (14 November 2008): A15-A16.

Flower, Linda. *Community Literacy and the Rhetoric of Public Engagement.* Carbondale: Southern Illinois University Press, 2008.

Fraser, Nancy. "Rethinking the Public Sphere: A Contribution to the Critique of Actually Existing Democracy." Pp. 89–110 in *Habermas and the Public Sphere,* edited by Craig J. Calhoun. Cambridge, Mass.: MIT Press, 1992.

Gecan, Michael. *Going Public.* Boston: Beacon Press, 2002.

Gilbert, Ben W. *Ten Blocks from the White House: Anatomy of the Washington Riots of 1968.* New York: Praeger, 1968.

Giroux, Henry A. "Neoliberalism, Corporate Culture, and the Promise of Higher Education: The University as a Democratic Public Sphere." *Harvard Educational Review* 72, no. 4 (Winter 2002): 425–463.

———. *Teachers as Intellectuals: Toward a Critical Pedagogy of Learning.* New York: Bergin & Garvey, 1988.

Global Exchange. Global Exchange. www.globalexchange.org (22 Nov 2002).

Grabill, Jeffrey T. *Writing Community Change: Designing Technologies for Citizen Action.* Cresskill, N.J.: Hampton Press, 2007.

Gramsci, Antonio, Quintin Hoare, and Geoffrey Nowell-Smith. *Selections from the Prison Notebooks of Antonio Gramsci.* 1st ed. New York: International Publishers, 1972; 1971.

Groundwork Anacostia River, DC. Facebook: GWARDC Information. www.facebook.com/pages/GWARDC-Groundwork-Anacostia-River-DC (10 August 2010).

Gurak, Laura J. *Persuasion and Privacy in Cyberspace: The Online Protests Over Lotus MarketPlace and Clipper Chip.* New Haven: Yale University Press, 1997.

Habermas, Jürgen. "Political Communication in Media Society: Does Democracy Still Enjoy an Epistemic Dimension? The Impact of Normative Theory on Empirical Research." *Communication Theory* 16 (2006): 411–426.

———. *The Structural Transformation of the Public Sphere: An Inquiry into a Category of Bourgeois Society.* Cambridge, Mass.: MIT Press, 1989.

Hammerback, John C., and Richard J. Jensen. *The Rhetorical Career of César Chávez.* College Station: Texas A & M University Press, 1998.

Harper's Magazine Foundation. "About Harper's Magazine." *Harper's Magazine.* (n. d.): www.harpers.org/harpers/about (18 August 2010).

Harris, Joseph. *Rewriting: How to do Things with Texts.* Logan, Utah: Utah State University Press, 2006.

Hauser, Gerard A. *Vernacular Voices: The Rhetoric of Publics and Public Spheres.* Columbia: University of South Carolina Press, 1999.

Hayduk, Ronald, and Benjamin H. Shepard. *From ACT UP to the WTO: Urban Protest and Community Building in the Era of Globalization.* London; New York: Verso, 2002.

Hines, Susan. "Shared Wisdom: Stone Soup." *Landscape Architecture* (June, 2005): 124–134.

Hirsch, E. D. Jr. *The Knowledge Deficit: Closing the Shocking Education Gap for American Children.* Boston: Houghton Mifflin, 2007.

Hirsch, E. D. Jr., Joseph F. Kett, and James S. Trefil. *The New Dictionary of Cultural Literacy,* 3rd ed. Boston: Houghton Mifflin, 2002.

———. *Cultural Literacy: What Every American Needs to Know.* New York: Vintage Books, 1988; 1987.

Hirsch, E. D. Jr., William G. Rowland, and Michael Stanford. *A First Dictionary of Cultural Literacy: What our Children Need to Know:* Houghton Mifflin, 1996.

Holmes, David. "Fighting Back by *Writing* Black: Beyond Racially Reductive Composition Theory." Pp. 44–52 in *Race, Rhetoric, and Composition,* edited by Keith Gilyard. Portsmouth, N.H.: Boynton, 1999.

hooks, bell. *Teaching to Transgress.* New York: Routledge, 1994.

Horton, Myles, Herbert R. Kohl, and Judith Kohl. *The Long Haul: An Autobiography.* New York: Teachers College Press, 1998.

Howard-Hassman, Rhoda E. The Great Transformation II: Human Rights Leap-Frogging in the Era of Globalization. *Globalization and Autonomy.* 2005. www .globalautonomy.ca (25 Oct. 2005).

Incite! Women of Color Against Violence. *The Revolution Will Not be Funded: Beyond the Non-Profit Industrial Complex.* Cambridge, Mass.: South End Press, 2007.

International Monetary Fund. Common Criticisms of the IMF: Some Responses. 2005. www.imf.org (27 Oct. 2005).

Janack, James A. "Mediated Citizenship and Digital Discipline: A Rhetoric of Control in a Campaign Blog." *Social Semiotics* 16, no. 2 (June 2006): 283–294.

Janofsky, Michael. "Federal Parks Chief Calls 'Million Man' Count Low." *New York Times,* Oct 21, 1995 1995, www.nytimes.com/1995/10/21/us/federal-parks-chief-calls-million-man-count-low.html (July 19, 2010).

Jones, Mark. "Can Technology Transform? Experimenting with Wired Communities." Pp. 354–383 in *Virtual Publics: Policy and Community in an Electronic Age,* edited by Beth Kolko. New York: Columbia University Press, 2003.

Jordan, June. "Nobody Mean More to Me than You and the Future Life of Willie Jordan." *Harvard Educational Review* 58, no. 3 (August 1988): 363–374.

Kameraad-Campbell, Susan. *Doc: The Story of Dennis Littky and His Fight for a Better School.* Alexandria, VA: Association for Supervision and Curriculum Development, 1989, 2005.

Kelderman, Eric. "Texas Push 'Em: Betting Big on Research Universities." *Chronicle of Higher Education* 56, no. 28 (16 March 2010): A1, A25-A27.

Kerr, Clark. *The University in America.* Santa Barbara, Calif.: Center for the Study of Democratic Institutions, 1967.

Klein, Naomi. "Conversation with Naomi Klein about the Anti-Corporate Movement." *Seattle Independent Media Center,* 7 Sept. 2000, Seattle.indymedia.org .

———. *No Space, no Choice, no Jobs, no Logo: Taking Aim at the Brand Bullies.* Boston: St. Martin's Press, 2000.

Kovach, Bill, and Tom Rosenstiel. *The Elements of Journalism:What Newspeople should Know and the Public should Expect.* New York: Crown Publishers, 2001.

Kuhn, Thomas S. *The Structure of Scientific Revolutions.* Chicago: University of Chicago Press, 1962.

Lakoff, George. *Don't Think of an Elephant! Know Your Values and Frame the Debate: The Essential Guide for Progressives.* White River Junction, Vt.: Chelsea Green, 2004.

Lakoff, George. *Moral Politics: How Liberals and Conservatives Think.*2nd ed. Chicago, Ill.: University of Chicago Press, 2002.

Levine, Peter. *The Future of Democracy: Developing the Next Generation of American Citizens.* Medford, Mass.: Tufts University Press, 2007.

Life Pieces to Masterpieces. Contact. n.d. www.lifepieces.org (Aug. 2010).

Life Pieces to Masterpieces. Our Model. n.d. www.lifepieces.org (Aug. 2010).

Lippmann, Walter. *Public Opinion.* New York: Free Press, 1965.

——. *The Phantom Public.* New York: Harcourt, Brace, 1925.

LoLordo, Ann. "Protesters Say their Mission was Accomplished in Seattle." *Baltimore Sun,* 5. Dec. 1999, A1.

Lorde, Audre. "The Uses of Anger." Pp. 124–133 in *Sister Outsider: Essays and Speeches* Santa Cruz: Crossing, 1984.

Lunsford, Andrea A., and Franklin E. Horowitz. *Easy Writer: A Pocket Reference.* 3rd ed. Boston: Bedford/St. Martin's, 2006.

Lyons, Scott R. "Rhetorical Sovereignty: What do American Indians Want from Writing?" *College Composition and Communication* 51, no. 3 (Feb. 2000): 447–468.

Marin, Peter. "Helping and Hating the Homeless." Pp. 305–318 in *Writing and Community Action,* edited by Thomas Deans. Boston: Longman, 1987, 2003.

Mathieu, Paula. *Tactics of Hope: The Public Turn in English Composition.* Heinemann, 2005.

Mathieu, Paula, and Diana George. "Not 'Going it Alone': Public Writing, Independent Media, and the Circulation of Homeless Advocacy." *College Composition and Communication* 61, no. 1 (September 2009): 130–149.

Metropolitan Police Department (DC). Citywide Crime Statistics: Annual Totals, 1993–2009. *DC Government.* 2009. mpdc.dc.gov/mpdc/cwp/view,a,1239,q,547256,mpdcNav_ GID,1556.asp.

Milbrath, Lester W. *Political Participation: How and Why do People Get Involved in Politics?* Chicago: Rand McNally, 1965.

Miriam's Kitchen. Miriam's Kitchen. miriamskitchen.org (28 July 2010).

Mitchell, Don. "The End of Public Space? People's Park, Definitions of the Public, and Democracy." *Annals of the Association of American Geographers* 85, no. 1 (March 1995): 108–133.

Mobilization for Global Justice. Affinity Groups, A-16, 2000. www.a16.org (22 Nov. 2002).

Modan, Gabriella G. *Turf Wars: Discourse, Diversity, and the Politics of Place.* Malden, Mass.: Blackwell, 2007.

Morton, Keith. "The Irony of Service: Charity, Project and Social Change in Service-Learning." *Michigan Journal of Community Service Learning* no. (Fall 1995): 19–32.

Morton, Keith, and Sandra Enos. "Developing a Theory and Practice of Community-Campus Partnerships." Pp. 20–41 in *Building Partnerships for Service-Learning,* edited by Barbara Jacoby. San Francisco, Calif.: Jossey-Bass, 2003.

Morton, Keith, and Sandra Enos. "Building Deeper Civic Relationships and New and Improved Citizens." *Journal of Public Affairs* 6, (2002): 83–102.

Moses, Robert P., and Charles E. Cobb. *Radical Equations: Civil Rights from Mississippi to the Algebra Project.* Boston: Beacon Press, 2001.

Murphy, Troy A. "Deliberative Civic Education and Civil Society: A Consideration of Ideals and Actualities in Democracy and Communication Education." *Communication Education* 53, no. 1 (January 2004): 74–91.

National Coalition for the Homeless. "Hate Crimes and Violence Against People Experiencing Homelessness." 2009. www.nationalhomeless.org/factsheets/hatecrimes .html (30 July 2010).

––––. "About Us." 2010. www.nationalhomeless.org/about_us/index.html (30 July 2010).

––––. Faces of Homelessness Speakers' Bureau. Washington, D.C., 2010. www .nationalhomeless.org/faces/index.html (30 July 2010).

––––. The Presentations: Faces of Homelessness Speakers' Bureau. Washington, D.C., 2010. www.nationalhomeless.org/faces/presentation.html (30 July 2010).

National Recreation and Park Service. n.d. *Marvin Gaye Park Backgrounder.* www .nrpa.org.

Nieto, Sonia. *Affirming Diversity: The Sociopolitical Context of Multicultural Education.* White Plains, N.Y.: Longman, 1992.

North American Street Newspaper Association. What is a Street Newspaper? 2010. www.nasna.org (19 August 2010).

Obama, Michelle. "Michelle Obama's Democratic Convention Speech." *Huffington Post,* 25 Aug. 2008, www.huffingtonpost.com/2008/08/25/michelle-obamas -democrati_n_121310.html (20 July 2010).

Obie, Brooke. The Right Wing Media Hate Alinsky, Except when He's Shaping their Movement. *Media Matters.* 10 Feb. 2010. mediamatters.org/blog/201002010041 (20 Aug. 2010).

Ogbu, John U. *Minority Status, Oppositional Culture, and Schooling.* New York: Routledge, 2008.

––––. *Black American Students in an Affluent Suburb: A Study of Academic Disengagement.* Mahwah, N.J.: L. Erlbaum Associates, 2003.

Pacyniak, Gabriel. "Lincoln Heights: Future Beacon on a Hill?" *East of the River,* May 2006, www.capitalcommunitynews.com/publications/eotr/2006-MAY/html/ Lincoln_Heights.cfm (15 May 2008).

Payne, Charles M. *I've Got the Light of Freedom: The Organizing Tradition and the Mississippi Freedom Struggle.* Berkeley: University of California Press, 1996.

Piccoli, Sean. "Urban Renewal Jewel: Meridian Park Gets Presidential Salute." *The Washington Times,* April 22 1994, C4.

Powell, Malea. "Blood and Scholarship: One Mixed-Blood Story." Pp. 1–16 in *Race, Rhetoric, and Composition,* edited by Keith Gilyard. Portsmouth, N.H.: Boynton, 1999.

Pratt, Mary L. "Arts of the Contact Zone." Pp. 581–595 in *Ways of Reading,* edited by David Bartholomae and Anthony Petrosky. Bedford: New York, 2001.

Putnam, Robert D. *Bowling Alone: The Collapse and Revival of American Community.* New York: Simon & Schuster, 2000.

Raja, Colin. "Globalism and Race at A16 in DC." *Colorlines: Race, Color, Action* 3, no. 3 2000).

Readings, Bill. *The University in Ruins.* Cambridge, Mass.: Harvard University Press, 1996.

Riedner, Rachel, and Kevin Mahoney. *Democracies to Come: Rhetorical Action, Neoliberalism, and Communities of Resistance.* Lanham, Md.: Rowman and Littlefield, 2008.

Rimmerman, Craig A. *The New Citizenship: Unconventional Politics, Activism, and Service.* 3rd ed. Boulder: Westview Press, 2005.

Rodman, Gilbert B. "The Net Effect: The Public's Fear and the Public Sphere." Pp. 9–48 in *Virtual Publics: Policy and Community in an Electronic Age,* edited by Beth Kolko. New York: Columbia University Press, 2003.

Rose, Mike. *Lives on the Boundary: A Moving Account of the Struggles and Achievements of America's Educational Underclass.* New York: Penguin Books, 1990; 1989.

Ryder, Phyllis M. "In(ter)Ventions of Global Democracy: An Analysis of the Rhetorics of the A-16 World Bank/IMF Protests in Washington, DC." *Rhetoric Review* 25, no. 4 (October 2006): 408–426.

Sandoval, Chela. *Methodologies of the Oppressed.* Minneapolis: University of Minnesota Press, 2000.

Schiappa, Edward. "Intellectuals and the Place of Cultural Critique." Pp. 26–32 in *Rhetoric, Cultural Studies, and Literacy,* edited by Frederick Reynolds. Hillsdale, N.J.: Erlbaum, 1995.

Silko, Leslie M. "Language and Literature from a Pueblo Indian Perspective." Pp. 434–440 in *Living Languages,* edited by Nancy Buffington, Marvin Diogenes and Clyde Moneyhun. Upper Saddle River, N.J.: Prentice, 1997.

Silver, David. "Communication, Community, Consumption: An Ethnographic Exploration of an Online City." Pp. 327–353 in *Virtual Publics: Policy and Community in an Electronic Age,* edited by Beth Kolko. New York: Columbia University Press, 2003.

Smitherman-Donaldson, Geneva. *Talkin and Testifyin: The Language of Black America.* Detroit: Wayne State University Press, 1977.

Sommers, Nancy, and Laura Saltz. "The Novice as Expert: Writing the Freshman Year." *College Composition and Communication* 56, no. 1 (September 2004): pp. 124–149.

Sotomayor, Sonia. "A Latina Judge's Voice." *Berkeley La Raza Law Journal* 13, no. 1 (Spring 2002): 87–94.

Stewart, Charles J. "The Evolution of a Revolution: Stokeley Carmichael and the Rhetoric of Black Power." *Quarterly Journal of Speech* 83, no. 4 1997): 429–446.

Stone Soup Films. 2009. *Life Pieces to Masterpieces—8 Min. Version.* Vol. Vimeo. com. vimeo.com/5143977: Vimeo.

Streeter, Thomas. *Selling the Air: A Critique of the Policy of Commercial Broadcasting in the United States.* Chicago: University of Chicago Press, 1996.

Sullivan, Andrew. "Why I Blog. " *Atlantic Monthly.* [Electronic], (November 2008): www.theatlantic.com/magazine/archive/2008/11/why-i-blog/7060/4/ (Aug. 2010).

Sullivan, Patricia. "Getting its Groove Back." *Washington Post,* 2 April 2006, www.washingtonpost.com/wp-dyn/content/article/2006/04/01/AR2006040101105.html (9 Nov. 2010).

Suskind, Ron. *A Hope in the Unseen: An American Odyssey from the Inner City to the Ivy League.* New York: Broadway Books, 1998.

Tannen, Deborah. *The Argument Culture: Moving from Debate to Dialogue.* New York: Random House, 1998.

Thurman, Rosetta. 28 Days of Black, Nonprofit Leadership: Mary Brown. *Rosetta Thurman: Presenting Now Generation Leadership for Social Change.* 4 Feb. 2010. www.rosettathurman.com/2010/02/28-days-of-black-nonprofit-leaders-mary-brown (Aug. 2010).

Trimbur, John. "Composition and the Circulation of Writing." *College Composition and Communication* 52, no. 2 (December 2000): 188–219.

Warner, Michael. *Publics and Counterpublics.* Cambridge, Mass.: Zone Books, 2005.

Warnick, Barbara. *Critical Literacy in a Digital Era: Technology, Rhetoric, and the Public Interest.* Mahwah, N.J.: Lawrence Erlbaum Associates, 2002.

Warshauer, Susan. "Community-Based Software, Participatory Theater: Models for Inviting Participation in Learning and Artistic Production." Pp. 286–326 in *Virtual Publics: Policy and Community in an Electronic Age,* edited by Beth Kolko. New York: Columbia University Press, 2003.

Washington Parks and People. Welcome. 2007. www.washingtonparks.net (Aug 2010).

Weiler, Kathleen. *Women Teaching for Change: Gender, Class & Power.* South Hadley, Mass.: Bergin & Garvey Publishers, 1988.

Weisser, Christian R. *Moving Beyond Academic Discourse: Composition Studies and the Public Sphere.* Carbondale: Southern Illinois University Press, 2002.

Welch, Nancy. "Living Room: Teaching Public Writing in a Post-Publicity Era." *College Composition and Communication* 56, no. 3 (Feb 2005): 470–492.

Wells, Susan. "Rogue Cops and Health Care: What do we Want from Public Writing?" *College Composition and Communication* 47, no. 3 (October 1996): 325–341.

West, Cornel. *Democracy Matters: Winning the Fight Against Imperialism.* New York: The Penguin Press, 2004.

———. *Race Matters.* New York: Vintage Books, 1994.

Wiggins, Todd. People for Fairness Coalition. Jun 2006. www.peopleforfairness.magnify.net/user/QD7495R46QD0GDM5 (28 July 2010).

Willis, Paul E. *Learning to Labor: How Working Class Kids Get Working Class Jobs.* New York: Columbia University Press, 1981; 1977.

World Bank Group. www.worldbank.org (22 Nov. 2002).

X, Malcolm. The Ballot or the Bullet. *EdChange Multicultural Pavillion.* 3 April 1964. www.edchange.org/multicultural/speeches/malcolm_x_ballot.html (May 20 2010).

Zinn, Howard. *S. N. C. C., the New Abolitionists.* Boston: Beacon Press, 1964.

Index

About The Author

Phyllis Mentzell Ryder is an associate professor of writing at The George Washington University.